THE MOST RUSTED NAME IN TRAVEL

Frommer's®

SANTA FE, TAOS & ALBUQUERQUE

By Erin Vivid Riley

FrommerMedia LLC

FROMMER'S STAR RATINGS SYSTEM

Every hotel, restaurant, and attraction listed in this guide has been ranked for quality and value. Here's what the stars mean:

- ♥ Recommended
- ♥♥ Highly Recommended
- ♥♥♥ A must! Don't miss!

AN IMPORTANT NOTE

The world is a dynamic place. Hotels change ownership, restaurants hike their prices, museums alter their opening hours, and buses and trains change their routings. And all of this can occur in the several months after our authors have visited, inspected, and written about these hotels, restaurants, museums, and transportation services. Though we have made valiant efforts to keep all our information fresh and up-to-date, some few changes can inevitably occur in the periods before a revised edition of this guidebook is published. So please bear with us if a tiny number of the details in this book have changed. Please also note that we have no responsibility or liability for any inaccuracy or errors or omissions, or for inconvenience, loss, damage, or expenses suffered by anyone as a result of assertions in this guide.

Dancers perform at Albuquerque's Indian Pueblo Cultural Center (p. 196)

CONTENTS

Downtown Santa Fe aglow at dusk.

A LOOK AT NORTHERN NEW MEXICO

Whoever originally dubbed New Mexico "the Land of Enchantment" must have coined the state's motto while taking in a blazing purple-orange-and-red sunset over Santa Fe. Or during a daybreak mass ascension near Albuquerque, when hundreds of brightly colored hot-air balloons take to the skies in unison. Or when they got their first look at Taos Pueblo, the ancient adobe complex set against an impossibly blue sky. There's a certain magic here that has long drawn artists, writers, spiritual pilgrims, and everyday travelers to the state's rugged terrain, its Native American pueblos and petroglyphs, and eye-popping natural juxtapositions of color and plays of light. As well, northern New Mexico offers visitors a cultural mix that is unique in the United States—where members of Pueblo, Navajo, and Apache tribes, long-established Hispanic communities, modern cowboys, and New Age-y seekers all blend to form a vibrant, quirky community that's rich with museums, spicy with chile-infused cuisine, and laid-back with its small-town ambiance. On these pages, we offer a small taste of what the region has in store. Visit, and be enchanted!

Hikers explore the recently reopened Kasha-Katuwe Tent Rocks National Monument (p. 116), southwest of Santa Fe.

SANTA FE

A block east of the Plaza, Santa Fe's massive Romanesque 19th-century cathedral is a charming anomaly in a downtown full of low-rise adobe buildings.

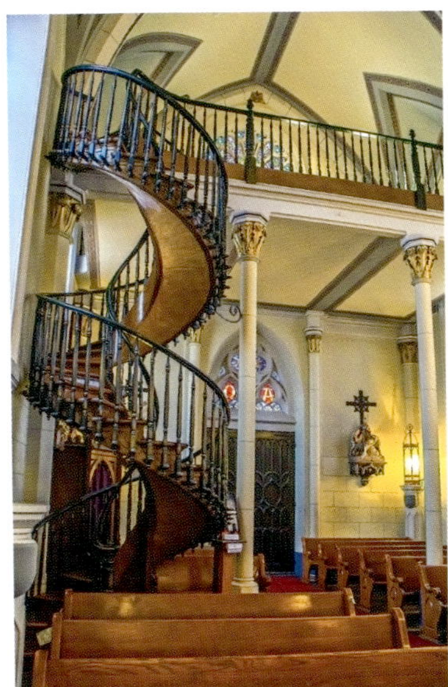

There's a remarkable legend behind this spiral staircase at the Loretto Chapel (p. 84), now a deconsecrated church run as a private museum.

Beneath the portico of the Palace of the Governors (p. 76), only authenticated Native American artisans can sell their jewelry, pottery, rugs, and other crafts.

In Santa Fe's historic arts district, Chiaroscuro Contemporary Art Gallery (p. 99) represents artists working in a variety of mediums and from many cultural traditions.

Santa Fe is known as a shopper's mecca. Among other luxury goods, turquoise and silver Native American jewelry can be found at galleries, gift shops, and outdoor markets.

A vendor shows her intricate needlework at the Indian Market in Santa Fe, the largest and most prestigious intertribal fine art market in the world. See p. 33.

Immersive experiences at Meow Wolf (p. 73) combine music, video, architecture, painting, and performance art.

When ordering a burrito in Santa Fe, ask for red and green chile sauces side by side, otherwise known as "Christmas."

The Inn and Spa at Loretto (p. 52) lit with farolitos, or luminary candles, at night. Built in 1975, the hotel was styled after the multistory Taos Pueblo.

The renowned Santa Fe Opera (p. 104) draws music lovers from around the world to its dramatic high desert amphitheater for five productions in July and August.

Bandelier National Monument (p. 120) offers an up-close look at prehistoric Indigenous ruins, along with trails where hikers can spot lots of New Mexican wildlife.

Exhibits at the Bradbury Science Museum in Los Alamos (p. 118) tell the inside story of the World War II Manhattan Project and its controversial director, J. Robert Oppenheimer.

TAOS

If you see only one Native American site in your northern New Mexico visit, make it Taos Pueblos (p. 148), where about 150 residents still live much as their ancestors did more than 700 years ago.

Artists have been drawn to the Taos community for over a century, and many of the artworks they produced here are on view at the Harwood Museum of Art (p. 151).

The design of San Francisco de Asís Church is a classic mix of Spanish and Native styles, with huge buttresses supporting the walls and bell towers adorned with white crosses. (See p. 148.)

In the Historic Taos Inn, Doc Martin's restaurant (p. 138) celebrates a slice of early Taos history, while also serving one of the town's best green chile cheeseburgers.

The adobe home of famed frontiersman Kit Carson is now the Kit Carson Home and Museum (p. 152), where exhibits tell of his sometimes controversial exploits.

At family-friendly Michael's Kitchen (p. 144), a Taos landmark since the 1970s, all-day breakfast is the star attraction, but the hearty lunch menu is also huge.

Taos Ski Valley (p. 155) is New Mexico's best and most famous ski area; many consider it the preeminent ski resort in the southern Rocky Mountains.

Art is everywhere in Taos, like this street mural of galloping mustangs racing along Ledoux Street.

A staple of northern New Mexican cuisine, chiles rellenos are green chile peppers, often breaded, then stuffed with cheese, deep-fried, and sometimes slathered in green chile sauce.

In the tiny village of Ojo Caliente, about 45 minutes from Taos, soak your troubles away in geothermal mineral waters ranging in temperature from 80 to 109 degrees. (See p. 160.)

The Cumbres & Toltec Scenic Railroad (p. 173) steam trains run through incredible mountain scenery and over the magnificent Toltec Gorge of the Rio de los Pinos.

The wild and wonderful Taos Box, a steep-sided canyon south of the Wild Rivers Recreation Area of Rio Grande del Norte National Monument, offers a series of class IV rapids. (See p. 160.)

ALBUQUERQUE

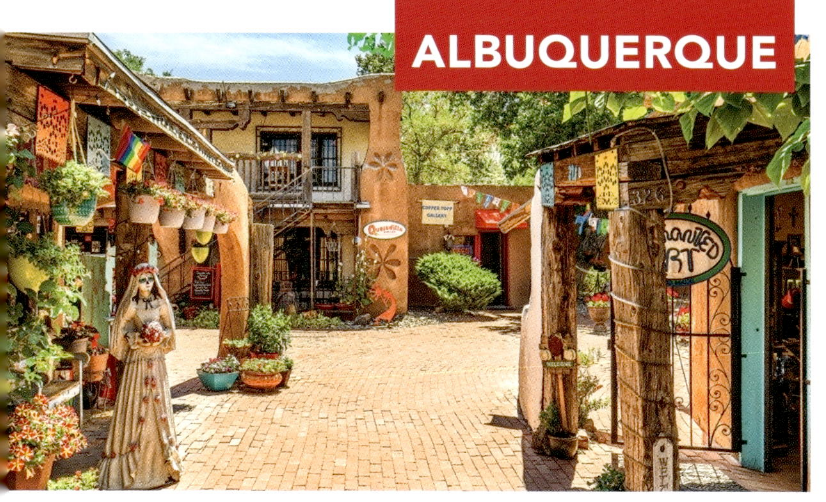

Albuquerque's original town site, known today as Old Town, is a central point of interest for visitors, with historic sites, restaurants, galleries, and crafts shops.

Penguin Chill is a popular (and refreshingly cool!) exhibit at the BioPark Zoo (p. 201).

Vintage businesses still operate along parts of historic Route 66, which runs right through downtown Albuquerque along Central Avenue.

For an unmatched panoramic view of Albuquerque and the surrounding mountains, a trip on the Sandia Peak Tramway (p. 198) is a must-do activity.

Along walking trails in the Boca Negra area of Petroglyph National Monument (p. 205), you can easily spot an incredible array of images—four-pointed stars, handprints, and a human-like mask.

Though it's not actually from the 1950s, retro neon-and-chrome decor at the 66 Diner (p. 193) sets the tone for a classic diner menu along Historic Route 66.

Balloons prepare to launch in a mass ascension at the Albuquerque International Balloon Fiesta (p. 210), held each October at Balloon Fiesta Park.

Elegant Southwestern furnishings and authentic art decorate the lobby of the Hotel Albuquerque at Old Town (p. 180)

Opened in 1927, the KiMo Theatre (p. 218) is an example of Pueblo Deco, a flamboyant architectural style using Pueblo Indian motifs in an Art Deco design.

In Albuquerque, handy New Mexico Rail Runner Express trains (p. 234) connect with Amtrak's Chicago-to-Los Angeles Southwest Chief service to take visitors to Santa Fe and other points of interest throughout northern New Mexico.

If you're visiting the area from November through March, head south to Bosque del Apache National Wildlife Refuge (p. 224), where vast numbers of many bird species winter.

Among the many intriguing prehistoric structures at Chaco Culture National Historical Park (p. 229), the astronomically aligned Casa Rinconada may have been used for major religious observances

THE BEST OF NORTHERN NEW MEXICO

1

Northern New Mexico is a land of contradictions, contrasts, and extremes in climate and culture. One day you're hiking among prickly pear cactus and sagebrush, hoping you brought enough drinking water. Next day you're speeding down a mountainside on skis as the falling snow fills the tracks you leave behind. Here you'll find Native Americans living much like their ancestors did hundreds of years ago, alongside Hispanic communities with deep Spanish roots, outdoor enthusiasts who work to play, artists drawn to the high-desert light, and nuclear scientists confronting a dark past and trying to chart a brighter future. As for entertainment, there are refined chamber music concerts, wild Texas two-steppin' bars, and practically everything in between.

As you explore northern New Mexico, you'll see the magical beauty in both land and spirit that has captured the hearts of so many artists, writers, and thinkers. And we hope you'll also experience some of that magic yourself, and take a little bit of it back home when you leave.

NORTHERN NEW MEXICO'S best AUTHENTIC EXPERIENCES

- **Taos Pueblo:** If you see only one Native American site in your northern New Mexico visit, this should be it. This awe-inspiring structure, where about 150 residents still live much as their ancestors did more than 700 years ago, is bold and imposing, with mud-built rooms poetically stacked to echo the shape of Taos Mountain behind them. You can visit resident artists' studios, munch on bread baked in a *horno* (a beehive-shaped oven), and wander past the fascinating ruins of the old church and cemetery. See p. 148.

- **Santa Fe Opera:** One of the finest opera companies in the United States has called Santa Fe home for more than a half-century. Performances are held during the summer months in a hilltop, open-air (but mostly under-roof) amphitheater. Have the full local's experience by "tailgating," or having a picnic, in the parking lot before a show. See p. 104.
- **Albuquerque International Balloon Fiesta:** The desert skies fill with color as the world's largest balloon rally assembles some 500 hot-air balloons. Highlights are the mass ascension at sunrise and the special shapes rodeo, in which balloons in all sorts of whimsical forms, from liquor bottles to cows, rise into the sky. See p. 210.
- **Ojo Caliente Mineral Springs Resort and Spa:** About 45 minutes southwest of Taos in the tiny village of Ojo Caliente, this spa resort is a perfect place to soak your troubles away in geothermal mineral waters, ranging in temperature from 80 to 105 degrees. Each of the resort's four springs contains a different mineral, and the nine communal pools are filled with combinations of the mineral waters. There's also a mud pool, a full-service spa, and private pools with fireplaces for chilly evenings. See p. 160.
- **High Road to Taos:** This spectacular 80-mile route between Santa Fe and Taos takes you through red-painted deserts, villages bordered by apple and peach orchards, and the foothills of 13,000-foot peaks. You can stop in Cordova, known for its woodcarvers, or Chimayo, famed for its weavers—even rub some healing dirt between your fingers at the fabled 200-year old church, **El Santuario de Chimayó.** See p. 123.
- **Northern New Mexican Enchiladas:** There are few things more New Mexican than the enchilada. They're covered with rich chile sauces seasoned with garlic and oregano—order red, green, or "Christmas" (half red, half green). See p. 30.

NORTHERN NEW MEXICO'S best MUSEUMS

- **Georgia O'Keeffe Museum:** This Santa Fe museum honors renowned modernist artist Georgia O'Keeffe. After falling in love with the deserts of the Southwest in the 1930s, she moved in 1949 to the isolated northern New Mexico community of Abiquiu, which inspired her best-known works—striking paintings of flowers, animal skulls, and stark landscapes. See p. 73.
- **Harwood Museum of Art:** For an overview of Taos's fascinating contemporary arts history, head to this small but mighty museum. You'll find a good representation of each modern era, from the early–20th century Taos Society of Artists right up to the present. See p. 151.
- **Indian Pueblo Cultural Center:** There's no better way to learn about New Mexico's history than from the source. This Albuquerque institution is

Northern New Mexico

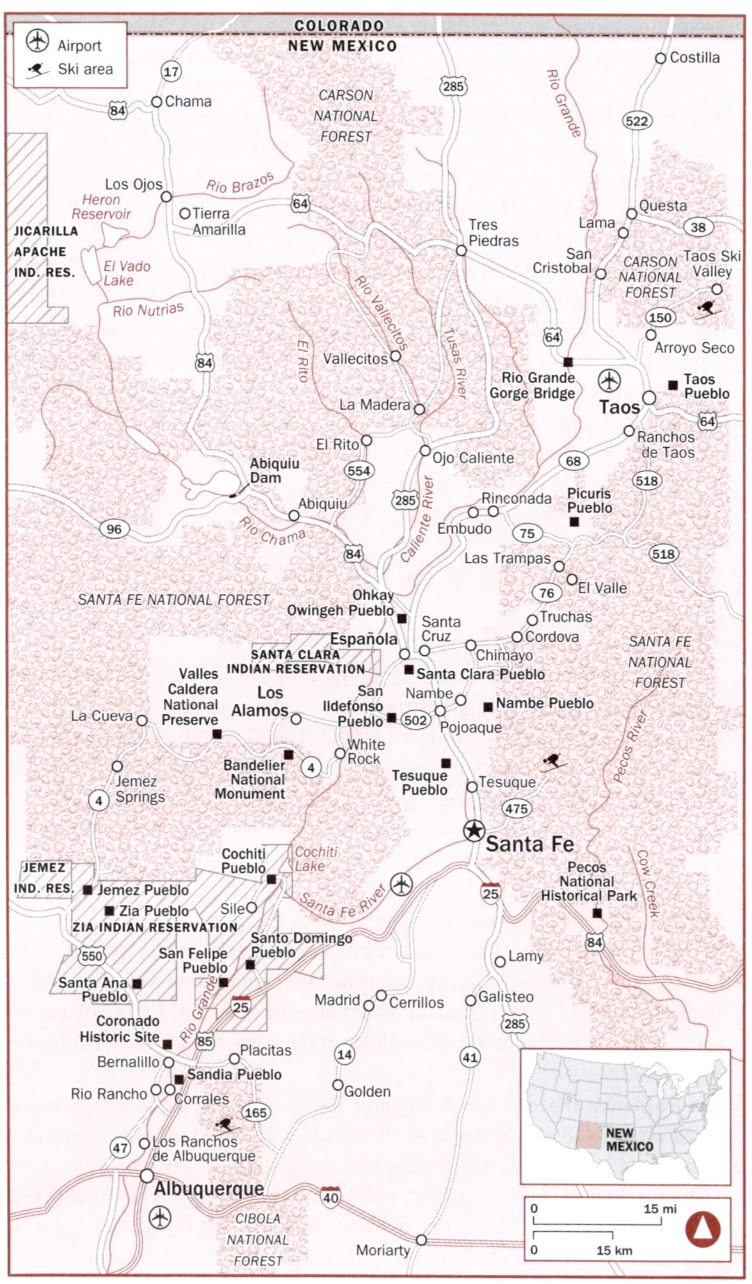

owned and operated by the state's 19 pueblos and draws from a collection of more than 2,500 pieces of pottery, jewelry, textiles, baskets, photographs, prints, paintings, and archaeological artifacts. There's also an excellent restaurant and gift shop, serving and selling authentic dishes and crafts. See p. 196.

- **Museum of International Folk Art:** Santa Fe's perpetually expanding collection of folk art is the largest in the world, with thousands of objects from more than 100 countries. You'll find an amazing array of imaginative works, ranging from Hispanic folk art *santos* (carved saints) to Indonesian textiles and African sculptures. See p. 78.
- **Millicent Rogers Museum:** This Taos museum is among the best collections anywhere of turquoise and silver American Indian jewelry, Navajo rugs, Pueblo pottery, and other Southwestern arts and crafts, born out of the personal collection of Standard Oil heiress Millicent Rogers. See p. 146.
- **New Mexico Museum of Natural History and Science:** Here you'll stroll through 12 billion years of natural history, from the very beginnings to the age of dinosaurs and beyond, with interactive exhibits, a planetarium, and a huge-screen theater. This Albuquerque science museum is actually fun, and (we'll say this quietly so the kids don't hear) educational. See p. 206.

NORTHERN NEW MEXICO'S best HOTELS

- **The Blake:** This premier hotel at the base of the lifts at Taos Ski Valley, named for the resort's founder Ernie Blake and his family, combines luxury and a casual simplicity befitting an Alpine-style ski resort. Most rooms have spacious walk-in showers and large windows providing spectacular views of the ski slopes and surrounding mountains. See p. 136.
- **La Fonda:** Settle into old Santa Fe at this historic hotel that combines all the modern conveniences you expect in a splurge-worthy hotel with enough vintage ambiance to knock your socks off. Head to the Bell Tower Bar for a drink, and enjoy a spectacular sunset view. See p. 54.
- **El Monte Sagrado:** With guest rooms, suites, and casitas set around a grassy "Sacred Circle," this eco-resort in Taos is the quintessence of a relaxing retreat. Every detail, from the waterfalls and chemical-free pool and hot tubs to the authentic theme decor in the rooms, has been created with care. See p. 130.
- **Los Poblanos Historic Inn & Organic Farm:** A stay at this boutique inn—listed on the National Register of Historic Places—ticks all the boxes for an unforgettable getaway. Its rooms and grounds have an understated yet authentic New Mexico character, and its setting—25 acres of formal flower gardens, ancient cottonwoods, fields of lavender, and organic vegetable gardens—feels wonderfully removed from the bustle of Albuquerque. See p. 181.

- **El Rey Court:** For historic charm and a lively scene (for Santa Fe), head to El Rey. Built in the 1930s as a motor lodge and added on to and upgraded over the years, it has a variety of room types, all different but nicely appointed, with a Route 66 ambience and nicely landscaped grounds. Its bar, La Reina, is one of the city's most popular hangouts, offering good live music and great people watching. See p. 56.
- **Sagebrush Inn & Suites:** This sprawling property about 3 miles south of Taos can please almost any taste, from old adobe rooms with kiva fireplaces to modern executive suites with all the 21st-century amenities. Set back from the highway with lovely landscaped grounds, Sagebrush Inn is a pleasant oasis to escape to at the end of a busy sightseeing day. The huge lobby bar is also a hotspot for country music and dancing. See p. 133.
- **Hotel Albuquerque at Old Town:** Just steps from Albuquerque's Old Town, this reasonably priced hotel has excellent service and artfully decorated rooms with Southwestern decor, plus good views of the Sandia Mountains. See p. 180.

NORTHERN NEW MEXICO'S best RESTAURANTS

- **Cafe Pasqual's:** Helmed by "the Alice Waters of Santa Fe," Katherine Kagel, this restaurant is as cozy and atmospheric as they come, with string-light ristras of red chiles and colorful Mexican papel picados hanging from the ceiling. If you have the time, go for both breakfast (order the *huevos barbacoa* made with beef cheeks) and dinner (order the *cochinita pibil,* a Yucatan-style dish with tangy marinated pork shoulder wrapped in a leaf and slow-cooked). See p. 62.
- **Campo at Los Poblanos:** For a delicious New American meal with New Mexican influences, head to this converted dairy farm set on the scenic grounds of Albuquerque's Los Poblanos hotel. Start with a cocktail featuring botanicals grown and distilled on site before enjoying a hearty meal that feels worth the price point. See p. 186.
- **El Chile Toreado:** For the best tacos in Santa Fe (and maybe the entire state), head to this food truck sporting a green-chile mustache parked off Cerrillos Road. Best bet: an *adovada*—pork marinated in chile adobo sauce—taco or burrito topped with the truck's signature chile sauce made of super-hot jalapeños. See p. 70.
- **The Compound:** This Canyon Road fine-dining classic (and a 2024 James Beard Award finalist) serves daring contemporary American food, combining regional ingredients with Mediterranean influences. You'll likely enjoy the roasted duck breast or the braised lamb shank. Even lunch entrees are a step above, such as the house-cured pastrami sandwich. See p. 64.
- **Doc Martin's:** Historic ambience, an inviting patio away from the traffic, and consistently excellent food all make Doc Martin's a long-time favorite

of Taos locals. The menu is fairly short, specializing in American and New Mexican dishes, and there's a good weekend brunch. We recommend the cornmeal-crusted rainbow trout, chile relleno, or what we consider one of the best green chile cheeseburgers in New Mexico. See p. 138.

- **Mary & Tito's Cafe:** Already an Albuquerque dining institution, this family-run restaurant continues to win over new devotees. For many, it's the best place in town to get a quintessential New Mexican dish: *carne adovada,* a stew of marinated roast pork that's slow-braised in red chile for hours. See p. 192.
- **Michael's Kitchen:** This casual eatery has been serving hearty, all-day New Mexican breakfasts to Taoseños since 1974. There's no more quintessential experience than loading up with an eggy enchilada plate overflowing with pinto beans and chile before a day at Taos Ski Resort, fly-fishing the Rio Grande, or hiking the Sangre de Cristo mountains. See p. 144.

NORTHERN NEW MEXICO'S best FREE THINGS TO DO

- **Browsing the Galleries Along Canyon Road:** Originally a Pueblo Indian route over the mountains and later an artists' community, Santa Fe's Canyon Road is now gallery central—the arts capital of the Southwest. The narrow one-way street is lined with more than 80 galleries, in addition to restaurants and private residences, where artwork ranges from the beautiful to the bizarre, from offbeat to world-class. See p. 99.
- **Experiencing a Pueblo Dance:** These traditional dances, related to the changing cycles of the earth, offer a unique chance to see how an indigenous culture worships and celebrates. Throughout the year, the Pueblo people participate in ceremonies ranging from harvest and deer dances to those commemorating the feast days of their particular saints—all in the mystical light of the northern New Mexico sun. See p. 110.
- **Exploring the Rio Grande Gorge:** You'll first see it as you come over a rise heading toward Taos, a colossal slice in the earth formed 130 million years ago. Drive about 35 miles north of town, near the village of Cerro, to the Wild Rivers Recreation Area, where you can hike down through millions of years of geologic history to dip your toes in the fabled *rio.* See p. 153.
- **Wandering Around Old Town:** Albuquerque's commercial center until about 1880, Old Town still gives a remarkable sense of what life was once like in a Southwestern village. Meander down crooked streets and narrow alleys, rest in the cottonwood-shaded plaza, and browse the art, jewelry, pottery, and weavings sold in the numerous shops. Don't miss the historic San Felipe de Neri Parish, built in 1793, with 5-foot-thick adobe walls. See p. 198.

NORTHERN NEW MEXICO'S best OF OUTDOORS

- **Taos Ski Valley:** World-renowned for its challenging runs and spectacular powder snow, Taos Ski Valley has long been a pilgrimage site for extreme skiers. Newer bowls now accommodate intermediate and beginning skiers. Taos welcomes snowboarders and has an excellent children's ski school. See p. 155.
- **Sandia Peak Tramway:** The world's longest tramway ferries passengers 2¾ miles, from Albuquerque's city limits to the summit of 10,378-foot Sandia Peak. On the way, you may see Rocky Mountain bighorn sheep and circling birds of prey. Go in the evening to watch the sun set, and then enjoy the glimmering city lights on your way down. See p. 198.
- **Bandelier National Monument:** These ruins provide a spectacular look into the lives of the ancestral Puebloan culture, which reached its peak in this area around C.E. 1100. Less than 15 miles south of Los Alamos, the ruins spread across a peaceful canyon populated by deer and rabbits. Make your way through the canyon to the most dramatic site, a kiva and dwelling in a cave 140 feet above the canyon floor. See p. 120.
- **Whitewater Rafting on the Rio Grande:** In spring and early summer, the region's most notorious whitewater trip, the Taos Box, takes rafters on an 18-mile jaunt through the Rio Grande Gorge. Less extreme types can enjoy a trip down the river from Pilar and still get plenty wet. See p. 160.
- **Hot-Air Ballooning:** One of the biggest treats about being in Albuquerque or Taos is waking most days and seeing colorful balloons floating serenely on the horizon. The experience of riding in one, however, is indescribable. You're literally floating, being carried along by nothing but the wind. Try it! See p. 210 or 157.
- **Bosque del Apache National Wildlife Refuge:** About 90 miles south of Albuquerque lies one of the nation's finest wildlife refuges. By late December, this riparian preserve may harbor as many as 45,000 snow geese, 60,000 ducks of various species, and close to 20,000 sandhill cranes. Seeing them "fly out" to the fields in search of food in the morning or "fly in" to the lakes in the evening is a life-altering experience. See p. 224.

NORTHERN NEW MEXICO'S best FOR FAMILIES

- **The Anderson-Abruzzo Albuquerque International Balloon Museum:** Fun and fascinating, entertaining and educational, this Albuquerque museum is a favorite of kids because of its many hands-on activities, multimedia technology, and the balloon flight simulator. See p. 196.
- **¡Explora!:** Part science center, part children's museum, part Grandma's attic and Grandpa's garage, Albuquerque's ¡Explora! scores big with kids

for its lively interactive experiences, many of which focus on the unique characteristics of elements, like "Moving Air" and "Water of Life." Younger children love the arts and crafts workshop, where they can make something to take home. See p. 206.

- **The Museum of International Folk Art:** Toys, toys, and more toys fill the Girard Wing of this world-class Santa Fe museum, the center of a collection of over 100,000 dolls, masks, dioramas, animals, and other objects gathered from over 100 countries. There's a play area and hands-on craft section for itchy fingers, as well as a gift shop that's almost overwhelming in its colorful selection. You may have to drag the kids out. See p. 78.
- **Riding the Cumbres & Toltec Scenic Railroad:** Step back to the days of the Wild West and get some cinders in your hair aboard this steam-powered train, which starts its trip into the Colorado mountains in Chama. Kids will have fun watching as the train chugs up the mountains, and especially enjoy the open gondola car. See p. 173.
- **The Santa Fe Children's Museum:** Interactive exhibits and hands-on activities here will keep the kids happy and busy. In the "Discovery" section are a microscope lab that allows kids to inspect fossil, rocks, and insects, as well as a carnivorous plant terrarium (where Cornelius the snake also lives). See p. 89.

NORTHERN NEW MEXICO'S best OFFBEAT EXPERIENCES

- **American International Rattlesnake Museum:** A natural fit for a desert capital like Albuquerque, this small museum displays living specimens of common, uncommon, and very rare rattlesnakes of North, Central, and South America, in naturally landscaped habitats. Some 30 species are included, along with oddities such as albino rattlesnakes. See p. 207.
- **The Burning of Zozobra:** Part of the annual early-September Las Fiestas de Santa Fe, this ritual draws crowds to the core of the city to cheer as "Old Man Gloom," a giant marionette, moans and struggles as he burns. The Fiestas also include Masses, parades, dances, food, and arts. See p. 33.
- **Theater Grottesco:** This Santa Fe theater troupe likes to shock, confuse, confound, and tickle its audience's funny bones. Their original works combine adept movement with sound, story, and, well . . . brilliance. See p. 105.
- **Meow Wolf:** Constantly evolving and changing, this interactive art installation in Santa Fe is otherworldly, somewhat bizarre, and entirely fascinating, combining every type of media one can imagine, from architecture to painting to performance to audio engineering. It also hosts great live music year-round. See p. 73.

NORTHERN NEW MEXICO IN CONTEXT

2

Although Santa Fe has claimed the title of "The City Different," all of northern New Mexico really qualifies as being different from anywhere else in America. When you wake up in Santa Fe, Taos, or even Albuquerque (probably the closest New Mexico gets to a "normal" community), you know you're not in Chicago, or Long Island, or even Los Angeles. The only similar example we can think of is the French Quarter of New Orleans, but even that's nothing like New Mexico.

In many ways, visiting northern New Mexico is like visiting a foreign country. The landscape is rugged and unforgiving, the weather unpredictable, and the customs, at least to some, are strange. Maybe that's why so many people love it.

From the moment you set foot in this 121,666-square-mile state, you're met with wildly varied terrain, temperature, and temperament. On a single day, you might experience temperatures from 25° to 75°F (-4° to 24°C). From the vast heat and dryness of White Sands in the summer to the subzero, snow-encrusted Wheeler Peak in the winter, New Mexico's beauty is carved by extremes.

Culturally, this is also the case. Pueblo, Navajo, and Apache tribes occupy much of the state's lands, many of them still speaking their native languages and observing the traditions of their people. Some even live as their ancestors did, without running water and electricity. Meanwhile, the local Hispanic people tend to remain deeply linked to their Spanish roots, practicing a devout Catholicism and speaking a centuries-old Spanish dialect; some still live by subsistence farming in tiny mountain villages.

New Mexico has its very own sense of time and its own social mores. People rarely arrive on time for appointments, and businesses don't always hold to their posted hours. In most cases, people wear whatever they want here: Even at formal occasions you'll see men wearing button-down shirts with bolo ties and neatly pressed jeans, and women in cowboy boots and broomstick skirts.

All this leads to a certain lost-and-not-caring-to-be-found spell that the place casts on visitors. We find ourselves standing amid the dust or sparkling light, within the extreme heat or cold, not sure whether to speak Spanish or English. That's when we let go completely of mainstream society's dictates. We slip into a kayak and let the river take us, or hike to a peak and look at the world from a new perspective. Or we climb into a car and drive past ancient ruins, past ghost mining towns, under hot-air balloons, and around hand-smoothed adobe *santuarios*—all on the road to nowhere, New Mexico's best destination. At some point in your travels, you'll likely find yourself on this road, and you'll realize that there's no destination so resonant, yet elusive.

NEW MEXICO TODAY

New Mexico is a cultural tapestry with many strands. First came the ancestral Puebloans (also called the Anasazi), an enigmatic people who inhabited this area from C.E. 1100 until the arrival of the Spanish conquistadors, around 1550. When the conquistadors arrived, they imposed a new foreign order on the resident Americans and their land, changing most Native American names, renaming the villages "pueblos," and forcibly converting native populations to Catholicism. When the Santa Fe Trail opened in 1821, Anglos began to move into the territory, and the United States gained possession in the 1840s during the Mexican War. Today, northern New Mexico is experiencing another transition, as the Anglo population soars and outside money and values again make their way in. The process continues to transform New Mexico's three distinct cultures, albeit in a much less violent manner than during the Spanish conquest.

Certainly, the newcomers—many of them from large cities—add a cosmopolitan flavor to life here. The variety of restaurants has greatly increased, as have entertainment options. For their relatively small sizes, the communities of Taos and Santa Fe offer a broad variety of cuisines and cultural events. Santa Fe has developed a strong dance and drama scene, with treats such as flamenco and opera, and Taos is where you want to go for chamber music. Albuquerque has an exciting downtown nightlife scene; you can walk from club to club and hear a wealth of jazz, rock, country, and alternative music.

For decades, many transplants, drawn by the adobe houses and exotic feel of the place, often bring only a loose appreciation for the area and fail to even try to blend in. Some tend to romanticize the lifestyle of the other cultures and trivialize their beliefs. Native American symbols are casually used as Southwestern decorative motifs (including the Zia symbol in the state's own flag; see "The Sun Worshippers of New Mexico," p. 12), and New Age groups appropriate traditional rituals, such as sweats (in which believers sit encamped in a very hot, enclosed space to cleanse their spirits). Cultural and economic change affect the countryside as well, where land is being developed at an alarming rate.

This transformation is also apparent in the number of new stores springing up. For some residents, these are a welcome relief from the ubiquitous Western clothing stores and provincial dress shops, but the downside is that historic city plazas, which once provided goods and services for the resident communities, are now jammed with T-shirt shops and galleries aimed at tourists. Many of these claim to sell authentic Native American crafts, jewelry in particular, but the goods are actually mass-produced abroad (be sure to ask the salesperson questions about an item's provenance). Many locals now rarely visit their plazas except during special events such as fiestas.

> **Impressions**
>
> "Things which apply elsewhere often do not apply in New Mexico."
>
> –Lew Wallace, governor of New Mexico Territory (1878–81) and author of *Ben-Hur*

Environmental threats are another regional reality. Nuclear waste issues are part of an ongoing conflict affecting the entire Southwest, and a section of southern New Mexico has been designated a nuclear waste site. Because much of the waste must pass through Santa Fe, the U.S. government, along with the New Mexico state government, constructed a bypass that directs some transit traffic around the west side of the city.

Still, population growth has also brought positive changes, and many locals have directly benefited from New Mexico's influx of wealthy newcomers and its popularity as a tourist destination. Businesses and industries large and small have come to the area, bringing money and jobs. Local artists and artisans have also benefited, and many craftspeople—furniture makers, tin workers, potters, and weavers—have expanded their businesses.

The influx of people and new ideas has broadened the sensibility of what would otherwise be a fairly provincial state. There's a general live-and-let-live attitude here, which has made the area a refuge for many in the LGBTQIA+ community, as well as for political exiles, such as Tibetans.

As northern New Mexico's popularity as a tourist destination has leveled out somewhat in the 21st century, some artists and businesspeople lament the loss of the crowds they saw back in the '80s, yet many residents are glad that wave has subsided. It's good news for travelers, too; you no longer have to compete so heavily for restaurant seats or space when hiking through ruins. Though parts of northern New Mexico have lost some of the unique charm that attracted so many to the area, the overall feeling is still one of mystery and a cultural depth unmatched in the country.

Preserving Cultural Identity

Faced with new challenges to their ways of life, both Native American and Latino people are marshaling forces to protect their cultural identities. A prime concern is language. Over the years, many Pueblo people have begun to speak more and more English, with their children getting little exposure to

THE sun worshippers OF NEW MEXICO

One of the simplest yet most easily recognized state flags in the U.S., New Mexico's official flag got its start in the 1920s with a flag-designing contest organized by the Daughters of the American Revolution. The winning design, officially proclaimed in 1925, turned out to be a red sun symbol, called a Zia, with a yellow background.

The design of the Zia is an interpretation of a sun image found on a late-19th-century water jar from Zia Pueblo. The image is a circle from which four points radiate, and each of the four points is made up of four themes: the four seasons of the year (spring, summer, autumn, winter); the four directions of earth (north, south, east, west); the four times of day (sunrise, noon, evening, night); and the four stages of life (childhood, youth, adulthood, old age), all tied together in the circle of life. For decades, the symbol has been appropriated in ways that the Zia people have felt to be disrespectful. Efforts by the Pueblo to copyright the emblem have been unsuccessful.

their native tongue. In a number of the pueblos, elders are working with schoolchildren in language classes. Some of the pueblos have even developed written dictionaries, the first time their languages have been presented in this form.

Some pueblos have introduced programs to conserve the environment, preserve ancient seed strains, maintain traditional crafts, and protect religious rites. Because their religion is tied closely to nature, a loss of natural resources threatens the entire culture. Certain rituals have been closed to outsiders, the most notable being some of the rituals of Shalako at Zuni, a popular and elaborate series of year-end ceremonies.

Hispanic people, through art and observance of cultural traditions, are also embracing their roots. In northern New Mexico, murals depicting important historic events, such as the 1848 Treaty of Guadalupe Hidalgo, adorn many walls. The **Spanish Market** in Santa Fe, held every July, has expanded into a grand celebration of traditional arts, from tin working to *santo* (icon) carving. Public schools have bilingual education programs, allowing students to embrace their Spanish-speaking roots.

Gambling Wins & Losses

Gambling, a fact of life and source of much-needed revenue for Native American tribes across the country, has caused controversy in northern New Mexico for a number of years. In 1994, then-Governor Gary Johnson signed a pact with tribes in New Mexico, ratified by the U.S. Department of the Interior, to allow full-scale gambling. **Tesuque Pueblo** (p. 108) was one of the first to begin a massive expansion, and many other pueblos followed suit.

Many New Mexicans are concerned about the tone gambling sets in their state. The casinos are often managed by outsiders. Though most residents appreciate the economic boost that gambling brings to the local tribes—it does provide some tribe members with jobs—critics wonder where gambling profits actually go, and if the casinos are really a good thing for the tribes long-term. Another negative is that the low-cost meals most casinos offer to get would-be gamblers through the doors have impacted locally run restaurants nearby, even driving some out of business.

Santa Fe Today

There's an inexplicable magic in Santa Fe. You'll sense it when you glimpse an old adobe building set against blue mountains and giant billowing thunderheads, when you hear a ranchero song come from a low-rider's radio, or you smell chile roasting in large cylinder cages at roadside vending booths at the start of fall. Although it's speeding up, the pace of life here is still a few steps slower than that of the rest of the country. Like a lot of countries south of the border, we use the word *mañana* to describe the pace—which doesn't mean "tomorrow" exactly, it just means "not today." There's also a level of creativity here that you'll find in few other places in the country. Artists who have fled big-city jobs come here to follow their passions, alongside locals who grew up making crafts and continue to do so. Conversations often center on how to plan one's day to take advantage of the incredible outdoors while still making enough money to survive.

However, Santa Fe's precipitous growth and enduring tourist popularity have led to conflict and squabbling. Outsiders have bought up land in the hills around the city, building housing developments and sprawling single-family homes. The hills that local populations claimed for centuries as their own are being overrun, while property taxes for all have skyrocketed. Local outcry has prompted the city to implement zoning restrictions on where and how development can proceed. Some of the restrictions include banning building on ridge tops and on steep slopes and limiting the size of homes built.

Only in recent years have Santa Fe's politicians become conscientious about the city's growth. Former mayor Debbie Jaramillo was one of the first local politicians to take a strong stand against growth. A fiery native of Santa Fe, she came into office in the 1990s as a representative of *la gente* (the people) and set about discouraging tourism and rapid development. Subsequent mayors have taken a middle-of-the-road approach, which has resulted in a calmer community and an increase in tourism and development. As in other popular mountain towns, efforts have been made to curb short-term rentals. In 2022, the Santa Fe County Commission introduced a temporary moratorium on new permits for property owners who don't live on site. The latest ordinance, as of this writing, allows non-residents to operate, but only allows 3% to 7% of a neighborhood's total number of properties to be rentals.

Taos Today

A funky town in the middle of a beautiful, sage-covered valley, Taos is full of narrow streets dotted with galleries and shops—and locals are determined to keep it that way. An unusually vocal and active contingent of Taos residents consistently work to block heavy development in the area. Several times since the 1980s they stalled plans to expand their airport, though eventually they lost; in the 1990s, they blocked plans for a $40-million golf course and housing development; and in 2003, they prevented a Super Walmart from opening. It's hard to say where Taos gets its rebellious strength; the roots may lie in the hippie community that settled here in the '60s, or possibly the Pueblo community around which the city formed. After all, Taos Pueblo was at the center of the 17th-century Pueblo revolt.

Still, changes occur, even in Taos. The blinking light that for years residents used as a reference point has given way to a real traffic signal north of town. You'll also see the main route through town becoming more and more like Cerrillos Road in Santa Fe, as fast-food restaurants and service businesses set up shop. Though the town is working on alternate routes to divert through-traffic around downtown, there's no feasible way to widen the main drag in the Taos Plaza area, because the street—which started out as a wagon trail—is bordered closely by historic buildings. Like Santa Fe, Taos has started capping short-term rentals, starting with a 2024 ordinance that limits new permits to 400.

Albuquerque Today

The largest city in New Mexico, Albuquerque is more like a suburb without a city. Sure, there are some relatively tall buildings and there is an old town surrounding a plaza, but it doesn't feel like a metropolis. It's an easy city to get around in, with shopping centers dotted among residential areas and plenty of parking. Many New Mexicans from outside Albuquerque primarily come for medical specialists and serious shopping. This is where you'll find Costco, Sam's Club, and the state's major furniture and appliance stores.

Of course, growth has had its effect. The city, which old-timers remember as being little more than a big town, now sprawls more than 20 miles, from the lava-crested mesas on the west side of the Rio Grande to the steep alluvial slopes of the Sandia Mountains on the east, and north and south through the Rio Grande Valley. New subdivisions seem to sprout up almost daily.

Despite the growth, Albuquerque is prized by New Mexicans for its authenticity. You'll find none of the self-conscious artsy atmosphere of Santa Fe here. Its traditional New Mexico feel is evident in the downtown area, where shiny skyscrapers are built around the original Route 66, which still maintains some of its 1950s charm.

The city's growing pains are symbolized by concerns over **Petroglyph National Monument** (p. 205), on the city's west side. Five extinct volcanoes in this area created lava flows that became a hunting and gathering place for prehistoric inhabitants, who left a chronicle of their beliefs etched in the dark basalt boulders; more than 25,000 petroglyphs have been found in the preserve. Yet it's difficult for visitors these days to ponder what life was like for those ancient peoples, when they're bombarded with the sound of traffic whizzing by and the sight of a trailer park nearby.

NEW MEXICO THROUGH TIME

The Pueblo tribes of the upper Rio Grande Valley are descendants of the people formerly called Anasazi, now better known as ancestral Puebloans. From the mid-9th to the 13th century, these people lived in the Four Corners Region, where the states of New Mexico, Arizona, Colorado, and Utah meet. On rock faces throughout northern New Mexico, you'll see the petroglyphs they left behind, symbols carved in sandstone—the wavy mark of Avanyu, the river serpent, or the ubiquitous Kokopelli playing his magic flute. The ancestral Puebloans built spectacular structures—you get an idea of their scale and intricacy at the ruins at **Chaco Canyon** (p. 229) and **Mesa Verde** in Colorado. It isn't known exactly why they abandoned their homes; some archaeologists believe it was due to drought, others claim it was social unrest, but most now believe it was likely a combination of both. Most theories suggest that they moved from these sites to such areas as Frijoles Canyon (**Bandelier National Monument,** p. 120) and **Puye** (p. 113), where they built villages resembling the ones they had left. Then several hundred years later, for reasons not yet understood, they moved down from the canyons onto the flat plain next to the Rio Grande. By the time the Spaniards arrived in the 1500s, the Pueblo culture was well established throughout what would become northern and western New Mexico.

Architectural style was a unifying mark of the otherwise diverse ancestral Puebloan and today's Pueblo cultures. Both built condominium-style communities of stone and mud adobe bricks, three and four stories high (five stories at Taos). Grouped around central plazas, the villages incorporated circular spiritual chambers called *kivas.* As farmers, the ancestral Puebloan and Pueblo peoples used the waters of the Rio Grande and its tributaries to irrigate fields of corn, beans, and squash. They also hunted deer, rabbits, and whatever else was in the area, and created elaborate pottery.

The Spanish Occupation

After conquering Mexico's Aztecs from 1519 to 1521, the Spanish ventured into the upper Rio Grande area. In 1540, Francisco Vázquez de Coronado led an expedition in search of the fabled Seven Cities of Cíbola, coincidentally introducing horses and sheep to the region. Neither Coronado nor a succession of fortune-seeking conquistadors could locate the legendary cities of gold, so the Spanish concentrated their efforts on exploiting the people already here.

Franciscan priests attempted to turn the Pueblo people into model peasants. Their churches became the focal points of every pueblo, with Catholic schools an essential adjunct. By 1625, there were approximately 50 churches in the Rio Grande Valley. (Two of the Pueblo missions, at Isleta and Acoma, are still in use today.) The Pueblos, however, weren't enthused about doing "God's work" for the Spanish—building new adobe missions, tilling fields, and weaving garments for export to Mexico—so Spanish soldiers came north to back the padres in extracting labor. In effect, the Pueblo people were forced into slavery.

Santa Fe was founded in 1610 as the seat of Spanish government in the upper Rio Grande. Governor Don Pedro de Peralta named the settlement La Villa Real de la Santa Fe de San Francisco de Asis (The Royal City of the Holy Faith of St. Francis of Assisi). The **Palace of the Governors** (p. 76) has been used continuously as a public building ever since—by the Spanish, Pueblos (1680–92), Mexicans, and Americans. Today it stands as the flagship of the state museum system.

Decades of oppression by the Spanish colonists led to Pueblo unrest. Uprisings in the 1630s in Taos and Jemez left village priests dead and triggered even more repression. In 1680, a unified Pueblo rebellion, orchestrated from Taos, succeeded in driving the Spaniards from the upper Rio Grande Valley. The leaders of the revolt defiled or destroyed the churches, just as the Spanish had destroyed the religious symbols of the native people. Revolutionaries took the Palace of the Governors, where they burned archives and prayer books, and converted the chapel into a kiva. They also burned much of the property in Santa Fe that had been built by the Europeans and laid siege to Spanish settlements up and down the Rio Grande Valley. Forced to retreat to Mexico, the colonists were not able to retake Santa Fe until 12 years later. Bloody battles raged for the next several years, but by the beginning of the 18th century, Nuevo Mexico was again firmly in Spanish hands.

In the mid-1700s, the Franciscan priests departed, exasperated by their failure to wipe out all vestiges of traditional Pueblo religion. Throughout the Spanish occupation, eight generations of Pueblos had clung tenaciously to their way of life. However, by the 1750s, the number of Pueblo villages had shrunk by half.

DATELINE

- **25,000 B.C.E.** Sandia people leave earliest evidence of humans in the land that will become New Mexico.
- **3000 B.C.E.** First evidence of stable farming settlements in region.
- **C.E. 700** Earliest evidence of ancestral Puebloan presence.
- **1540** Francisco Vázquez de Coronado marches north from Mexico in search of a "city of gold." When he leaves 2 years later, he declares his mission a failure.
- **1598** In what is considered the founding of New Mexico, Juan de Oñate establishes the first Spanish capital north of present-day Española. In **1608,** Oñate is removed as governor and sent to Mexico City to face charges of abuse of power and mistreatment of the Native Americans.
- **1610** Immigration to New Mexico from Mexico increases; Don Pedro de Peralta establishes Santa Fe as the capital.
- **1680** Pueblo tribes revolt against the Spanish, driving the colonists back to Mexico. The colonists finally recapture Santa Fe in **1692.**
- **1706** Albuquerque is established.
- **1743** First French traders enter Santa Fe.

The Arrival of the Anglos

The first Anglos to spend time in the upper Rio Grande Valley were mountain men: itinerant hunters, trappers, and traders. At the forefront of the U.S. westward expansion, they began settling in New Mexico in the first decade of the 19th century. Many married into Pueblo or Hispanic families.

Perhaps the best known was **Kit Carson,** a sometime federal agent, sometime scout, whose legend is inextricably interwoven with that of early Taos. Though he seldom stayed in one place for long, he considered the Taos area his home. It is believed he was married three times, to women in the Arapaho and Cheyenne tribes, and finally to Josepha Jaramillo, the Hispanic daughter of a leading Taos citizen. Later he became a prime force in the final subjugation of the Navajos, responsible for what was called the "Long Walk," the forced march of Navajo people that resulted in thousands of deaths. The Taos home where he lived off and on for 40 years, until his death in 1868, is now a museum (see p. 152).

Wagon trains and eastern merchants followed Carson and the other early settlers. Santa Fe, Taos, and Albuquerque, already major trading and commercial centers at the northern end of the **Chihuahua Trail** (the Camino Real from Veracruz, Mexico, 1,000 miles south), became the western terminals of the new **Santa Fe Trail** (from Independence, Missouri, 800 miles east).

After Mexico gained its independence from Spain in 1821, the newly independent Mexico granted the Pueblo people full citizenship and abandoned restrictive trade laws instituted by their former Spanish rulers. Nevertheless, over the subsequent 25 years of direct rule from Mexico City, things were still not peaceful in the upper Rio Grande. Instead, they were marked by ongoing rebellion against severe taxation, especially in Taos. Neither did things quiet

1807 Zebulon Pike leads the first Anglo-American expedition into New Mexico.

1821 Mexico gains independence from Spain; Santa Fe Trail opened to international trade.

1828 Kit Carson, the legendary frontiersman, arrives in Taos; first major gold discovery in the western United States is made in the Ortiz Mountains south of Santa Fe.

1841 Soldiers from Texas invade New Mexico and claim all land east of the Rio Grande for Texas, but are driven out by New Mexico forces.

1846 The Mexican-American War breaks out; Gen. Stephen Kearny takes possession of New Mexico for the United States. In **1847,** Governor Charles Bent is killed in Taos during a revolt against U.S. control. In **1848,** with the Treaty of Guadalupe Hidalgo, Mexico officially cedes New Mexico to the U.S.

1864 Navajos relocate to Bosque Redondo Reservation, at Fort Sumner in eastern New Mexico, by what is known as the infamous "Long Walk," in which thousands die of disease and starvation. Those that survive will return to their native homeland in **1868.**

continues

down when the United States assumed control of the territory during the Mexican-American War (1846–1848). Shortly after General Stephen Kearney occupied Santa Fe (in a bloodless takeover) on orders of President James Polk in 1846, a revolt in Taos in 1847 led to the slaying of Charles Bent, the new U.S. governor of New Mexico. At the end of the war, in 1848, the Treaty of Guadalupe Hidalgo officially transferred title of New Mexico, along with Texas, Arizona, and California, to the United States.

Aside from Kit Carson, perhaps the two most notable personalities of 19th-century New Mexico were priests. **Father Antonio José Martínez** (1793–1867) was one of the first local-born priests to serve his people. Ordained in Durango, Mexico, he jolted the Catholic church after assuming control of the Taos parish. Martínez abolished the obligatory church tithe (a donation of 10% of one's income) because it was a hardship on poor parishioners. In 1835 he published the first newspaper in the territory, and after the United States annexed the territory, he fought large land acquisitions by Anglos.

Impressions

"In New Mexico he always awoke a young man; not until he rose and began to shave did he realize that he was growing older."

–Archbishop Latour in Willa Cather's *Death Comes for the Archbishop*, 1927

On all these issues, Martínez was at odds with **Bishop Jean-Baptiste Lamy** (1814–88), a Frenchman appointed in 1851 to supervise the affairs of the first independent New Mexican diocese. Lamy, upon whose life Willa Cather based her novel *Death Comes for the Archbishop,* served the diocese for 37 years. Lamy didn't take kindly to Martínez's independent streak and, after repeated conflicts, excommunicated the maverick priest in 1857. But Martínez was steadfast in

1878–81 Lincoln County War erupts, which epitomizes the lawlessness and violence of the Wild West.

1879 Atchison, Topeka, and Santa Fe Railroad routes main line through Las Vegas (NM), Albuquerque, El Paso, and Deming, where connection is made with California's South Pacific Line.

1886 Apache chief Geronimo is captured, signaling the end of New Mexico's Indian wars.

1898 Painters Ernest Blumenschein and Bert Phillips arrive in Taos. In **1914** they found the Taos Society of Artists.

1912 New Mexico becomes the 47th state.

1916 Mexican revolutionary Pancho Villa raids Columbus, New Mexico, leaving 17 Americans dead.

1924 Native Americans granted full U.S. citizenship, although they will not be allowed to vote in state elections until **1948.**

1943 Los Alamos National Laboratory built; "Manhattan Project" scientists spend 2 years in complete seclusion developing nuclear weapons. The first atomic bomb is exploded at Trinity Site in **1945.**

1947 Reports of a flying saucer crash near Roswell make national headlines, despite the U.S. Air Force's denials that it occurred. Not until his preaching. He established an independent church and continued as northern New Mexico's spiritual leader until his death.

Lamy made many positive contributions to New Mexico, especially in the fields of education and architecture. Santa Fe's Romanesque **Basilica Cathedral of St. Francis of Assisi** (p. 80) and the nearby Gothic-style **Loretto Chapel** (p. 84) were constructed under his direction. But he was adamant about adhering to strict Catholic religious tenets, while Martínez embraced folk traditions, including the craft of *santero* (religious icon) carving, and tolerated the Penitentes, a flagellant sect that had flourished since the Franciscans' departure.

The Railroad Boom & the 20th Century

With the advent of the **Atchison, Topeka and Santa Fe Railway** in 1879, New Mexico began to boom. Albuquerque, in particular, prospered in the wake of major gold strikes in the Madrid Valley, close to ancient turquoise mines. By the time the gold lodes began to shrink in the 1890s, cattle and sheep ranching had become well entrenched. The territory's growth culminated in statehood in 1912.

Territorial governor **Lew Wallace,** who served from 1878 to 1881, was instrumental in promoting interest in the arts, which today flourish in northern New Mexico. While occupying the Palace of the Governors, Wallace penned the great biblical novel *Ben-Hur.* In the 1890s, Ernest Blumenschein, Bert Phillips, and Joseph Sharp launched the **Taos Art Colony;** it boomed in the decade following World War I when Mabel Dodge Luhan, D. H. Lawrence, Georgia O'Keeffe, Willa Cather, and many others visited or established residence here.

During World War II, the federal government displaced Pueblo villages and Mexican-American ranching communities to establish the **Los Alamos**

1994 will the U.S. Air Force, under pressure from Congress, reopen its investigation, which eventually concludes that the debris found was likely from tests of a secret Cold War spy balloon. UFO believers allege a cover-up.

1972 Pioneer balloonist Sid Cutter establishes the Albuquerque International Balloon Fiesta.

1982 Space shuttle Columbia lands at White Sands Space Harbor near Alamogordo.

1984 New Mexico's last remaining section of famed Route 66, near San Jon, is abandoned.

1990 New Mexico's last uranium mine, near Grants, closes.

2010 Santa Fe celebrates its 400-year anniversary; Governor Bill Richardson announces that he will not pardon famed outlaw Billy the Kid.

2021 Virgin Galactic launches its first human spaceflight from Spaceport America, in the New Mexico desert north of Las Cruces.

2024 Around 65,000 gather in Santa Fe to celebrate the 100th anniversary of the **Burning of Zozobra** (see p. 33), an annual September tradition that symbolizes the start of a new beginning.

> **Impressions**
>
> "I am become death, the shatterer of worlds."
>
> –J. Robert Oppenheimer, quoting from ancient Hindu texts, shortly after the successful detonation of the first atomic bomb

National Laboratory, where the Manhattan Project and other top-secret atomic experiments were developed and perfected. The impact of the lab is still felt among these communities; recent plans to ramp up production of plutonium pits, the base radioactive material of nuclear weapons, has troubled residents who have long questioned the potential health impacts of living near the site.

This legacy of scientific research and military support continues today; Albuquerque is among the nation's leaders in attracting defense contracts and high technology. The relatively unsettled desert landscape here has attracted such projects as the Karl G. Jansky Very Large Array, the world's most powerful radio telescope, which began operations in 1981, and the Waste Isolation Pilot Project, the nation's first deep-geologic repository for permanent disposal of radioactive waste, which began storage operations in 1998. Holloman Air Force Base, near White Sands National Monument, served as the landing space for the U.S. space shuttle *Columbia* in 1982, and Spaceport America, the world's first purpose-built base for commercial outer-space transport, began development in 2006 in the desert 45 miles north of Las Cruces. The site hosted Virgin Galactic's first human spaceflight in 2021, which the company celebrated by displaying the Zia symbol, sacred to the Zia people and featured on the state's flag, on the vessel's exterior.

ART & ARCHITECTURE

Land of Art

It's all in the light—or at least that's why many artists say they were drawn to northern New Mexico. In truth, the light is only part of the attraction: Nature in this part of the country, with its awe-inspiring thunderheads, endless expanse of blue skies, and rugged desert, is itself a canvas. To record the wonders of earth and sky, the ancestral Puebloans imprinted images—in the form of **petroglyphs** and **pictographs**—on the sides of caves and on stones, as well as on the sides of pots shaped from clay dug in the hills. Today's Pueblo tribes carry on that legacy, and other more recent arrivals copy those motifs.

Life in northern New Mexico is shaped by the arts. Everywhere you turn, you see pottery, paintings, jewelry, and weavings. You're liable to meet an artist whether you're having coffee in a Taos cafe or walking along Canyon Road in Santa Fe. Oh, and be careful driving along the dirt back roads—you wouldn't want to run over a painter at his easel or a photographer hovered over her tripod.

Each pueblo has a trademark design, such as the black pottery from **Santa Clara** (p. 113) and **San Ildefonso** (p. 111), or needlepoint silver work from **Zuni Pueblo,** on the western edge of New Mexico. Bear in mind that the images used often have deep symbolic meaning. When purchasing art or an artifact, you may want to talk to its maker about what the symbols mean. Hispanic villages are also distinguished by their artistic identities. **Chimayo** (p. 123) has become a center for Hispanic weaving, while the village of **Cordova** (p. 124) is known for its *santo* (icon) carving. *Santos, retablos* (paintings), and *bultos* (sculptures), as well as works in tin, are traditional devotional arts tied to the Roman Catholic faith. Sometimes, these works are sold out of artists' homes, an opportunity for you to glimpse the lives of the artists and the surroundings that inspire them.

Many non-native artists have also flocked here, particularly during the 20th and 21st centuries, and established important art societies. One of the most notable is the **Taos Society of Artists.** Its founders, artists **Bert Phillips** and **Ernest L. Blumenschein,** were traveling through the area from Colorado on a mission to sketch the Southwest when their wagon broke down north of Taos. The scenery so impressed them that they abandoned their journey and stayed. Joseph Sharp joined them, and still later came Oscar Berninghaus, Walter Ufer, Herbert Dunton, and others. You can see a brilliant collection of some of their romantically lit portraits and landscapes at the **Taos Art Museum** (p. 148). Another major player in Taos's artistic development was writer and arts patron **Mabel Dodge Luhan,** who in the 1920s held court for many notables, including Georgia O'Keeffe, Willa Cather, and D. H. Lawrence. These elements explain why this town of just under 6,000 inhabitants has so many arts-and-crafts galleries, as well as numerous resident painters, sculptors, photographers, and writers.

Santa Fe's own art society was begun in the 1920s by a nucleus of five painters who became known as **Los Cinco Pintores.** Jozef Bakos, Fremont Ellis, Walter Mruk, Willard Nash, and Will Shuster lived in the area of dusty Canyon Road (now the de facto arts center of Santa Fe). Despite its relatively small size, Santa Fe today is considered one of the top art markets in the United States.

Perhaps the most celebrated artist associated with northern New Mexico is **Georgia O'Keeffe** (1887–1986), a painter who worked and lived here most of her later years. O'Keeffe's first sojourn to New Mexico in 1929 inspired her sensuous paintings of the area's desert landscape and bleached animal skulls. She lived in the small, picturesque community of Abiquiu, about 42 miles northwest of Santa Fe, on US 84. The **Georgia O'Keeffe Museum** (p. 73), the only museum in the United States dedicated entirely to an

Impressions

"[Sun-bleached bones] were most wonderful against the blue—that blue that will always be there as it is now after all man's destruction is finished."

–Georgia O'Keeffe, on the desert skies of New Mexico

internationally renowned woman artist, opened in Santa Fe in 1997. In response to ever-increasing visitation, the museum is currently building a much larger home, also in the historic downtown area.

Santa Fe is also home to the **Institute of American Indian Arts,** where many of today's leading Native American artists have studied, including the Apache sculptor Allan Houser (whose works you can see near the State Capitol building, at a sculpture garden south of town, and in other public areas in Santa Fe). Possibly the best-known Native American painter is the late R. C. Gorman, an Arizona Navajo who made his home in Taos for more than 2 decades and became known for his bright, somewhat surreal depictions of Navajo women. Also in the spotlight is Dan Namingha, a Hopi artist who weaves images of native symbols into contemporary designs. Other notable local artists include Tammy Garcia, a young Taos potter who for years swept the awards at Indian Market with her intricately shaped and carved pots; Cippy Crazy Horse, a Cochiti jeweler who has acquired a steady following for his silver creations; and noted muralist and Santa Fe native Frederico Vigil, whose frescoes are all around the area.

Art is for sale everywhere, from small shows at the pueblos to major markets such as the annual **Spanish Market** (p. 33) and **Indian Market** (p. 33) in Santa Fe. Under the portals along the Santa Fe and Albuquerque plazas, you'll find a variety of works in silver, stone, and pottery created by Native artists who've undergone a certification process; you'll also find city streets lined with galleries, some very slick, some more modest. If you're interested in buying art, however, some caution should be exercised; there's a lot of schlock out there, targeting the tourist trade. It seems that every year brings news reports of another arrest for selling counterfeit Native American jewelry and pottery, usually manufactured overseas. Yet if you persist, you're likely to find much inspiring work as well. Try to buy directly from the artisans themselves.

A Rich Architectural Melting Pot

Northern New Mexico's distinctive architecture reflects the diversity of cultures that have left their imprint on the region. The first people in the area, the ancestral Puebloans, built stone and mud homes at the bottom of canyons and inside caves. **Pueblo-style adobe architecture** evolved and became the basis for traditional New Mexican homes: sun-dried clay bricks mixed with straw for strength, mud-mortared, and covered with additional protective layers of mud. Roofs are supported by a network of *vigas*—long beams whose ends protrude through the outer facades—and *latillas,* smaller stripped branches layered over the vigas. Other adapted Pueblo architectural elements include plastered adobe-brick kiva fireplaces, *bancos* (adobe benches that protrude from walls), and *nichos* (small indentations within a wall in which religious icons are placed). These adobe homes are characterized by flat roofs and soft, rounded contours.

THE lure of turquoise

Those of us who live in the Southwest have a tendency to think of turquoise, and especially the beautiful turquoise jewelry you'll see in practically every museum and shop here, as our own. We know that it has been mined in this region for hundreds of years, and people make pilgrimages from around the world to buy jewelry and other decorative items created with turquoise. Therefore, this must be the center of the turquoise universe, right?

No, we've been wrong.

Turquoise was mined in Egypt some 4,000 years ago, and it can be found on every continent except Antarctica, according to turquoise expert Jacob Lowry, director of the **Turquoise Museum** in Albuquerque (p. 199). He tells us that the most common color for turquoise is not the blue or green we're used to, but white. He adds that, throughout history, turquoise has been an important trade item, and there are a variety of legends regarding its mystical qualities.

When the Indian Arts and Crafts Board of the U.S. Department of the Interior decided to publish a brochure about turquoise—whether it's natural or treated; what makes one stone more valuable than another; and how to buy quality stones—it sought out the assistance of another turquoise expert, Joe Dan Lowry, Jacob Lowry's father.

Natural turquoise is the stone that comes out of the ground, and accounts for about 15% of the world's turquoise, according to the Indian Arts and Crafts Board's brochure. Turquoise that has been darkened, stabilized, or is composed of tiny chips of turquoise glued together is considered treated, the brochure states, adding that the value of turquoise is determined in part by uniformity and deepness of color, the presence of tiny veins or dots (called matrix), and its clarity.

The board's buying tips include choosing a dealer with a good reputation; examining the stone for color, clarity, and matrix; requesting a written receipt that includes detailed information about the artist and stone, such as the mine it came from and whether it is natural, stabilized, or treated; and to remember that genuine handmade turquoise pieces can be expensive—be cautious if a price seems too good to be true. Of course, the main reason to buy a piece of turquoise is because you love it.

Spaniards wedded many elements to Pueblo style, such as portals (porches that often run the length of a home) and enclosed patios, as well as the simple sculptural shapes of Spanish mission arches and bell towers. They also brought elements from the Moorish architecture found in southern Spain: heavy wooden doors and elaborate *corbels*—carved wooden supports for the vertical posts.

With the opening of the Santa Fe Trail in 1821, and later the 1860s gold boom, more Anglo settlers arrived, launching the next wave of building. They contributed architectural elements such as the Greek Revival and Victorian influences popular in the United States at the time. What came to be known as **Territorial-style** architecture introduced one significant new feature: pitched rather than flat roofs. Territorial style also included brick facades and cornices as well as porches, often placed on the second story; also note millwork on doors, wood trim around windows and doorways, double-hung windows, and Victorian bric-a-brac. In **Santa Fe Plaza** (p. 76), you can see these two architectural styles converge: On the west side is a Territorial-style balcony, while the Palace of the Governors is marked by Pueblo-style vigas and oversize Spanish/Moorish doors.

In Santa Fe, many other styles flourish: Compare the Romanesque architecture of the **Basilica Cathedral of St. Francis of Assisi** (p. 80) to the Gothic-style **Loretto Chapel** (p. 84), brought by Archbishop Lamy from France, as well as the railroad station built in the **Spanish Mission style** popular in the early part of the 20th century. Since 1957, however, strict city building codes have required that all new structures within the circumference of the Paseo de Peralta conform to one of two revival styles: Pueblo or Territorial. The regulation also limits the height of the buildings and restricts the types of signs permitted, and it requires buildings to be topped by flat roofs.

Albuquerque also has a broad array of styles, most evident in a visit to **Old Town** (p. 198). There, you'll find the large Italianate brick house known as the **Herman Blueher home,** built in 1898; throughout Old Town you'll find little *placitas,* homes, and haciendas built around courtyards, a strategy developed not only for defense purposes, but also as a way to accommodate several generations of the same family in different wings of a single dwelling. The **San Felipe de Neri Parish** at the center of Old Town is situated between two folk Gothic towers. This building was begun in a cruciform plan in 1793; subsequent architectural changes resulted in an interesting mixture of styles.

The most notable architecture in Taos is **Taos Pueblo** (p. 148), the site of two structures emulated in homes and business buildings throughout the Southwest. Built to resemble Taos Mountain, which stands behind it, the two structures are pyramidal in form, with the different levels reached by ladders. Also quite prevalent is architecture echoing colonial hacienda style, such as the **Martinez Hacienda** (p. 152), an example of a hacienda stronghold. Built without windows facing outward, it originally had 20 small rooms, many with doors opening out to the courtyard. One of the few refurbished examples of colonial New Mexico architecture, the hacienda is on the National Historic Registry. You can also wander through artist **Ernest Blumenschein's home** (p. 150), built in 1797 and restored by Blumenschein in 1919. It represents another New Mexico architectural phenomenon: homes that were added onto year after year. Doorways are typically low, and floors rise and fall at the whim of the earth beneath them.

As you head into villages in the north, you'll see steep-pitched roofs on most homes. This is because the common flat-roof style doesn't shed snow; the water builds up and causes problems. In just about any town in northern New Mexico, you may detect the strong smell of tar, a sure sign that another resident is laying out thousands to fix his enchanting but frustratingly flat roof.

IS THAT REAL adobe?

Today, especially in Santa Fe and Albuquerque, few new homes are actually built of adobe. Instead, most are constructed with wood frames and plasterboard, and then stuccoed over to look like adobe. A keen eye can see the difference: True adobe buildings have rounded corners—what locals call feminine lines—while fake adobe buildings have more sharp and clear-cut lines.

A number of northern New Mexico architects and builders today are employing innovative architectural designs to create a Pueblo-style feel. They incorporate straw bales, pumice-crete, rammed earth, old tires, and even aluminum cans in the construction of homes. Most of these elements are used in the same way bricks are used, stacked and layered, and then covered over with plaster and made to look like adobe. West of Taos, a number of "earthships" have been built. Many of these homes are constructed with alternative materials; most are bermed into the sides of hills, utilizing the earth as insulation. Many are off-the-grid, relying on the sun and wind for power.

A visitor could spend an entire trip to northern New Mexico focusing on the architecture, and some do. As well as relishing the wealth of architectural styles, you'll find more subtle elements everywhere. You may encounter an ox-blood floor, for example. An old Spanish tradition, ox blood is spread in layers and left to dry, hardening into a glossy finish that's known to last centuries. You're also likely to see coyote fences—narrow cedar posts lined up side by side, a system early settlers devised to keep their animals safe. Winding around homes and buildings you'll see *acequias,* ancient irrigation canals still maintained by locals for watering crops and trees. And throughout the area you'll notice that old walls are whimsically bowed, and windows and floors are often crooked, constant reminders of the effects time has had on even these stalwart structures.

ANTHROPOLOGY 101: BELIEFS & RITUALS

Spirituality has always been a defining element in the life of the Pueblo people. Within the cosmos, which they view as a single whole, all living creatures are mutually dependent. Thus, every relationship a human being may have, whether with a person, an animal, or a plant, has spiritual significance. A hunter prays before killing a deer, asking the creature to sacrifice itself to the tribe. A slain deer is treated as a guest of honor, and the hunter performs a ritual in which he sends the animal's soul back to its community, so that it may be reborn. Even the harvesting of plants requires prayer, thanks, and ritual.

The Pueblo people believe that their ancestors originally lived under the ground, which, as the place from which plants spring, is the source of all life.

According to their beliefs, the original Pueblos, encouraged by burrowing animals, entered the world of humans—the so-called "fourth" world—through a hole, a *sipapu.* The ways in which this came about and the deities that the Pueblo people worship vary from tribe to tribe. Most, however, believe this world is enclosed by four sacred mountains, where four sacred colors—coral, black, turquoise, and yellow or white—predominate.

There is no single great being ruling over this world; instead, it is watched over by a number of spiritual elements. Most common are Mother Earth and Father Sun. In this desert land, the sun is an element of both life and death. The tribes watch the skies closely, tracking solstices and planetary movements, to determine the optimal time for crop planting.

Ritualistic dances are occasions of great symbolic importance. Usually held in conjunction with the feast days of Catholic saints (including Christmas Eve), Pueblo ceremonies demonstrate how Christian elements were absorbed without surrendering traditional beliefs. To this day, communities enact medicine dances, fertility rites, and prayers for rain and for good harvests. The spring and summer corn, or *tablita,* dances are among the most impressive. Most ceremonies begin with an early-morning Mass and procession to the plaza; the image of the saint is honored at the forefront. The rest of the day is devoted to song, dance, and feasting, with performers masked and clad as deer, eagles, or other creatures.

Visitors are usually welcome to attend Pueblo dances, but they should call to confirm and if allowed to pay witness, respect the tribe's requests not to be photographed or recorded. It was exactly this lack of respect that led the Zunis to ban outsiders from attending many of their famous Shalako ceremonies.

danse MACABRE

The **Dance of the Matachines,** a ritualistic dance performed at northern New Mexico pueblos and in many Latino communities, reveals the cultural mixing, identities, and conflicts that characterize northern New Mexico. It's a dark and vivid ritual in which a little girl, Malinche, is wedded to the church. The dance, depicting the taming of the native spirit, is difficult even for historians to decipher.

Brought to the New World by the Spaniards, the dance has its roots in the painful period during which the Moors were driven out of Spain. However, some symbols seem obvious: At one point, men bearing whips tame "El Toro," a small boy dressed as a bull who has been charging about rebelliously. The whip-men symbolically castrate him and then stroll through the crowd, pretending to display the dismembered body parts, as if to warn villagers of the consequences of disobedience. At another point, a hunched woman-figure births a small troll-like doll, perhaps representative of the union between Indian and Hispanic cultures.

The Dance of the Matachines ends when two *abuelo* (grandparent) figures dance across the dirt, holding up the just-born baby, while the Matachines, adorned with bishop-like headdresses, follow them away in a recessional march.

Catholicism, imposed by the Spaniards, infused northern New Mexico with another elaborate set of beliefs. This is a Catholicism heavy with iconography, expressed in carved *santos* (statues) and beautiful *retablos* (paintings) adorning the altars of many cathedrals. Catholic churches are the focal points of most northern New Mexico villages. If you take the high road to Taos, be sure to note the church in **Las Trampas** (p. 124), as well as one in **Ranchos de Taos** (p. 125); both have 3- to 4-foot-thick walls sculpted from adobe and old-world interiors with beautiful *retablos* on the walls.

Many Latino people in northern New Mexico maintain strong family and Catholic ties, and they continue to honor traditions associated with both. Communities plan elaborate celebrations such as the *quinceañera* for young girls reaching womanhood, and weddings with big feasts and dances in which well-wishers pin money to the bride's elaborately laced gown.

If you happen to be in the area during a holiday, you may even get to see a religious procession or pilgrimage. Most notable is the pilgrimage to the **Santuario de Chimayó** (p. 124), an hour's drive north of Santa Fe. Constructed in 1816, the sanctuary has long been a pilgrimage site for Roman Catholics who attribute miraculous healing powers to the earth found in the chapel's anteroom. Several days before Easter, fervent believers begin walking the highway to Chimayo, some carrying large crosses, others carrying nothing but small bottles of water.

In recent years, New Mexico has also become known (and in some circles, ridiculed) for **New Age pilgrims and celebrations.** The roots of the local movement are hard to trace. It may have something to do with northern New Mexico's centuries-old reputation as a place where rebel thinkers come to enjoy freedom of beliefs, or maybe it's a relic of the hippie invasion of the 1960s. Pueblo spirituality and a deeply felt connection to the land have also drawn New Agers. At any rate, there's a thriving New Age network here with alternative churches, centers, and schools. You'll find all sorts of alternative medicine and fringe practices, from aromatherapy to Rolfing (a form of massage that realigns the muscles and bones in the body), and chelation therapy (in which an IV drips ethylene diamine tetra-acetic acid into the blood to remove heavy metals).

These New Age practices are often the butt of local humor. One pointed joke asks: "How many New Agers does it take to change a light bulb?" Answer: "None. They just form a support group and learn to live in the dark." For many, however, there's much good to be found in the movement. The Dalai Lama visited Santa Fe because the city is seen as a healing center and has become a refuge for Tibetans. Notable speakers such as Ram Dass and Thomas Moore have also come to the area. Many spiritual seekers find exactly what they are looking for in the receptive northern New Mexico desert and mountains.

BOOKS, FILMS, TV & MUSIC

Books

Many well-known writers made their homes in New Mexico in the 20th century. In the 1920s, the most celebrated were **D. H. Lawrence** and **Willa Cather,** both short-term Taos residents. Lawrence, the controversial English novelist, spent time here between 1922 and 1925; he reflected on his sojourn in *Mornings in Mexico* and *Etruscan Places.* Lawrence's Taos period is also described in *Lorenzo in Taos,* written by his patron, Mabel Dodge Luhan. Cather, a Pulitzer-Prize winner famous for her depictions of the pioneer spirit, was inspired to write *Death Comes for the Archbishop*—a fictionalized account of 19th-century Santa Fe bishop Jean-Baptiste Lamy—by her stay in the region. **Frank Waters** (1902–95), a part-time resident from the 1930s on, gives a strong sense of Pueblo tradition in his classics *People of the Valley* and *The Man Who Killed the Deer.*

Many contemporary authors also live in and write about New Mexico. **John Nichols,** of Taos, whose *Milagro Beanfield War* was made into a Robert Redford movie in 1987, writes insightfully about the problems of poor Latino farming communities. The late **Tony Hillerman** of Albuquerque for decades wove mysteries around Navajo tribal police in books such as *Listening Woman* and *A Thief of Time.* More recently, **Sarah Lovett** has followed in his footsteps with a series of gripping mysteries, most notably *Dangerous Attachments.*

The Hispanic novelist **Rudolfo Anaya's** *Bless Me, Ultima* (1972) and Pueblo writer **Leslie Marmon Silko's** *Ceremony* (1977) capture the lifestyles of their respective peoples. A coming-of-age story, **Richard Bradford's** *Red Sky at Morning* (1968) juxtaposes the various cultures of New Mexico. **Edward Abbey** wrote of the desert environment and politics; his *Fire on the Mountain* (1962), set in New Mexico, was one of his most powerful works.

For general histories of the state, try **Myra Ellen Jenkins and Albert H. Schroeder's** *A Brief History of New Mexico* (University of New Mexico Press, 1974) and **Marc Simmons's** *New Mexico: An Interpretive History* (University of New Mexico Press, 1988).

Films & TV

Over the years, so many movies have been filmed in New Mexico that we can't list them all, but here's a sampling: *Silverado* (1985), a lighthearted Western; the heartfelt miniseries *Lonesome Dove* (1989), based on a Larry McMurtry novel; Billy Bob Thornton's film adaptation (2000) of the novel *All the Pretty Horses;* Ron Howard's film version of *The Missing* (2003); Billy Crystal in *City Slickers* (1991), and Christopher Nolan's biopic *Oppenheimer* (2023).

Favorite classics include *Butch Cassidy and the Sundance Kid* (1969), filmed in Taos and Chama; *The Cowboys* (1972), with John Wayne; Clint Eastwood's *Every Which Way But Loose* (1978); and Dennis Hopper and Peter Fonda in the 1960s classic *Easy Rider* (1969). Popular TV shows include *Breaking Bad*, *Better Call Saul*, and *Roswell.*

For a comprehensive list of movies and TV shows filmed at least partly in New Mexico, see **nmfilm.com**, then click on "Filmography."

Music

Such musical legends as Bo Diddley, Buddy Holly, Roy Orbison, and the Fireballs basked in New Mexico's light for parts of their careers. More recent musicians whose music really reflects the state include Manzanares, two brothers who grew up in Abiquiu, known for their Spanish guitar and soulful vocals. Look for their album *Nuevo Latino.* Master flute player Robert Mirabal's music is informed by the ceremonial music he grew up with at Taos Pueblo. Check out his 2006 Grammy Award–winning album *Sacred Ground.* Using New Mexico as his creative retreat since the 1980s, Michael Martin Murphey often plays live in Red River, north of Taos, where fans always cheer for his most notable song, "Wildfire." *The Best of Michael Martin Murphey* gives a good taste of his music.

EATING & DRINKING IN NORTHERN NEW MEXICO

You know you're in a food-conscious place when the local newspaper uses chile peppers (and onions) to rate movies, as does Santa Fe's *New Mexican.* A large part of that city's cachet as a chic destination derives from its famous cuisine, while Taos and Albuquerque are developing tasty reputations themselves. Competition among restaurants is fierce, giving visitors plenty of options from which to choose. Aside from establishments serving regional New Mexican cuisine, there are also French, Italian, Asian, and Indian restaurants, as well as interesting hybrids of those. And not all restaurants are high-end; several hidden gems satisfy your taste buds without emptying your wallet.

Dinner reservations are always recommended at the higher-end restaurants and are essential during peak seasons. Most restaurants are casual, so almost any attire is fine, though for the more expensive ones you'll probably feel more comfortable being at least a little dressed up. Only a few restaurants serve late—try to plan dinner before 8pm. If you arrive late at ABQ Sunport and are starving, you're better off grabbing a bite there (Albuquerque has

TRADITIONAL bread baking

While visiting the pueblos in New Mexico, you'll probably notice adobe beehive-shaped outdoor ovens, known as *hornos,* which Native Americans have used for hundreds of years to bake bread. Usually in the evening, the bread dough (made of white flour, lard, salt, yeast, and water) is made and kneaded; the loaves are shaped, set to rise, and in the morning placed in the oven heated by a wood fire. They bake for about an hour. If you would like to try a traditional loaf, you can buy one at the **Indian Pueblo Cultural Center in Albuquerque** (see p. 196) and at many of the pueblos.

24-hr. Denny's and IHOP restaurants). Santa Fe has a Denny's that's open until 3am on weekdays and 24 hours on weekends, but get into Taos late and you're simply out of luck.

New Mexican regional cuisine isn't the same as Mexican cuisine or even its American variations, Tex-Mex and Cal-Mex. New Mexican cooking is a product of Southwestern history. Native Americans taught the Spanish conquerors about corn—how to roast it and how to make corn pudding, stewed corn, cornbread, cornmeal, and *posole* (hominy)—and they also taught the Spanish how to use chile peppers, an indigenous crop, having been first harvested in the Andean highlands as early as 4000 B.C.E. Meanwhile, the Spaniards brought the practice of eating beef to the area. Later newcomers introduced other elements: From Mexico, for instance, came an interest in seafood. Regional New Mexican cuisine blends elements such as sauces from Mexico's Yucatán Peninsula or Central American dishes such as fried bananas served with beans.

The basic ingredients of New Mexico cooking are three indispensable, locally grown foods: **chile, beans,** and **corn.** Of these, perhaps the most crucial is the **chile,** whether brilliant red or green and with various levels of spicy bite. (See the box on below.) Spotted or painted **pinto beans** with a nutty taste are simmered with garlic, onion, cumin, and red chile powder and served as a

YOU SAY chili, WE SAY chile

You'll never see "chili" on a menu in New Mexico. Or you shouldn't. Real New Mexicans are adamant that *chile,* the Spanish spelling of the word, is the only way to spell it—no matter what your dictionary may say.

Virtually anything you order in a restaurant is likely to be topped with a chile sauce. Chile forms the base for the red and green sauces that top most New Mexican dishes, such as enchiladas and burritos. One is not necessarily hotter than the other; spiciness depends on the type, and where and during what kind of season (dry or wet) the chiles were grown. Some of the best come from the tiny community of Hatch, along I-25 toward the state's southern border; many restaurants make a point of bragging that they use Hatch chile.

If you're not accustomed to spicy foods, certain varieties will make your eyes water, your sinuses drain, and your palate feel as if it's on fire. ***Warning:*** No amount of water or beer will alleviate the sting; it just spreads it. Dairy products work best. Drink milk or add grated cheese or sour cream to your food. A *sopaipilla* drizzled with honey, which often takes the place of a traditional bread basket, is also helpful.

But don't let these words of caution scare you away from genuine New Mexico chiles. The pleasure of eating them far outweighs the pain. Start slowly, with salsas and chile sauces first, perhaps *rellenos* (stuffed green chile peppers) next. You can also ask your servers how "hot" the chile is today, and in some cases, you can have it served on the side and add it gradually.

In 1999, the New Mexico State Legislature passed a memorial adopting, "Red or green?" as the official state question, and if you order practically any genuine New Mexico food you'll most likely be asked. The correct answer is "red," "green," or "Christmas," which means both.

side dish. When mashed and refried in oil, they become *frijoles refritos.* **Corn** supplies the vital dough, called *masa,* for tortillas and tamales. New Mexican corn comes in six colors, of which yellow, white, and blue are the most common.

Even if you're familiar with Mexican cooking, the dishes you know are likely to be prepared differently here, and every restaurant has its own little twists on our regional standards. The following is a rundown of some regional dishes, a number of which aren't widely known outside the Southwest.

BISCOCHITO A cookie made with anise and lard, especially popular at Christmastime, but served at all special occasions including weddings. (If you get an anise cookie that doesn't contain lard, it's not a biscochito.)

BREAKFAST BURRITO Scrambled eggs, potatoes, some kind of meat (usually bacon or sausage) wrapped in a flour tortilla with red or green chile sauce and melted cheese. You can choose to eat your breakfast burrito either hand-held, with the chile inside, or "smothered" on a plate and covered with chile sauce.

CARNE ADOVADA Tender pork marinated in red chile sauce, herbs, and spices, and then baked.

CHILE RELLENOS Green chile peppers, often breaded, then stuffed with cheese, deep-fried, and sometimes covered with green chile sauce.

EMPANADA A fried pie with nuts and currants. An *empanadita* is a small version.

ENCHILADAS Tortillas either rolled or layered with chicken, turkey, beef, and/or cheese, topped with chile sauce, and often baked as a casserole.

GREEN CHILE CHEESEBURGER Practically every restaurant in the state claims to offer the world's best green chile cheeseburger. Lately, some fancy restaurants have been adding items to their green chile cheeseburgers, such as aioli mayonnaise, caramelized onions, or pineapple. Don't buy it! A green chile cheeseburger is just that—a good-quality burger with cheddar cheese, topped with green chile (usually chopped but sometimes whole), and served on a bun. A strip or two of bacon, maybe, but that's it.

GREEN CHILE STEW Green chiles cooked in a stew with chunks or shredded chicken, turkey, or pork (rarely beef), plus beans and potatoes. Usually served with a tortilla on the side to mop up the goop.

HUEVOS RANCHEROS Fried eggs on corn tortillas, topped with cheese and red or green chile, served with pinto beans.

PAN DULCE A sweet Native American bread.

POSOLE A corn soup or stew (called hominy in parts of the South), sometimes prepared with pork and chile, usually red.

SOPAIPILLA A lightly fried puff pastry served with honey, or better yet, a honey-butter mixture. It's served as a side, a dessert, or stuffed with meat and vegetables as a main dish.

TACOS Spiced chicken or beef, served either in soft tortillas or crispy shells, with cheese and chile. If you see fish tacos on the menu, you're in a Mexican, not New Mexican, restaurant.

TAMALES A dish made from cornmeal mush, wrapped in corn husks and steamed. (It tastes a lot better than this description makes it sound!) Add a New Mexican flavor to your Thanksgiving or Christmas dinner by stuffing your turkey with tamales (remember to remove the husks first), and then rub the bird with red chile powder to complete the flavor. Your gravy will be extra tasty with the chile flavored drippings.

WHEN TO GO

Forget any preconceptions you may have about the New Mexico "desert." The high desert climate of this part of the world is generally dry, but not always warm. Santa Fe and Taos, at 7,000 feet above sea level, have **midsummer** highs in the 80s (20s Celsius) and lows in the 50s (teens Celsius).

This tends to be the busiest time of year in New Mexico, when most cultural activities are in full swing and prices and temperatures rise. This period also coincides with monsoon season, which usually entails brief but intense showers and gorgeous sunsets. You'll want to make hotel reservations well in advance, and avoid some major events, such as fiestas, culture festivals, and hot-air balloon rallies, unless you have a great desire to participate in them.

Spring and fall are some of New Mexico's most pleasant seasons, with highs in the 60s (teens Celsius), and lows in the 30s (as low as –1°C). Spring can be quite windy, but the skiing is often still excellent, with sunny days and the season's accumulated deep snow. Fall is a particularly big draw because the aspens and cottonwoods turn a brilliant gold.

Winter can be delightful in northern New Mexico, when typical daytime temperatures are in the 40s (single digits Celsius), and overnight lows are in the teens (–7°C and below). The snowy days here are some of the prettiest you'll ever see, and during a good snow year (more than 300 inches at Taos Ski Valley), skiers can't get in enough slope time. However, during holidays the ski areas can be jammed.

During all the seasons, temperatures in Albuquerque, at 5,300 feet, often run about 10° warmer than elsewhere in the northern region, and snow often melts by noon.

Average Temperatures (High/Low) & Annual Rainfall (In.)

		JAN	APR	JULY	OCT	RAINFALL
ALBUQUERQUE	TEMP (°F)	51/25	74/42	94/66	74/45	9.4
	TEMP (°C)	11/–4	23/6	34/19	23/7	
SANTA FE	TEMP (°F)	42/17	64/32	85/55	66/35	14.1
	TEMP (°C)	6/–8	18/0	29/13	19/2	
TAOS	TEMP (°F)	41/11	63/30	86/52	66/32	12.3
	TEMP (°C)	5/–11	17/–1	30/11	19/0	

Northern New Mexico Calendar of Events

A good resource for events is **www.newmexico.org/events**; also see each city's Exploring chapter. Here are some favorites.

APRIL

Gathering of Nations Powwow, Expo New Mexico and Tingley Coliseum. Albuquerque. North America's largest powwow and Native American competition in singing and dancing. Plus arts and crafts, native food, and music. gatheringofnations.com. ✆ **505/836-2810.** Late April.

JULY

Fiestas de Taos. The celebration begins with a Friday-night Mass at Our Lady of Guadalupe Church behind Taos Plaza, where the fiesta queen is crowned. Over the weekend, there are candlelight processions, Masses, music, dancing, parades, crafts, and food booths. fiestasdetaos.com. Third weekend in July.

Spanish Market. Santa Fe Plaza. More than 500 traditional and contemporary Hispanic artists from New Mexico and southern Colorado exhibit and sell their work in this lively community event, with demonstrations, traditional Hispanic music, dance, and food. traditionalspanishmarket.org. ✆ **505/836-0306.** Last full weekend in July.

AUGUST

Indian Market. Santa Fe Plaza. The largest and most prestigious intertribal fine art market in the world brings more than 1,000 artisans together to display their baskets and blankets, jewelry, pottery, woodcarvings, rugs, sand paintings, and sculptures. Watch the spectacular costumed tribal dancing and crafts demonstrations. The market is free. Hotels are booked months in advance. Produced by the **Southwestern Association for Indian Arts.** swaia.org. ✆ **505/983-5220.** Mid-August.

SEPTEMBER

Fiesta de Santa Fe. An exuberant combination of spirit, history, and general merrymaking, Las Fiestas are billed as the oldest community celebration in the United States. The first fiesta was celebrated in 1712, 20 years after the resettlement of New Mexico by Spanish conquistadors in 1692. Included are Masses, a parade for children and their pets, a historical/hysterical parade, mariachi concerts, dances, food, and arts. **Zozobra** (burnzozobra.com), "Old Man Gloom," a 50-foot-tall effigy made of wood, canvas, and paper, is burned at dusk on Thursday. santafefiesta.org. ✆ **505/470-6325.** Labor Day weekend.

New Mexico State Fair and Rodeo. Expo New Mexico in Albuquerque. One of America's top state fairs, it features a nationally acclaimed rodeo, entertainment by top country artists, livestock shows, arts and crafts, a fun midway carnival, and more. Get advance tickets online or by phone. statefair.exponm.com. ✆ **505/222-9700.** Two weeks in early September.

Taos Fall Arts Festival. Highlights include arts and crafts exhibitions and competitions, studio tours, gallery openings, lectures, concerts, and plays. At about the same time, the **Wool Festival** (taoswoolsfestival.com) is held in Kit Carson Park and **San Geronimo Day** at Taos Pueblo (taospueblo.com). taosfallarts.com. Mid-September to the first week in October.

OCTOBER

Albuquerque International Balloon Fiesta. The skies are alive with the colors of balloons at this 9-day festival (p. 210). Some 600 balloons rise over the city in the largest balloon rally in the world. There are races and contests, mass ascensions at sunrise, "balloon glows" in the evening, balloon rides for those desiring a little lift, and various other special events. Balloon Fiesta Park (at I-25 and Alameda NE) on the north side of Albuquerque. balloonfiesta.com. ✆ **505/821-1000.** First full week in October.

Taos Mountain Balloon Rally. Taos. Anywhere from 35 to 50 vibrantly colored balloons soar above the Taos Valley in early morning and at dusk on Saturday for a "balloon glow." There is usually a tethered balloon ride for kids. taosballoonrally.com. ✆ **575/737-8846.** Last full weekend in October.

NOVEMBER

Festival of the Cranes. Bosque del Apache National Wildlife Refuge, 77 miles south of Albuquerque via I-25. Migratory birds, especially sandhill cranes, winter here, and this is the time they are arriving. People come from all over the world to see them, and take advantage of the numerous photography, art, and ecology workshops. friendsofbosquedelapache.org. ✆ **575/405-8434.** Mid-November.

SUGGESTED NORTHERN NEW MEXICO ITINERARIES

3

You may already have an idea of how you want to spend your time in New Mexico—power shopping for one-of-a-kind art and crafts, perhaps, or time-traveling through ancient cultures. Once you're here, however, you just might realize that there's more to this magical place than you expected. To make sure you don't miss the essentials, here are three possible driving itineraries, each starting in Albuquerque.

Northern New Mexico offers an amazing range of museums, some excellent opportunities to enjoy a live music or theater performance, plus other indoor activities. But to really experience it, you need to get out and see the people, observe some of the customs and traditions, breathe the pristine air of the mountains, and watch the sun drop below the distant horizon. With this in mind, these itineraries combine scenic drives with city stays. Take your time—linger at a cafe, take a short hike, or wander a plaza. You might be surprised at how easily northern New Mexico seeps into your psyche.

NORTHERN NEW MEXICO IN A WEEK

A week in northern New Mexico isn't quite long enough to do justice to the area's rich and varied landscape, but if that's all the time you have, you can certainly hit some of the highlights. Gaze at ancient drawings etched into stone at Petroglyph National Monument, browse the shops around a plaza, and marvel at the play of light on the Rio Grande Gorge in Taos. See map on p. 37.

Days 1 & 2: Albuquerque

If it's early enough and you have some energy left after arriving, head to **Old Town** (p. 198), where you can wander the **plaza** and peruse the shops. Be sure to duck into some of the back alleyways and little nooks—you'll uncover several of the city's most innovative shops in these areas. Or, head over to the **Indian Pueblo Cultural Center** (p. 196) for a historical view of the Pueblo world and a look at the art and craftsmanship they are producing today.

On **DAY 2,** start out at **ABQ BioPark** (p. 200) in the vicinity of **Old Town Plaza.** You can easily spend a couple of hours here exploring the aquarium and strolling the botanic gardens. Next, head west of town to **Petroglyph National Monument** (p. 205). (If you visit in summer, head here first, before the day heats up.) If the weather's really lousy (unusual here in the Land of Enchantment, but it does happen) or you're more of a history or art buff, visit the **Albuquerque Museum** (p. 194) for a unique look at how art and history intersect. In the late afternoon, find your way to Central Avenue, just south of Old Town, and drive east on **Historic Route 66.** It takes you straight through downtown and the Nob Hill district, where many of the city's best restaurants and bars are, and eventually reaches the foothills of the Sandia Mountains. Finish your day with a ride up the **Sandia Peak Tramway** (p. 198). Once on top, you might hike along the crest, though this isn't safe for young kids. Ideally, you should ride up in daylight, watch the sunset, and then ride back down for a dazzling view of the city lights. You may even want to dine up on the peak at **Ten 3** (p. 188)—practically every table has a great view.

Day 3: The Turquoise Trail & Santa Fe

For a prettier and more relaxing drive than you'll get on the interstate, strike out for the ghost towns and other sights along the **Turquoise Trail** (p. 221) on your way to Santa Fe. Stop in **Madrid** (p. 222) and browse through a few of the galleries, and when you reach **Cerrillos** (p. 222), grab a bite at **Black Bird Saloon** and take a short side trip to **Cerrillos State Park.** This will put you in Santa Fe in time to do a little shopping and sightseeing. Head straight to the **plaza** and take our walking tour (p. 76). While browsing the wares for sale from the Native Americans under the Palace of the Governors' portal, you might inquire about the significance of symbols on pottery or in the jewelry design. Eat dinner at the **Paloma** (p. 64).

Day 4: Santa Fe Arts

In the morning, take a stroll and do some shopping on **Canyon Road,** with its top-notch assortment of art galleries. For lunch, head to **El Chile Toreado** (p. 710) for the best tacos in town. Time now to head up to Museum Hill, where you can take your pick from four unique museums: the **Museum of International Folk Art** (p. 78), the **Museum of Indian Arts and Culture** (p. 77), the **Wheelwright Museum of the American Indian** (p. 79), and the **Nuevo Mexicano Heritage Arts Museum** (p. 78). Take a break with a stroll through the **Santa Fe Botanical Garden at Museum Hill** (p. 79). At sunset during the warmer months, a smart option is to enjoy a gin cocktail on the patio of **Bar Norte,** tucked within Los Poblanos' Farm Shop Norte (p. 99).

Northern New Mexico in a Week

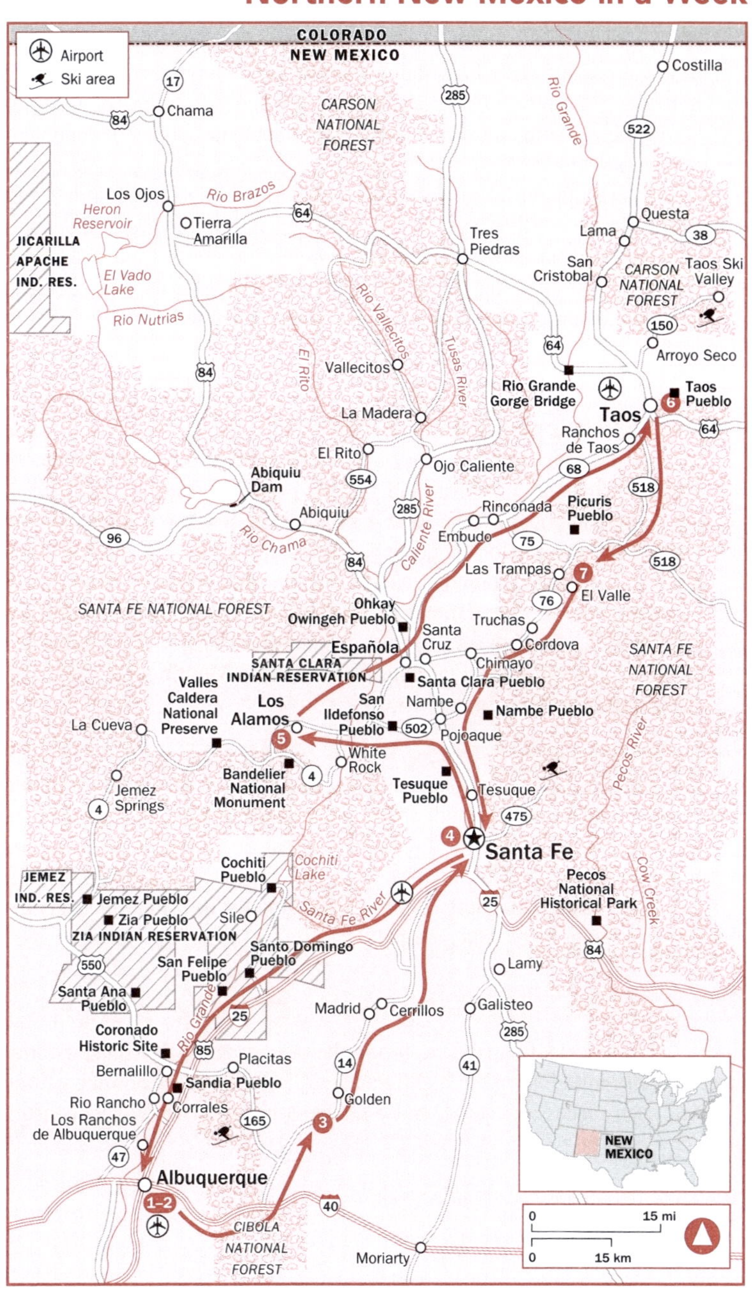

3

SUGGESTED NORTHERN NEW MEXICO ITINERARIES | Northern New Mexico in a Week

Day 5: Los Alamos & Valles Caldera National Preserve

Head northwest out of town to **Los Alamos** (p. 117). If it's not a Sunday, time your visit to take Los Alamos Historical Society's 11am docent-led tour focused on the Manhattan Project; you'll also visit the homestead-era Romero Cabin and see an Ancestral Pueblo site. Then continue west to **Valles Caldera National Preserve** (p. 122), stopping at Valle Grand Overlook along NM 4 for sweeping views of the huge crater at the heart of the preserve. The easy 1.5-mile Cerro La Jara Loop circles the area's smallest volcanic dome. Head out by the mid-afternoon and make your way to Taos, stopping for a look at **San Francisco de Asis Church** (p. 148) at sunset, before heading to **Mante's Chow Cart** (p. 143) for dinner.

Day 6: Taos

Start the day exploring **Taos Pueblo** (p. 148) when the sun strikes the face of the four- and five-story adobe. Then head out to the **Millicent Rogers Museum** (p. 146), and if time permits, make a quick trip to see—and walk out on—the **Rio Grande Gorge Bridge** (p. 153). You can then ditch your car for the afternoon and step out on foot. Wander **Taos Plaza,** do some shopping, check out the **Kit Carson Home and Museum** (p. 152), the **Harwood Museum of Art** (p. 151), or the **Taos Firehouse Collection** (p. 153). At cocktail time, head to the **Adobe Bar** (p. 165), and follow that up with dinner at **Doc Martin's** (p. 138), both in the **Historic Taos Inn** (p. 133).

Day 7: The High Road

On your last day, enjoy a real Taos breakfast at **Michael's Kitchen** (p. 144) and then head south on the **High Road to Taos** (p. 123). Be sure to spend some time at the lovely **Santuario de Chimayó** (p. 124) and touch its miraculous healing dirt. Then stop for lunch at **Rancho de Chimayó** (p. 124). Depending on your flight time the next morning, stay the night in Santa Fe or Albuquerque.

NORTHERN NEW MEXICO IN 2 WEEKS

If you have 2 weeks to spend exploring the region, consider yourself fortunate. In addition to hitting the highlights, you'll be able to spend time getting to know such places as Los Alamos and ride a historic narrow gauge steam train. See map on p. 39.

Days 1–4: Albuquerque & Santa Fe

For days 1 to 4, follow the previous itinerary, "Northern New Mexico in a Week."

Northern New Mexico in 2 Weeks

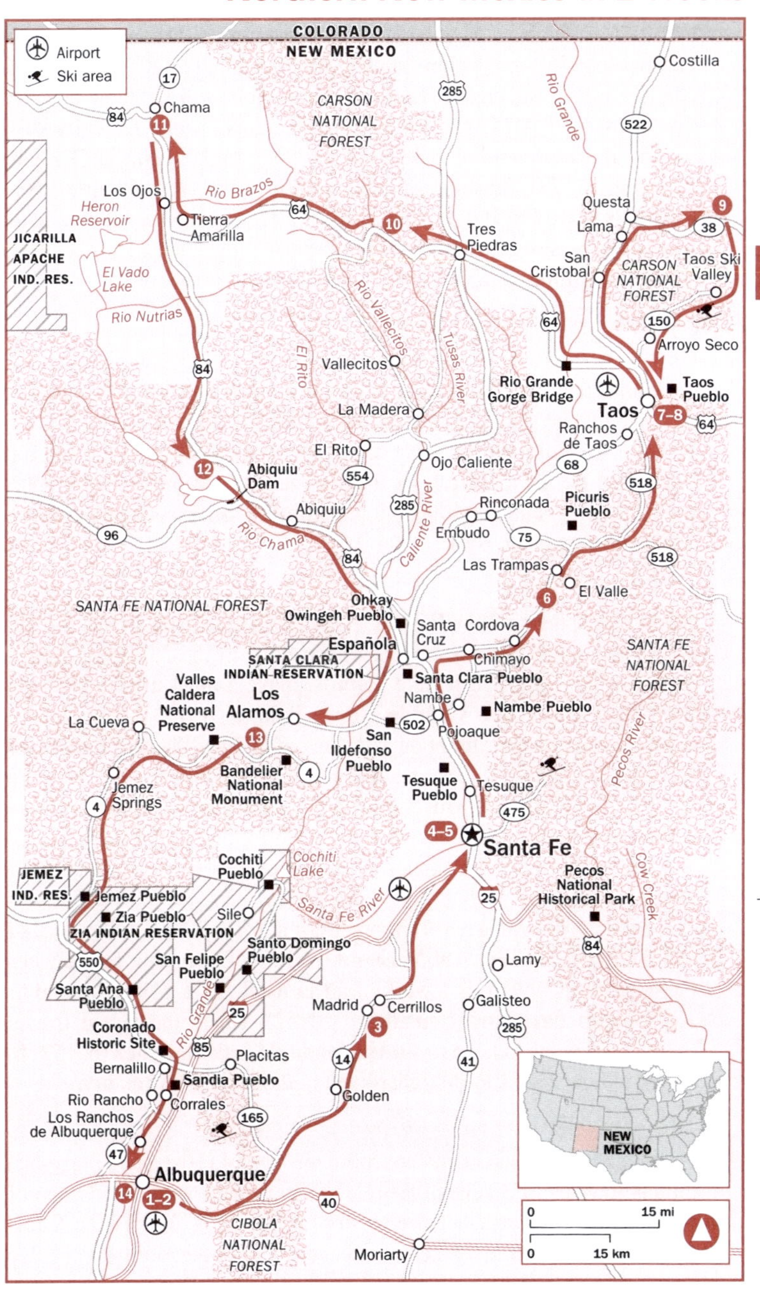

Day 5: Santa Fe

In the morning, browse around the Plaza area some more, spending a little time at the **New Mexico History Museum** (p. 74) and the **Loretto Chapel** (p. 84). Or, if you're looking for something totally different and edging towards the bizarre, head to **Meow Wolf** (p. 73). Chow down on the "Mother of All Green Chile Cheeseburgers" at the **Cowgirl BBQ** (p. 66). In the afternoon, make your way over to the **Georgia O'Keeffe Museum** (p. 73), finishing off with a visit to the "Roundhouse," **New Mexico's State Capitol** (p. 86) and the only round capitol building in the United States. For an excellent New Mexican dinner, spend an evening at **The Pink Adobe** (p. 65).

Day 6: High Road to Taos

On **DAY 6,** travel the **High Road to Taos** (see p. 123), stopping to visit the **Santuario de Chimayó** (p. 124) and touch its miraculous healing dirt, and maybe sampling real northern New Mexico cuisine for lunch at **Rancho de Chimayó** (p. 124). On the way into Taos, stop at the **San Francisco de Asis Church** (p. 148) to gaze at the most-photographed back side of a church, with its huge buttresses, perhaps having dinner at **The Love Apple** (p. 140).

Days 7 & 8: Taos

Begin by exploring **Taos Pueblo** (p. 148) when the sun strikes the face of the four- and five-story adobe. Then head to the **Millicent Rogers Museum** (p. 146), and if time permits, make a quick trip to see—and walk out on—the **Rio Grande Gorge Bridge** (p. 153). You can then ditch your car for the afternoon and step out on foot. Wander **Taos Plaza,** do some shopping, check out the **Kit Carson Home and Museum** (p. 152), the **Harwood Museum of Art** (p. 151), or the **Taos Firehouse Collection** (p. 153). At cocktail time, head to the **Adobe Bar** (p. 165), and follow that up with dinner at **Doc Martin's** (p. 138), both in the Historic Taos Inn.

Start **DAY 8** with a real Taos breakfast at **Michael's Kitchen** (p. 144) and then visit the **Taos Art Museum** (p. 148). The Fechin Home where the museum is housed is a work of art in itself. Take a stroll around the **Kit Carson Park and Cemetery** (p. 152), where the famed frontier scout is buried, then head to **La Hacienda de Los Martinez** (p. 152) for a look at how a well-to-do trader lived in the early 19th century.

Day 9: The Enchanted Circle

Take the 90-mile loop from Taos north through old Hispanic villages and mining towns to see some of the region's most picturesque landscapes. If you're a literary type, be sure to stop at the **D. H. Lawrence Ranch** (p. 150), and if you're a hiker, stretch your legs at the **Wild Rivers Recreation Area** (p. 170). You can lunch in either Red River or Eagle Nest.

Day 10: West to Chama

If you're traveling in the spring, summer, or fall, take a scenic—not speedy—drive west through the mountains to **Chama.** Stop at one of the overlooks when you top out, stretch your legs, and gaze at the huge formation called the Brazos Box. Once in Chama, stroll around town and the depot to get a feel for the area's steam train history, and prepare for tomorrow's ride on the **Cumbres & Toltec Scenic Railroad** (p. 173). Volunteers are sometimes on hand to relate stories about the train and its history. Be sure to make your train reservations well in advance. As well as offering a great ride, the Cumbres & Toltec is a living train museum, so sit back and enjoy your ride into yesterday.

Or, if you're not a train buff, stay in Taos and take a whitewater raft trip through the exciting **Taos Box** (p. 160). In winter, when the trains aren't running, here's an excellent high-desert option: Stay in Taos and head to **Taos Ski Valley** (p. 155) for a day of skiing.

Day 11: Cumbres & Toltec Scenic Railroad

Spend the day riding the **Cumbres & Toltec Scenic Railroad** (p. 173). You can ride the train to the luncheon stop at Osier Pass and turn around and come back, or continue on the train all the way to Antonito, Colorado, and return to Chama by bus. Spend the night in Chama. If you opted to stay in Taos, take a **horseback ride** (p. 160), or (in winter) spend another day on the slopes at **Taos Ski Valley** (p. 155).

Day 12: Head South to Los Alamos

Drive south through stupendous scenery, passing through Georgia O'Keeffe country: **Abiquiu** and the crimson-and-white hills she painted (see p. 144). When you reach **Los Alamos** (p. 117), be aware that you've left ancient history behind and entered a town that didn't exist before World War II. But there's plenty to see before you bed down for the night.

Day 13: Bandelier National Monument

You might make a side trip to **Valles Caldera National Preserve** (p. 122), before driving to **Bandelier National Monument** (p. 120), where you'll hike among ancient ruins. Follow the Main Loop Trail through the ruins, making sure you stop to climb the ladders to the dwellings perched high on the canyon wall. Finally, drive back to Albuquerque.

Day 14: Albuquerque

A great finale to your visit would be to take a **balloon ride** (p. 210) first thing in the morning. (Be sure to make your reservations well in advance.) Then head to the **Anderson-Abruzzo Albuquerque International Balloon Museum** (p. 196) to learn about ballooning's history. Finish the afternoon cooling off at your hotel pool, or if you're feeling energetic, visit the **National Hispanic Cultural Center** (p. 197). Have dinner at **Campo** at Los Poblanos hotel (p. 186).

AN ACTIVE TOUR OF NORTHERN NEW MEXICO

Anyone who skis, hikes, mountain bikes, or rafts knows that all of the Southwest is unsurpassed in its offerings for outdoor enthusiasts. New Mexico is no exception, and the highest concentration of these sports and outdoor activities lies in the north. You can ski world-class terrain at **Taos Ski Valley,** fly-fish or bike the edge of the **Rio Grande Gorge,** and hike the mountains among the ancestral Puebloan ruins at **Bandelier National Monument.** Be aware that the region is known for its mercurial weather conditions—always be prepared for extremes. Also, most of northern New Mexico is over 6,000 feet in elevation, so it may take you time to catch your breath. Be patient on the long upward hills. The sports you do will, of course, depend a lot on the season. For the full benefit of this trip, take it in late March or early April. With a little advance preparation, you might be able to ski and river raft on the same trip! See map on p. 43.

Days 1 & 2: Albuquerque

When you arrive in Albuquerque, you may want to get acclimated to the city by strolling through **Old Town** (p. 198) and visiting the **ABQ BioPark** (p. 200) to get a sense of the nature in the area. A visit to the **Indian Pueblo Cultural Center** (p. 196) will acquaint you with some of the traditions and customs you'll encounter as you head north. On **DAY 2,** for a truly unique experience, you may want to schedule a **balloon ride** (p. 210) first thing in the morning. Just be sure to make advance reservations for this exhilarating activity. If you're a hiker, head to **Petroglyph National Monument** (p. 205) to see thousands of symbols etched in stone. In the evening, ride the **Sandia Peak Tramway** (p. 198) and go hiking along the crest. If you like, you can have dinner at **Ten 3** (p. 188) and view the city lights as you come down.

Day 3: The Turquoise Trail to Santa Fe

For a prettier and more relaxing drive than you'll get on the interstate, strike out for the ghost towns and other sights along the **Turquoise Trail** (p. 221) on your way to Santa Fe. Stop in **Madrid** (p. 222) and browse through a few of the galleries, and when you reach **Cerrillos** (p. 222), grab a bite at **Black Bird Saloon** and take a short side trip to the **Cerrillos State Park** for a quick hike. This will put you in Santa Fe in time to do some sightseeing. Head straight to the **plaza** (p. 76), the **Palace of the Governors** (p. 76), and the **Cathedral Basilica of St. Francis of Assisi** (p. 80). While browsing the wares for sale from the Native Americans under the Palace portal, you might inquire about the significance of symbols on pottery or in the jewelry design. Eat dinner at **The Shed** (p. 68).

An Active Tour of Northern New Mexico

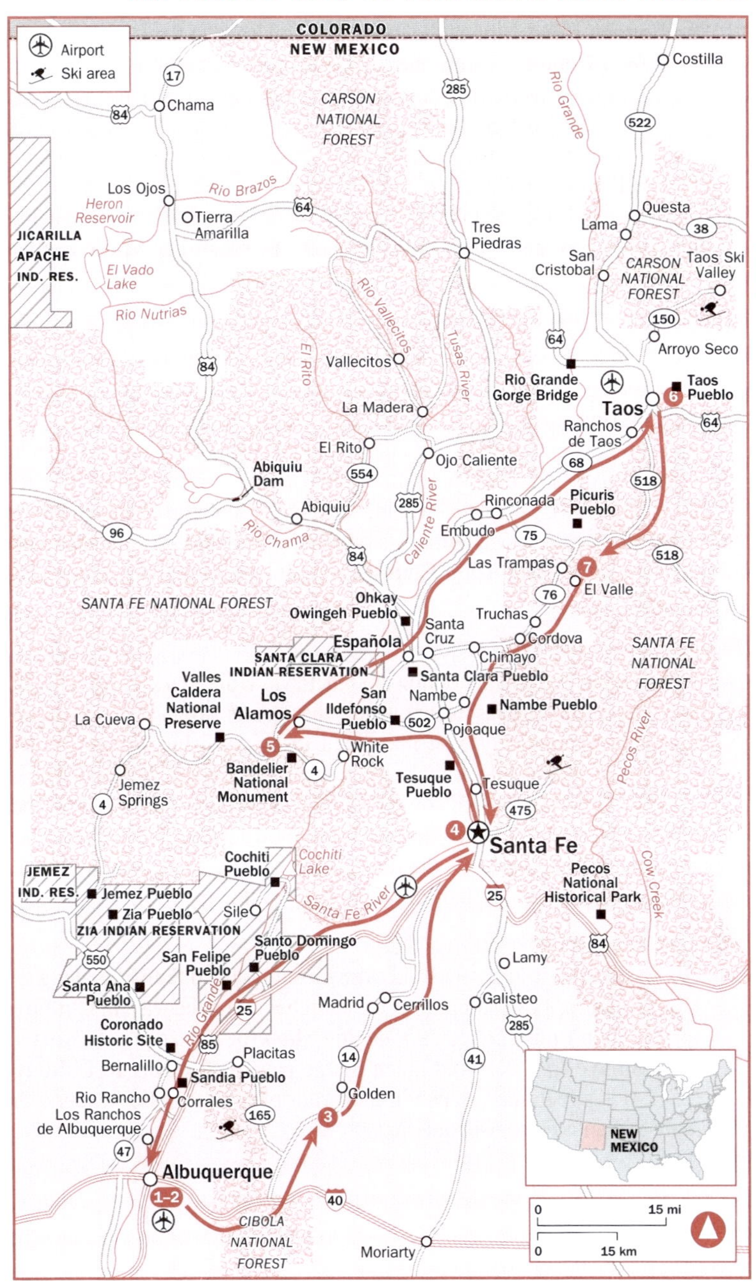

3

SUGGESTED NORTHERN NEW MEXICO ITINERARIES | An Active Tour of Northern New Mexico

Day 4: Santa Fe

Use your own bike or rent a cruiser in town to ride around the plaza and up **Canyon Road.** Stop at the top of Canyon Road at the **Randall Davey Audubon Center & Sanctuary** (p. 87) to do some bird-watching and hiking. Alternatively, you may want to head to the mountains to do some hiking on the **Borrego Trail** (p. 95) or, if it's winter, some skiing at **Ski Santa Fe** (p. 97). Finish your day with a soak in one of the mineral pools at **Ten Thousand Waves** (p. 97). In the evening, depending on the season, you may want to take in some of Santa Fe's excellent arts, such as the **Santa Fe Opera** (p. 104) or the **Santa Fe Chamber Music Festival** (p. 105).

Day 5: Bandelier National Monument

Head out from Santa Fe to **Bandelier National Monument** (p. 120) and hike among ancient ruins. Follow the Main Loop Trail as far up as you'd like, making sure you stop to climb the ladders to the dwellings perched high on the canyon wall. Hikers should take the Falls Trail up Frijoles Canyon to a striking waterfall. From Bandelier, drive along the Rio Grande to Taos. Spend the evening strolling around the **plaza** (p. 161) to get a feel for the town, perhaps stopping for a libation and to hear some local music at **The Alley Cantina** (p. 166) or Taos Inn's **Adobe Bar** (p. 165).

Day 6: Taos

Sports lovers have many options in this town. **Horseback rides** will take you out on the mesas or exploring the forests around the ski valley (p. 160). Alternatively, you may want to go fly-fishing along the Rio Grande, or hike on one of the many trails in the **Carson National Forest** (p. 154). If it's ski season, you'll definitely want to spend the day at **Taos Ski Valley** (p. 155), or if you're visiting in the spring and the rivers are running high and fast, take the full-day heart-throbbing romp through the **Taos Box** (p. 160) or a half-day float trip at **Pilar** (p. 170).

Day 7: The High Road to Taos

On your last day, take a leisurely drive south toward Santa Fe along the **High Road** (p. 123), stopping at the churches along the way. In **Chimayo** (p. 123) don't miss **Ortega's Weaving Shop** (p. 123), or the **Santuario de Chimayó** (p. 124). And lunch on the patio at **Rancho de Chimayó** (p. 124) is a real treat. Depending on your plane reservations, spend the night in Santa Fe or Albuquerque.

SANTA FE ESSENTIALS

4

After visiting Santa Fe, humorist Will Rogers reportedly said, "Whoever designed this town did so while riding on a jackass backwards and drunk." Well, we can't argue with that. You, too, may find yourself perplexed when maneuvering through the meandering lanes and one-way streets of the oldest capital city in the United States. But Santa Fe's crooked streets, combined with its stunning setting at the base of rugged mountains, provide a sense of exotic sophistication. On its historic central plaza, you'll see Native Americans selling crafts, locals cruising along in souped-up low-riders and vintage pickup trucks, and people young and old just hanging out. Such diversity, coupled with the variety of architecture—which ranges from Pueblo style to Romanesque to Gothic—prompted the tourism promotion people to label Santa Fe "The City Different."

Remember to pack your walking shoes, because exploring Santa Fe by foot is the best way to enjoy its idiosyncrasies. And if you do get lost, ask one of the roughly 90,000 people living here—7,000 feet above sea level—for directions.

ORIENTATION

Visitor Information

Official **Santa Fe Visitor Information Centers** are located at the Convention Center, 201 W. Marcy St. (✆ **505/955-6200**); on the south side of the plaza in Plaza Galeria, 66 E. San Francisco St., Suite 3 (✆ **505/955-6215**); and at the Water Street Visitor Center, 100 E. Water St. (✆ **505/955-6200**). You can also log on to the city's visitor information website at www.santafe.org or call ✆ **800/777-2489.**

The **American Automobile Association (AAA),** 3517 Zafarano Dr., Suite D (www.aaa.com; ✆ **877/222-1020** or 505/471-6620), provides free maps and other information to members.

City Layout

MAIN ARTERIES & STREETS The limits of downtown Santa Fe are loosely defined on three sides by the horseshoe-shaped **Paseo de Peralta** and on the west by **St. Francis Drive,** otherwise

Santa Fe Orientation

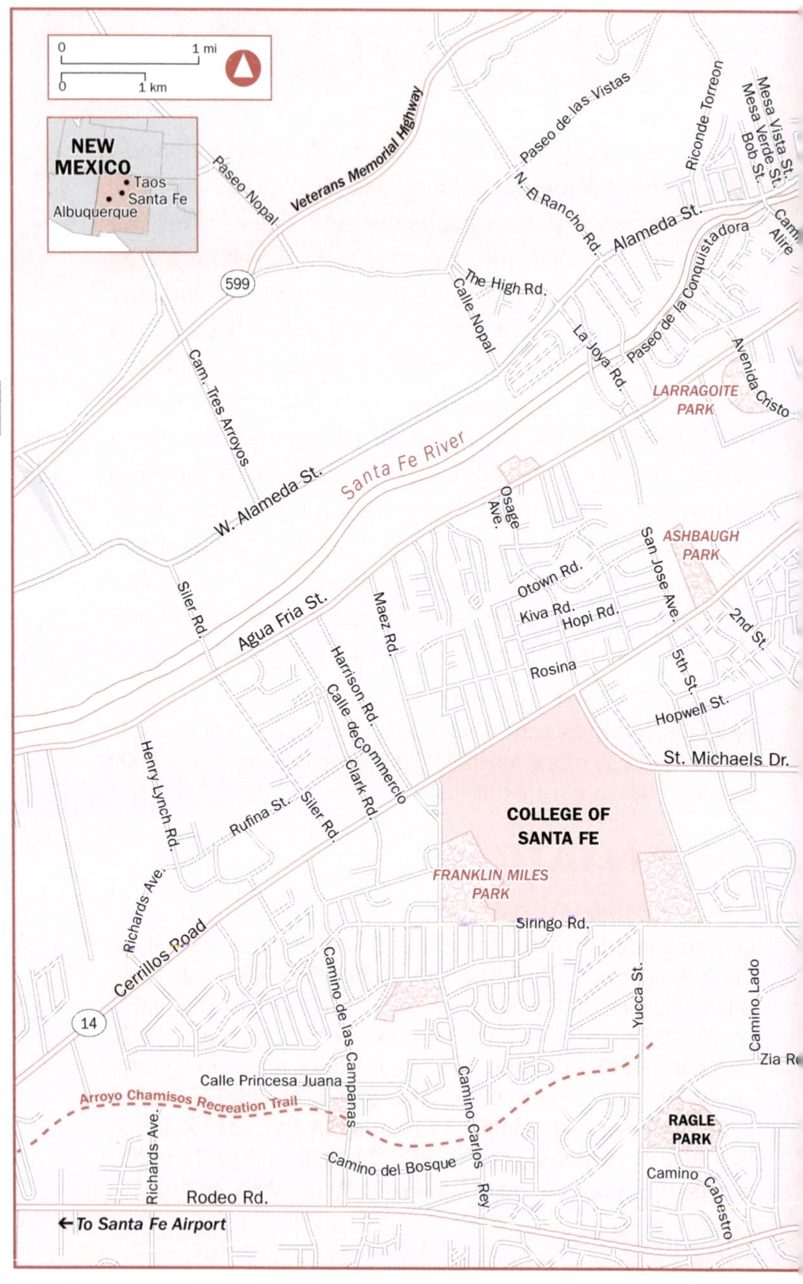

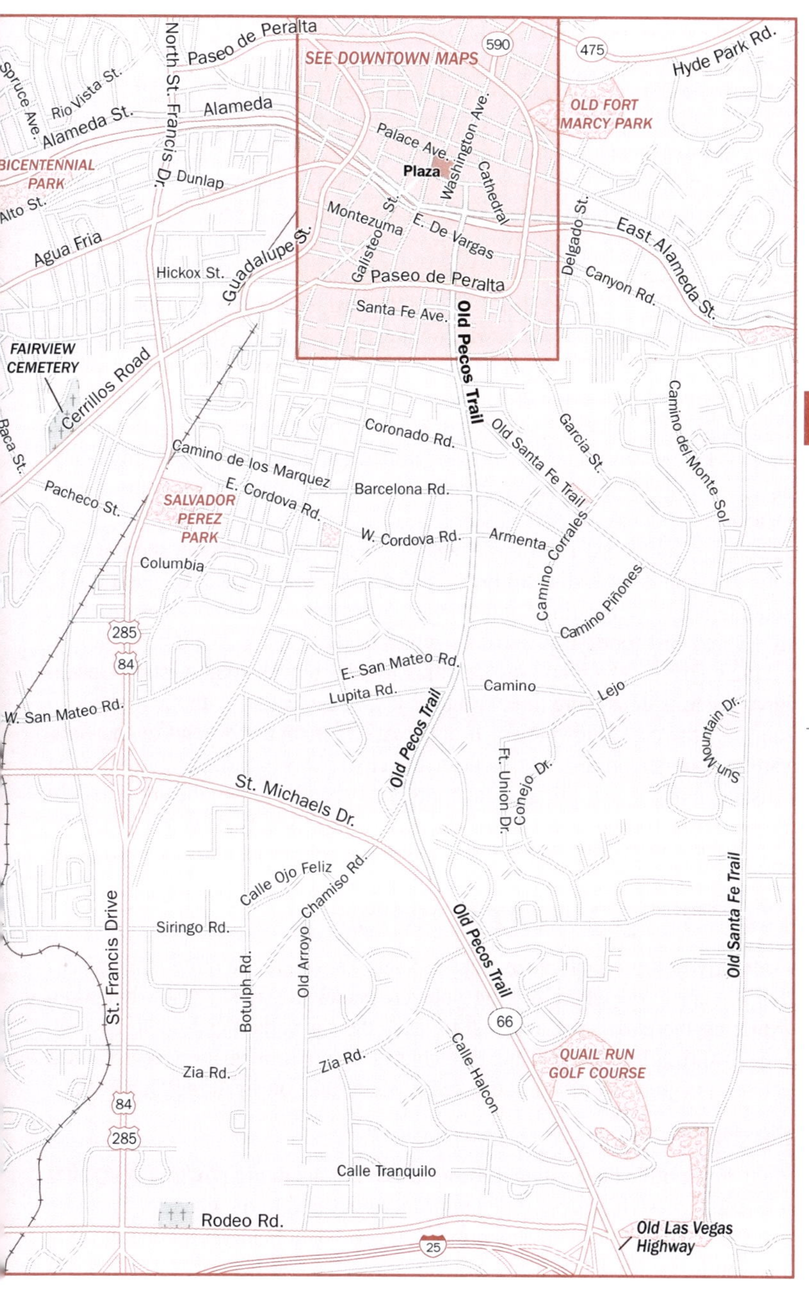

4 SANTA FE ESSENTIALS | Orientation

known as US 84/285. **Alameda Street** runs along the north side of the Santa Fe River through downtown. The State Capitol and other government buildings are on the south side of the river, while most buildings of historic and tourist interest are on the north, east of Guadalupe Street.

Santa Fe Plaza is the city's universally accepted point of orientation. Here, you'll find tall shade trees, lots of grass, and plenty of tourists. Its four diagonal walkways meet at a central fountain. If you stand in the center of the plaza looking north, you'll be facing the Palace of the Governors. In front of you is Palace Avenue; behind you, San Francisco Street. To your left is Lincoln Avenue, and to your right is Washington Avenue, which divides the downtown avenues into east and west. The Cathedral Basilica of St. Francis of Assisi is the massive Romanesque structure a block east, down San Francisco Street. Two full blocks south of the plaza, running east-west, are Alameda Street and the **Santa Fe River,** a tiny tributary of the Rio Grande that runs most of the year. Near the intersection of Alameda Street and Paseo de Peralta, you'll find **Canyon Road,** a narrow, mostly one-way street packed with galleries and shops. Once it was the home of many artists, and today you'll still find some at work within gallery studios. A number of fine restaurants are in this district as well.

Leading southwest from the downtown area, beginning opposite the state office buildings on Galisteo Street, is **Cerrillos Road.** Once the main north-south highway connecting Santa Fe with Albuquerque, it is now a 6-mile-long motel and fast-food strip, most of which ends at the I-25 interchange. **St. Francis Drive,** which crosses Cerrillos Road 3 blocks southwest of Guadalupe Street, is a far more direct route to I-25, intersecting with the highway 4 miles southwest of downtown. It also marks the southwest end of the Railyard, a commercial district that hosts the city's weekly farmers', artists', and artisans' markets, as well as restaurants, shops, and a movie theater. The **Old Pecos Trail,** on the east side of the city, also connects downtown and the freeway. **St. Michael's Drive** crosses all three arteries south of downtown.

GETTING AROUND

Overall, you'll probably need a car in Santa Fe—there are quite a few places you'll want to go where driving yourself makes the most sense—but when exploring the plaza area, it's best to leave the car parked and do so on foot. Free **walking-tour maps** are available at visitor information centers (see above); for guided walking tours, see p. 88, or take our walking tour, p. 90.

By Bus

Santa Fe's public bus system, **Santa Fe Trails** (santafenm.gov/transit; ✆ **505/955-2001**), has 10 routes; although primarily geared to the needs of Santa Fe residents, they are also an economical way for visitors to get around the city. The **Santa Fe Pick-Up,** a free shuttle service geared towards visitors, is an ideal way to explore downtown; it runs every 30 minutes daily, 8:30am to 6:30pm, making 28 stops that include Canyon Road, the Plaza, and the

Railyard district. Other buses serve the plaza area, Museum Hill, and Cerrillos Road. One trip for adults costs $1; a 1-day pass costs $2, and a 31-day pass costs $20. Rates are half that for seniors 60 and older and people with disabilities, and U.S. military veterans ride free. Fares must be paid in cash on the buses; checks and credit cards are accepted if you buy a pass at the bus system office, 2931 Rufina St. Most buses operate Monday to Friday 6am to 10pm and Saturday 8am to 8pm. There is limited service on Sunday and holidays.

By Car

Street parking is difficult to find during summer months, especially near the plaza, but the city has about 1,850 off-street parking spaces in downtown Santa Fe. Metered parking may be costlier during special events, but the basic fee is $2 per hour, collected 8am to 6pm Monday through Saturday (free on Sundays and major holidays). There's a 24-hour metered lot a block south of the plaza at 100 E. Water St., and two nearby parking garages (216 W. San Francisco St., 2 blocks west of the plaza, and 119 S. Federal Place, 2 blocks north of the plaza at the convention center) are open daily 7am to midnight. At the Santa Fe Railyard, there's a parking garage at the north end, and a lot toward the south. Santa Fe visitor information centers (see p. 45) can give you a printed guide to Santa Fe parking areas, or you can get specific directions at santafenm.gov/public-works/parking.

Driving Warning

New Mexico has one of the highest per-capita rates of traffic deaths in the nation (mostly due to drunk driving), and also a high rate of uninsured motorists. It's a good idea to be especially cautious while driving, especially at intersections.

The State Highway and Transportation Department has a toll-free **Road Advisory Hotline** (✆ **511** or 800/432-4269) and also a website—www.nmroads.com—that provides current information on road closures and driving conditions.

By Bicycle

Riding a bicycle is somewhat challenging in downtown Santa Fe due to its narrow streets and limited number of bike paths. However, it is a good way to get around for experienced city riders. You can rent bikes from **Raworks,** 418 Cerrillos Rd. (raworkshc.com; ✆ **505/772-0524**) and **Bike-N-Sport,** 504C Cordova Rd. (nmbikensport.com; ✆ **505/820-0809**).

[Fast FACTS] SANTA FE

Car Rentals **Avis** has an outlet at the Santa Fe Airport (✆ 505/471-5892) and another at 1946 Cerrillos Rd. (✆ 505/820-7943) shared with **Budget** (✆ 505/984-1596). **Hertz** has an outlet at the airport (✆ 505/471-7189) and also at 2010 Cerrillos Rd. (✆ 505/438-4650). **Enterprise** is located at 3961 Cerrillos Rd. (✆ 505/424-1134) and at 1611 St. Michaels Dr. (✆ 505/986-1414). See

p. 235 in chapter 10 for more information on car rentals.

Currency Exchange You can exchange foreign currency at **Wells Fargo** at 241 Washington Ave. (✆ **505/984-0500**).

Doctors For a medical emergency, dial ✆ **911**. For other medical issues, a highly rated urgent care facility is **Railyard Urgent Care,** 831 S. St. Francis Dr. (www.railyardurgentcare.com; ✆ **505/501-7791**), open daily 8am to 7pm.

Emergencies For police, fire, or medical emergencies, dial ✆ **911.**

Hotlines Available hotlines include UNM **Poison and Drug Info Center** (✆ **800/222-1222**) and **Sexual Assault** (✆ **505/986-9111**).

Libraries **The Santa Fe Public Library** is half a block from the plaza, at 145 Washington Ave. (https://santefelibrary.org; ✆ **505/955-6781**). The Oliver La Farge Branch library is at 1730 Llano St., just off St. Michael's Drive, and the Southside Library is at 6599 Jaguar Dr., at the intersection of Country Club Road.

Newspapers The ***New Mexican***—Santa Fe's daily paper—is the oldest newspaper in the West (santafenewmexican.com; ✆ **505/983-3303**). The weekly ***Santa Fe Reporter,*** 1512 Pacheco St. (sfreporter.com; ✆ **505/988-5541**), published on Wednesdays and available at stands all over town, is often more controversial, and its entertainment listings are excellent.

Police In case of emergency, dial ✆ **911.** For all other inquiries, contact the **Santa Fe Police Department,** 2515 Camino Entrada (santafenm.gov/police; ✆ **505/428-3710**). The **Santa Fe County Sheriff,** with jurisdiction outside the city limits, is at 35 Camino Justicia (santafecountynm.gov/sheriff; ✆ **505/986-2455**).

Post Offices The **main post office** is at 120 S. Federal Place, 2 blocks north and 1 block west of the plaza. It's open Monday to Friday 8am to 5:30pm and Saturday 9am to 4pm. The **Coronado Station branch,** at 2071 S. Pacheco St., is open Monday to Friday 8am to 6pm and Saturday 9am to 4pm. For additional locations, see usps.com or call ✆ **800/275-8777.**

Taxis There are no city-run taxicab companies currently operating in Santa Fe, but both **Uber** (uber.com) and **Lyft** (lyft.com) operate their ride-share businesses in the city. Availability can be limited.

WHERE TO STAY IN SANTA FE

The City Different offers a broad range of accommodations. From downtown hotels to Cerrillos Road motels, ranch-style resorts to quaint bed-and-breakfasts, the standard is almost universally high, and usually so are the prices.

Accommodations are often booked solid through the summer months, the Christmas holiday, and Easter, and most places raise their prices accordingly. Rates increase even more during Indian Market, the third weekend of August, and some properties even raise them during the Albuquerque International Balloon Fiesta in early October. During these periods, it's essential to make reservations well in advance and to expect to pay premium. But the other side of the coin is also true: If you're not particularly interested in Indian Market, the balloon fiesta, summer, or holiday events, you can save quite a bit by visiting at other times. You'll also miss the crowds and long lines at restaurants. The lowest rates are usually from November through March, except for Christmas, of course. Be sure to check hotel websites for seasonal discounts and packages.

CHAIN MOTELS in santa fe

In Santa Fe, you'll find a handy string of chain motels along Cerrillos Road, offering a decent alternative to the city's more expensive hotels if you want to save a few bucks. Although you won't be as close to Santa Fe Plaza as you might like, Santa Fe just isn't that big, so nothing's really far away. Note that the lower street numbers on Cerrillos Road—say, in the hundreds—are closer to the downtown attractions than the higher numbers, in the thousands, which are down at the south end of Cerrillos, near where it meets I-25.

We're fans of the La Quinta chain, now part of the Wyndham family, in part because La Quintas generally accept pets with no extra charge—not to be confused with the $75 per night pet fee you'll pay at some downtown properties—but also because we have found these facilities to be clean, generally well-maintained, and a good value. The **La Quinta by Wyndham ♥♥** is an especially attractive property, located at 4298 Cerrillos Rd. (lq.com or wyndham hotels.com; ✆ **800/753-3757** or 505/471-1142); it offers free Wi-Fi and all the usual amenities, with winter rates of $70 to $110 double and summer rates of $98 to $115 double.

Other popular chains include the **Santa Fe Courtyard by Marriott ♥♥**, 3347 Cerrillos Rd. (santafecourtyard.com; ✆ **505/473-2800**), offering winter rates of $110 to $160 double and summer rates of $120 to $225 double; and **Best Western Plus Inn ♥**, 3650 Cerrillos Rd. (bestwestern.com; ✆ **800/454-3213** or 505/438-3822), with year-round rates of $130 to $195 double. A **Comfort Inn ♥** is located at 4312 Cerrillos Rd. (choicehotels.com; ✆ **877/424-6423** or 505/474-7330) with winter rates of $73 to $101 and summer rates of $111 to $168.

There's a **Motel 6 ♥** at 646 Cerrillos Rd. (motel6.com; ✆ **800/899-9841** or 505/982-3551), with rates of $60 to $90 double; and a **Quality Inn ♥** at 3695 Cerrillos Rd. (choicehotels.com; ✆ **877/424-6423** or 505/596-9044), with rates of $61 to $156 double.

No matter the season, discounts are often available to seniors, members of AAA, active and retired military, corporate employees, and others, especially at the chain motels (see above).

A little-known way to obtain relatively inexpensive lodging is to bed down at commercial campgrounds in what are usually called **"camping cabins."** You'll usually need to bring your own linens and sometimes share the campground bathhouses, but these cabins can be very nice and are usually more affordable than traditional motels and hotels. See "RV Parks & Campgrounds," p. 59.

A combined **city-state tax** of about 15.2% is added to every hotel bill in Santa Fe. And unless otherwise indicated, all recommended accommodations come with a private bathroom and free parking.

RESERVATION SERVICES The best all-around reservation service in Santa Fe is the official Santa Fe website—**www.santafe.org**—where you can find a list of lodgings, restaurants, outdoor activities, and events. It's operated by the Santa Fe Convention and Visitors Bureau. Click on "Accommodations" at the top of the page, then choose the type of accommodation you want, such as hotels and motels, bed and breakfasts, vacation rentals, or campgrounds, and a large number of choices will pop up from which you can choose.

Downtown

With Santa Fe Plaza at the center, everything within the horseshoe-shaped Paseo de Peralta, along Canyon Road, and in and near the Railyard is considered downtown Santa Fe for the purposes of this book.

EXPENSIVE

Hotel St. Francis ♥♥ St. Francis of Assisi was a rich aristocrat who gave up a life of luxury to follow an ascetic path of devotion. The hotel named after him offers the best of these two extremes, combining a simple, historic aesthetic with modern luxury. Pillar candles flicker on the plaster walls and wide stone floors in the lobby, while the rooms are sparely but tastefully decorated, with high ceilings and casement windows. The three-story National Historic Register property offers a relaxed cosmopolitan vibe and a multilingual concierge. (Don't miss the cherubs above the Victorian fireplace in the lobby, a motif that's repeated elsewhere.) Some of the rooms are small. The hotel has a **Gruet Santa Fe tasting room** in which you can relax and sip premium Gruet wines, as well as the **Market Steer Steakhouse** and **Secreto Lounge,** an award-winning wine and cocktail bar with a loggia patio that's a local favorite for drinks and streetside people-watching.

210 Don Gaspar Ave. hotelstfrancis.com. ✆ **800/529-5700** or 505/983-5700. 81 units. $145–$560 double plus $30 service fee. Dogs accepted ($75 per day; $35 per day for a second pet). **Amenities:** Restaurant; lounge; business center; valet parking, shuttle to pools and fitness centers at sister properties; free Wi-Fi.

Inn and Spa at Loretto ♥♥♥ Don't be surprised if you're 2 blocks from the plaza in downtown Santa Fe and suddenly think you've spotted a Native American pueblo. That's the Inn and Spa at Loretto, built in 1975 and styled after the multi-story Taos Pueblo, all shadow-catching corners and flat roofs on the outside. Inside, it's an elegant hotel. The rooms are generously sized, with Native design touches like kiva fireplaces and modern amenities such as iPhone docks and slate-floored bathrooms. Some units have balconies—especially inviting are the ones on the northeast side with views of the Cathedral Basilica of St. Francis of Asis and the Loretto Chapel next door. Spring for a junior suite if you can. The **Living Room** lounge hosts live music in front of the fireplace Thursday, Friday, and Saturday nights; the **Luminaria** restaurant serves upscale Southwestern dishes; and the Living Room Spa offers a long list of high-end treatments. There are also complimentary weekend walking tours of downtown Santa Fe.

211 Old Santa Fe Trail. hotelloretto.com. ✆ **866/582-1646** or 505/988-5531. 136 units. $165–$695 double plus $30 resort fee. Pets accepted ($75 per day plus $35 per day for a second dog). **Amenities:** Restaurant; lounge; concierge; 24-hour fitness center; business center; outdoor pool (heated year-round); room service; spa; free Wi-Fi.

Downtown Santa Fe Hotels

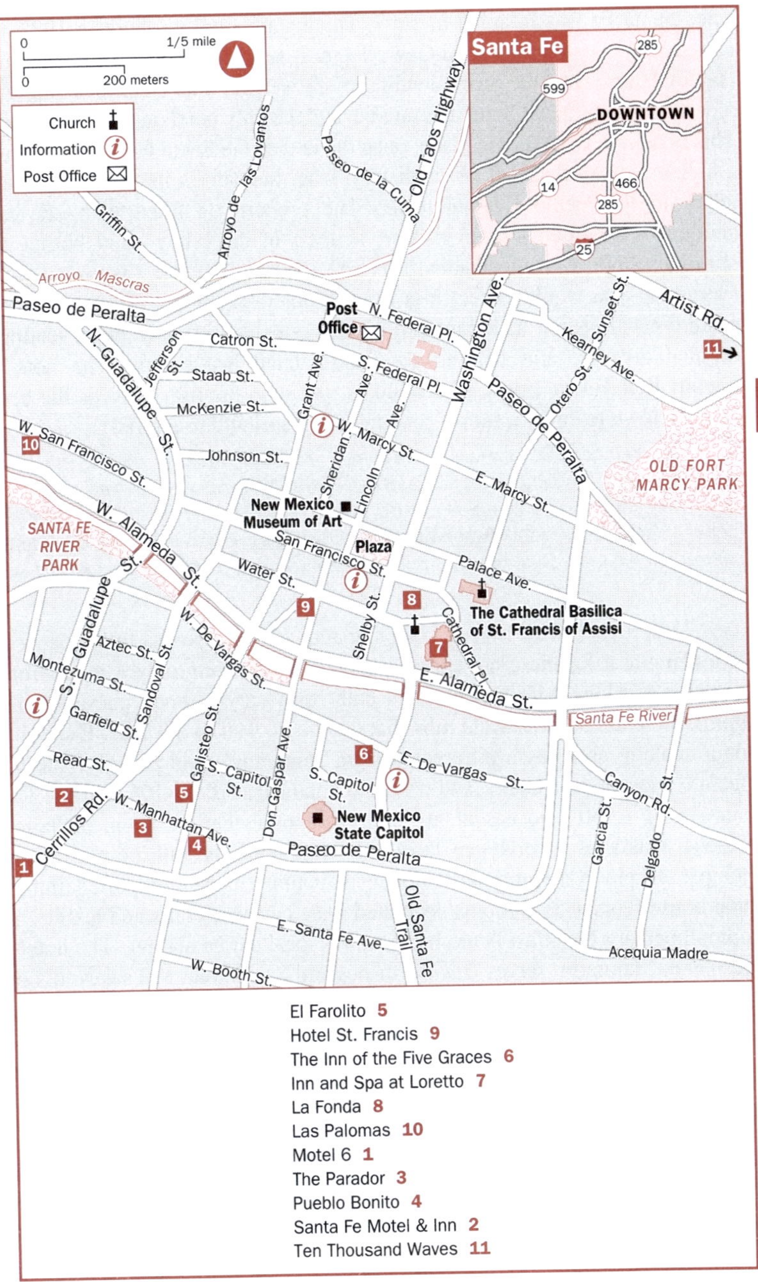

La Fonda ♥♥♥ According to the historical record, there has been a *fonda,* or inn, at this location—on the southeast corner of the plaza—almost since Santa Fe was founded in 1607. This incarnation was built in 1922 by famed Santa Fe architect John Gaw Meem. It served as a railway hotel and a Harvey House over the years, lending more weight to its claim of being the oldest and best-known hotel in Santa Fe, and the only hotel on Santa Fe Plaza. This is definitely an iconic place, once the end of the Santa Fe Trail and now a high-end hotel that still oozes history, from the cafe in its time-warp tiled lobby to its Pueblo Revival tower. The property is filled with art and antiques—and often ogling visitors, at least in the lobby—and boasts an unusually high level of personal service. All the rooms are luxurious, with everything you would expect in a top-tier hotel. There is a wide variety of room types (thus the wide range of nightly rates) but all have plush seating, original artwork, and delightfully hand-painted headboards. The hotel's famous **Bell Tower Bar,** on La Fonda's roof atop the fifth floor, is the best place in town to enjoy a sunset cocktail (open spring through fall).

100 E. San Francisco St. lafondasantafe.com. ✆ **800/523-5002** or 505/982-5511. 180 units. Doubles $190–$500, suites $300–$600. Children 12 and under stay free in parent's room. Self and valet parking $30 per day (max. vehicle height 6'6"). Pets accepted (under 45 lb., $50 per night). **Amenities:** Restaurant; 2 lounges; babysitting; car rentals; concierge; exercise room; hot tub; outdoor heated pool; room service; free art and history tours; sauna; spa, business center; free Wi-Fi.

Ten Thousand Waves ♥♥ Staying at this 20-acre retreat truly does feel like being at a Japanese hot springs resort, despite being only 4 miles from downtown. Along with a communal bath open only to hotel guests (8am–9pm), there are seven private tubs that can be booked in advance. Each outdoor soaking area has a different design; some have cold plunges; and all feature a sauna, deck chairs, and waters maintained at 104 to 106 degrees. The spa-centric resort also has plenty of treatments to choose from, including Shiatsu massages and oxygen facials. Dotted along the hillside of fragrant juniper and piñon are minimalist wooden structures, made of imported timber, that house ryokan-style rooms decorated with Japanese crafts and textiles. A complimentary breakfast bento box features local coffee and tea. The hotel's restaurant, **Izanami,** serves *izakaya* dishes and a wide range of sakes. It's by far the best Japanese you'll find in Santa Fe.

21 Ten Thousand Waves Way. tenthousandwaves.com. ✆ **505/982-9304.** 14 units. $370–$460 double plus $30 service fee. 2-night minimum. Dogs accepted ($40 per day). **Amenities:** Restaurant; breakfast; free Wi-Fi.

MODERATE

Santa Fe Motel & Inn ♥♥ The Santa Fe Motel & Inn boasts a central location, relatively reasonable prices, and clean and comfortable rooms, always a good combination in this pricey city. Although technically a motel, it feels like a B&B, with friendly service, antique furnishings, and a free healthy breakfast including oatmeal, yogurt parfait, granola bars, bizcochito

FAMILY-FRIENDLY hotels

El Rey Court (p. 56) Covered picnic tables in a nicely landscaped courtyard set back from the street, plus an outdoor pool, make this a nice place for families to commune in summer.

Santa Fe Motel & Inn With its companion rubber duckies and some rooms that feature enclosed patios, this is a good spot for families.

cookies, fresh fruit, cereals, juices, and coffee. Rooms are tastefully decorated in Southwest style, with fresh flowers and radiant baseboard heat, and one or two queen-size beds or one king. All have a refrigerator, microwave, and a smart TV so guests can access their own TV services, and some come with working fireplaces. You'll also find a companion rubber ducky in all tubs and showers. Some units are pet friendly with enclosed patios (call for details). There are also several patio rooms available in three historic casitas, plus a free-standing studio apartment and a two-bedroom two-bath home suitable for two couples traveling together (call for rates). The motel is making an effort to be as environmentally friendly as possible, and reports that it is almost 100% free of single use plastic.

510 Cerrillos Rd. santafemotel.com. ✆ **800/930-5002** or 505/982-1039. 24 units. $99–$279 double. Free parking. **Amenities:** Free Tesla/EV charging stations; free Wi-Fi.

INEXPENSIVE

Pueblo Bonito ♥♥ This traditional adobe compound consisting of three buildings between the Plaza and the Railyard district is a great deal for its central location and authentic feel. Each of its rooms feature Casper mattresses, Pendleton blankets, and Roku TVs with Netflix and Hulu. Beyond these comforts, the rooms have a lot of character, with decor from New Mexican artisans, like punched-tin wall hangings, photography, and ceramics. Many have wood-fired kiva fireplaces (though there's a $15 "usage fee"), some have fully stocked kitchenettes, and all feature Smeg mini fridges and beautifully tiled bathrooms.

138 W. Manhattan Ave. pueblobonitoinn.com. ✆ **505/984-8001.** 19 units. $92–$240 double. Free parking. No pets except for service animals. **Amenities:** Free Wi-Fi.

Outside Downtown

Santa Fe's main artery from downtown south to I-25 and Albuquerque is Cerrillos Road, NM 14. Once the main route to and from Albuquerque, NM 14 becomes very scenic south of I-25, as it skirts the mountains on the east. North of I-25, however, it's a commercial strip with lots of chain hotel and fast-food options. It's about 5¼ miles from the plaza to the Santa Fe mall at the corner of Cerrillos and Rodeo roads, which marks the southern boundary of the city. Most motels are on this strip, although several of them are to the east, closer to St. Francis Drive (US 84) or the Las Vegas Highway.

MODERATE

El Rey Court ♥ This historic adobe property, which opened as a motor lodge on the Original Route 66 in 1936, is pure Santa Fe, or as the management says, "Dennis Hopper meets Georgia O'Keeffe." It has traditional northern New Mexico thick adobe walls, corner kiva fireplaces, massive log vigas, beautiful woodwork, and understated Southwestern furnishings. Some suites have kitchenettes. The El Rey sits on 5 nicely landscaped acres, with a pool, a lively bar that features music and a hip crowd most weekends, and a backyard that hosts Tender Fire, a local's favorite pizza truck, on Sundays and Mondays. No two rooms are alike—fun for repeat visitors—and you'll want to request a room back from busy Cerrillos Road. The best units here surround the Spanish Colonial courtyard. The two-story main inn does not have an elevator, so those with mobility issues should specify ground-floor rooms, of which there are plenty.

1862 Cerrillos Rd. elreycourt.com. ✆ **800/521-1349** or 505/982-1931. 86 units. $130–$359 doubles; suites from $350. **Amenities:** Lounge, exercise room; hot tub; outdoor pool (summer only); sauna; free Wi-Fi.

Hyatt Place Santa Fe ♥♥ No "Santa Fe charm" here, but a very nice, modern hotel with spacious and well-appointed rooms sporting light colors, large windows, and separate living and sleeping areas. It's the sort of place you could move into long-term, and although its main purpose is to serve business and extended-stay guests, the Hyatt Place also works well for vacationers. Rooms have two queen-size beds or one king, plus an oversize sofa-sleeper or sofa; and because the hotel caters to business travelers, each unit has a separate work area and remote printing. Located near the south end of Cerrillos Road, it is not within walking distance to most of Santa Fe's attractions, but is a good option if you have a car.

4320 Cerrillos Rd. hyattplacesantafe.com. ✆ **800/993-4751** or 505/474-7777. 92 units. $160–$270 double. Children 18 and younger stay free in parents' room. Rates include breakfast. Pets accepted (2 max., up to 50 lb. for 1 dog or 75 lb. for 2, for up to 1 week; $75 per stay). $100 cleaning fee for stays more than 1 week. **Amenities:** Restaurant; concierge; 24-hr. exercise room; indoor pool; business center; room service; free Wi-Fi.

INEXPENSIVE

Santa Fe International Hostel ♥ This non-profit offers the most affordable lodging we can recommend in Santa Fe, and, although simple and basic in true hostel style, the accommodations here are quite pleasant. You can choose from a basic dormitory bed to a small private room with bath (shower only, no tub). There are also private rooms with shared bath and private rooms with half baths (sink and toilet only). The common bathhouses have private showers. Each dormitory is single sex and sleeps up to six people. Rooms are non-smoking and quiet hours are 11pm to 7am. Food, beverages, and sleeping bags are not permitted in the rooms. There is no maid service; all guests are required to clean their rooms before they leave and help clean the common areas. We especially like the outdoor courtyard where you can sit and have

Hotels & Restaurants on Cerrillos Road

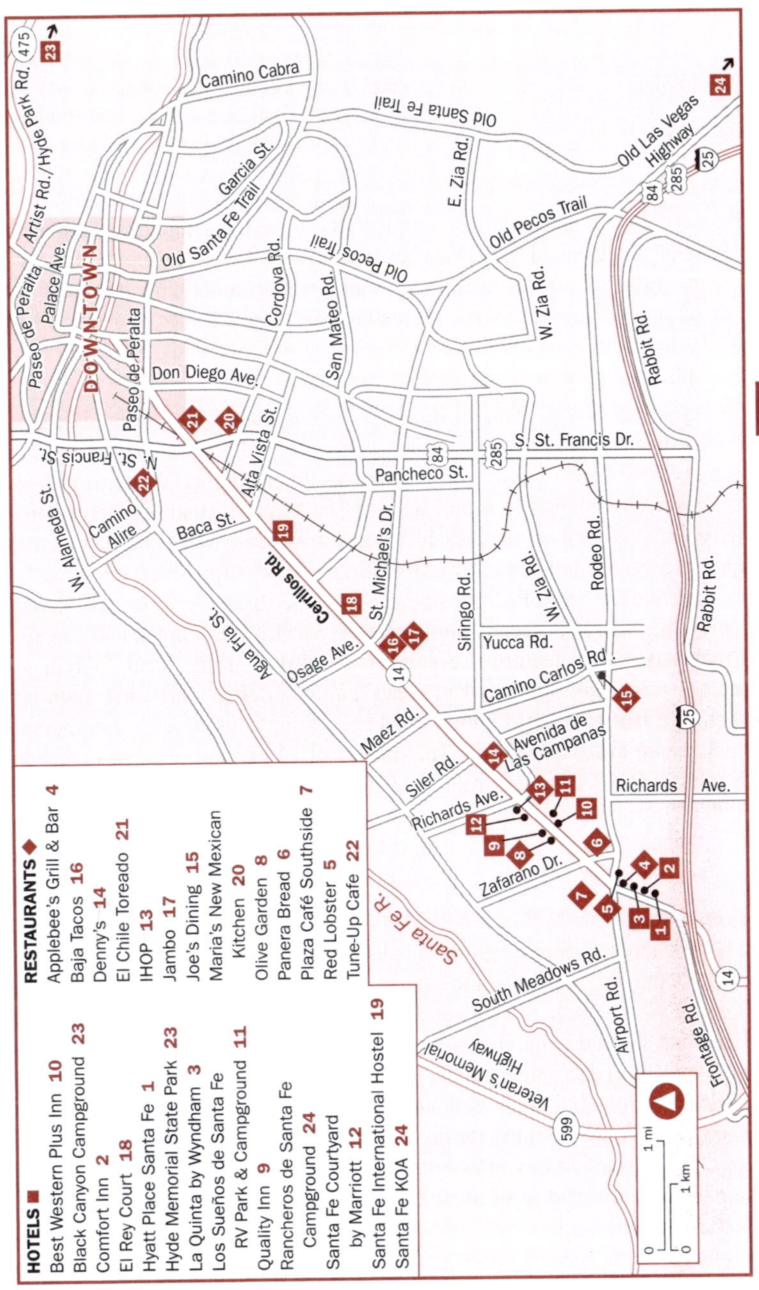

dinner or morning coffee under a giant cherry tree. The hostel has an international feel, and because its mission is to support educational travel, lodging is not available to New Mexico residents. There is a 2-night minimum stay.

1412 Cerrillos Rd., across from the Santa Fe Indian School. hostelsantafe.org. ✆ **505/988-1153.** Dorm bed $25, double with shared bath $35, with half bath $40, with private bath $45. Accompanied children 12 and under $5. Cash only; no credit cards. **Amenities:** Communal kitchen stocked with food staples (free); coin-op laundry; free Wi-Fi.

Bed & Breakfasts

If you prefer a homey, intimate setting to the sometimes impersonal ambience of a large hotel, one of Santa Fe's bed-and-breakfast inns may be right for you. We have also found that B&B owners and staff are among the best people to ask for recommendations for restaurants and things to see and do. All the B&Bs listed here are in or close to the downtown area and offer comfortable accommodations at moderate to expensive rates.

El Farolito ♥♥♥ One of the top B&Bs in Santa Fe—an intimate compound of gardens and sunny walled patios—is only a few blocks from the plaza. Rooms are outfitted in different styles, including Western, folk art, Spanish Colonial, Native American, and Santa Fe. All share a tasteful artistic sensibility, as well as features like beeswax-rubbed walls and hand-carved furniture. Seven units have kiva fireplaces, with wood provided free (mid-Oct to Apr), and the Santa Fe Suite has a gas fireplace usable year-round. All units have either shared or private garden patios. Service is top-notch and attentive. Breakfasts, often featuring Southwestern dishes using local ingredients, include fresh fruit, home-baked bread, gourmet coffee, and a hot main dish such as a frittata or eggs with corned beef hash. Complimentary homemade cookies are available all day. The owners of El Farolito also own the **Four Kachinas B&B Inn,** a six-room bed and breakfast 2 blocks from El Farolito, with comparable accommodations and amenities.

514 Galisteo Dr. farolito.com. ✆ **888/634-8782** or 505/988-1631. 8 units. $119–$319 double, suites $265–$365. Rates include breakfast. **Amenities:** Free Wi-Fi.

Inn of the Five Graces ♥♥♥ For a splurge, consider this jewel box of a hotel. Stepping onto its grounds is like entering the maximalist mind of its owners, the antique-collecting couple behind the city's famed design store Seret & Sons. Each room is an explosion of color, patterns, and textures. Elaborate mosaics, inlaid woodwork, and Southwestern and Central Asian pieces seem to decorate every surface. The hotel is set among a series of old stone and adobe buildings in Santa Fe's historic Barrio de Analco neighborhood, a half-mile from the Plaza. The prices put the property into ritzy territory, but it's a place you won't soon forget. Turndown service includes homemade chips and salsa and a dreamcatcher in lieu of chocolate. Breakfast features quintessential New Mexican dishes and can be delivered to your room, served in a shaded courtyard in summer or a kiva firelit dining room in winter. There's also a new spa that is very on-theme, with Buddha statues at every turn and treatments like Himalayan salt stone massages.

150 E. De Vargas St. fivegraces.com. ✆ **505/992-0957.** 25 units. $656–$1,175 double plus $30 service fee. Rates include breakfast. Dogs accepted ($100 per day). **Amenities:** Restaurant; valet parking; 24-hr. concierge; fitness room; complimentary laundry and dry cleaning; free Wi-Fi.

Las Palomas ♥♥ No two rooms are alike at this series of compounds dating back to the mid-1900s. Whether you choose an artful studio in the main adobe building or a Victorian-home-turned-rustic-casita featuring a full kitchen, expect a lot of character, a fireplace, and superb service. The hotel's age shows in certain rooms that are a little worse for wear, but it's hard to deny its value, with relatively reasonable rates for a central but quiet location between downtown and the Railyard district. The Southwestern-themed breakfast includes delicious green chile breakfast burritos, fresh fruit, homemade granola, and full coffee selection. Las Palomas also stands out for its thoughtful nods to beloved Santa Fe institutions—scoops from local-favorite Taos Cow Ice Cream, coffee from Iconik Roasters, and work by Doug Coffin, a Potawatomi and Creek Indian artist who created an original piece for each casita and sculptures throughout the garden walkways.

460 W. San Francisco St. laspalomas.com. ✆ **505/982-5560.** 60 units. $139–$319 double. 2-night minimum. Dogs accepted ($40 per day). **Amenities:** Cafe; free Wi-Fi.

The Parador ♥♥ This early 19th-century adobe farmhouse is located in historic downtown Santa Fe, on a quiet side street within easy walking distance of many of the city's top attractions and restaurants. Rooms and suites are decorated with rugs, weaving, art, and other bright touches, with warm reds, muted yellows, inviting greens. Some of the rooms feature skylights, balconies, and kiva fireplaces. The two suites are in a separate building, a century-old brick coachman's house that is on New Mexico's list of Historically Significant Properties. There's a quiet garden courtyard with flowers and native plants and a walled-in patio with large evergreens. Breakfast usually features a choice of four made-to-order options such as veggie-and-egg quinoa bowls and biscuits and gravy.

220 W. Manhattan Ave. paradorsantafe.com. ✆ **505/988-1177.** 15 units. $207–$277 double, suites $277–$356. Rates include breakfast. **Amenities:** Concierge; free Wi-Fi.

RV Parks & Campgrounds

There are several commercial RV parks plus camping in a state park and the nearby national forest for RVers and tenters visiting Santa Fe. For the commercial campgrounds, rates vary by type of site and season, with the highest rates usually from Memorial Day weekend through Labor Day weekend and even higher during special events. Be sure to book ahead at busy times. All the campgrounds and RV parks listed here accept pets in the campsites, and the commercial campgrounds have specific dog-walking areas.

Black Canyon Campground ♥♥ This Santa Fe National Forest campground, administered by the national forest's Española District, is next to Hyde Memorial State Park (see below). Due to its proximity to Santa Fe and beautiful forest setting, it is one of the region's most popular federal campgrounds and can fill up quickly. There are 36 drive-in RV and car sites and 6 walk-in tent sites; several of the drive-in sites are doubles that can accommodate groups of up to 16 individuals. A very pleasant 1-mile-loop hiking trail leaves from the back of the campground. There is a campground host on-site but no dump station or electric hookups. Reservations are available (recreation.gov; ✆ **877/444-6777** or 518/885-3639).

Off Hyde Park Rd., Santa Fe. recreation.gov. ✆ **505/438-5300** or 505/753-7331 (Española District office). 45 campsites. $10 per night. Closed Dec–Apr. **Amenities:** Vault toilets; drinking water.

Hyde Memorial State Park ♥♥♥ If you can do without the amenities of a commercial campground and just want the beauty and serenity of a mountain forest, this is the spot for you. Located about 8 miles northeast of downtown Santa Fe, it feels like it's 100 miles from the city lights and sounds. The campsites are what you would expect in a national park; seven of them even have electric hookups. Hyde Memorial has 4.2 miles of hiking trails, a playground, and a visitor center. In winter you can cross-country ski and snowshoe. Elevations at the park range from 8,300 feet to 9,400 feet, so expect cool to cold nighttime temperatures, even in summer. Camping reservations can be made through the state park website (see below) with a $4 per night fee (maximum $12).

740 Hyde Park Rd. (follow Artist Rd. from downtown). recreation.gov. ✆ **505/983-7175.** 50 campsites. $10 basic campsite, $14 with electric hookup. **Amenities:** Picnic tables; group shelters; vault toilets; water; dump station.

Los Sueños de Santa Fe RV Park & Campground ♥ This commercial RV park offers full RV hookups at all sites and has all the usual commercial campground amenities. There are trees, a picnic table at each site, and a covered pavilion for campers' use. The park has a convenient location, just 3 miles south of the plaza, and easy access to Santa Fe's walking and biking trails. Although it's on Cerrillos Road, one of Santa Fe's busiest thoroughfares, it is set back from the road and fairly quiet.

3574 Cerrillos Rd. lossuenosrv.com. ✆ **505/473-1949.** 92 RV campsites. $66–$90 daily. **Amenities:** Restrooms; showers; laundry; free Wi-Fi.

Rancheros de Santa Fe Campground ♥♥ Among northern New Mexico's most scenic commercial campgrounds, Rancheros de Santa Fe sits on 22 acres of piñon and juniper, with open and wooded sites for motor homes and trailers of all sizes, plus secluded tent sites nestled among the trees. It offers close to a national forest or national park experience with all the amenities you'd expect in a commercial campground. A bit of trivia: Part of the 1978 Clint Eastwood film *Every Which Way But Loose* was filmed in the campground. Camping cabins, which share the campground's bathhouse, are also available ($80–$100 double), and there is an enclosed dog run.

736 Old Las Vegas Hwy. (I-25 exit 290, east ½ mile). rancherosdesantafe.com. ✆ **505/466-3482.** 127 campsites. Tent sites (no hookup) $40; RV hookup sites $60–$75. Rates for 2 people; $3 for additional people over 3 years old. Bathhouse and store closed Nov to mid-Mar, some full hookup back-in RV sites remain open Nov to mid-Mar ($25 per night). **Amenities:** Cable TV hookup (full RV hookup sites only); grills; grocery store; coin-op laundry; nature trails; nightly movies mid-May to Sept; picnic tables; playground; outdoor pool (summer only); propane; recreation room; gift shop; restrooms; showers; free Wi-Fi.

Santa Fe KOA ♥ A member of the well-respected KOA chain, this commercial campground provides exactly what you would expect from a KOA. There's no pool, but it does have a playground, putting green, and enclosed dog run. About 11 miles northeast of Santa Fe, it sits among the foothills of the Sangre de Cristo Mountains in a pine-filled high desert. It offers some attractive camping cabins, where you'll either share a bathhouse with other campers or have your own private bathroom.

934 Old Las Vegas Hwy. (I-25 exit 294, west ¼ mile). koa.com. ✆ **800/562-1514** or 505/466-1419 for reservations. 62 campsites. RV hookup sites $60–$105, tent sites $43–$53; cabins $75–$105 (no bathroom), $165 (full bathroom). Max. RV or vehicle/trailer length 65 ft. Closed early-Nov to Feb. Pets accepted in some cabins ($10 per night). **Amenities:** Cable TV hookup; dump station; gift shop; game room; coin-op laundry; picnic tables; playground; propane; restrooms; showers; free Wi-Fi.

WHERE TO EAT IN SANTA FE

Santa Fe abounds in dining options, with hundreds of restaurants in all categories. That's the good news. What's the bad news? The fierce competition means that not all survive for long. We suggest calling ahead to check not only on whether a particular restaurant is still there, but what the current hours are, since restaurants here frequently change their hours of operation.

Many of the long-time favorites serve traditional northern New Mexican cuisine, which emphasizes chile sauces. If you're not used to spicy food, you may want to ask the servers how hot the chile is; many restaurants will either bring you a sample to taste, or put the chile on the side. There's also a variety of American restaurants here, as well as those specializing in European, Mexican, South American, and Japanese cuisine. Especially during peak tourist seasons, dinner reservations may be essential; reservations are always recommended at better restaurants.

In New Mexico you'll find that many restaurants serve beer and wine but no spirits; that's because a beer and wine license is easier to obtain and cheaper than a full liquor license.

Looking for a familiar chain? Many are on the south end of town, on or near Cerrillos Road. You'll find **Olive Garden** ♥ at 3781 Cerrillos Rd. (✆ **505/438-7109**); **Applebee's Grill & Bar** ♥♥ at 4246 Cerrillos Rd. (✆ **505/473-7551**); and **Red Lobster** ♥ at 4450 Rodeo Rd. (✆ **505/473-1610**). If you're getting in late, leaving early, or just hungry at 2am, there's a **Denny's ♥♥** at 3004 Cerrillos Rd. (✆ **505/471-2152**) that's open until 3am weekdays and 24 hours on Friday and Saturday. An excellent choice for a healthy sandwich or soup to take back to your room or on a hike (or eat on-site) is the well-respected chain **Panera Bread ♥♥♥**, with its Santa Fe branch at 3535 Zafarano Dr. (✆ **505/471-9396**).

For restaurants in the downtown and Canyon Road areas, see map on p. 63. For restaurants in the Cerrillos Road area, see map on p. 57.

Expensive

The Bull Ring ♥♥♥ STEAKHOUSE There are quite a few northern New Mexico restaurants that serve good steak, but for the very best you'll have to go to the Bull Ring. For years, the Bull Ring, then located next to the state capitol, was famous as the hangout of the state legislature and other New Mexico movers and shakers. In 1995 it moved downtown near the plaza and, more importantly, owner Harry Georgeades decided to change the menu, which had been good but not a standout, to feature the best beef available. Today, the Bull Ring serves corn-fed USDA prime beef, hand-cut daily. The large dining room is simply decorated—you can't help but notice the large pieces of pottery—with nicely upholstered chairs and circular booths. You can also eat in the bar or, in warm weather, on the outside patio. Beef is the star here, of course, but you'll find a good selection of other entrees as well. For lunch, our choice is the locally famous half-pound Bull Burger, served with hand-cut fries; you might prefer the salmon salad, with the fresh catch just lightly blackened, or possibly a prime-rib sandwich or fried chicken. For dinner, you'll probably want beef, such as the 12-ounce filet, 14-ounce New York strip, or 16-ounce prime rib. Other dinner options include barbecue baby back ribs, grilled salmon fillet, and lamb chops; you can add a lobster tail onto any entree for an additional price. Portions are generous, and service is excellent. Monday through Friday 3 to 6pm there are happy hour-specials on appetizers, beer, and wine, and the Bull Ring offers full liquor service.

150 Washington Ave., in courtyard of New Mexico Bank and Trust. santafebullring.com. ✆ **505/983-3328.** Lunch $12–$26, dinner entrees $28–$55, bar menu items mostly under $20. Mon–Thurs 11:30am–8pm; Fri–Sat 11:30am–9pm; Sun 4–8pm.

Cafe Pasqual's ♥♥♥ NEW MEXICAN/MEXICAN For nearly 50 years, James Beard Award-winning chef Katherine Kagel—known as the "Alice Waters of Santa Fe" for her seasonal approach—has run this tiny corner restaurant in the Plaza. Looking into the wide windows from its cheerful vermillion adobe exterior will make you think you're visiting Mexico during Christmas, with string-light *ristras* (strung arrangements of red chiles) and colorful Mexican *papel picados* hanging from the ceiling, and wooden tables arranged as if the guest-list grew last minute. It can be hard to choose which meal to have here, but most locals will go for breakfast and take out-of-town visitors for dinner. The wide-ranging menus offer an exciting change from the standard fare at other New Mexican restaurants in the city, with even typical

Downtown Santa Fe Restaurants

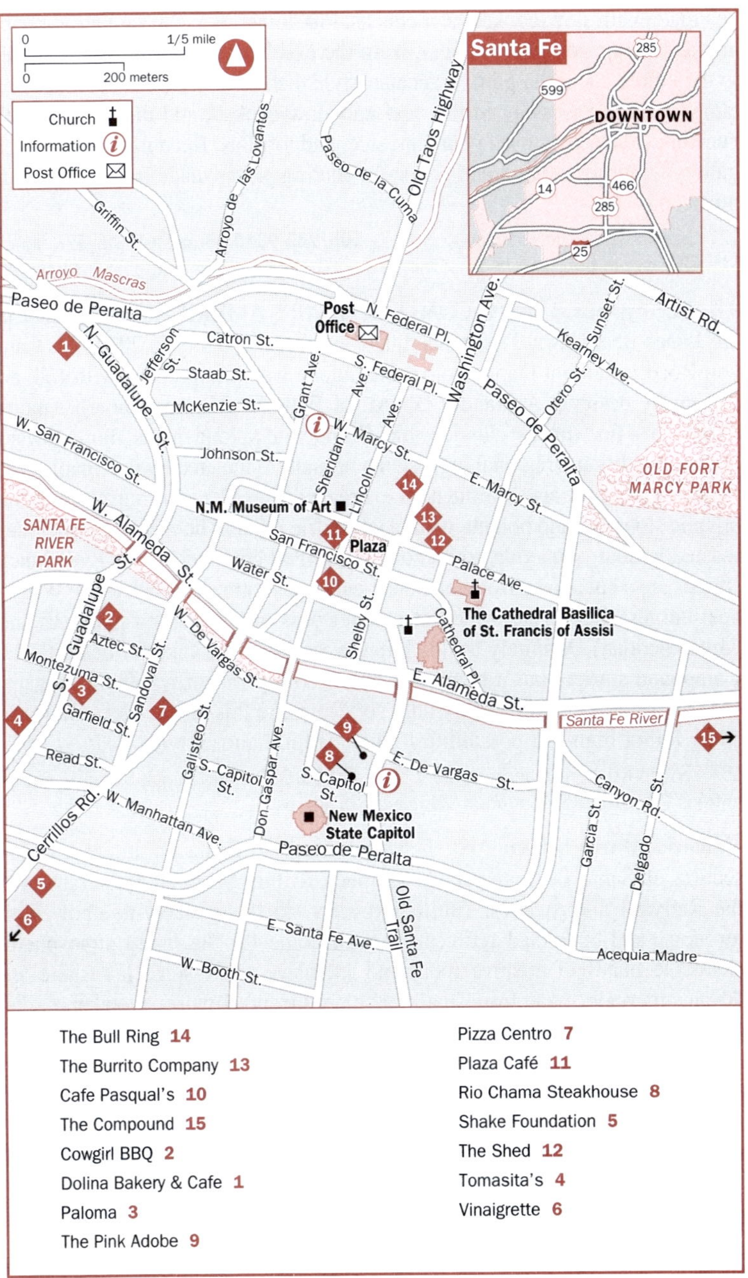

dishes featuring a unique ingredient or two. Take, for example, the cornmeal pancakes, served with both maple syrup and mole sauce, or the huevos barbacoa made with slow-cooked beef cheeks. For dinner, you can't go wrong with any dish wrapped in banana leaf, from the excellent vegetable tamale starter to the entree cochinita pibil, a Yucatan-style dish in which pork shoulder in a tangy marinade is wrapped in a leaf and slow-cooked, and then served with zucchini calabacitas, fried plantains, rice, and tortillas. Head upstairs to find a gallery featuring artwork and pottery, including pieces made from indigenous micaceous clay.

121 Don Gaspar Ave. pasquals.com. ✆ **505/983-9340.** Breakfast $15–$27, lunch $19–$29, dinner entrees $25–$57. Daily (except Tues) 8am–3pm and 5:30–9:30pm.

The Compound ♥♥♥ CONTEMPORARY AMERICAN A finalist in the James Beard Award's Outstanding Restaurant category in 2024, this Canyon Road restaurant features old white adobe walls, brightened with folk art chosen by designer Alexander Girard (of Folk Art Museum fame). Among Santa Fe's fine-dining classics, the Compound's food leans more toward homey. Traditional regional ingredients brought to the area by the Spanish are joined by Mediterranean influences to create dishes like wild mushrooms and organic stone-ground polenta with black truffle relish. The menu also includes roasted halibut, sous-vide pork chop, and grilled beef tenderloin. Even lunch entrees are a cut above, from the house-cured pastrami sandwich to the Wagyu beef burger. (If you order the latter, don't pass on the roasted poblanos and white cheddar.) Definitely try the bittersweet chocolate cake for dessert. The Compound's prices put it in splurge-only territory for many, but the elegant-yet-comfortable setting and friendly service make this an excellent choice in a city full of high-end possibilities. There is full liquor service.

653 Canyon Rd. compoundrestaurant.com. ✆ **505/982-4353.** Lunch $16–$30, dinner entrees $32–$58. Mon–Sat noon–2pm and 5–8:30pm.

Paloma ♥♥♥ MEXICAN Few restaurants in Santa Fe attract a cross-section of Santa Fean characters as much as this Mexican restaurant near the Railyard district does. You'll find artsy ski bums elbow-to-elbow with turquoise-and-linen-clad retirees, who all come for the lively atmosphere, shareable plates of creative food, and extensive agave-spirit list (there are 50-plus mezcals, many from small-batch producers). Textiles, wooden masks, and murals adorn the white adobe walls of the small dining room, which includes a bar area that offers full dinner service, and leads to a casual patio (closed in winter) strung with Christmas lights. The best dishes feature masa using heirloom corn that's nixtamalized in-house—try small plates like the squash-blossom quesadillas or the *sopecitos,* featuring two masa cakes topped with adobo-roasted mushrooms. As for entrees, you can't go wrong with roasted chicken doused in mole negro or tacos with beer-battered rockfish and jalapeño slaw.

401 S. Guadalupe St. palomasantafe.com. ✆ **505/467-8624.** Main courses $20–$38. Sun, Tues–Thurs 5–9pm; Fri–Sat 5–10pm.

The Pink Adobe ♥♥ NEW MEXICAN/AMERICAN Named for the pink hue of its 350-year-old adobe walls, the Pink Adobe has been a local favorite since it was opened by New Orleans transplant Rosalea Murphy in 1944. Each of several small dining rooms has its own kiva fireplace, and hand-carved wood furnishings and heavy log vigas add to the building's historic charm. In typical northern New Mexico fashion, even some traditional American dishes get spiced up a bit, such as the pork tenderloin, which is prepared with red mole. The restaurant's most popular (and most expensive) selection, Steak Dunigan, is a charbroiled 13-ounce New York strip, topped with sautéed mushrooms and, of course, green chile. Looking for traditional northern New Mexico cuisine? Try the Plato Mexicano, a filling sampler that includes a cheese enchilada, chile relleno, and chicken taco, with red or green chile, rice, posole, and pinto beans. The chile served here is extra hot; if in doubt, ask for a sample before ordering. The restaurant's signature dessert is hot French apple pie topped with rum hard sauce. The Pink Adobe's Dragon Room Bar is a real local hangout thanks to its tableside guacamole, taco flights, and stellar margarita list.

406 Old Santa Fe Trail. thepinkadobe.com. ✆ **505/983-7712.** Main courses $24–$50. Tues–Fri 5–9:30pm; Sat–Sun 8am–2pm and 5–9:30pm (bar Tues–Sun 4–midnight).

Rio Chama Steakhouse ♥♥ STEAK/SEAFOOD Among the best places in Santa Fe for prime rib, this steakhouse is loaded with Santa Fe charm, with soft adobe walls, lots of wood, and a handmade tin chandelier; the bar has the atmosphere of a mountain lodge. There's a limited amount of prime rib nightly, so get there early. The prime rib is a rib-eye beef roast brined with herbs and spices for 48 hours, grilled whole over an open flame and then slow roasted. It's accompanied by the steakhouse's signature whipped horseradish cream and natural jus, and served with a loaded baked potato and broccoli. The dinner menu also includes several steaks and wild salmon with a charred tomato vinaigrette. For a late lunch, starting at 3pm there are sandwiches, salads, burgers, and entrees such as sun-dried tomato and artichoke pasta. The weekend brunch features egg dishes, including house-made corned beef hash with eggs, a six-cheese fondue with dipping vegetables, and burgers. Full liquor service is available.

414 Old Santa Fe Trail. riochamasteakhouse.com. ✆ **505/955-0765.** Main courses $21–$75, brunch $15–$27. Mon–Sat 3–9pm; Sun 11am–9pm (Sun brunch 11am–2:30pm).

FAMILY-FRIENDLY restaurants

Cowgirl BBQ (p. 66) A casual atmosphere, lots of old photos of cowgirls, and the ice cream baked potato makes for a fun time for kids and their parents.

Dolina Bakery & Cafe (p. 66) A relaxed atmosphere, lots of baked goodies, and a varied menu pleases both kids and parents.

Plaza Cafe (p. 68) Burgers, sandwiches, a funky atmosphere, and an old-fashioned ice cream–style counter make this a kids' favorite.

Moderate

Cowgirl BBQ ♥ AMERICAN/BARBECUE Good food in a fun and funky cafe atmosphere: low ceilings, lots of photographs of cowgirls and other Western memorabilia covering the adobe walls, and something sparkly in the wall paint. There's patio dining in warm weather. The service is good and the menu includes solid American fare plus some excellent—albeit spicy hot—Southwestern choices. We recommend the mesquite-smoked baby back ribs, sliced beef brisket on Texas toast, or for a bit of everything BBQ, the barbecue sampler platter. Other good choices include a grilled salmon filet with bourbon glaze and one of the fajitas platters—choose from chicken breast, flat iron steak, or mushroom. There are also burgers, including what the restaurant calls the "Mother of All Green Chile Cheeseburgers," a blend of all-natural beef, local bison, and applewood-smoked bacon, with melted brie and truffled green chile, served in a brioche chile bun. Save room for a fun dessert: ice cream baked potato—a chunk of good vanilla ice cream molded into the shape of a potato, rolled in cocoa, placed in a pool of chocolate sauce, and topped with whipped cream and shaved pistachios, and a square of golden frosting tucked into it like a pat of butter. Happy hour is weekdays from 3 to 6pm. There is full liquor service and usually live music every afternoon during summer.

319 S. Guadalupe St. cowgirlsantafe.com. ✆ **505/982-2565.** Main courses $11–$30. Sun, Tues–Thurs 11:30am–10pm, Mon, Fri–Sat 11:30am–11pm.

Dolina Bakery & Cafe ♥♥ NEW MEXICAN/SLOVAKIAN While a menu featuring both New Mexican and Eastern European staples might sound peculiar, Slovakian-born chef Annamaria Brezna O'Brien makes it all come together at this roadside brunch spot located between a dry cleaner and a fast-food restaurant. Despite its parking-lot exterior, the cheerful dining room is whitewashed and airy, with canteen-style seating and a lively atmosphere. There's almost always a wait on weekends (it doesn't take reservations), but you can order a coffee and pastry while you wait. Dolina is well known for its baked goods, with the best menu items featuring items made in-house, like the orechovnik French toast and breakfast croissant. There's nothing quite like starting your day with a heartwarming Slovak-inspired favorite, such as the savory paprikash or morning soup with lamb-bone broth and wild rice, topped with a poached egg. Every Santa Fean will have a different answer to the "best" breakfast burrito in the city, but most will agree that Dolina's ranks high, likely due to the perfectly crisp hash browns that line the tortilla. Those looking for more standard diner fare have a choice of omelets and sandwiches, plus excellent buttermilk fried chicken and cornmeal waffles that come with a side of green apple and fennel slaw.

402 N. Guadalupe St. dolinasantafe.com. ✆ **505/982-9394.** Main courses $12–$19. Mon, Wed–Sat 7am–2:30pm; Sun 8am–2:30pm.

Jambo ♥♥ AFRICAN Chef Ahmed Obo, who hails from the Kenyan island of Lamu, is beloved by the community. In a city where it can be difficult to find authentic international cuisines, Jambo is a multicultural explosion that reflects Obo's upbringing, with influences from Africa, the Mediterranean, India, and the Caribbean. The restaurant is located in a sprawling strip mall off Cerillos Road, but its warm dining room reflects the restaurant's wide-ranging flavors, with art from an in-house bazaar that also sells stew and spice mixes. The same menu is served all day, with a variety of sandwiches and wraps for lunch. For dinner starters, you can't go wrong with the fried cornmeal plantain crab cakes or the phyllo pastry stuffed with feta, chickpeas, and vegetables. Entrees range from classics like jerk chicken and kebobs to curries and stews. The Moroccan lamb stew is a standout, served with chickpeas, raisons, apricots, and sweet potatoes over curried couscous and topped with a ginger chutney. Many items come with your choice of coconut basmati rice or a roti. If you're on the south side of town, check out Obo's newest venture, **Bobcat Bite,** which serves casual breakfast and lunch options, including the chef's special iterations of the breakfast burrito (it swaps out the tortilla for a roti) and green-chile cheeseburger (featuring a Chimayo red-chile aioli).

2010 Cerrillos Rd. jambocafe.net. ✆ **505/473-1269.** Main courses $17–$25; sandwiches $14–$16. Mon–Sat 11am–9pm.

Joe's Dining ♥ AMERICAN It used to be called Joe's Diner, a name we liked better, but whatever they call it, this casual and comfortable eatery is unpretentious and easy to like. Decor is '50s diner, complete with red vinyl upholstery and a checkerboard linoleum floor. The menu is old-time diner as well, but what's surprising is that the food quality is definitely a step above what you might expect. The owners are committed to using sustainable, local ingredients as much as possible, and claim to be the biggest restaurant buyer of farmers' market products in Santa Fe. We believe them. Try the roasted chicken with mole, grass-finished New Zealand rack of lamb, or one of the nifty burgers such as the green chile cheeseburger. There are weekday blue plate lunch specials, including meatloaf on Wednesdays and fish and chips on Fridays; Friday evenings feature prime rib. Joe's also offers pizzas and good basic breakfasts. Beer and wine are available.

2801 Rodeo Rd., in Rodeo Plaza. joesdining.com. ✆ **505/471-3800.** Breakfast/brunch $8–$19, lunch and dinner main courses $11–$39, pizzas from $12. Daily 8am–8pm. Closed some holidays.

Maria's New Mexican Kitchen ♥ NEW MEXICAN Maria's was opened back in 1950, which explains its somewhat odd location just off the busy intersection of Cordova Road and St. Francis Drive. No matter—Maria's is a Santa Fe tradition, with creaking wood floors and dependable New Mexican comfort food like blue-corn enchiladas, tacos, hand-rolled tamales, grilled ruby trout, and burgers. Specialties also include spareribs, baked slowly in a mild red chile barbecue sauce; and fajitas—beef, chicken, shrimp, or vegetarian—cut into bite-size strips and sautéed, served with a cup of soupy beans, guacamole, pico de gallo, and house-made flour tortillas. Maria's is famous for its margaritas—a separate menu lists over a hundred choices, all made with 100% agave tequila. For the full experience, sit in the cozy bar area, lit with wagon-wheel lights and neon beer signs, and tuck into chile rellenos and a Silver Coin margarita. There is full liquor service.

555 West Cordova Rd. marias-santafe.com. ✆ **505/983-7929.** Main courses $14–$26. Wed–Sun 11:30am–8pm.

Plaza Café ♥♥ AMERICAN/NEW MEXICAN/GREEK Santa Fe's oldest continuously operating restaurant, opened in 1905 by Greek immigrants the Razatos family, offers the best diner food in Santa Fe. It's served in a suitably funky atmosphere, too, with colorful ceiling lights, linoleum-top tables, a neon wall clock, old black-and-white photos, and a soda-fountain-style counter with red vinyl-covered stainless steel stools. Plaza Café serves traditional American and New Mexican breakfasts—the blue corn piñon pancakes make a nice change—or go with the traditional steak and eggs or huevos rancheros. Lunch and dinner items include tortilla soup—avocado, tortilla strips, and Mexican cheeses—plus a good choice of salads and specialties such as chicken-fried steak, spicy fish and chips, grilled chicken, burgers, and sandwiches. The restaurant claims that its spaghetti sauce recipe is over 100 years old. There are several Greek items available, including moussaka—a casserole of eggplant, spiced meat, and a creamy béchamel sauce. Beer and wine are available.

54 Lincoln Ave. www.plazacafesantafe.com. ✆ **505/982-1664.** Main courses $14–$25. Daily 7am–9pm.

Plaza Café Southside ♥ AMERICAN/NEW MEXICAN Off Cerrillos Road at the south end of Santa Fe, this sister restaurant to the downtown Plaza Café is a good option for when you're on that side of town. The wide-open restaurant has a 1950s diner look, with strong colors, vintage black-and-white photos, a row of old automobile hubcaps on the wall, and a mural with a sort of Day of the Dead motif. Breakfasts here are special, ranging from traditional bacon and eggs to pancakes and French toast. The yogurt parfait features layers of fresh fruit, honey-flavored Greek yogurt, and house-made pumpkinseed granola. There are also breakfast burritos, huevos rancheros, and other New Mexican dishes. For lunch and dinner there are burgers, a good choice of salads, sandwiches, and New Mexican dishes such as an enchilada platter. (Note that the Plaza Café Southside serves only cage-free eggs.) The menu warns diners that its red and green chile sauces come either medium hot or extra hot; you can ask for a sample or request that your sauce be served on the side. Most baked goods are prepared in-house, and they serve the very best restaurant sticky bun we have ever eaten. There is a full bar.

3466 Zafarano Dr., at back of San Isidro Plaza shopping center. www.plazacafesouth.com. ✆ **505/424-0755.** Main courses $14–$25. Mon–Thurs 9am–8pm, Fri–Sat 8am–9pm, Sun 8am–8pm.

The Shed ♥♥♥ NEW MEXICAN Long lines, even at lunch, are proof that this local institution just east of the plaza is something special. The restaurant is set inside a rambling hacienda, built in 1692, and decorated with bright, folky paintings. The Shed is known for its shaded brick patio and its rich and spicy New Mexican cooking. The red chile is a regular local prizewinner, best paired with the house's signature enchiladas. Another sure bet is the green chile stew, brimming with pork and potatoes. Sandwiches and burgers are also offered at lunch, though not dinner. Every traditional entree is served with blue corn tortillas and, oddly, garlic bread, which is a restaurant tradition. Save room for a piece of homemade mocha cake, one of Santa Fe's best desserts. Full liquor service is available. The margaritas are among the best in town. The restaurant doesn't take reservations, but starts a dinner waitlist at 4pm—put your name down and have a glass of organic white at nearby wine bar La Mama (225 E. Marcy St.).

113½ E. Palace Ave. sfshed.com. ✆ **505/982-9030.** Main courses $12–$33. Mon–Sat 11am–2:30pm and 5–9pm.

Tune-Up Café ♥♥ NEW MEXICAN/AMERICAN For a strong margarita, diner-length menu, and no-frills dishes enjoyed among regulars, head to this quaint cafe in a residential neighborhood near the Railyard. Helmed by chef Jesus Rivera, who hails from El Salvador and cooked at **Cafe Pasqual's** (p. 62) before opening his own place, Tune-Up serves a mix of standard American fare, New Mexican staples, and Salvadoran specialties. In addition to common breakfast options like huevos rancheros and steak and eggs are standouts like the smoked duck hash with cheesy hash browns. Lunch features a variety of enchiladas, burgers, pizzas, and sandwiches, while dinner has a lot of the same options but also steaks and pastas. Tune-Up's chile relleno, a cheese-stuffed roasted and fried green chile, is beloved, served with roasted tomato salsa, guacamole, corn tortillas, and rice and beans. It comes with eggs and refried beans for breakfast. The cafe's tres leches cake is a local favorite and often sells out early.

1115 Hickox St. tuneupsantafe.com. ✆ **505/983-7060.** Breakfast $9–$16, lunch $11–$17, dinner main courses $10–$21. Mon–Fri 7am–10pm, Sat–Sun 8am–10pm.

Vinaigrette ♥ SALAD Tucked away off Cerrillos Road, this casual salad bistro offers up-to-the-minute-fresh ingredients in concoctions like duck confit tossed with baby arugula, and "Eat Your Peas," with bacon and Asiago cheese mixed with sweet green peas. Much of the produce comes from the owner's 10-acre farm in Nambe Pueblo. Proteins such as lemon-herb chicken breast, grilled flank steak, diver scallops, or grilled tofu are also available. Seasonal salad options are always changing—watch for the winter kale with ricotta and chicken when it's available. Several healthy sandwiches are also on the menu, including a hot turkey sandwich and a tuna melt. Vinaigrette's dining room has a modern, playful atmosphere, with a green-tiled wine bar. On the back patio you can eat under an old apricot tree. Beer and wine are available.

709 Don Cubero Alley. vinaigretteonline.com. ✆ **505/820-9205.** Main courses $15–$24. Mon–Sat 11am–9pm.

Inexpensive

Baja Tacos ♥ NEW MEXICAN/AMERICAN Known for its millionaires and billionaires living in multi-million dollar hillside homes, Santa Fe also has plenty of regular folk, and Baja Tacos has been one of their restaurants-of-choice for about a half-century. (At our most recent visit we parked next to a local plumber's truck.) Until 2019 it was a tiny take-out-only restaurant, but then a building that had housed a Wendy's restaurant became available and Baja Tacos had a new home, complete with tables and chairs! It sells tacos, of course (beef, chicken, fish, and tofu and bean) plus enchiladas, burritos, and the like, and, surprising for an inexpensive fast-food joint, prepares hand-formed hamburgers from scratch and also makes its own guacamole and salsa daily. The most expensive item on the menu is a half-pound burger combo at $12, which comes with lettuce, tomato, onion, cheese, New Mexico green chile, plus fries and a soft drink. The breakfast burrito is good, and the bacon roll burrito (crispy bacon, cheese, and chile wrapped in a flour tortilla) is especially popular. No alcohol is served.

2621 Cerrillos Rd. bajatacossantafe.com. ✆ **505/471-8762.** Main courses $3–$12. Daily 7am–7pm (dining room closes 6:30pm, drive-up open until 7pm).

The Burrito Company ♥ AMERICAN/NEW MEXICAN Located just off Santa Fe Plaza, this family-owned fast-food eatery has been a favorite of locals and tourists alike since it opened in 1978. It's noisy, busy, and fun, with red vinyl booths and colorful Mexican-style murals on the walls. You order at the counter, find a place to sit, and they bring you your food. Most breakfast items are served all day, including the popular breakfast burrito, either with or without meat, and the you'll-only-find-this-in-Santa-Fe Washington Street Burrito: scrambled egg whites, sautéed spinach, tomatoes, and turkey bacon, rolled in a whole-wheat tortilla and topped with New Mexico–style chile and Swiss cheese. Lunch items include burritos, tacos, burgers, several sandwiches, some tasty and even healthy salads, and to honor the chef-owner's Salvadoran roots, the El Salvador Combo—two house-made corn masa *pupusas* stuffed with squash, beans, and cheese, plus one chicken tamale wrapped in a banana leaf and served with a side of mixed rice and beans. Beer and wine are available.

111 Washington Ave. burritocompanysf.com. ✆ **505/982-4453.** Main courses $8–$16. Mon–Tues 7:30am–3:30pm, Wed–Fri 7:30am–9pm, Sat 8am–9pm, Sun 8am–3:30pm.

El Chile Toreado ♥♥♥ MEXICAN Look for a white food truck sporting a green-chile moustache parked on a side street off Cerrillos Road. There you'll find the flavor-packed creations of Luis Medina, who moved his family from Chihuahua, Mexico, to Santa Fe in 2003 and has run this beloved food truck ever since. Toreado, which means "bullfighting," is a nod to the truck's super-hot jalapeños, which are also used in the chile sauce available at the self-service toppings counter. For breakfast, choose between vegetarian, bacon, sausage, or mixed Polish sausage (or if you can't decide on a meat, order the Luis Mix, which is all three), served either in a hefty burrito or four tacos. Each combination comes with eggs, potatoes, Hatch green chile, and Monterey jack cheese. The lunch menu is organized into burritos, tacos, quesadillas, and hot dogs, with a variety of options under each meat or veggie category. The *al pastor* (pork marinated in adobo with pineapple), *adovada* (pork marinated in chile adobo sauce), and *barbacoa* tacos can't be beat. And if you've never tried a Kielbasa sausage topped with baked pinto beans or chile, this is your chance. Behind the truck are a few picnic tables, though grabbing a bench at the nearby Railyard Park might be more pleasant. In addition to the original downtown location, there's an outpost at the southern end of Santa Fe (131 Siler Rd., closed Sun–Mon).

807 Early St. elchiletoreado.com. ✆ **505/500-0033.** Breakfast/lunch $11–$13. Mon–Fri 7:30am–2:30pm, Sat 7:30am–2pm.

Pizza Centro ♥ PIZZA Tucked away inside the Santa Fe Design Center, Pizza Centro turns out an excellent hand-tossed New York–style pizza in a suitably modern, no-frills setting. The restaurant makes its own dough and marinara sauces, with a menu full of specialty combos named after New York neighborhoods, like the Soho (roast chicken, mushroom, sun-dried tomato, onion, truffle oil, and fresh basil) and the Central Park (spinach, sun-dried tomato, basil, garlic, and ricotta). There's also the Hell's Kitchen: sausage, flash-fried eggplant, green chile, jalapeño, roasted red pepper, and feta. There are vegetarian selections and gluten- and dairy-free options as well. Sandwiches, calzones, and salads round things out. There's also outside dining at picnic tables. Beer and wine are served. Another branch of Pizza Centro can be found at San Isidro Plaza, 3470 Zafarano Dr., off Cerrillos Road (✆ **505/471-6200**).

418 Cerrillos Rd. pizzacentronys.com. ✆ **505/988-8825.** Pizzas $11–$26. Daily 11:30am–8:30pm.

Shake Foundation ♥ BURGERS & SHAKES This is fast-food Santa Fe style, and one of the top spots to get a genuine New Mexico–style green chile cheeseburger. The burgers aren't huge, but they are tasty. All the patties are made with a mix of prime sirloin and brisket, the fresh-cut shoestring fries are perfectly crispy, and all food is prepared to order. You can also get a lamb or turkey burger, a deep-fried portobello mushroom burger stuffed with Muenster cheese, or a fried oyster sandwich with red chile mayo. Yes, the Shake Foundation has just about everything…except a dining room. Step up to the window to order and sit at a picnic table outside under the awning, or in your car, or you can opt to take your food back to your room. Save room for an Adobe Mud Shake made with organic ice cream—topped with piñon nuts, of course. No alcohol is served.

631 Cerrillos Rd. ✆ **505/988-8992.** Burgers and sandwiches $4–$9. Mon–Thurs 11am–6:30pm, Fri–Sat 11am–7pm, Sun 11am–6pm.

Tomasita's ♥♥ NEW MEXICAN Occupying a 19th-century former railroad depot on the "Chile Line," this local standby cooks up fresh red and green chile every day. No surprise, then, that both are often voted the best in

Santa Fe. Tomasita's has been run for over 40 years by the same family, so they know what they're doing, using recipes handed down from generation to generation. The restaurant reflects its brick railroad station origins on the outside; inside, it's a homey place with hanging chile *ristras* (a string of dried chile peppers), brass light fixtures, brick walls, colorful art, high windows, and light wood accents. There's also a pleasant outdoor patio. The food is nothing fancy, just solid northern New Mexican cooking, as in the combination plate: a red chile cheese enchilada, taco, Spanish rice, posole, pinto beans, and green chile. Entrees come with one of the best sopapillas in the city, served with honey butter. Known for its margaritas, Tomasita's has full liquor service. A mariachi band plays every Sunday at 6pm.

500 S. Guadalupe St. tomasitas.com. ✆ **505/983-5721.** Main courses $11–$20. Mon–Thurs 11am–9pm, Fri–Sat 11am–10pm.

EXPLORING SANTA FE

One of the oldest cities in the United States, Santa Fe has long been a center for the creative and performing arts, so it's not surprising that most of its major sights are related to local history and the arts—the Museum of New Mexico, art galleries and studios, historic churches, and cultural sights associated with local Native American and Latino communities. It would be easy to spend a full week sightseeing in the city without ever heading out to any nearby attractions.

5

WHAT TO SEE & DO IN SANTA FE

The Top Attractions

Georgia O'Keeffe Museum ♥♥♥ MUSEUM Some artists will always be connected to specific places: Ansel Adams to Yosemite, Claude Monet to his gardens at Giverny, and Georgia O'Keeffe to New Mexico. O'Keeffe (1887–1986) fell in love with the Southwest deserts in the 1930s, and in 1949 she moved from the East Coast to Abiquiú, about 70 miles northwest of Santa Fe. Her paintings of flowers, skulls, and stark landscapes, simultaneously voluptuous and semi-abstract, made her an international art icon who is now considered the "Mother of American Modernism." This museum, set in a former Baptist church, rotates its works on view throughout the year, featuring pieces from its large collection, including O'Keefe's art and personal materials, such as her paint brushes and animal bones. While you're here, you can also book guided tours of her historic home and studio in Abiquiú, which is just south of I-84, slightly more than an hour's drive away. Reserve your tickets up to 60 days in advance, as limited same-day tickets often sell out quickly. As of writing, the museum has begun building a new, larger building nearby.

217 Johnson St. okeeffemuseum.org. ✆ **505/946-1000.** Adults $22, ages 6–18 and students $10, free for children 5 and under. Daily 10am–5pm. Closed New Year's Day, Easter, Thanksgiving, and Christmas.

Meow Wolf ♥♥ MULTIMEDIA INSTALLATION There's something almost other-worldly here—Disneyland with a twist.

This arts and entertainment group has created, in their words, "an immersive interactive art experience that transports audiences of all ages into a fantastic realm of storytelling." This huge art installation—it encompasses some 20,000 square feet—combines a plethora of media including architecture, audio engineering, costuming, cross-reality, music, narrative writing, painting, performance, photography, sculpture, video production, and whatever else is needed to complete the artists' vision. Installations change and evolve, but will always pull you in. It's also Santa Fe's go-to concert venue, with shows scheduled most weekends throughout the year.

1352 Rufina Circle. meowwolf.com. ✆ **505/395-6369.** Adults $50 ($40 for timed entry); discounts for NM residents. Sat–Mon, Thurs 10am–7pm, Fri–Sat 10am–8pm. Closed New Year's Day, Easter, Thanksgiving, and Christmas.

New Mexico History Museum ♥♥♥ MUSEUM Few places in the U.S. have a richer cultural history than New Mexico, and this museum is one of the best places to explore it. From prehistoric peoples and more modern Native Americans to the various waves of Spanish, Mexican, European, and American colonists that have swept through, New Mexico has seen it all, and this panorama is well represented. The museum's campus combines three connected buildings: the historic Palace of the Governors, the modern Pete V. Domenici Building, and the 1907 Fray Angélico Chávez Library. Plan for at least half a day's browsing, with immersive, interactive exhibits (permanent and changing) on indigenous cultures, the Santa Fe Trail, Spanish Colonial painted hides, and a working printing press—you name it. All the displays are clearly laid out, with photos, historical artifacts, and videos to help explain the complex tapestry of New Mexico.

113 Lincoln Ave. nmhistorymuseum.org. ✆ **505/476-5200.** Adults $12, free for ages 16 and under; free 5–7pm 1st Fri of month. Daily 10am–5pm (closed Mon Nov–Apr; open until 7pm 1st Fri of month). Closed New Year's Day, Easter, Thanksgiving, and Christmas.

New Mexico Museum of Art ♥♥ MUSEUM "New Mexico" and "art" go together like, well, any two things that go very, very well together. This immensely photogenic state has inspired artists for centuries, so assembling a representative regional collection was no small task. This museum, formerly the Museum of Fine Arts, does an admirable job with its 20,000-piece permanent collection. Visitors here find drawings, paintings, photographs, furniture, prints, and sculptures by the usual suspects—Georgia O'Keeffe, Ansel Adams, Ernest Blumenschein—and many others, including Francisco de Goya, Gustave Baumann, and artists commissioned during the New Deal. Rotating exhibits change from month to month. The 1917 building itself is a work of art, one of the city's oldest Pueblo Revival structures, featuring a wonderfully peaceful inner courtyard with flowers, WPA murals, sculptures, and flowing water. This is a nice place to easily pass an hour or two.

107 W. Palace (at Lincoln Ave.). nmartmuseum.org. ✆ **505/476-5063.** Adults $12, free for ages 16 and under, free 1st Fri of month. Ticket includes same-day admission to Vladem Contemporary, below (except on free Fri). Daily 10am–5pm (open until 7pm 1st Fri of month). Closed New Year's Day, Thanksgiving, and Christmas.

Downtown Santa Fe Attractions

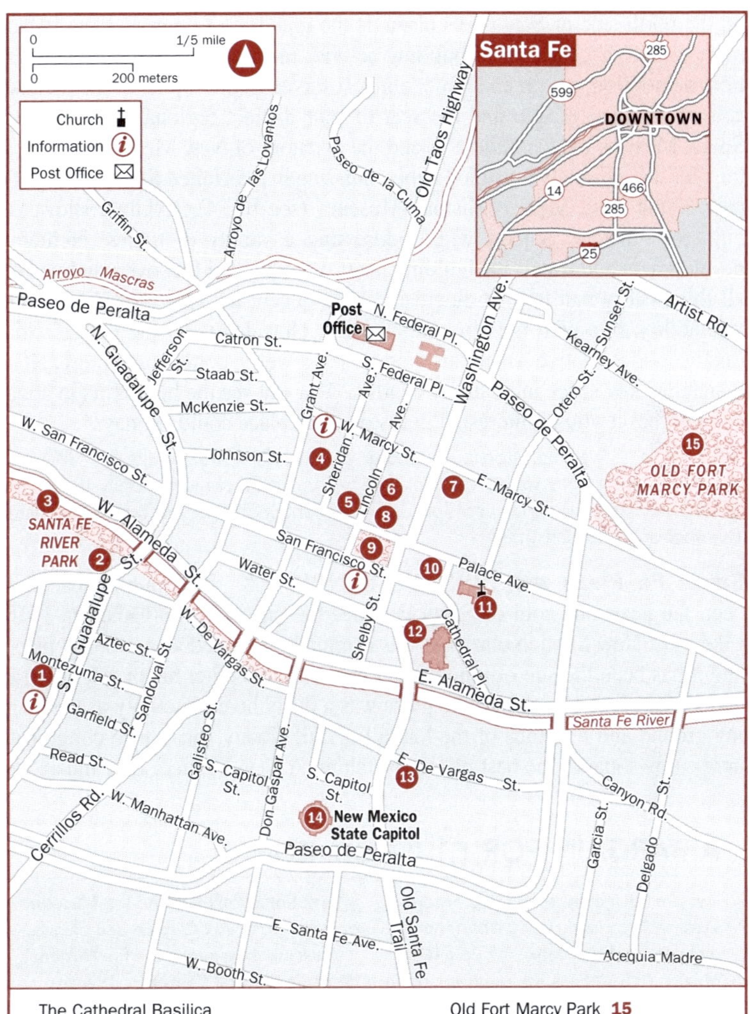

The Cathedral Basilica of St. Francis of Assisi **11**
Georgia O'Keeffe Museum **4**
IAIA Museum of Contemporary Native Arts **10**
Loretto Chapel Museum **12**
New Mexico History Museum **6**
New Mexico Museum of Art **5**
New Mexico State Capitol (Roundhouse) **14**
Old Fort Marcy Park **15**
Palace of the Governors **8**
San Miguel Chapel **13**
Santa Fe Plaza **9**
Santa Fe Public Library **7**
Santa Fe River Parkway **3**
Santuario de Nuestra Señora de Guadalupe **2**
Vladem Contemporary **1**

Palace of the Governors ♥♥ HISTORIC SITE In an ancient city filled with lots of oldest thises and oldest thats, the Palace of the Governors, on the north side of Santa Fe's plaza, is the grandest of them all. The Palace represents four centuries of building activity including periods of deterioration, demolition, repair, and remodeling. It served as the capital of the Spanish colony of New Mexico and the seat of four distinct regional governments: Spain, Mexico, the Confederacy, and the Territory of New Mexico, making it the oldest continually occupied public building in the United States. Today it's part of the New Mexico History Museum (see p. 74). Exhibits showcase numerous historic objects while addressing a variety of topics, including development and use of the building itself. Visitors who feel overwhelmed by all this history can have it elucidated by a docent-led tour (based on guide availability, free with museum admissions). Outside, under the palace's distinctive portal, Native American vendors sell jewelry, pottery, and more, all of which has met strict authenticity controls. You can see the highlights in about an hour, but if you're interested in history, this place could fill days.

105 W. Palace Ave. nmhistorymuseum.org. ✆ **505/476-5100.** Adults $12, NM residents $7, free for ages 16 and younger; free 5–7pm 1st Fri of month. Daily 10am–5pm (closed Mon Nov–Apr; open until 7pm 1st Fri of month). Closed New Year's Day, Easter, Thanksgiving, and Christmas.

Santa Fe Plaza ♥♥ HISTORIC LANDMARK This public space has been the heart and soul of Santa Fe since the city was established in 1610. Like most New Mexico plazas, it was originally designed as a meeting place, and it has been the site of innumerable festivals and other historical, cultural, and social events. Long ago the plaza was a dusty hive of activity as the staging ground and terminus of the Santa Fe Trail. Today, those who congregate here enjoy some of the best people-watching in New Mexico. Live music and

A BARGAIN FOR museumgoers

If you're a fan of museums and historic sites, and especially if you'll be touring other areas of the state, pick up a **New Mexico CulturePass,** which covers some 15 museums and historic sites across the state. The cost is $30 per person and entitles the bearer to one visit at each of the properties in a 12-month period. You can buy the CulturePass online at newmexicoculture.org or at any of the participating museums and historic sites.

Sites included in the Santa Fe area are the **New Mexico History Museum, New Mexico Museum of Art, Vladem Contemporary,** and the **Palace of Governors** (see above), and the **Museum of International Folk Art** and the **Museum of Indian Arts and Culture** (see below).

Sites in Albuquerque are the **National Hispanic Cultural Center** (p. 197) and the **New Mexico Museum of Natural History and Science** (p. 206).

Other sites included in the pass are the **New Mexico Museum of Space History** in Alamogordo, the **New Mexico Farm and Ranch Heritage Museum** in Las Cruces, and six historic parks: **Bosque Redondo Memorial/Fort Sumner Historic Site, Coronado Historic Site, Fort Selden Historic Site, Jemez Historic Site,** and **Lincoln Historic Site.**

dancing are often staged on the gazebo-turned-bandstand in summer, and at Christmastime the plaza is decked out with lights.

At the corner of San Francisco St. and Lincoln Ave. Open daily 24 hr.

Vladem Contemporary ♥♥ MUSEUM When the New Mexico Museum of Art began outgrowing its early-century building in the Plaza a decade ago, the search began for a space that could house the collection's contemporary pieces. In 2023, that annex opened in the Railyard District as Vladem Contemporary. Even with its clay-colored walls, the building's modern exterior stands out among all the adobe. But its open, airy design is well-suited to the large-scale, multimedia, installation, and performance works that make up most of its rotating exhibits, which focus on Southwestern works created after the 1980s. Art from members of New Mexico's great movements, like those by the Taos Society of Artists and the Santa Fe art colony, as well as Indigenous and LGBTQIA-plus communities, inform most of the exhibit themes. From May through October, the museum hosts docent-led walking tours of the city that focus on both art and architecture ($20 per person; includes museum admission).

404 Montezuma Ave. nmartmuseum.org. ✆ **505/476-5062.** Adults $12, free for ages 16 and under, free last Fri of month. Ticket includes same-day admission to New Mexico Museum of Art, p. 74 (except on free Fri). Daily 10am–5pm (open). Closed New Year's Day, Thanksgiving, and Christmas.

Museum Hill

As the real estate people like to say, it's all about "location, location, location." Museum Hill is a group of four museums with Spanish Colonial and American Indian themes—which, of course, could be said for a great many museums in northern New Mexico. What makes Museum Hill special, however, is that because they're so close together, it's easy to see all four of the major museums here in a single morning or afternoon. And when you need a break from information overload, cross the street to Santa Fe Botanic Gardens where you can wander among flowers, shrubbery, and trees for a breath of fresh air. For information on what's happening on Museum Hill, see www.museumhill.net.

Museum of Indian Arts and Culture ♥♥ MUSEUM The Southwest's unique legacy of Native American culture is the focus of this state-run museum, which traces the culture's development from ancient times to the modern day through artifacts, music, video, and live demonstrations. A tunnel-like entrance, symbolizing the *sipapu* portal between spiritual worlds, leads into the current exhibits, curated from more than 75,000 objects in the museum's total collection. Exhibits are varied and change periodically, with current exhibit information available online. Displays may include centuries-old pottery, silver jewelry, intricate weavings, and more, all created by Native craftspeople. There's a recreation of a trading post and a traditional Pueblo kitchen, and the outstanding multimedia "Here, Now and Always" exhibition, which combines story, song, artifacts, and the voices of Indigenous elders to tell the complex, ongoing story of these people and their place in the United States.

710 Camino Lejo. indianartsandculture.org. ✆ **505/476-1269.** Adults $12 ($7 for NM residents), free for ages 16 and under. Daily 10am–5pm (closed Mon Nov–Apr). Closed New Year's Day, Easter, Thanksgiving, and Christmas.

Museum of International Folk Art ♥♥♥ MUSEUM Kids of all ages will enjoy this world-class museum with exhibits that encourage hands-on activities, engaging and challenging the imagination. The Tree of Life area has peek-a-boo art windows, miniature tree houses, puppets, and lots of books. A perennial favorite is the "Multiple Visions: A Common Bond" display; no matter how often one visits, the more than 10,000 objects dazzle and intrigue, with something new always catching your eye. These objects are drawn from the museum's 100,000-plus dolls, masks, ceramics, animals, and more, gathered from over 100 countries and donated by architect and interior designer Alexander Girard and his wife Susan. A multimedia tour highlights certain displays within the Multiple Visions exhibit. Several galleries are devoted to rotating exhibits, all exploring diverse cultures from around the world. Free docent tours are offered at 10:30am on Wednesdays, Thursdays, Fridays, and occasional weekends. This branch of the Museum of New Mexico is the main destination on Museum Hill, and for good reason: There's nowhere else like it in the world. Expect to spend at least an hour here, although if you have kids, you might end up staying the whole afternoon. The on-site gift shop is almost overwhelming in its colorful selection.

706 Camino Lejo. moifa.org. ✆ **505/476-1200.** Adults $12, free for ages 16 and under. Daily 10am–5pm (closed Mon Nov–Apr). Closed New Year's Day, Easter, Thanksgiving, and Christmas.

Nuevo Mexicano Heritage Arts Museum ♥ MUSEUM Thank the Spanish Colonial Art Society, founded in Santa Fe in 1925, for the unequaled collection on display here. This is the only museum in the U.S. dedicated to Spanish Colonial art, with a prime spot on Museum Hill next to the Folk Art and Indian Arts and Culture museums. It's a (relatively) small building, meaning only a fraction of the 4,000-piece collection is visible at a time, but that includes holy images called *retablos* (painted) and *santos* (carved), furniture,

Cultural Chow

If you get hungry while visiting the **Museum of Indian Arts & Culture,** the **Museum of International Folk Art,** the **Wheelwright Museum of the American Indian,** or the **Nuevo Mexicano Heritage Arts Museum** (all located together, on a hilltop southeast of the Plaza), you can subdue that growling stomach at the **Museum Hill Café ♥,** 710 Camino Lejo (museumhillcafe.net; ✆ **505/984-8900**). It's open Tuesday through Sunday, 11am to 3pm, with upscale Santa Fe selections including salmon tostadas, duck flautas, a steak sandwich, and of course, the almighty burger.

weaving, ceramics, and tinwork that date to between the 16th and 20th centuries. A trip here feels like visiting the house of a very dedicated collector. The grounds include an authentic circa-1780 Mexican Colonial house from the state of Michoacán, one of only three in the country. The gift shop sells works by artists who gather for the Traditional Spanish Market every July.

750 Camino Lejo. nmheritagearts.org. ✆ **505/982-2226.** Free admission, donations appreciated. Wed–Fri noon–4pm, Sat 10am–4pm. Closed Easter, Thanksgiving, Christmas, and month of Jan.

Santa Fe Botanical Garden at Museum Hill ♥♥ GARDENS You'll enter into the Orchard Gardens, with its centerpiece fruit orchard surrounded on three sides by a sturdy retaining wall and flanked by a meadow garden and a xeric garden. Plants were chosen not only for beauty but for their ability to thrive in the high desert climate of Santa Fe. The botanical garden straddles the Arroyo de los Pinos via a historic "red bridge"—built in 1913 for San Miguel County—which spans the arroyo, allowing pedestrians easy movement from garden to garden. Interested in ethnobotany? Visit the Ojos y Manos (eyes and hands) Garden to explore, through hands-on experiences and observation, the shared history of people and plants in northern New Mexico. Children especially can get involved and enjoy themselves here. Adjacent is the newest development at the gardens: the Pinyon-Juniper Woodland, where visitors can learn about New Mexico's predominant coniferous ecosystem through innovative interpretive graphics and programs. Forthcoming plans include numerous paths—many handicap accessible—and trails with benches so visitors can enjoy the distant views of the Sangre de Cristo Mountains; an area where children can play and learn year-round is also in the works.

715 Camino Lejo. visitsfbg.org. ✆ **505/471-9103.** Adults $13, ages 4–17 $8, children 3 and under free. Apr–Oct daily 9am–5pm, Nov–Mar Wed–Sun 10am–4pm. Closed Thanksgiving and Christmas.

Wheelwright Museum of the American Indian ♥♥ MUSEUM On Museum Hill, the Wheelwright is a small but extraordinary museum of contemporary and iconic Native American art. The original building's octagonal shape is inspired by the Navajo *hooghan* or hogan, the traditional home and setting for ceremonies; its doors face east toward the rising sun. Founded in 1937 with the help of a Navajo medicine man, the collection's original aim was to preserve Navajo cultural artifacts. Since then it has expanded to include works by living artists of all Indian cultures, with one gallery devoted permanently to Indigenous jewelry, and two others hosting up to four changing exhibits annually. On the lower level, the Case Trading Post is a gift shop modeled on the classic posts that served as stores, banks, and meeting places across the Western frontier. It offers the finest contemporary jewelry, pottery, paintings, textiles, and more, from items for tourists to pieces for the discerning collector.

704 Camino Lejo. wheelwright.org. ✆ **505/982-4636.** Adults $10, free for Native Americans, kids 12 and under, students with ID, veterans, and active military. Free admission 1st Sun of month. Tues–Sat 10am–5pm. Closed New Year's Day, Thanksgiving, and Christmas.

More Attractions

MUSEUMS

IAIA Museum of Contemporary Native Arts (MoCNA) ♥♥ MUSEUM After a few days in New Mexico, it's good to be reminded that Native art is more than just pottery, blankets, and kachina dolls. This museum, run by the Institute of American Indian Arts, is the largest assemblage of contemporary Native art in the country, located right in the heart of downtown Santa Fe, 1 block from the Plaza. MoCNA represents a unique, dynamic population of Indigenous artists and houses a vibrant and edgy collection of approximately 8,500 works collected since the 1960s. Exhibitions rotate regularly, with works including photographs, paintings, prints, sculptures, and much more. Some works embody the struggle to bridge the old and new, the traditional and the contemporary. Don't miss the outdoor sculpture garden, featuring works by Allan Houser.

108 Cathedral Place. iaia.edu/museum. ✆ **505/983-1777.** Adults $10; seniors (62+), students, and ages 16 and under $5, free every Fri. Mon and Wed–Sat 10am–5pm, Sun 11am–4pm. Closed New Year's Day, Easter, Thanksgiving, and Christmas.

New Mexico Military Museum ♥♥ MUSEUM New Mexico has a long military history, going back at least to the 1500s with the arrival of the Spanish conquistadores. Then there was the Battle of Glorieta Pass during the Civil War (see Pecos National Historic Park, p. 113) and Pancho Villa's invasion of the border town of Columbus, New Mexico in 1916. The state's citizens played major roles in both world wars, including the infamous Bataan Death March in World War II, plus the Vietnam War and more recent military action. This museum, housed in the former headquarters of the New Mexico National Guard and the state's World War II induction center, honors the state's soldiers, sailors, airmen, Marines, and members of the Coast Guard. Changing and permanent exhibits tell the stories of New Mexicans who fought for their country, including exhibits on New Mexico women who served. A replica of the Vietnam Veterans Memorial Wall in Washington, D.C., which lists the names of the more than 58,000 servicemen and women who died in the Vietnam War, is displayed, along with a shipping crate from the replica's national tour, upon which many people wrote notes about the individuals listed on the monument. The museum's campus also includes a meditation garden, a 300-seat auditorium (see website for scheduled events), and a reference library available for public use.

1050 Old Pecos Trail. newmexicomilitarymuseum.com. ✆ **505/629-5199.** Free; donations appreciated. Mon–Fri 10am–3pm. Closed New Year's Day, Thanksgiving, and Christmas.

CHURCHES

The Cathedral Basilica of St. Francis of Assisi ♥♥♥ CHURCH Santa Fe's grandest religious structure is an architectural anomaly in Santa Fe because its design is French. Just a block east of the plaza, it was built between 1869 and 1887 by Archbishop Jean-Baptiste Lamy (see box p. 85) in

FETISHES: gifts OF POWER

According to Zuni lore, before human existence, the Sun and Moon sent down their two children to assist pre-people from the watery underworld. When they emerged and turned human, sea monsters followed them to the surface. To save them, the children shot lightning bolts at the predators, turning them to stone and instructing them to help the humans they once hunted. For generations, Zunis, traveling across their lands in western New Mexico, have found stones shaped like particular animals, and Zuni legend maintains that these stones are the remains of those long-lost predators, still containing their souls or last breaths.

In some shops in Santa Fe, you too can pick up a carved animal figure called a *fetish.* According to belief, the owner of the fetish is able to absorb the power of that creature. Many fetishes were long ago used for protection and power while hunting. Today, a person might carry a bear for health and strength, or an eagle for keen perspective. A mole might be placed in a home's foundation for protection from elements underground, a frog buried with crops for fertility and rain, or a ram carried in the purse for prosperity. For love, some locals recommend pairs of fetishes—often foxes or coyotes carved from a single piece of stone.

Many fetishes, arranged with bundles on top and attached with sinew, serve as an offering to the animal spirit that resides within the stone. Fetishes are still carved at many of the pueblos. A good fetish is not necessarily one that is meticulously carved—some fetishes are barely carved at all, as the original shape of the stone already contains the form of the animal. When you have a sense of the quality and elegance available, decide which animal (and power) suits you best. Zuni Pueblo people caution, however, that the fetish cannot be expected to impart an attribute you don't already possess. Instead, it will help elicit the power that already resides within you.

An excellent source for fetishes is **Keshi** ♥, 227 Don Gaspar Ave. (keshi.com; ✆ **505/989-8728**). Expect to pay $30 to $75 or more.

the style of the great cathedrals of Europe. French architects designed the Romanesque building—named after Santa Fe's patron saint—and Italian stonemasons assisted with its construction. In 2005 the cathedral was elevated by the Pope to basilica status, as a church of particular importance due to its historical efforts in spreading Catholicism. The cathedral was built over and around an older church, Our Lady of the Assumption, founded along with Santa Fe in 1610; the only remaining portion of that church can be found on the northeast side of the cathedral, the small adobe **Our Lady of the Rosary chapel,** built in a Spanish style in 1807.

Take some time to admire the cathedral's **front doors,** which feature 16 carved panels of historic note and a plaque memorializing the 38 Franciscan friars who were martyred during New Mexico's early years. Just inside the front doors are a small gift shop and religious bookstore. Seven archbishops, including Lamy, are buried in the sanctuary. In the wall of the north chapel, don't miss the wooden icon set in a niche, **Our Lady of Peace,** believed to be the oldest representation of the Madonna in the United States. Rescued from

Greater Santa Fe Attractions

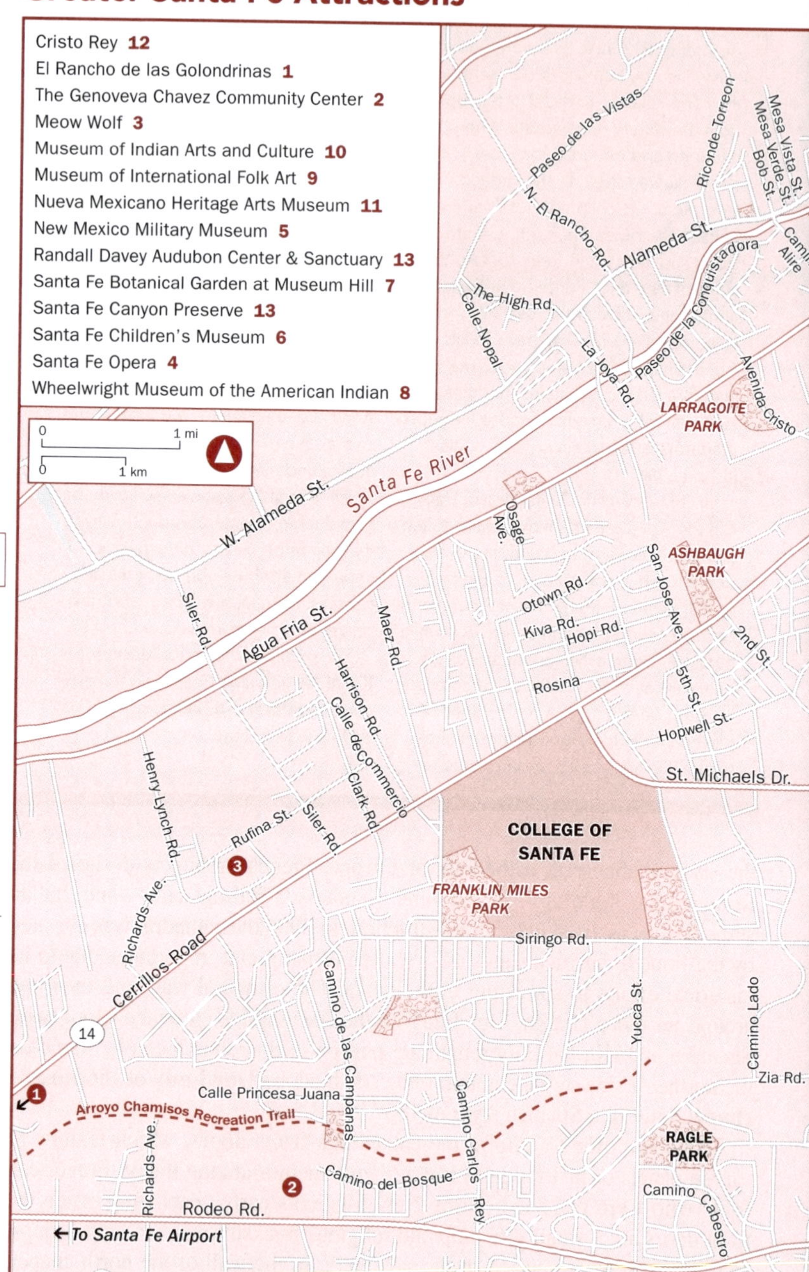

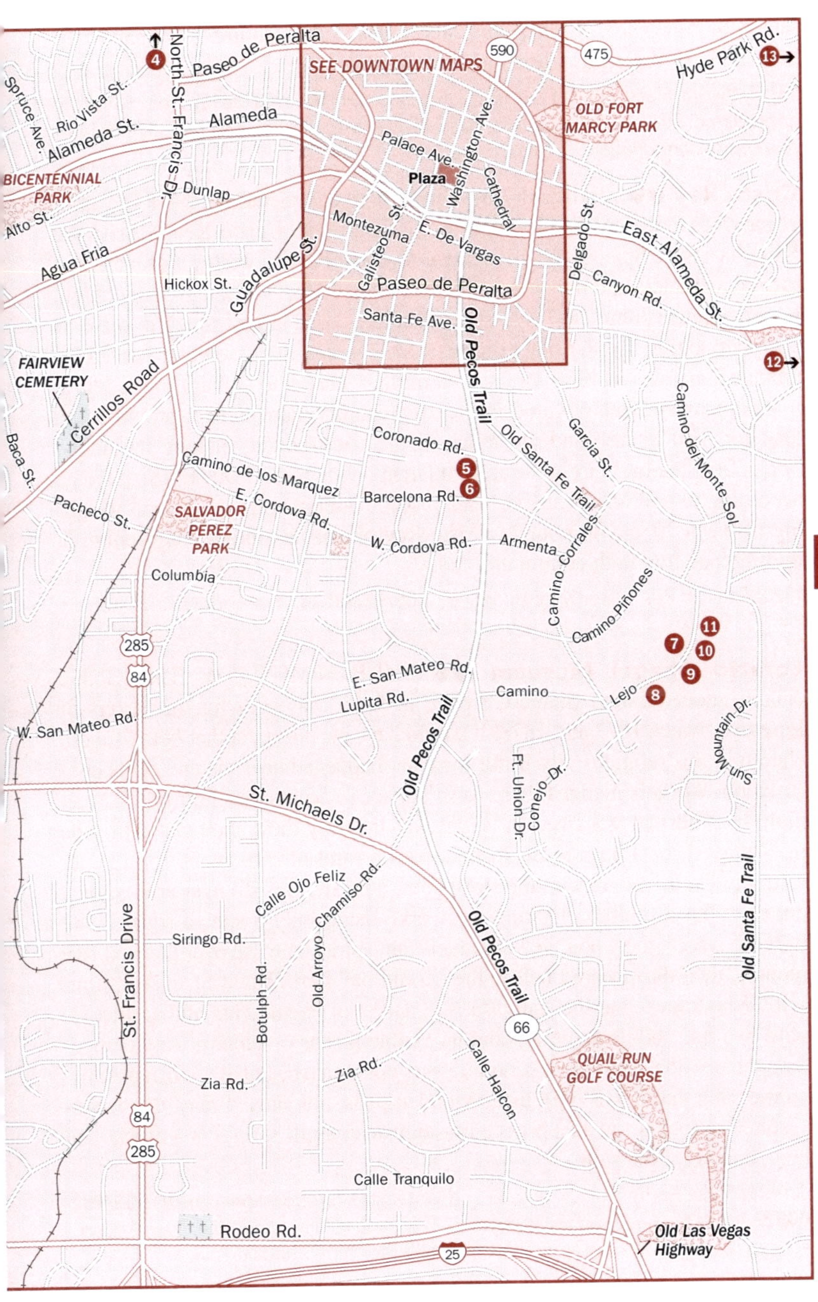
SEE DOWNTOWN MAPS
Paseo de Peralta
North St. Francis Dr.
Spruce Ave.
Rio Vista St.
Alameda St.
Alameda
BICENTENNIAL PARK
Alto St.
Dunlap
Agua Fria
Hickox St.
Guadalupe St.
Palace Ave.
Plaza
Washington Ave.
Cathedral
Montezuma
Galisteo St.
E. De Vargas
Paseo de Peralta
Santa Fe Ave.
OLD FORT MARCY PARK
Hyde Park Rd.
Delgado St.
East Alameda St.
Canyon Rd.
FAIRVIEW CEMETERY
Cerrillos Road
Baca St.
Old Pecos Trail
Coronado Rd.
Old Santa Fe Trail
Garcia St.
Camino del Monte Sol
Camino de los Marquez
Barcelona Rd.
Pacheco St.
SALVADOR PEREZ PARK
E. Cordova Rd.
W. Cordova Rd.
Armenta
Camino Corrales
Columbia
Camino Piñones
E. San Mateo Rd.
Lupita Rd.
Camino
Lejo
W. San Mateo Rd.
Sun Mountain Dr.
Ft. Union Dr.
Conejo Dr.
St. Michaels Dr.
Calle Ojo Feliz
Chamiso Rd.
Old Arroyo
Siringo Rd.
Botulph Rd.
St. Francis Drive
Old Santa Fe Trail
Zia Rd.
Zia Rd.
Calle Halcon
QUAIL RUN GOLF COURSE
Calle Tranquilo
Rodeo Rd.
Old Las Vegas Highway
590
475
285
84
66
25
4
5
6
7
8
9
10
11
12
13

the old church during the 1680 Pueblo Rebellion, it was brought back by Don Diego de Vargas when the Spanish colonists reconquered the capital 12 years later—thus the name. Today, Our Lady of Peace plays an important part in the annual Feast of Corpus Christi in June and July.

131 Cathedral Place, at San Francisco St. cbsfa.org. ✆ **505/982-5619.** Free; donations appreciated. Tues–Fri 9:30am–4pm, Sat 9:30am–3pm. Check website or call for Mass and confession schedule.

Cristo Rey ♥♥ CHURCH Built in 1940 to commemorate the 400th anniversary of Coronado's exploration of the Southwest, **Cristo Rey (Christ the King)** is a huge Spanish-Pueblo revival-style adobe. The walls range from two to nine feet thick, and the nave is 125 feet long, 40 feet wide, and 33 feet high. Local architect John Gaw Meem designed the space large enough to serve as a proper setting for the magnificent stone *reredos* (altar screen); carved by unknown artisans in 1760 for use in a military chapel to be built in the Plaza, it was recovered and restored in the 20th century. Parishioners provided the land for their church and did much of the construction, making the adobe bricks from the best dirt in the area and then laying some 1,000 bricks per day, according to oral history. More than 150,000 adobes were used, each weighing between 20 and 40 pounds. Cristo Rey remains a vibrant, multi-cultural, multi-generation faith community today.

1120 Canyon Rd. cristoreyparish.org. ✆ **505/983-8528.** Free admission. Mon–Fri 8am–5pm; Mass Sat 4:30pm and Sun 10am.

Loretto Chapel Museum ♥♥ CHURCH/MUSEUM This Gothic church, modeled after Sainte-Chapelle in Paris, was built for the Sisters of Loretto between 1873 and 1878. It would have been just another beautiful old church in this religious city if not for what happened near the end of its construction. Workers realized there wasn't space to access the choir loft, 22 feet high, by a normal staircase—a ladder was the only thing that would fit. The nuns prayed for 9 days to St. Joseph, patron saint of carpenters, for a better solution. On the 9th day, as the story goes, a mysterious stranger arrived on a donkey with a toolbox, looking for work. Using only a saw, a square, and water to season the wood, he built an elegant spiral staircase over the next few months, then disappeared before they could pay him. Was it St. Joseph himself? Who knows, but the staircase is a marvel of engineering and aesthetics, with two full 360-degree turns and no visible means of support. Any competent stair builder can explain how it was constructed, but it's still amazing, considering that it was built using wooden pegs, not nails. Today, the deconsecrated chapel is run as a private museum with a gift shop. It's a quick visit here, but worth the stop.

207 Old Santa Fe Trail (btw. Alameda and Water sts.). lorettochapel.com. ✆ **505/982-0092.** Adults $5, seniors (65+) $4, ages 7–17 $3, ages 6 and under free. Daily 9:30am–4:30pm. Chapel closes for special events; call for current schedule.

San Miguel Chapel ♥ CHURCH To really get the feel of Spanish Colonial Catholicism, visit this church—you won't be disappointed. First constructed around 1610, it was partially destroyed during the Pueblo Revolt of 1680 (p. 112), but by 1710 it had been fully restored. The church has massive adobe walls, high windows, an elegant altar screen (erected in 1798), and a 780-pound San José bell (now found inside), which was cast in Spain in 1356. It also houses buffalo-hide and deerskin Bible paintings used by Franciscan missionaries in the 1600s. It is believed to be the oldest active church in the United States. Anthropologists have excavated near the altar, down to the original floor that some claim to be part of a 12th-century pueblo. The *Schola Cantorum* of Santa Fe sings Vespers and a Gregorian chant at 4pm on the third Sunday of the month.

401 Old Santa Fe Trail (at E. De Vargas St.). sanmiguelchapel.org. ✆ **505/983-3974.** Free; donations appreciated. Mon 11am–3pm, Tues–Sat 10am–3pm, Sun noon–3pm; Mass Sun 3pm in Latin, 5pm in English.

Santuario de Nuestra Señora de Guadalupe ♥ CHURCH This church, built between 1776 and 1796 at the end of El Camino Real by Franciscan missionaries, is believed to be the oldest shrine in the United States honoring the Virgin of Guadalupe, the patron saint of Mexico. Better known

SANTA FE'S french connection

In the 19th century, New Mexico, including Santa Fe, was first ruled by Spain, then Mexico, and finally the United States. So how is it that one of the most influential and important people of that time was a Frenchman?

Bishop Jean-Baptiste Lamy was the first bishop and archbishop of the Diocese of Santa Fe. Born in 1814 to a religious family in Lempdes in Auvergne, a region in southern France, Lamy entered a seminary that specialized in training priests for foreign missions, and in 1839 Lamy and a small group of priests and nuns made their way to America. Lamy's first assignment was to a parish in Danville, Ohio, where he oversaw the construction of several churches.

After the New Mexico Territory became part of the United States, the Catholic Church leadership petitioned the Vatican to establish a provisional diocese in New Mexico. The Vatican did so in 1850, and Lamy was rewarded for his work in Ohio by being appointed vicar. When the Diocese of Santa Fe was officially created in 1853, he was named its bishop.

While bishop of Santa Fe, Lamy was known for his many confrontations with the local Mexican clergy, many of whom he considered too worldly. He didn't like or trust them, and they didn't like or trust him. These confrontations included a long-running dispute with Father Antonio José Martínez of Taos, whom Lamy excommunicated in 1858. Martínez, however, refused to recognize the excommunication and continued to celebrate Mass in private chapels.

Lamy disliked New Mexico's adobe architecture, so in the 1860s when it came time to build the St. Francis Cathedral (p. 80), Lamy chose a stone Romanesque style instead. He also was responsible for the Gothic style of Loretto Chapel (p. 84).

Elevated to archbishop by the Vatican in 1875, Lamy retired in 1884 and died in Santa Fe in 1888. Perhaps his widest fame came after his death, as the model for Willa Cather's 1927 novel *Death Comes for the Archbishop.*

as Santuario de Guadalupe, the shrine has adobe walls that are almost 3 feet thick; the deep-red plaster wall behind the altar was dyed with oxblood in traditional fashion when the church was restored early in the 20th century. The building has gone through several transformations over time, with styles ranging from flat-topped pueblo to New England town meeting to today's northern New Mexico style. On one wall is a famous oil painting, *Our Lady of Guadalupe,* created in 1783 by the renowned Mexican artist José de Alcíbar. Painted expressly for this church, it was brought from Mexico City by mule caravan. One of Santa Fe's newest landmarks, the graceful 12-foot, 4,000-pound statue of Our Lady of Guadalupe by Mexican sculptor Georgina "Gogy" Farías was erected in front of the church in 2008. This historic church is now an art and history museum containing the Archdiocese of Santa Fe's collection of New Mexican santos (carved images of the saints), Italian Renaissance paintings, and Mexican baroque paintings.

100 S. Guadalupe St. solg.org. ✆ **505/983-8868.** Free; donations appreciated. Mon–Tues, Thurs–Fri 9am–4pm.

HISTORIC SITES

El Rancho de las Golondrinas ♥♥ HISTORIC HOME A fascinating place to visit, particularly during its festivals and other special events, El Rancho de las Golondrinas—The Ranch of the Swallows—takes us back to New Mexico's Spanish Colonial and Territorial days. The 200-acre ranch includes an 18th-century hacienda, its rooms surrounding a central placita where most day-to-day living and working took place, plus a 19th-century home complete with outbuildings. Numerous other buildings—molasses mill, blacksmith shop, wheelwright shop, schoolhouse, and several water-powered grist mills—round out the story of life in Spanish Colonial and Territorial New Mexico. The ranch was an important overnight stop on the 1,000-mile Camino Real, or Royal Road, between Mexico City and Santa Fe. Craft demonstrations take place, and there are live farm animals to see. A walk around the entire property is 1¾ miles, with amazing scenery. A daily guided tour, included in the price of admission, is offered at 10:30am, except during special events. Check the website for upcoming festivals; they're worth fitting into your travel schedule.

334 Los Pinos Rd. Take exit 276 from I-25, go N on NM 599, turn left at 1st traffic light on W. Frontage Rd. then right on Los Pinos Rd. golondrinas.org. ✆ **505/471-2261.** Adults $8; seniors, veterans, and ages 13–17 $6, free for kids 12 and under. Higher fees during special events. June–Sept Wed–Sun 10am–4pm (closed Nov–Mar). Private tour by reservation only (call ext. 101) 2 weeks in advance.

New Mexico State Capitol (Roundhouse) ♥♥ LANDMARK Built in 1966, this is the only entirely round capitol building in the U.S., and there's a reason behind its design—it's the shape of a Zia Pueblo emblem, or sun sign, which is also the state symbol and is on the state flag. (See "The Sun Worshippers of New Mexico," p. 12). Surrounding the capitol is a lush, nearly 10-acre garden boasting more than 100 varieties of plants, including roses, plums, almonds, nectarines, Russian olives, and sequoias. Inside you'll find the House and Senate chambers and the Governor's office, plus a 500-piece art collection by New Mexico artists on permanent display in the public areas. The Rotunda and the fourth-floor Governor's Gallery feature rotating exhibits. Guided tours are available by appointment; all tours and self-guided brochures are free.

490 Old Santa Fe Trail, at Paseo del Peralta. nmlegis.gov. ✆ **505/986-4589.** Free. Mon–Fri 7:30am–5:30pm; Sat 9am–5pm June–Aug. Free parking in garage at 420 Galisteo St.

PARKS & REFUGES

Old Fort Marcy Park ♥ PARK Marking the 1846 site of the first U.S. military installation in the Southwest, this park overlooks the northeast corner of downtown. Only a few mounds remain from the fort, but the Cross of the Martyrs, at the top of a winding brick walkway from Paseo de Peralta near Otero Street, is a popular spot for bird's-eye photographs. The cross was erected in 1920 by the Knights of Columbus and the Historical Society of New Mexico to commemorate the Franciscans killed during the Pueblo Rebellion of 1680. It has since played a role in numerous religious processions.

617 Paseo de Peralta. Open daily 24 hr.

Randall Davey Audubon Center & Sanctuary ♥♥ NATURE CENTER This is Audubon's leading education and wildlife sanctuary in New Mexico, attracting more than 10,000 visitors each year. In 1983 the site was given to the National Audubon Society by the heirs of the Santa Fe artist Randall Davey, who in 1920 bought an 1847 sawmill and converted it into his home and studio. An excellent escape from the bustle of the city, the center and sanctuary now occupies 135 acres at the mouth of Santa Fe Canyon just a few minutes' drive from the plaza. More than 125 species of birds and 120 types of plants live here, and varied mammals have been spotted, including black bears, mule deer, mountain lions, bobcats, raccoons, and coyotes. Trails winding through more than 100 acres of the nature sanctuary are open to day hikers, although no dogs are allowed. Tours of Davey's home and art studio are available Fridays at 2pm for a $5 fee; guided bird walks are led on Saturdays at 8:30am. There's also a gift shop.

1800 Upper Canyon Rd. randalldavey.audubon.org. ✆ **505/983-4609.** Free; donations appreciated. Mon–Sat 8am–4pm. Closed multiple holidays; check website.

Santa Fe Canyon Preserve ♥♥♥ NATURE PRESERVE Covering some 525 acres just 2 miles from Santa Fe Plaza, this peaceful preserve managed by the Nature Conservancy offers hiking and biking trails, wildflowers, ponderosa pine, and a grove of cottonwoods and willows. There are also remnants of two dams: Old Stone Dam, built in 1881, and Two-Mile Dam, built in 1893, the first of four dams built on the Santa Fe River to store its seasonal flow for city use. Some 140 species of birds call the preserve home; there are deer, and an occasional bear and beavers, plus their dams and lodges, are a common sight. The **Dale Ball Foothill Trail System,** which runs through the preserve, includes some 22 miles of multi-use trails, and these trails connect to several other trails, including the 5.2-mile Atalaya Trail, the 1.5-mile Dorothy Stewart Trail, and a 1.3-mile **interpretive loop trail** that meanders along the remains of Two Mile Dam to an overlook of a pond—all that's left of the reservoir that once served Santa Fe. Note that dogs and bicycles are not permitted in the preserve except on the Dale Ball Foothill Trail System.

Cerro Gordo Rd., at intersection with Upper Canyon Rd. Nature Conservancy office, 212 E. Marcy St., 3200. nature.org. ✆ **505/988-3867.** Free admission. Daily sunrise–sunset.

Santa Fe River Parkway ♥ PARK This is a lovely pathway along the Santa Fe River, and incidentally Alameda Street which pretty much follows the river, in downtown Santa Fe. It meanders its way for about 2.5 miles from Patrick Smith Park near Canyon Road in a westerly direction to St. Francis Drive—perfect for an early morning jog, a tree-shaded midday walk, or perhaps a sack lunch at a picnic table.

Open daily 24 hr.

Organized Tours

Walking is the best way to see downtown Santa Fe, and we highly recommend the self-guided walking tour on p. 90. But if you prefer a guide who can fill you in on the historic tidbits of this old city, the best is **Historic Walks of Santa Fe** ♥ (historicwalksofsantafe.com; ✆ **505/986-8388**). Many of the guides are local museum docents. The private tours cost $40 per person, have a two-person minimum (free for children under 16 with parent), and require reservations. They last 1 hour and 45 minutes, starting at 10am daily at the Plaza. The company also offers various special tours, including a ghost tour, shopping tour, and a Canyon Road art tour. Details are on the company's website.

Another option for walking tours—and to familiarize yourself with trail locations to explore more on your own—is offered by **Vámonos: Santa Fe Walks,** a free urban walking program on public trails in the city. The Santa Fe Walking Collaborative, convened by the Santa Fe Conservation Trust, has put together some 25 walks in and around the city's parks and nearby environs. They take place May through October, last about an hour, and are led by interesting locals. Check the website (sfct.org) for the schedule.

Feet getting sore but don't want to fight the Santa Fe traffic? An open-air tram tour of the city with **Loretto Line** ♥ (toursofsantafe.com; ✆ **505/982-0092, ext. 1**) may solve the problem. The company has been running tours here since 1992. Tours last a little over an hour, covering the main historic sites and other places of interest, and are offered daily from March through October. They depart at 10am, noon, and 2pm Wednesday through Monday from the Loretto Chapel and a half-hour later from La Fonda Hotel. The cost is $25 for adults and $15 for children 12 and under with an adult. Tours are not given during Spanish Market (late July) and Indian Market (the third weekend in August).

CLASSES FOR culture vultures

Looking for a deeper dive into New Mexico's culture? Try one of these classes.

You can master the flavors of Santa Fe with an entertaining 3-hour demonstration class at the **Santa Fe School of Cooking** ♥, 125 N. Guadalupe St. (www.santafeschoolofcooking.com; ✆ **800/982-4688** or 505/983-4511). It offers several classes, each including tidbits about the flavors and history of traditional New Mexican and contemporary Southwestern cuisines. Prices are $100 to $120. (Hands-on classes cost a bit more.) Check the website for class descriptions and the current schedule.

If Southwestern art has you hooked, consider taking a drawing and painting class led by a Santa Fe artist, organized by **Jane Shoenfeld's Art Adventures in the Southwest** ♥ (skyfields.net; ✆ **505/986-1108**). Students paint such outdoor subjects as the Santa Fe landscape and adobe architecture. In case of inclement weather, classes are held in the studio. Classes generally last for 3 hours, and art materials are included in the fee, which starts at $175. All levels of experience are welcome; private lessons can also be arranged.

Also see "Special-Interest Tours," p. 237.

Especially for Kids

Don't miss taking the kids to the **Museum of International Folk Art** (p. 78), where they'll love the international dioramas and the toys. Kids are also sure to enjoy **El Rancho de las Golondrinas** (p. 86), a living 18th- and 19th-century Spanish village with a hacienda, a village store, a schoolhouse, and several chapels.

The Genoveva Chavez Community Center ♥ RECREATION CENTER On the south side of Santa Fe, this city-run, full-service family recreation center offers many options for kids. The complex includes a 50m pool, a leisure pool, a therapy pool, an ice-skating rink, three gyms, a workout room, racquetball courts, and an indoor running track, as well as a spa and sauna. For hours, prices, and more info, check the center's website.

3221 Rodeo Rd. santafenm.gov/community-services. ✆ **505/955-4000.**

Santa Fe Children's Museum ♥ MUSEUM This museum is based on a very simple idea: Children learn by doing. The focus is to bring parents and children together in a spirit of challenging play. It offers interactive exhibits and hands-on activities in the arts, humanities, and science, plus a number of weekly programs in which kids of all ages can play with model trains, dig around and learn about gardening, study the night sky in a mobile planetarium, or play with Cornelius the snake (yes, a live snake). Call or check the website for the schedule.

1050 Old Pecos Trail. santafechildrensmuseum.org. ✆ **505/989-8359.** Adults $12; children $9; free for infants under 1 year old.; free for all Thurs 4–6pm. Wed–Sat 10am–6pm, Sun noon–5pm (shorter hours in winter). Closed New Year's Day, Easter, July 4, Thanksgiving, and Christmas.

Santa Fe Public Library ♥ LIBRARY/COMMUNITY CENTER Special programs, such as storytelling and magic shows, can be found here, especially in summer. Check the website or call for the current schedule. The main library is in the center of town, 1 block from the plaza.

145 Washington Ave. santafelibrary.org. ✆ **505/955-6781.** Mon, Fri–Sat 10am–6pm, Tues–Thurs 10am–8pm.

A SANTA FE STROLL

Santa Fe Plaza is the heart and soul of the city. For centuries it's where residents have come to shop, eat, and meet, and although in recent times the plaza has become a mecca for tourists as well as residents, it's still where you must go if you're going to say you saw Santa Fe. Because everything is so close (and because parking is sometimes a challenge) it's best to leave your car at your hotel or in a lot and explore the plaza area on foot.

WALKING TOUR: THE PLAZA AREA

START:	**The Plaza**
FINISH:	**Loretto Chapel**
TIME:	**1 to 5 hours, depending on the length of visits to the museums and churches**
BEST TIMES:	**Any morning before the afternoon heat, but after the Native American traders have spread out their wares at the Palace of the Governors**

1 The Plaza ♥♥

This historic square (p. 76) offers a look at Santa Fe's everyday life as well as many types of architecture, ranging from the Pueblo-style Palace of the Governors to the Territorial-style row of shops and restaurants on its west side.

Facing the plaza on its north side is the:

2 Palace of the Governors ♥♥

Today the flagship of the New Mexico State Museum system (p. 76), the Palace of the Governors has functioned continually as a public building since it was erected in 1610 as the capitol of Nuevo Mexico. Every day, Navajo and Pueblo artisans spread out their crafts for sale beneath its portal and share insight into their process.

North of the Palace at the corner of Lincoln and Palace aves., you'll find the:

3 New Mexico History Museum ♥♥♥

Continue your time-traveler's tour of New Mexico at this landmark institution (p. 74), where immersive, interactive exhibits trace 400 years of the region's history, from its Indigenous beginnings and the Spanish colonization to the merchants, cowboys, and scientists that make up New Mexico's rich tapestry.

Walking Tour: The Plaza Area

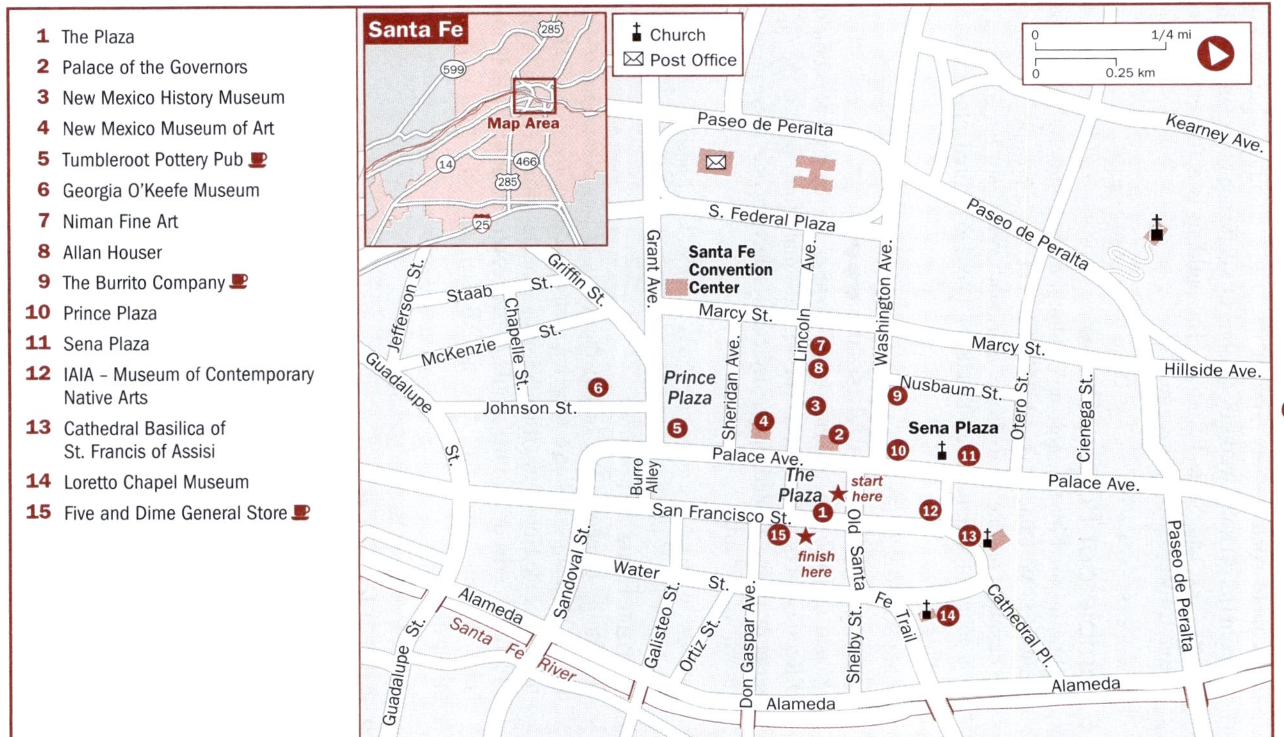

Virtually across the street is the:

4 New Mexico Museum of Art ♥♥

For a more contemporary look at the state's cultural influence, this museum (p. 74) holds works by Georgia O'Keeffe and other famed 20th-century Taos and Santa Fe artists. The building is a fine example of Pueblo revival–style architecture.

Go west on Palace Ave. to Grant Ave. On the corner on your right is:

5 Tumbleroot Pottery Pub ♥

Feeling inspired by the morning's cultural digest? Stop by this pottery studio, 135 W. Palace Ave. (✆ **505/982-4711**) for a breather, to browse the ceramics on sale, or to create your own work of art. For $15, you'll get a pound of sculptural clay that doesn't need to be fired, plus access to shaping tools.

Head 1 block north on Grant Ave. and make a left onto Johnson St. to reach the:

6 Georgia O'Keeffe Museum ♥♥♥

Opened in 1997, this museum (p. 73) houses the largest collection of O'Keeffe works in the world. The 13,000-square-foot space is the only museum in the United States dedicated solely to one internationally known woman artist.

Head back to Grant Ave. turn left and go to W. Marcy St., turn right and go to Lincoln Ave. Turn right onto Lincoln to find:

7 Niman Fine Art ♥

This family-owned gallery houses the works of Dan Namingha, one of the most acclaimed Native American artists working today (p. 100). A member of the Hopi-Tewa tribe, Namingha creates abstract paintings and sculptures derived from the motifs of his people, traditions, and homeland. The artist's two sons, Arlo and Michael, also show their works at this spare space.

Just a few storefronts south on Lincoln Ave. is:

8 Allan Houser ♥

This small flagship gallery features the work of Allan Houser (p. 99), considered one of the 20th century's most renowned Native American modernist sculptors. His abstract figures, inspired by Chiricahua-Apache traditions, are also on display at a by-appointment-only sculpture garden 20 miles south of town.

Return to W. Marcy St., turn right, then make another right onto Washington Ave. to find:

9 The Burrito Company ♥

Stop for refreshments at **The Burrito Company,** 111 Washington Ave. (burritocompanysf.com; ✆ **505/982-4453**), a busy, fun, family-owned spot that's popular with locals and visitors. The burritos are hearty, and beer and wine are available.

Across Washington Ave., you'll notice the entrance to the Palace of the Governors Museum Shop, a good place to purchase quality regional memorabilia. Continue down Washington to the Plaza and turn left (east) on Palace Ave. A short distance farther on your left, at 113 E. Palace Ave., is:

10 Prince Plaza ♥

A former governor's home, this Territorial-style structure, which now houses the **Shed** (a great lunch or dinner spot; p. 68), once had huge wooden gates to keep out tribal attacks.

Next door is:

11 Sena Plaza ♥

This city landmark offers a quiet respite from the busy streets, with its parklike patio and over 20 boutiques, galleries, and salons. **La Casa Sena** restaurant (a good place to stop for lunch or dinner) is the primary occupant of what was once the 31-room Sena family adobe hacienda, built in 1831. The Territorial legislature met in the hacienda in the 1890s.

Turn right (south) on Cathedral Place to no. 108, which is the:

12 IAIA Museum of Contemporary Native Arts ♥♥

Here you'll find the world's most comprehensive collection of contemporary Native American art (p. 80).

Across the street, step through the doors of the:

13 The Cathedral Basilica of St. Francis of Assisi ♥♥♥

Santa Fe's grandest religious edifice (p. 80) was built in Romanesque style between 1869 and 1886 by Archbishop Lamy. Look for its famous 17th-century wooden Madonna, known as Our Lady of Peace.

Go south on Cathedral Place and west on Water St., walking around the backside of the illustrious La Fonda Hotel (p. 54). After 1 block, turn left on the Old Santa Fe Trail, where you'll see the:

14 Loretto Chapel ♥♥

More formally known as the Chapel of Our Lady of Light, this chapel (p. 84) was another project of Archbishop Lamy (p. 85), built for the Sisters of Loretto. It is remarkable for its "miraculous" spiral staircase, which has no central or other visible support.

Follow Old Santa Fe Trail north back to the Plaza. At its southwest corner, check out:

15 Five and Dime General Store ♥

Finish your walking tour with a stop at Five and Dime General Store, 58 E. San Francisco St. (fiveanddimegs.com; ✆ **505/992-1800**), located near where the Plaza's F. W. Woolworth's store once stood. Like Woolworth's, the store serves a cherished local delicacy called Frito pie: a bag of Fritos smothered in chile con carne, served in a plastic bag with a spoon and a napkin.

SPORTS & RECREATION

Set between the granite peaks of the Sangre de Cristo Mountains and the volcanic Jemez Mountains, with the Rio Grande flowing through, the Santa Fe area offers many opportunities to play outdoors. Here in the high desert, temperatures vary with the elevation, allowing for a full range of activities throughout the year. You can find information on the city's parks and trails at santafenm.gov/community-services/recreation.

If the weather turns against you but you still want to keep up with your exercise routine, stop by the city's premier rec center, the **Genoveva Chavez Community Center** (p. 89), on the city's south side at 3221 Rodeo Rd.

Biking

You can cycle along main roadways and paved country roads year-round in Santa Fe, but be aware that traffic is particularly heavy around the plaza. Mountain-biking interest has blossomed here and is especially popular in the spring, summer, and fall; the high-desert terrain is rugged and challenging, but mountain bikers of all levels can find exhilarating rides. The Santa Fe Visitor Information Centers (p. 45) can supply you with bike maps; you can also get information and some maps from the Santa Fe Tourism website (santafe.org).

You can rent bikes from **Raworks,** at the Design Center at 418 Cerrillos Rd. (raworkshc.com; ✆ **505/772-0524**) and **Bike-N-Sport,** 504-C Cordova Rd. in the same shopping center as Trader Joe's (nmbikensport.com; ✆ **505/820-0809**).

Some of the best mountain-biking here is in the **Dale Ball Trail System ♥♥** (p. 87). Another good option for biking or hiking is the 3.7-mile paved **Arroyo de los Chamisos Trail ♥**, which meanders through the southwestern part of the city and is easily accessible to those staying in hotels along Cerrillos Road. It follows a chamisa-lined arroyo and has good mountain views. Begin at Santa Fe High School on Yucca Street or on Rodeo Road near Sam's Club.

Bird-Watching

The best bird-watching in Santa Fe is at the Nature Conservancy's **Santa Fe Canyon Preserve ♥♥♥** and the nearby **Randall Davey Audubon Center ♥♥** (see "Parks & Refuges," p. 87).

Fishing

In the lakes and waterways around Santa Fe, anglers typically catch trout, bass, perch, and kokanee salmon. The most popular fishing holes are the Cochiti and Abiquiu lakes, as well as the Rio Chama, Pecos River, and the Rio Grande. For a weekly fishing report, plus information on licenses and special fishing proclamations, check with the **New Mexico Department of Game and Fish** (wildlife.dgf.nm.gov; ✆ **505/476-8000**).

For gear, licenses, and experienced guides, contact **High Desert Angler,** 460 Cerrillos Rd. (highdesertangler.com; ✆ **505/988-7688**), open Monday through Saturday 9am to 6pm, Sunday 11am to 4pm.

Indoor/Outdoor Adventuring

If you're one of those people who wants it all, and you don't mind spending money to have someone organize everything, consider hooking up with **Santa Fe Mountain Adventures ♥♥** (santafemountainadventures.com; ✆ **505/988-4000**), which offers programs combining outdoor adventures with arts and cultural experiences. You might start the day with fly-fishing or whitewater rafting, and then in the afternoon take a cooking or pottery-making class, or even possibly a spa treatment. Families especially enjoy the guided petroglyph hiking adventures at La Cieneguilla and near Santa Fe or at White Rock Canyon along the Rio Grande. Prices start at $200 per person for a half-day.

Golf

Top golf courses in the Santa Fe area include the 27-hole **Marty Sanchez Links de Santa Fe ♥♥**, 205 Caja del Rio Rd. (linksdesantafe.com; ✆ **505/955-4402**); the 18-hole **Santa Fe Country Club ♥** 3950 Country Club Rd. just off Airport Rd. (santafecountryclub.com; ✆ **505/471-0601**); and the 27-hole **Towa Golf Club ♥**, Buffalo Thunder Resort, 12 miles north of Santa Fe on US 285/84 (hiltonbuffalothunder.com; ✆ **505/455-9000**), with its splendid views of the Jemez and Sangre de Cristo mountains. Avid golfers don't mind the drive to the highly rated 18-hole **Cochiti Golf Club ♥** at Cochiti Pueblo, 5200 Cochiti Hwy., Cochiti Lake (cochitigolfclub.com; ✆ **505/934-6367**), about 35 miles southwest of Santa Fe. Take I-25 south to exit 264; head west on NM 16; at the stop sign turn right onto NM 22 and it's about 10 miles.

Hiking

For in-town hiking and walking, the hands-down top spots are the Nature Conservancy's **Santa Fe Canyon Preserve ♥♥♥**, which connects you with the **Dale Ball Trail System ♥♥**, and the nearby **Randall Davey Audubon Center & Sanctuary ♥♥** (see "Parks & Refuges," p. 87). Trails in the Dale Ball Foothill Trail System are open to those with leashed dogs.

It's hard to decide which of the 1,000 or so miles of nearby national forest trails to tackle. Among the most popular areas are the **Pecos Wilderness,** with 223,000 acres, and the 58,000-acre **Jemez Mountain National Recreation Area.** Information on these and other U.S. Forest Service areas is available from the **Santa Fe National Forest Headquarters,** 11 Forest Ln. (fs.usda.gov/santafe; ✆ **505/438-5300**).

A popular but challenging hike in the national forest is the **Borrego Trail ♥**, which runs 22 miles through aspens and ponderosa pines up onto Borrego Mesa, climbing in and out of four canyons along the way. The average grade is 8%, with a maximum grade of 26%, and a total elevation gain of 4,183 feet to 9,275 feet. For those not inclined to go the distance, there's a pretty creek about 4 miles up that makes a good turnaround point. It's easy to find the trail

ONE-STOP SHOP FOR outdoor rec

A valuable resource for information on outdoor recreation is the **Public Lands Information Center,** on the south side of Santa Fe at 301 Dinosaur Trail (publiclands.org; ✆ **877/276-9404** or 505/954-2002). Here, adventurers can find out what's available on lands administered by the National Forest Service, the Bureau of Land Management, the Fish and Wildlife Service, the National Park Service, the New Mexico Department of Game and Fish (which sells hunting and fishing licenses), and New Mexico State Parks. To get there, drive south on Cerrillos Road; just past the entrance to I-25, turn left onto Rancho Viejo Blvd., then left again onto Dinosaur Trail. The office is on the corner.

head: head up Hyde Park Road toward Ski Santa Fe, just over 8 miles northeast of the city. Before going, check with the forest service regarding current trail conditions.

Also on Hyde Park Rd. near Ski Santa Fe is **Hyde Memorial State Park** ♥♥, New Mexico's first state park, with a nice campground (p. 60), a playground, visitor center, toilets, and 4.2 miles of hiking trails. These include the half-mile **Waterfall Trail** ♥, which follows a small creek to—you guessed it—a pretty waterfall, and the **West Circle Trail** ♥♥, a difficult 2.2-mile hike with a 1,000-foot elevation gain in 1 mile; the payoff is a splendid view of Santa Fe through the pines. The **East Circle Trail** ♥ completes the circle in a pleasant and fairly easy 1 mile. The highway splits the circle into its east and west parts. The park day use fee is $5 per vehicle. For information, see nmparks.com or call ✆ **505/983-7175.**

Horseback Riding

Want to experience the high desert terrain from the back of a horse? About 20 miles south of downtown just off the Turquoise Trail (aka NM14), in the historic mining town of Cerrillos, **Broken Saddle Riding Company** ♥♥ (brokensaddle.com; ✆ **505/424-7774**) offers a variety of rides, including evening outings to enjoy a sunset and/or the moonlight. You'll ride with experienced wranglers and see the West like cowboys did more than 100 years ago, rambling through the stunning Galisteo Basin south of Santa Fe.

Indoor Climbing

Santa Fe Climbing Center ♥ (3008 Cielo Court; climbsantafe.com; ✆ **505/986-8944**) is a full-service climbing center for kids (at least 5 years old) and adults. It's a perfect place to practice your rock climbing out of the rain, snow, or blazing sun. There are auto belays, top ropes, lead climbing, bouldering, and kids' walls with routes for all levels of climbers. They also have a workout space to practice yoga or take a fitness class. A day pass costs $20 for adults, $15 for children 5 to 11. Check the website or call for hours.

Skiing

There's something available for every ability level at **Ski Santa Fe** ♥ (skisanta fe.com; ✆ **505/982-4429**), about 16 miles northeast of Santa Fe at the end of NM Highway 475/Hyde Park Rd. While not as large as Taos or most Colorado resorts, it's still a fun place to ski, with 20% beginner, 40% intermediate, and 40% more advanced terrain. Lots of locals ski here, particularly on weekends, so if you can, go on a weekday. With 660 acres available, you can easily split off from and later reconnect with your group. Built on the upper reaches of 12,000-foot Tesuque Peak, the area has an average annual snowfall of 176 inches and a vertical drop of 1,725 feet. Seven lifts, including a 5,000-foot triple chair and a quad chair, serve 86 runs. Base facilities, at 10,350 feet, center on **La Casa Cafe,** with a cafeteria, full-service rental shop, boutique, and Baz coffee shop. **Totemoff's,** the mid-mountain bar and grill, has live music weekends on the patio. The ski area is open daily 9am to 4pm, usually

GETTING PAMPERED: THE spa SCENE

If traveling, skiing, or other activities have left you weary, Santa Fe has a number of relaxation options. **The Spa at Hotel Santa Fe** ♥♥, 1501 Paseo De Peralta (hotelsantafe.com; ✆ **505/955-7844**), is the only Native-owned wellness offering in Santa Fe, featuring a menu inspired by Indigenous healing practices. Treatments include a warm-stone massage, a squash-blossom body wrap and scrub, and the "Sacred Indulgence" treatment, which begins with a cedar-and-wild-sage body polish (targeting dehydrated skin and other high-altitude conditions), then a body mask of juniper, piñon, and cedar oils, followed by a full-body massage. The staff are all master-level therapists with more than a decade of experience; they use only natural and organic products in their treatments. The tranquility of the spa carries on into the outdoor pool, which is surrounded by a lush garden dotted with Native American art. The spa is open Monday to Saturday 9:30am to 6pm. Prices start at $105 for a neck and shoulder massage, $155 for a 1-hour massage, or $180 for a facial, while 2-hour rituals start at $315.

Another spa option is **Ten Thousand Waves** ♥♥, about 3½ miles northeast of Santa Fe on Hyde Park Road (ten thousandwaves.com; ✆ **505/982-9304**). This serene retreat, nestled in a grove of piñon trees, offers hot baths, saunas, and cold plunges, plus a variety of massage and other bodywork techniques. The mixed communal bath is only available for hotel and massage guests, but visitors can reserve a timed-entry 90-minute slot for community soaking in a shared private tub Monday through Thursdays at 10:45am or 7:30pm ($62 per person; book 72 hr. in advance). Seven private baths are available for $82 per person for 90 minutes. You can also arrange therapeutic massage, herbal wraps, salt glows, and facials. Most of the offerings have a Japanese influence: Japanese organic facials, the much-praised Japanese Hot Stone Massage, Shiatsu and Thai massages, Yasuragi head and neck treatment, and the Ashi Anma foot treatment. The spa is open daily 9am to 9pm. Reservations are recommended. The hotel's restaurant, which has a great selection of sake, serves lunch and dinner except Tuesdays.

from Thanksgiving to early April, depending on snow conditions. Full-day lift tickets start at $102 for adults, $82 for ages 13 to 23 and 62 to 71, $68 for children 6 to 12, and free for children under 5 or seniors over 72. For 24-hour reports on snow conditions, call ✆ **505/983-9155.** For current snow conditions, check the website.

Cross-country skiers find seemingly endless miles of snow to track in the **Santa Fe National Forest,** especially along Hyde Park Rd., and there are also suitable trails in **Hyde Memorial State Park** (see "Hiking," p. 96).

Swimming

In addition to the many pools at local hotels and motels, Santa Fe has several public city-run pools. In summer try the **Bicentennial Outdoor Swimming Pool,** 1121 Alto St. (✆ **505/955-4779**), with both a main pool and one for tots. Public indoor pools open year-round include a 25-yard pool in the **Fort Marcy Recreation Complex,** 490 Bishop's Lodge Rd. (✆ **505/955-2500**), and three pools at the **Genoveva Chavez Community Center** (p. 89). For additional information, see the City of Santa Fe website, santafenm.gov/recreation.

SANTA FE SHOPPING

Shopping in Santa Fe can be both exciting and intimidating, with myriad shops and galleries greeting you at seemingly every turn. You could easily spend several days wandering among the shops and not see them all, but with perseverance, a good eye, and a bit of luck, you should be able to find that special item or items that will make an ideal gift or be the perfect memento of your time in the Land of Enchantment.

Your first port of call should be Santa Fe Plaza, the heart of Santa Fe for more than 4 centuries. Traders battled the heat and dangers of the Santa Fe Trail every year to bring their goods here, as had earlier traders bringing goods from Mexico along the Camino Real. In and around the Plaza you'll find everything from fine art to folk art to kitschy souvenirs, but beware of a number of sellers claiming to sell Native-made items that are counterfeit pieces, often mass-produced abroad. For a guarantee of authenticity, head to the north side of the plaza, under the portal of the Palace of the Governors, where Native American artisans display their jewelry, pottery, hand-tooled leather, and other transportable goods for sale. They'll be happy to talk with you about their wares.

Don't forget the museum shops, often excellent places to find top-quality crafts. Galleries selling a superb range of fine art cluster along Canyon Road. If you're still not shopped out, head to some of the small shopping malls scattered about the city, such as DeVargas Center (see p. 100).

And don't worry about having to lug your purchases home—practically every shop and gallery can easily ship them for you.

The Top Art Galleries

Allan Houser Gallery ♥♥ Considered one of the most important American artists of the 20th century, the late Allan Houser, a Chiricahua Apache, was a fine painter and teacher, but is probably best known for his bronze sculptures. You can see and purchase them here. 125 Lincoln Ave., Ste. 112. allanhouser.com. ✆ **505/982-4705.**

Charlotte Jackson Fine Art ♥ With the works of some 30 artists, this gallery presents contemporary American and European art in a wide variety of styles—concrete, light and space, monochrome, modernism, and color field painting. 554 S. Guadalupe St. charlottejackson.com. ✆ **505/989-8688.**

Chiaroscuro Contemporary Art ♥ Specializing in contemporary abstraction, this gallery represents artists working from a variety of perspectives, including Native American, Australian Aboriginal, and American Southwestern. You'll also find large-scale photography, textile, wood, glass, and ceramic art. 558 Canyon Rd. chiaroscurogallery.com. ✆ **505/992-0711.**

Gerald Peters Gallery ♥♥♥ Many consider this Santa Fe's top gallery, displaying a wide range of fine art. Works include classic Western, 20th-century modernism, American impressionism, Ashcan and American realism, contemporary, naturalism, sculpture, photography, and jewelry, with the founders of the Taos Society of Artists and Santa Fe Art Colony well represented. 1011 Paseo de Peralta. gpgallery.com. ✆ **505/954-5700.**

LewAllen Galleries ♥♥ Among Santa Fe's top galleries, this spot displays works by modernists from the late 1800s to the mid–20th century, plus contemporary artists, in a magnificent 14,000-square-foot space. You'll see a variety of paintings, sculptures, and works on paper and glass. 1613 Paseo de Peralta. lewallengalleries.com. ✆ **505/988-3250.**

Manitou Galleries ♥ Contemporary representational paintings, many depicting the Southwest, are the theme at this large gallery, which also has prints, sculpture, glass, and extremely fine jewelry. 123 W. Palace Ave. www.legacygallery.com. ✆ **505/986-0440;** also 225 Canyon Rd. ✆ **505/986-9833.**

A Welcome Albuquerque Import

Heavy-duty shopping can be tiring, so if you need a recharge, stop at the offshoot of the Albuquerque hotel Los Poblanos (p. 181), which opened an outpost of its **Farm Shop** in a renovated 1930s gas station at 201 Washington Ave. in Santa Fe. Beyond the displays of honey, soaps, and home items is **Bar Norte** ♥♥ (✆ **505/808-1713**), a cozy retro tasting room that showcases the hotel's inhouse line of gins distilled with ingredients from its beloved farm, including piñon, rose, hawthorn, chamomile, and lavender. There's also coffee, tea, and light bites, including a cheeseboard. The shop is open Tuesday through Saturday 11am to 9pm, Sunday and Monday 11am to 6pm. The bar is open Tuesday through Friday 3 to 9pm, Saturday and Sunday noon to 9pm.

Morning Star Gallery ♥♥ Looking for genuine Native American artworks? This is the place to come. From New Mexican antiques, Southwestern textiles, and beadwork to works by today's young Pueblo potters and silversmiths, everything that's Native American is represented here. 513 Canyon Rd. morningstargallery.com. ✆ **505/982-8187.**

Niman Fine Art ♥ The works of the acclaimed Hopi-Tewa painter and sculptor Dan Namingha are on display at this small gallery, which also hosts the modern and carved works of his two sons, Arlo and Michael. 125 Lincoln Ave. namingha.com. ✆ **505/988-5091.**

Peyton Wright Gallery ♥ To see a wide variety of art in one place, stop at this fine gallery, housed in a historic building near the plaza. Although it specializes in 20th-century postwar and modern American art, it also has a fine collection of Spanish Colonial devotional art, Spanish Colonial silver, pre-Columbian objects, and works from around the world. 237 E. Palace Ave. peytonwright.com. ✆ **800/879-8898** or 505/989-9888.

photo-eye Gallery ♥ Contemporary photography is the main thrust of this excellent gallery, though it also shows some earlier works. Photography styles vary considerably, with both established and beginning photographers represented; it's practically guaranteed that you'll see photos you love as well as some works that you think belong in the trash can. 541 S. Guadalupe St. photoeye.com. ✆ **505/988-5159, ext. 202.**

SITE Santa Fe ♥ This sleek and sprawling space kicked off the Railyard Arts District, an offshoot cultural hub that's now home to several galleries. A lot of big names have come through here, including local stars like Bruce Nauman and Jeffrey Gibson as well as national artists like Ed Ruscha and Jenny Holzer. 1606 Paseo De Peralta. sitesantafe.org. ✆ **505/989-1199.**

Malls & Shopping Centers

DeVargas Center ♥♥ This is your all-around shopping center, with specialty shops, clothing boutiques, an upscale jewelry store, a cooking shop and school, beauty salons and spa, and of course eateries from healthy to pizza to fast food standards. There's also a Starbucks, Sprouts, Baskin Robbins, CVS Pharmacy, even a U.S. Post Office. Not to mention a pet boutique! N. Guadalupe St. and Paseo de Peralta. www.frpltd.com. ✆ **505/982-2655.**

Markets

Santa Fe Artists Market ♥ Every summer Saturday, a rotating display of work from over 100 local artists and craftspeople sets up along the railroad just north of the water tower, selling everything from gallery-standard paintings to small knickknacks that make for good souvenirs. Look out for Lynda Ferman's bright, wheel-thrown, red earthenware ceramics; wooden jewelry by Griffith Evans; and Laura Star's printed textiles. Santa Fe Railyard, north of the water tower. Mar–Dec Sat 9am–2pm. santafeartistsmarket.com. ✆ **505/737-9311.**

Santa Fe Farmers' Market ♥♥ A large space with a list of vendors as long as your arm, this farmers' market has everything from fruits, vegetables, and flowers to cheeses, cider, and salsas. If you're an early riser, wander through and enjoy good coffee and excellent breakfast burritos. Open 8am to 1pm on Saturdays year-round, also on Tuesdays from May through November, plus occasional special market days. Santa Fe Railyard, off Paseo de Peralta. santafefarmersmarket.com. ✆ **505/983-4098.**

More Shopping A to Z

BOOKS

Collected Works Bookstore & Coffeehouse ♥ Stop in for an espresso, or if caffeine isn't your friend, an organic apple cider or chai. While you're sipping, peruse the many shelves containing books on the Southwest, travel, nature, cooking, and even novels. The shop offers readings, book signings, and occasional lectures. 202 Galiseo St. cwbookstore.com. ✆ **505/988-4226.**

Garcia Street Books ♥ Here you can browse a fine selection of titles on the Southwest, plus biographies, collectibles, cookbooks, and more, although there isn't much in the way of novels. The staff is very knowledgeable and happy to help. 376 Garcia St. garciastreetbooks.com. ✆ **505/986-0151.**

CRAFTS

Good Folk ♥ The brightly colored animals are real eye-catchers—this small shop is filled with them, not to mention the crazy snakes all over the wall. There is Mexican, New Mexican, and Navajo folk art, and a few other things thrown in just for variety. 141 Lincoln Ave. at Marcy St. goodfolknm.com. ✆ **505/983-1660.**

Nambé Outlet ♥ First sand-cast and handcrafted at the Nambé Pueblo, this metal alloy has since been fashioned into almost every cooking, serving, and decorating piece imaginable. It's quite lovely, but also quite soft, so be sure to ask about the care required to keep it shining. 104 W. San Francisco St. nambe.com. ✆ **505/988-3574.** Also at 924 Paseo de Peralta. ✆ **505/988-5528.**

FOOD

The Chile Shop ♥♥ Chile ristras, dried chile powder and pods, chile jelly (it's great with cream cheese and crackers), green chile stew mix—everything chile can be found in this fun little shop. It also stocks cookbooks, pottery, dinnerware, table linens, and other housewares. 109 E. Water St. thechileshop.com. ✆ **505/983-6080.**

Kakawa Chocolate House ♥♥ There's no better combination—or one that better captures the region—than chocolate and chile, and the husband-and-wife duo behind this shop puts it on full display with creations inspired by Aztec and Mayan flavors. In addition to assorted chocolates candies (try the red chile caramels), Kakawa is known for its elixirs, which are less sweet hot chocolates with interesting profiles. The Mesoamerican elixir, for example, is made with spices and herbs. 1050 Paseo De Peralta. kakawachocolates.com. ✆ **505/982-0388.**

Got Rocks?

A timeless adventure tucked into a small space just off the southwest side of Santa Fe Plaza, the **Meteorite, Mineral and Fossil Gallery,** 110 Don Gaspar Ave. (meteoritefossilgallery.com; ✆ **505/988-3299**), is part shop, part museum, and a fascinating experience for collectors and students. Rockhound Charlie Snell has been hunting fossils, minerals, and meteorites for 25 years, traveling around the world in search of items for his collection, which he displays and sells here. He likes to educate people about finding meteorites and saving fossils, and his fossil room is set up in a geological timeline. There is also a striking collection of sculpture from India and Tibet, and large items suitable for the yard or inside.

Señor Murphy Candymaker ♥ Everybody knows that chocolate is the most important food group. And Señor Murphy's law is to always use the best and freshest ingredients in small, handmade batches. Add to that the Southwestern flavors of chile and piñon nuts, and you have an unbeatable combination. 100 E. San Francisco St. at the La Fonda Hotel. senormurphy.com. ✆ **505/982-0461.** Also in the DeVargas Center (✆ **505/780-5179**).

GIFTS & SOUVENIRS

Cutlery of Santa Fe ♥♥ These knives are almost too beautiful to use—but use them you should. The variety runs the gamut from practical to decorative, functional to fun in this tiny shop wedged into a corner of La Fonda Hotel. 107 Old Santa Fe Trail. cutleryofsantafenm.com. ✆ **505/982-3262.**

Double Take ♥♥ Since its opening in 1987, the Double Take has become the choice for many travelers, locals, collectors, and bargain hunters. As New Mexico's largest and most complete consignment store, the Double Take blends retail and resale with a bit of everything, from the ordinary to the extraordinary—Western stuff, fetishes, home furnishings, affordable vintage and designer women's clothing, accessories, books, and more. Come in and browse. 321 S. Guadalupe St. santafedoubletake.com. ✆ **505/989-8886.**

HOME DECOR

Artesanos Imports Company ♥ Colorful tiles from Mexico, for every imaginable use from house numbers to countertops, are found here. There's a huge selection of Talavera tile and pottery, as well as tinwork, light fixtures, and many other accessories for the home. 1414 Maclovia St., west of Cerrillos Rd. and a bit south of St. Michael's Dr. artesanos.com. ✆ **505/471-8020.**

Casa Nova ♥ Amid this wild gathering of unusual yet attractive furnishings and accessories, you'll find everything from tableware to jewelry, furniture to weavings—all in geometric patterns or bright colors. 530 S. Guadalupe St. (in the Gross Kelly Warehouse). casanovagallery.com. ✆ **505/983-8558.**

Green River Pottery ♥♥ This studio and gallery features stoneware ceramics by Theo Helmstadter, whose works are wheel-thrown from New

Mexico clay, highly fired, and designed for daily use. His designs are simple, usable, and elegant, from teaware and bowls to platters and large-scale vessels. The studio also offers workshops, classes, and individual sessions. 1710 Lena St. greenriverpottery.com. ✆ **505/614-6952.**

Jackalope ♥♥ You have to see this to believe it. Innumerable items from India, Mexico, Thailand, Bali, Africa, China, and Egypt are carried at this international bazaar, with clothing and jewelry, pottery and textiles, garden decor and folk art, furniture and fountains spread all over. It's fascinating and fun. The owner has been traveling and buying stuff to sell here since 1976. 2820 Cerrillos Rd. jackalope.com. ✆ **505/471-8539.**

Seret & Sons ♥♥ After living in Afghanistan for 2 decades, exporting sheepskin coats, cotton dhurries, and other specialty crafts from the region to the U.S., Ira Seret and his wife, Sylvia, decided to settle in Santa Fe. Their 80,000-square-foot shop houses one of the country's largest collections of crafts from Central and South Asia, a colorful assemblage of mosaics, inlaid woodwork, and one-of-a-kind Silk Road pieces. 224 Galisteo St. seretandsons.org. ✆ **505/988-9151.**

Stone Forest ♥♥ You'll find marvelously crafted designs for the bath, kitchen, and garden sculpted from stone, bronze, copper, iron, and wood in this out-of-the-way shop behind the railway station. 213 South St. Francis Dr. stoneforest.com. ✆ **505/986-8883.**

JEWELRY

Tresa Vorenberg Goldsmiths ♥♥ Over 30 artists are represented in this fine jewelry store. The stunning pieces, with some delightfully imaginative designs, are all handcrafted, and custom commissions are welcome. 656 Canyon Rd. tvgoldsmiths.com. ✆ **505/988-7215.**

WEARABLES

Back at the Ranch ♥ You want cowboy boots? This is the place for you, with an incredible array of handmade boots, plus chic Western wear. 209 E. Marcy St. backattheranch.com. ✆ **505/989-8110.**

4Kinship ♥ Founded by Amy Denet Deal, a Diné designer, this Canyon Road boutique is the first Native-owned clothing store in the city. Along with Deal's signature upcycled hand-dyed pieces, the shop stocks jewelry and accessories by other Indigenous designers. 812 Canyon Rd. 4kinship.com.

O'Farrell Hat Company ♥♥ O'Farrell's has been making custom felt hats for over 30 years. The fit, style and shape, materials, and skill and craftsmanship that go into each hat make an O'Farrell hat just about the best you can find. 111 E. San Francisco St. ofarrellhatco.com. ✆ **505/989-9666.**

Overland Sheepskin Company ♥ For leather coats, blazers, hats, purses, or other finely made leather items, plus sheepskin slippers, coats, and more, this is the place to visit. Overland has been making these goods since 1973. 74 E. San Francisco St. overland.com. ✆ **505/986-0757.**

THE PERFORMING ARTS IN SANTA FE

The performing arts have recently become so strong, they almost eclipse the visual art scene in Santa Fe. Numerous companies call the City Different home, including the world-renowned Santa Fe Opera, and there are also festivals galore. Many companies perform in a variety of venues, and ticket prices vary tremendously. Specifics are available on websites, or by calling the phone number listed.

Classical Music

Desert Chorale ♥♥ This marvelous vocal group performs a repertoire spanning seven centuries of music from early polyphony to contemporary works. Singers from all over the United States audition for a place in the 24-member ensemble. There are summer and winter festivals, with performances at various locations in Santa Fe and throughout the Southwest. desertchorale.org. ✆ **505/988-2282.**

Santa Fe Opera ♥♥♥ For over 60 years, opera lovers have been drawn to the City Different to enjoy world-class opera in a spectacular setting. With breathtaking views in all directions, the fusion of nature and art leaves an enduring impression on all who visit. Although the dramatic adobe theatre has a roof these days, the open-air feel remains, with the amphitheater's sides still open, as well as the back of the stage (depending on the opera being performed). When there's a lightning storm—as there often is in this high-desert setting—it certainly adds to the drama taking place on stage. To help opera-goers better follow the drama, the Crosby Theatre's next-generation electronic libretto system provides individual seatback screens which translate performances into English or Spanish. Many patrons come early to enjoy a festive "tailgate picnic" in the parking lot before heading to the performance. Five operas are presented in repertory each July and August, in a blend of new, rarely performed, and standard works. Near the end of the season, apprentice artists take the stage for two evenings of fully staged scenes from this repertoire. For anyone not already an opera buff, these apprentice performances can be a perfect introduction to this magical music. 7 miles N of Santa Fe off U.S. 84/285 exit 168; follow signs to parking lot. santafeopera.org. ✆ **800/280-4654** or 505/986-5900.

A Home for the Arts

Santa Fe's year-round cultural hub is the Moorish-style 1931 movie palace turned state-of-the-art performance space, the **Lensic Performing Arts Center** (211 W. San Francisco St.; lensic.org; ✆ **505/988-1234** box office, 505/988-7050 information). Its events calendar offers everything from theater, music, and dance performances to literary happenings, films, and lectures. There's a complete schedule on their website.

Santa Fe Pro Musica Chamber Orchestra & Ensemble ♥♥ Pro Musica brings together outstanding musicians to delight and educate audiences of all ages. Its September–April season offers a variety of classical music programs in historic Santa Fe venues, including performances by orchestra, string quartet, chamber ensemble, and vocalists. santafepromusica.com. ✆ **505/988-4640.**

Santa Fe Symphony Orchestra and Chorus ♥ Founded in 1984, this professional group continues to offer great performances of classical and popular works. The season runs from September to May. santafesymphony.org. ✆ **505/983-3530** or 505/988-1234 box office.

Dance

Aspen Santa Fe Ballet ♥ This company brings classically trained dancers and choreographers from around the world to produce new and adventuresome pieces in both Santa Fe and Aspen, Colorado. Performances take place at the **Lensic Performing Arts Center** (p. 104). Office 550B St. Michael's Dr. aspensantafeballet.com. ✆ **505/983-5591.**

Music Festivals & Concert Series

Santa Fe Chamber Music Festival ♥♥ This festival brings together exceptional artists from around the world. Concerts are offered from mid-July to late August in the St. Francis Auditorium and the Lensic Performing Arts Center, with programs featuring new music by a composer in residence, plus free youth concerts, preconcert lectures, and open rehearsals. sfcmf.org. ✆ **505/982-1890** ticket office.

Theater Companies

Santa Fe Playhouse ♥ With uninterrupted seasons since its founding in 1922, the Santa Fe Playhouse claims to be "the oldest continuously running theatre west of the Mississippi." Although it has undergone many transformations over the years, it continues, through live theater, to celebrate the rich texture of the many diverse peoples that make up the Santa Fe community. The stage is never dark, and offers almost every genre of theatrical arts over the course of the season. 142 E. De Vargas St. santafeplayhouse.org. ✆ **505/988-4262.**

Theater Grottesco ♥♥ This troupe writes all of its plays as a collective, creating a new kind of performance that is visual, explosive, and full of surprise. They rely on the art of clowning—as well as dance, movement, and gestural communication—more than on a scripted narrative. The end result can be disconcerting, as nothing they present is typical of traditional American theater. Expect to be shocked, confused, or confounded, but above all, struck silly with laughter. Performances take place at whatever venue seems most appropriate. theatergrottesco.org. ✆ **505/474-8400.**

SANTA FE NIGHTLIFE

In addition to the clubs and bars listed below, a number of hotels and restaurants have bars and lounges that get lively after the sun goes down (see "Where to Stay in Santa Fe," p. 50). Entertainment schedules and cover charges vary.

CAVA Santa Fe Lounge ♥♥ Billing itself as Santa Fe's community living room, this bar in the Eldorado Hotel & Spa has an excellent wine list, good food, and live entertainment most Wednesday through Saturday evenings. The type of music varies, but it won't be heavy metal. At the Eldorado Hotel & Spa, 309 W. San Francisco St. eldoradohotel.com. ✆ **505/988-4455.**

Cowgirl BBQ ♥♥ If you're going to bump into someone you know in Santa Fe, chances are it'll be at the Cowgirl. It's that kind of place: raucous, sprawling, and popular with both visitors and locals. Happy hour is 3 to 6pm Monday through Friday, offering $2 off seasonal appetizers, the house margarita for $4.50, and more. There's a great front patio (heated and enclosed in winter, open in the summer) and a kid-friendly eating area in the back with a playground. Inside there are pool tables and a rambling bar/dining room with live music, karaoke, or a DJ most days, and a menu of barbecue favorites. For drinks, try a green chile margarita with a red chile salt rim, or a "lava lamp," which mixes a beer float with a margarita. See you at the Cowgirl! 319 S. Guadalupe St. cowgirlsantafe.com. ✆ **505/982-2565.**

Del Charro Saloon ♥ What's better than cozying up with a margarita next to a fireplace on a chilly Santa Fe evening? The signature house margarita is made with 100% agave tequila and real juice, which you can enjoy at this laid-back saloon attached to the Inn of the Governors. The burgers and the green chile chicken chowder are both tasty and satisfying, whether you're by the fire or at one of the copper-topped tables in the semi-enclosed patio dining room. At the Inn of the Governors, 101 W. Alameda St. delcharro.com. ✆ **505/954-0320.**

Santa Fe Brewing Company ♥ You may have seen Santa Fe Brewing's beers at a supermarket or liquor store, but it's always better at the source. Founded in 1988 by thirsty people desperate for a good beer, the brewery's sprawling headquarters is off Highway 14—the extension of Cerrillos Road—at the south end of Santa Fe, away from the hubbub of downtown; there's also **The Brakeroom,** 510 Galisteo St. (✆ **505/780-8648**), a smaller in-town outpost with a lively patio and nightly food trucks. The focus is on beer, of course, with over a dozen varieties available—seasonal brews and other unusual varieties, like the English-style Nut Brown Ale, the full-bodied Java Stout (with its extra punch of locally roasted New Guinea coffee beans), or the Chicken Killer, a smooth barley wine beer with twice the ingredients of the brewery's other beers and only half their liquid extracted, giving it a deep ruby red color. The headquarters also offer free tours and tastings of small-batch brews, available upon request. 35 Fire Pl. santafebrewing.com. ✆ **505/424-3333.**

Second Street Brewery ♥♥ After a hot summer hike or a day on the ski slopes, nothing hits the spot like a pint of ale and a plate of loaded potato skins. Second Street Brewery offers both in a convivial setting, often with live music on weekends. There are rotating seasonal brews, and eight drafts on tap—the cream stout is a standout—plus a menu of serviceable bar fare like turkey wraps and fish and chips. If you can't choose among the brews, order a sampler. The original Second Street location is a big, lively space, especially when the music is happening in the evenings. Another location in the Railyard (1607 Paseo de Peralta, #10, ✆ **505/989-3278**) has similar fare, and at least eight beers on tap—the website lists the current offerings. 2920 Rufina St. secondstreetbrewery.com. ✆ **505/930-5192.**

Secreto Lounge ♥♥♥ The bar in the historic Hotel St. Francis (p. 52) is a not-so-secret destination for an expertly made craft cocktail. The staff uses local herbs, fresh fruits, vegetables, bitters, and local spirits in many of the concoctions, like the As Soon As I Get Home, a combination of chamomile-infused tequila, lemon juice, ginger-and-agave syrup, and emulsified honey powder. Of all the drinks, the best may be the signature Smoked Sage Margarita, especially enjoyable while people-watching on the outdoor patio. Inside, wooden-cross light fixtures provide a faux-rustic vibe. Guests can order food from the hotel restaurant Wolf and Roadrunner—try the bison croquettes or orzo risotto made with wild-boar bacon, roasted garlic cream, spinach, and aged gouda. The service can be somewhat casual, so don't plan to be anywhere else in a hurry. In the Hotel St. Francis, 210 Don Gaspar Ave. hotelstfrancis.com. ✆ **505/983-5700.**

EXCURSIONS FROM SANTA FE

One of the things that makes Santa Fe such a popular destination is the variety of things to see and do in the surrounding areas. So, after you've seen what seems like every American Indian pot, piece of Hispanic folk art, and work of fine art in the world, take a break and hit the road. Head to a pueblo or two to see where those pots are actually made and the people who make them. Check out the birthplace of the atomic bomb, poke around historic ruins that show the clashes of cultures in New Mexico's past, or visit some old Spanish villages along the High Road to Taos that have barely changed in a hundred years.

Exploring the Northern Pueblos

Of the eight pueblos in northern New Mexico, six of them—Tesuque, Pojoaque, Nambe, San Ildefonso, Ohkay Owingeh, and Santa Clara—are within about 30 miles of Santa Fe. Picuris (San Lorenzo) is on the High Road to Taos (p. 123), and Taos Pueblo is just outside the town of Taos (see chapter 7, p. 148).

You can easily get to each of the six pueblos described in this section in day trips from Santa Fe. While you may not have time to visit them all, if you only

Pueblo Etiquette

Personal dwellings and/or important historic sites at pueblos must be respected as such. Obey the signage—if it says "off limits," it is. Many of the structures are old and fragile, so please don't climb on them. Remember that you are a guest here and peeking into doors or windows is rude. Don't enter sacred grounds, such as cemeteries and kivas.

If you attend a dance or ceremony, remain silent while it is taking place and refrain from applause when it's over. Many pueblos prohibit photography or sketches; others require you to pay a fee for a permit. If you don't respect the privacy of the people who live there, you'll be asked to leave.

have one day free, you can get a good feel for the ancient Indian lifestyle by combining visits to San Ildefonso, with its broad plaza, and Ohkay Owingeh, the birthplace of Pope (Poh-*pay*), who led the Pueblo Revolt of 1680.

For additional information on each of these pueblos, plus others in the state, go to **indianpueblo.org**. Select "New Mexico's 19 Pueblos" from the menu at the top. All the pueblos are periodically closed to the public; call to check their schedules and current hours.

TESUQUE PUEBLO ♥

Excavations confirm that a pueblo has existed here since at least the year C.E. 1200; accordingly, this pueblo is now on the National Register of Historic Places. The 800 residents at Tesuque (Te-*soo*-keh) Pueblo (✆ **505/983-2667**), about 10 miles north of Santa Fe on US 84/285, remain faithful to their traditional religion, rituals, and ceremonies. The Tesuque people played an important part in the 1680 Pueblo Revolt, with two of its members carrying the news of the uprising to all corners of the territory.

When you come to the welcome sign at the pueblo, turn right, go a block, and park on the right. You'll see the plaza off to the left. There's not a lot to see; in recent years renovation has brought a new look to some of the homes around it. There's a big open area where dances are held, and the **San Diego Church,** completed in 2004 on the site of an 1888 structure that burned down. It's the fifth church on the pueblo's plaza since 1641. Visitors are asked to remain in this area. You'll find many crafts at a gallery on the plaza's southeast corner; some Tesuque women are especially known for their skilled pottery. Ignacia Duran's black-and-white and red micaceous pottery and Teresa Tapia's miniatures and pots with animal figures are especially noteworthy.

You'll know that you're approaching the pueblo when you see a large store near the highway. If you're driving north and you get to the unusual Camel Rock formation, you've missed the pueblo entrance. Admission to the pueblo is free; photography, sketching, and painting are not permitted.

One of New Mexico's newest casinos is **Tesuque Casino** (tesuquecasino.com; ✆ **800/462-2635**), offering over 800 slot machines plus ten table games. It's located just north of the Santa Fe Opera, at U.S. 84/285 exit 171.

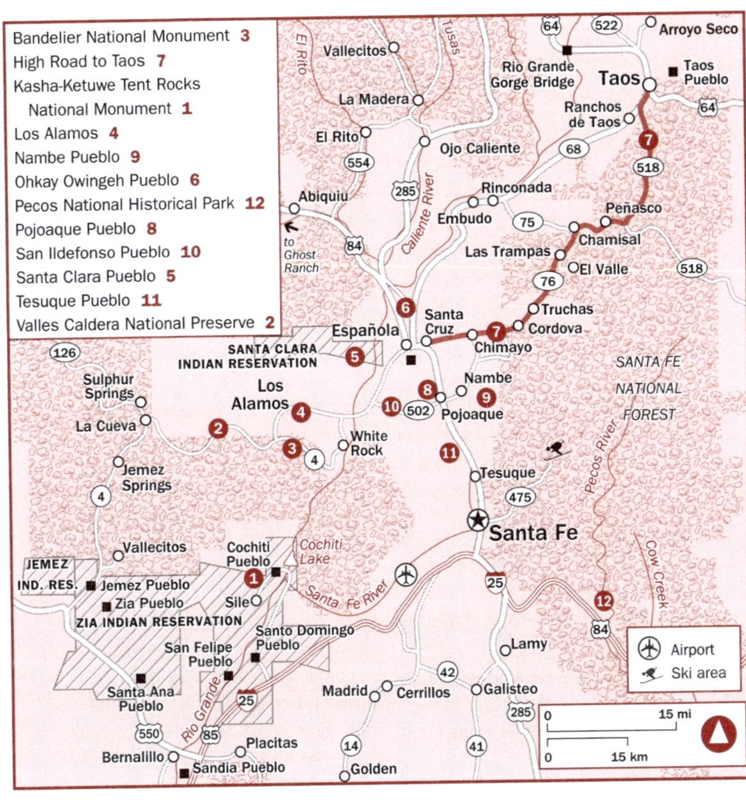

POJOAQUE PUEBLO ♥

Though small and without a definable village, Pojoaque (Po-*hwa*-keh) Pueblo (pojoaque.org; ✆ **505/455-4500**) is important as a center for traveler services; in fact, Pojoaque, in its Tewa form, means "water-drinking place." It's about 6 miles north of Tesuque Pueblo on US 84/285, at the junction of NM 502. The historical accounts of the Pojoaque people are uncertain, but we do know that in 1890 smallpox took its toll on them, forcing most pueblo residents to abandon their village. Since the 1930s, the population has gradually increased, and in 1990, a war chief and two war captains were appointed. Today, the **Poeh Cultural Center and Museum** (poehcenter.org; ✆ **505/455-5041**), on US 84/285, operated by the pueblo, provides a good roadside peek into pueblo arts, offering a museum, cultural center, and artists' studios. It's situated within a complex of adobe buildings, including the three-story Sun Tower that houses the sculptural works of renowned artist Roxanne Swentzell. There are frequent artist demonstrations, exhibitions, and, in the warmer months,

feast days THROUGH THE YEAR

Pueblos have special feast days throughout the year; visiting a pueblo on one of these days can be quite a special experience indeed, because you'll see the pueblo people celebrating in a very genuine way—these dances are the real thing, not some show for tourists. However, be aware that there are often special restrictions, such as no photography, and some areas of the pueblos will be off-limits to outsiders. Times of dances and ceremonies are determined by nature and/or a sequence of events, not by the 24-hour clock non-Puebloans typically run on: Any published time is approximate. Also, the specific dances to be performed are occasionally changed depending on events known only to the tribal members. Call a few days ahead to check if a specific dance is important to you. (Contact phone numbers are available at indianpueblo.org.)

Here's a calendar of many of the northern pueblos' feast days:

January 1: Transfer of Canes to New Pueblo Tribal Officials is marked with dances at most pueblos.

January 23: San Ildefonso Pueblo's Annual Feast Day features buffalo and deer dances.

April: Easter weekend features basket and corn dances at most pueblos.

June 24: Ohkay Owingeh Pueblo's San Juan Feast Day features buffalo and Comanche dances.

August 4: Santo Domingo Pueblo's St. Dominic Feast Day is celebrated with corn dances.

August 9 and 10: Picuris Pueblo celebrates San Lorenzo Feast Days with mass and sunset dances.

August 12: Santa Clara Pueblo has corn and harvest dances on Santa Clara Feast Day.

October 4: Nambe Pueblo celebrates Saint Francis of Assisi Feast Day with buffalo and deer dances.

November 12: Tesuque Pueblo observes San Diego Feast Day with harvest, buffalo, deer, flag, or Comanche dances.

December 12: Pojoaque Pueblo celebrates the annual feast day of Our Lady of Guadalupe with a buffalo dance.

Christmas Eve: Most pueblos offer dances, some with torchlight processionals following mass.

December 25: Ohkay Owingeh Pueblo performs the Matachines dance (p. 26), depicting the subjugation of the Pueblo people by the Spaniards, followed on **December 26** by a turtle dance ceremony.

December 28: Picuris Pueblo observes Holy Innocents Day with special children's dances.

For feast days at **Taos Pueblo,** see p. 149.

traditional ceremonial dances. Indigenous pottery, embroidery, silverwork, and beadwork are available for sale at the Buffalo Thunder Resort & Casino 3 miles south.

Admission to the pueblo is free; photography, sketching, and painting are not permitted. The pueblo also operates a casino, **Cities of Gold Casino** (citiesofgold.com; ✆ **800/455-0515**).

NAMBE PUEBLO ♥

The name means "round earth," and this 700-year-old Tewa-speaking pueblo, with a solar-powered tribal headquarters, sits at the foot of the Sangre de Cristo range. Drive north on US 84/285 about 3 miles from Pojoaque to NM 503, turn right, and travel until you see a sign for Nambe Falls. Turn right on NP 101 for another 2 miles to reach Nambe Pueblo (nambepueblo.org; ✆ **505/455-4400**). Only a few original pueblo buildings remain, including a large round kiva, used today in ceremonies. Pueblo artisans make woven belts, beadwork, and brown micaceous pottery. A 2-mile trail loops around a former bison pasture and offers sweeping views of the pueblo's lands and surrounding mountains. The **Nambe Falls & Lake Recreation Area** (✆ **505/455-2304**), usually open April through October, includes **Nambe Falls,** a stunning three-tier drop through a cleft in a rock face about 4 miles beyond the pueblo. You can reach the falls via a 15-minute hike on a rocky, clearly marked path leaving from the picnic area. A recreational site at the reservoir offers fishing, boating (non-motor or electric motor boats only), hiking, camping, and picnicking.

Admission to the pueblo is free. Admission to the recreation area is $20 per vehicle for day use; fishing, boating, and camping fees are separate and varied. Bring cash, as the Pueblo does not accept checks or credit cards. Photography, filming, sketching, and painting are allowed in the recreation area; in the pueblo, taking videos is prohibited, and still photography, sketching, or painting requires a permit. Check with the Nambe Pueblo Governor's Office for the permitting process. Remember: cameras and phones can be confiscated. It's open 8am to 5pm when the gate closes, but always call ahead to confirm access.

SAN ILDEFONSO PUEBLO ♥♥

Rebellious San Ildefonso was one of the last pueblos to succumb to the reconquest spearheaded by Don Diego de Vargas in 1692. Seen from the pueblo, the volcanic Black Mesa came to be a symbol of the San Ildefonso people's strength: whenever the pueblo felt itself threatened by enemy forces, the residents, along with members of other pueblos, would take refuge on the butte, returning to the valley only when starvation set in. From Pojoaque, head west on NM 502 and drive about 6 miles to the turnoff for San Ildefonso Pueblo (www.sanipueblo.org; ✆ **505/455-3549**), or *Pox Oge,* as it is called in its own Tewa language, meaning "where the water cuts through"—possibly named such because of the way the Rio Grande cuts through the mountains nearby before flowing into White Rock Canyon to the south. This pueblo has a broad, dusty plaza, with a kiva on one side, ancient dwellings on the other, and a church at the far end. It's nationally famous for its matte-finish, black-on-black pottery, developed by San Ildefonso's legendary potter Maria Martinez in the 1920s. A few shops surround the plaza, and the **San Ildefonso Pueblo Museum,** tucked away in the governor's office beyond the plaza, open Monday through Friday during pueblo visiting hours. Many craftspeople also sell

THE GREAT PUEBLO revolt

By the 17th century, the Spanish subjugation of the Native tribes in the region had left them virtual slaves, forced to provide corn, venison, cloth, and labor. They were also forced to participate in Spanish religious ceremonies and to abandon their own religious practices. Under no circumstances were their ceremonies allowed; those caught participating in them were severely punished. In 1676, several Puebloans were accused of sorcery and jailed in Santa Fe. Later they were led to the plaza, where they were flogged or hanged. This incident became a turning point in Indian-Spanish relations, generating an overwhelming feeling of rage in the community. One of the accused, an Ohkay Owingeh Pueblo religious leader named Pope (Poh-*pay*), became a leader in the Great Pueblo Revolt of 1680, which resulted in freedom from Spanish rule for 12 years.

out of their homes; pick up information for a self-guided walking tour from the museum.

Admission costs $5 per person or $20 per car, and there are additional fees for photography, sketching or painting, and fishing. The pueblo is generally open daily from 9am to 4pm, though as always, calling ahead is a good idea.

OHKAY OWINGEH PUEBLO (SAN JUAN) ♥

The largest of the Tewa-speaking pueblos and headquarters of the Eight Northern Indian Pueblos Council (enipc.org; ✆ **505/747-1593**), Ohkay Owingeh (formerly called San Juan Pueblo by non-Puebloans) is 25 miles north of Santa Fe on US 84/285; turn off on NM 68 just before Española, then drive north to NM 74. Ohkay Owingeh (✆ **505/852-4400**) is situated on the east side of the Rio Grande, opposite the site of San Gabriel, the first Spanish settlement west of the Mississippi River and the first capital of New Spain. In 1598, the Spanish, impressed with the openness and helpfulness of the people of the pueblo, decided to establish a capital there (it was moved to Santa Fe 10 years later), making Ohkay Owingeh the first pueblo to be subjected to Spanish colonization. The Puebloans were generous, providing food, clothing, shelter, and fuel—they even helped sustain the settlement when its leader Conquistador Juan de Oñate became preoccupied with his search for gold and neglected the needs of his people. The leader of the eventual 1680 pueblo revolt against the Spanish (above) was from Ohkay Owingeh, although the revolt was organized in Taos and Ohkay Owingeh played no special role. Today the pueblo is known for its micaceous pottery, weaving, and painting. The Ohkay Owingeh people live comfortably in 21st-century America while retaining their traditional culture and worldview. Thus, two rectangular kivas flank the church in the main plaza, and *caciques* (pueblo priests) share power with civil authorities.

Admission is free; ask about fees for photography, sketching, painting, or access to tribal lakes. The pueblo runs the **Ohkay Casino Resort Hotel** (ohkay.com; ✆ **505/747-1668**).

SANTA CLARA PUEBLO ♥

There's an intriguing mix of the old and the new at the big Santa Clara Pueblo (✆ **505/753-7326**), south of Española on NM 30. Its village sprawls across the river basin near the beautiful Black Mesa, rows of tract homes surrounding an adobe central area. Although it's in an incredible setting, the pueblo itself is not much to see; however, a trip through it will give a real feel for the contemporary lives of the community, where artisan elders work with children to teach them their native Tewa language, which is on the brink of extinction because so many now speak English. On the main route to the old village, stop by the visitor center, also known as the neighborhood center, to get directions to small shops that sell distinctive black incised Santa Clara pottery, red burnished pottery, baskets, and other crafts. One stunning sight here is the cemetery, on the west side of the church: Look over the 4-foot wall to admire this primitive site, with plain wooden crosses and some graves adorned with plastic flowers.

The past comes to life at the well-preserved **Puye Cliff Dwellings** ♥♥ (puyecliffdwellings.com; ✆ **505/917-6650**), located on Santa Clara Pueblo land (from the Puye Cliffs Welcome Center on NM 30, head about 7 miles west on Indian Route 601/NM 5). Stop first at the Harvey House and exhibit hall, which tells some of the history of the site. Separate tours take you to centuries-old cliff dwellings (this includes a fairly steep hike up to a 200-foot cliff face), and up to the top of the mesa. It's believed that these dwellings were occupied from the 900s to about C.E. 1580; at its height Puye had about 1,500 residents and was the center for a number of villages on the Pajarito Plateau. Guides, descendants of those people, help interpret the history. The site is open daily 8am to 6pm April through September, 8am to 4pm the rest of the year. Tours start on the hour beginning at 9am (the last starts 2 hr. before closing); reservations are not required but are recommended for groups. The 2-hour Adventure Tour, which encompasses both the shorter Cliffside and Mesa Top tours, includes both 10-foot and 30-foot ladders plus a narrow ledge carved out of the stone—not for the faint of heart. It is closed the week before Easter, June 13, August 12, and Christmas Day. The Adventure tour costs $35 for adults, $33 for seniors over 54, college students, and military personnel. Fees for the Cliffside and Mesa Top tours are $40 for adults and $36 for seniors, students, and military personnel. Puye is closed during the pueblo's feast days on June 13 and August 12, as well as Christmas Day; inquire about permits for photography, sketching, and painting.

Pecos National Historical Park ♥♥

An easy half-hour's drive east of Santa Fe, Pecos National Historical Park takes us from prehistoric times through Spanish colonization up to the early 20th century, preserving well over 1,000 years of human history. The park includes Ancestral Puebloan sites, mission churches built by the Spanish, a Santa Fe Trail trading post, the Civil War battlefield of the Battle of Glorietta Pass, and an early-20th-century cattle ranch.

GEORGIA O'KEEFFE & NEW MEXICO: a desert romance

In June 1917, during a short visit to the Southwest, the painter Georgia O'Keeffe (born 1887) visited New Mexico for the first time. She was immediately enchanted by the stark scenery; even after her return to the energy of New York City, her mind wandered frequently to New Mexico's arid land and undulating mesas. However, it wasn't until 12 years later, when she was coaxed by the arts patron and "collector of people" Mabel Dodge Luhan, that O'Keeffe returned to the multihued desert of her daydreams.

O'Keeffe was reportedly ill, both physically and emotionally, when she arrived in Santa Fe in April 1929. New Mexico seemed to soothe her spirit and heal her physical ailments almost magically. Two days after her arrival, Luhan persuaded O'Keeffe to move into her Taos home. There, she would be free to paint and socialize as she liked.

In Taos, O'Keeffe began painting what would become some of her best-known canvases—close-ups of desert flowers and objects such as cow and horse skulls. "The color up there is different . . . the blue-green of the sage and the mountains, the wildflowers in bloom," O'Keeffe once said of Taos. "It's a different kind of color from any I've ever seen—there's nothing like that in north Texas or even in Colorado." Taos transformed not only her art, but also her personality. She bought a car and learned to drive. Sometimes, on warm days, she ran naked through sage fields. That August, a rejuvenated O'Keeffe rejoined her husband, photographer Alfred Stieglitz, in New York.

The artist returned to New Mexico year after year, spending time with Luhan as well as staying at the isolated Ghost Ranch in Abiquiú, some 70 miles northwest of Santa Fe. She drove through the countryside in her snappy Ford, stopping to paint in her favorite spots along the way. Until 1949, O'Keeffe always returned to New York in the fall. Three years after Stieglitz's death, O'Keeffe relocated permanently to New Mexico, spending each winter and spring in her house in Abiquiú and each summer and fall at nearby Ghost Ranch. Georgia O'Keeffe died in Santa Fe in 1986.

Many of O'Keefe's iconic images were inspired by the colorful landscape in the Abiquiú area, and today, **Ghost Ranch Education & Retreat Center** (ghostranch.org; ✆ **877/804-4678** or 505/685-1000) offers guided tours to some of O'Keeffe's favorite spots. Tours are by bus, foot, or horse, and prices range from $5 to $130. To get to Abiquiú from Santa Fe, drive north on US 285/84 to Española. When the routes split, stay on US 84 north about 25 miles to Abiquiú. It's another 10 miles to the ranch turn-off between mile markers 224 and 225; follow the signs to the Ghost Ranch Welcome Center. In addition to the O'Keefe tours there are hiking trails, a labyrinth, and two museums on-site. A $10 conservation fee, payable at the Welcome Center, grants access to two museums. The **Florence Hawley Ellis Museum of Anthropology** displays ancient artifacts from Paleoindian cultures of 10,000 years ago, through ancestral Puebloan times to present-day pottery and weavings from local pueblos. The **Ruth Hall Museum of Paleontology** offers numerous exhibits, photographs, and life-size replicas of dinosaurs found on the ranch. Both are open Tuesday through Saturday 9am to 5pm (closed for lunch noon–1pm), and Sunday 1 to 5pm. For visitors wishing to spend a few days here, the ranch offers overnight lodging, from rooms with private bath to those using a communal bathroom, plus an RV campground.

Here's the history in a nutshell. Nomadic hunter-gatherers had been attracted to this area for thousands of years before pit houses began to appear in the 9th century. Then, in the 12th century, the pueblo of Pecos began taking shape. Although it started as many small villages in the Pecos Valley, protection and other issues initiated a move to consolidate the villages. By 1450, Pecos Pueblo had become one of the largest and most important Southwestern pueblos, a walled compound standing five stories high that housed some 2,000 people. The people of Pecos grew corn, beans, squash, and cotton, and traded with Apache and other Plains tribes, as well as other pueblos. By the late 1500s they were also trading with the Spanish, who visited Pecos in 1540 on their first foray into New Mexico in search of the fabled cities of gold.

Although the Spanish conquistadores did not find gold, they did discover what they believed were souls that needed saving, and by the late 1500s began setting up missions to convert the Pueblo people to Christianity. In all, four mission churches were built at Pecos, including the last one, built in 1717, whose remains can still be walked through today.

The people of Pecos and other New Mexico pueblos, however, did not appreciate being told by the Franciscan missionaries that their religious views and ceremonies, which they had practiced for centuries, were wrong. The demand that they pay tribute to this new religion was bad enough, but that was soon compounded by the introduction of European diseases and a drought and resulting famine. Eventually, the native peoples had enough, deciding to join forces and revolt against the Spanish. This culminated in the Pueblo Revolt of 1680. At Pecos, the priest was killed and the mission church, which had been the most impressive in the region, was destroyed.

The Spaniards returned 12 years later to retake New Mexico. Although their reconquest caused bloodshed at some pueblos, the takeover of Pecos Pueblo was largely peaceful, and a new Pecos mission, built on the foundation of the old one, was the first mission reestablished after the revolt. The Franciscans now treated the Indians better, but disease, raids by other Indian tribes, and other problems led to the decline of Pecos. In 1838, its few remaining tribal members abandoned Pecos to join Jemez Pueblo, about 80 miles to the west.

Today, the visitor center's **museum** contains exhibits on the pueblo, missions, and other aspects of the park, including a number of prehistoric Indian and Spanish Colonial artifacts that were discovered during excavations. A short introductory film is shown, and there is also a bookstore. A **1.25-mile round-trip self-guiding trail** leads from the visitor center through the ruins of Pecos Pueblo and the Spanish mission church. The two reconstructed kivas in the pueblo may also be entered. A trail guide is available at the visitor center.

There's also a **self-guided 2.3-mile Civil War Battlefield Trail,** visiting two sites from the Battle of Glorieta Pass, which took place in March 1862. It's considered the decisive battle of the Civil War for New Mexico in that it prevented the Confederates from overrunning the Southwest. Ask a ranger at the visitor center for the gate code to access the trail. A trail map and guide is also available at the visitor center bookstore for $2. In late March there is a **Civil War Encampment,** with a living history camp, kids' games and crafts, black powder demonstrations, and talks by historians.

The park also includes several early Ancestral Puebloan sites, the remains of a 19th-century Spanish settlement, a section of the Santa Fe Trail (complete with wagon wheel ruts), and a stage station along the trail. Some of these sites can be seen only on **guided tours** (free). These tours also visit the **Forked Lightning Ranch,** a cattle ranch from the early 1900s. Tours are offered year-round, but some require a reservation and can fill quickly in summer; call ahead to secure your place.

Pecos National Historical Park is open daily 8am to 6pm (until 4:30pm Labor Day to Memorial Day). It's closed New Year's Day, Thanksgiving, and Christmas. Admission is free. For information, see nps.gov/peco or call the park visitor center (✆ **505/757-7241**). The park is about 25 miles east of Santa Fe. Take I-25 south to exit 307, then go 4 miles north on NM 63 to the park entrance.

Kasha-Katuwe Tent Rocks National Monument ♥♥♥

Bordering Cochiti Pueblo, Kasha-Katuwe Tent Rocks National Monument is a geological wonder of cone-shaped tent rocks, also known as hoodoos, formed by eruptions from the Jemez volcanic field 6 to 7 million years ago. The hoodoos are made of pumice, ash, and tuff deposits, and many are topped with boulder caps that protect the softer rock below. The name, Kasha-Katuwe, means "white cliffs" in the Keresan language, spoken in a number of New Mexico's Pueblos, many of which have ancestral ties to the area. The site is about 40 miles southwest of Santa Fe, off of I-25.

Despite a total size of 5,000 acres, the monument has only two short trails, making it an easy and quick stop on the drive between Santa Fe and Albuquerque. Both routes start at the parking lot, where there are picnic tables shaded by juniper trees. The easier of the two, the 1.2-mile **Cave Loop Trail,** follows a wide circular path that stays relatively flat as it passes the signature rock formations, before reaching a cave that was once used by Ancestral Puebloans. About halfway through the Cave Loop Trail you can branch off on the **Canyon Trail,** a 3-mile out-and-back route that follows a slot canyon's meandering path through hoodoos that reach up to 90 feet high. This route is more challenging, due to a steep 630-foot climb to the mesa top, as well as some mild climbing throughout the narrow canyon using natural footholds.

When the area was designated a national monument in 2011, a provision was attached stating that it would be managed in close cooperation with Cochiti Pueblo. The site was, however, largely run by the Bureau of Land Management, until a closure at the start of the COVID pandemic prompted the BLM and Cochiti Pueblo to renegotiate how it would be operated. After a 4-year closure, Kasha-Katuwe reopened in late 2024 with the tribe taking on day-to-day operations. Visitors are now required to make reservations online in advance, which includes booking a $5 timed slot on recreation.gov (free for America the Beautiful passholders and ages 15 and under), as well as a Tribal Access Pass for $20 per adult, $10 per person 2 to 16 years old (free for visitors under 2). After making a booking on recreation.gov, a link will direct users to a link (purplepass.com; type "Cochiti Pueblo" in search bar), where the Tribal Access Pass can be purchased. A Tribal Access Pass can also be purchased in person at the **Cochiti Visitor Center** (1101 State Rd. 22; ✆ **505/318-6255**), 2 miles before the monument's entrance. A limited number of reservations are available each day. Visitors must check in at the visitor center before following a vehicle escort to the site's entrance.

Los Alamos ♥♥

Pueblo tribes lived in the rugged Los Alamos area for well over 1,000 years, and an exclusive boys' school operated atop the 7,300-foot plateau from 1918 to 1943. But the fascination most Americans have with this town stems from the **Los Alamos National Laboratory,** established here in secrecy during World War II to develop the world's first atomic bombs. The site has sparked renewed interest since the 2023 blockbuster film *Oppenheimer* (see "Los Alamos, Hollywood Style," p. 119).

Code-named Site Y of the Manhattan Project, the hush-hush Los Alamos project was led by director J. Robert Oppenheimer, later succeeded by Norris E. Bradbury. Thousands of scientists, engineers, and technicians worked here to produce the pioneering—and controversial—atomic bombs, which ended World War II with two mighty explosions at Hiroshima and Nagasaki, Japan. The community remained completely under federal government ownership until the 1960s, when the residents were finally allowed to buy land and buildings. This town of 12,000 people remains a "government town" today, its main purpose still being scientific research into nuclear energy for weaponry, energy production, and medicine, as well as space, atmospheric studies, supercomputing, and theoretical physics.

Sitting on the Pajarito Plateau, between the Jemez Mountains and the Rio Grande Valley, Los Alamos is about 35 miles west of Santa Fe and 65 miles southwest of Taos. From Santa Fe, take US 84/285 north approximately 16 miles to the Pojoaque junction, then turn west on NM 502. As NM 502 enters Los Alamos from Santa Fe, it follows Trinity Drive, where accommodations, restaurants, and other services are located. Central Avenue parallels Trinity Drive and has restaurants, galleries, shops, and museums.

The Los Alamos Commerce and Development Corporation operates the **Los Alamos Visitor Center,** 475 20th St., Suite A (visitlosalamos.org; ✆ **505/662-8105**), in the Los Alamos Community Building. It's open Friday through Monday 10am to 3pm. The visitor center produces one of the best visitor guides in the state, with real information and very little "aren't we wonderful!" gushing. You can view it online, ask for a hard copy to be mailed to you, or pick one up at most northern New Mexico visitor centers.

A free self-guided **walking tour** of the **Los Alamos Historic District** is available for download from visitlosalamos.org, or you can buy tickets for a docent-guided 1½-hour tour, offered Monday through Friday at 10am and 1:30pm (adults $25, free for those 18 and under with a ticketed adult). Tours are limited to 16 people. Tours visit most of the sites below, as well as walking past the Oppenheimer house, currently closed for restoration.

Bradbury Science Museum ♥♥ MUSEUM Operated by Los Alamos National Laboratory, this fun educational museum draws nearly 80,000 visitors a year. More than 60 interactive exhibits trace the history of the World War II Manhattan Project; highlight the Laboratory's current and historic research projects related to defense and technology; and focus on research related to national and international economic, environmental, political, and social concerns. The TechLab Discovery Room features hands-on activities and special displays on categories like nanotechnology and biosecurity. There's also a good exhibit on lasers and displays on supercomputers, including the vintage Cray 1A supercomputer, which was state-of-the-art back in 1977. You can see a 1939 letter from Albert Einstein to President Franklin Roosevelt, suggesting research into uranium as an energy source, and exhibits on Fat Man and Little Boy, the two bombs that were dropped on Japan.

1450 Central Ave., at 15th St. www.lanl.gov/engage/bradbury. ✆ **505/667-4444.** Free. Tues–Sat 10am–5pm, Sun 1–5pm. Closed New Year's Day, Thanksgiving, and Christmas.

Fuller Lodge Art Center ♥ Built in 1928 as the dining hall for the Los Alamos Ranch School, Fuller Lodge was designed by prominent architect John Gaw Meem, who personally chose the 771 massive pine trees used in its construction. Step inside the lodge to see the vertical-log and stone building with a 19-foot ceiling, stone fireplace, New Mexico weavings, and period decor. Fuller Lodge Art Center is in the south wing of the lodge (closest to the Oppenheimer and Groves statues and Central Avenue). The center offers adult and kids classes year-round, plus an 8-week Summer Art Camp for ages 4–18. Changing exhibits in the Main and Portal galleries showcase various artists, and the gallery shop downstairs offers beautiful handmade items created by over 100 local and regional artists. The Art Center hosts three annual Arts & Crafts Fairs in the spring, summer, and fall, a family-focused kit festival every April, and a very popular Affordable Art Show each winter.

2132 Central Ave. losalamosartscouncil.org. ✆ **505/662-1635.** Free. Tues–Wed noon–6pm, Thurs–Sat 10am–6pm, Sun noon–4pm.

Los Alamos History Museum ♥♥ The human history of Los Alamos and the Manhattan Project is just as fascinating, or maybe more so, than the scientific milestones that occurred here. Housed in historic log and stone buildings, this museum presents exhibits on the Ancestral Puebloan people, homesteaders, the Los Alamos Ranch School, the Manhattan Project, and Los Alamos and the Cold War. The main museum building, dating from 1918, was formerly an infirmary and later a guest cottage for the Los Alamos Ranch

School and the Manhattan Project. The museum's Harold Agnew Cold War Gallery is set in the nearby Hans Bethe House, previously home to two Nobel Prize winners.

1050 Bathtub Row (next to Fuller Lodge). losalamoshistory.org. ✆ **505/662-6272.** Adults $5; free for ages 18 & under and active duty military. Mon–Fri 9am–5pm, Sat 10am–4pm. Closed New Year's Day, Thanksgiving, and Christmas.

Manhattan Project National Historical Park ♥♥ HISTORIC SITE A massive, top-secret national mobilization of scientists, engineers, technicians, and military personnel, the Manhattan Project was charged with producing a deployable atomic weapon during World War II. Coordinated by the U.S. Army, its activities were spread across the continent, and this multidestination national park includes Los Alamos along with two other significant locations: Oak Ridge, Tennessee; and Hanford, Washington. While Oak Ridge and Hanford focused on providing the plutonium, Los Alamos was where scientists worked to design and build the atomic bomb. The "device" was tested on July 16, 1945 at Trinity Site in southern New Mexico, and a few weeks later atomic bombs were dropped on Hiroshima and Nagasaki, Japan, effectively bringing the war in the Pacific to an end.

The park at Los Alamos includes three Department of Energy areas: one associated with the design of the "Little Boy" bomb, the facility used to assemble the Trinity device, and one used for plutonium chemistry research. There's no public access to these identified sites, but the Visitor Contact Station offers information and a map for a historical walking tour of Los Alamos.

475 20th St. nps.gov/mapr. ✆ **505/661-6277.** Free. Dec–Feb daily 10am–3pm; Mar–Sept daily 10am–4pm (closed Mon March to Memorial Day). Closed Oct–Nov; closed New Year's Day and Christmas.

Pajarito Mountain Ski Area ♥ RECREATION Started in the late 1950s as a ski club for employees of Los Alamos National Laboratory and other locals, this fun little resort is rarely crowded and offers good tree skiing and great bump skiing. There are 300 acres of cleared skiable terrain with 53 named trails, a terrain park, five lifts, and a rope tow. Trails are rated 20%

LOS ALAMOS, hollywood style

An excellent drama, and a fairly accurate account of the Manhattan Project, is the 1989 film *Fat Man and Little Boy*, starring Paul Newman. The title comes from the code names given to the two bombs made in Los Alamos, which were eventually dropped on Hiroshima and Nagasaki, Japan. In 2023, *Oppenheimer*, a dramatization of J. Robert Oppenheimer's life directed by Christopher Nolan and starring Cillian Murphy, won seven Academy Awards and was one of the year's highest-grossing films. Many exterior scenes were filmed in Ghost Ranch, while some interior shooting took place in Los Alamos.

easy, 50% intermediate, and 30% difficult, with a vertical drop of 1,440 feet from the peak elevation of 10,440 feet.

397 Camp May Rd., 7 miles W of Los Alamos via NM 502. skipajarito.com. ✆ **505/662-5725.** Full-day lift tickets $15–$35, free for kids 12 and under. Check website for seasonal hours.

Bandelier National Monument ♥♥♥

Less than 15 miles south of Los Alamos via NM 4, Bandelier National Monument is in many ways the antithesis of that controversial 20th-century site: It offers an up-close look at prehistoric American Indian ruins, several hikes—including one to a picturesque waterfall—and opportunities to see New Mexican wildlife.

The main reason to come here is to see the fascinating 13th-century Ancestral Puebloan ruins, including a large pueblo, cliff dwellings, and a variety of rock art. The 1.2-mile **Main Loop Trail** begins just outside the **Frijoles Canyon Visitor Center,** where you can get a trail guide ($2) discussing the 21 numbered stops you'll be passing. This trail leads through the ruins of **Tyuonyi Pueblo**—an almost perfectly round pueblo, built in the 1300s and occupied into the early 1500s, which once had about 400 rooms. By the time Spanish explorers arrived later in the 16th century, it had already been abandoned. Anthropologists believe that the pueblo was a mix of one, two, and three stories, built around a large central plaza in which there were three small kivas, or underground ceremonial chambers. There were probably no windows on the compound's exterior walls, and only one ground-level exterior entrance.

The Delight Makers

Bandelier National Monument is named for Adolph Francis Alphonse Bandelier, a self-taught anthropologist-historian who left his native Switzerland in 1880 to study the early peoples of the American Southwest. Enthralled with the ruins he found here, he used them and the canyon in which they were built as the setting for a novel, *The Delight Makers,* a story of Native American life before the arrival of the Spanish in the 1500s.

From Tyuonyi Pueblo, the trail continues to a series of **cliff dwellings,** built into a south-facing canyon wall that caught the warming winter sun. From here you have a choice of a level, easy walk with views up at the cliff dwellings, or a paved but somewhat steep and narrow trail along the cliff side, with ladders providing access to some dwellings. Canyon walls here are composed of *tuff,* a soft, pinkish volcanic rock that weathers easily, producing holes that the prehistoric residents enlarged for storage and living quarters. These caves were often used as back rooms of more formal houses, constructed on the cliff face from *talus,* the broken chunks of rock deposited at the cliff base. One talus home has been reconstructed.

Continuing along the trail, you'll come to **Long House,** believed to have been a condominium-style community. Extending about 800 feet along the side of the cliff are rows of holes dug into the rock to support roof beams, called *vigas,* which show clearly the outline of the multistoried cliff dwelling. Also along the cliffside are a number of petroglyphs and a large pictograph, likely created by people standing on roofs. (*Petroglyphs* are designs chipped or pecked into a rock surface, while *pictographs* are images painted onto a rock surface.) Above the pictograph is a tall, narrow cave, which in summer is home to a colony of bats.

From the Long House cliff dwellings, the path returns to the visitor center via a shady **nature trail,** with signs describing the area's plant and animal life. A side trail leads to another cliff dwelling called **Alcove House** (formerly Ceremonial Cave), a natural cave that was enlarged by the prehistoric residents, who constructed clusters of rooms and a small kiva. Located about 150 feet above the canyon floor, it is accessed by a level dirt trail plus a steep 140-foot climb up a series of ladders and steps. This side trip adds about 1 mile round-trip to the Main Loop Trail.

The 1.5-mile **Frey Trail** starts at Juniper Campground, heads to the canyon edge, and switchbacks its way to the canyon floor—a total elevation drop of 550 feet—where it connects to the Main Loop Trail. This was the main route into the canyon before the entrance road was built in the 1930s, and provides excellent bird's-eye views of Tyuonyi. The trail has little shelter and is very hot in summer, so carry plenty of water. Instead of making the arduous climb back to the top, in summer you can ride a shuttle from the visitor center to the campground.

Several other sections of the monument are well worth visiting. Beginning at the end of the Backpacker's parking lot near the visitor center, the easy-to-moderate **Falls Trail hike** offers wonderful scenery and the possibility of seeing wildlife as it follows the Frijole Canyon—named for the beans ancestral Puebloans grew here—to two picturesque waterfalls, passing through a lush forest of juniper, ponderosa pine, and cottonwoods; in the falls area, yucca, cactus, and sagebrush predominate. The trail crosses Frijoles Creek on wooden bridges several times. It's an easy 1.5 miles to the dramatic Upper Falls, which plunges 70 feet; at the falls viewing area, you'll turn around and head back.

About 12 miles north of the main park entrance, the **Tsankawi Trail** is a 1.5-mile loop that is generally easy and fairly level, but it does include some narrow passages between rocks and involves climbing a 12-foot ladder. Passing among juniper, piñon, brush, and yucca, the trail offers views of petroglyphs including images of birds, humans, and four-pointed stars, as well as the mounds of dirt and rock that mark the unexcavated ruins of a pueblo, probably built in the 1400s, that contained about 350 rooms.

In addition to the park's main trails there are about 70 miles of backcountry trails, most of which are in the **Bandelier Wilderness,** a designated wilderness area that comprises over 70% of the monument's 32,737 acres. It's best to check at the visitor center for current conditions, as there are regular area closures due to flood hazard. The terrain is rugged, with steep canyons, but trails take hikers to relatively secluded sections of the monument where there are additional archaeological sites and excellent chances of seeing wildlife. Seen year-round are Steller's jays, western scrub jays, northern flickers, common ravens, canyon wrens, pygmy nuthatches, and both spotted and canyon towhees. In the warmer months, look for western bluebirds, violet-green swallows, white-throated swifts, broad-tailed hummingbirds, and turkey vultures. In wooded areas you're likely to see various squirrels, including Abert's, rock, golden-mantled ground, and red; plus their cousins, the least and Colorado chipmunks. Also watch for coyotes, raccoons, porcupines, mule deer, and elk. Numerous lizards inhabit the drier areas, plus a few snakes, including the poisonous western diamondback rattler. Detailed maps, additional information, and the required permits for overnight trips can be obtained at the visitor center.

For delightful **camping,** head to Juniper Campground, in a forest of junipers, with 55 nicely spaced campsites, each with a picnic table and fireplace. There are no RV hookups or showers, but there are restrooms with flush toilets and an RV dump station. Reservations for two of the three camping areas open up to 6 months in advance, while one area is available as first-come-first-serve. The cost is $20 per night, $10 for Interagency Senior and Access card holders, and is payable by credit card only at the self-registration kiosk on your way in.

The park is open year-round from dawn to dusk; visitor center hours are 9am to 6pm in summer, closing an hour earlier in winter. From mid-May through mid-October, daily 9am to 3pm, park visitors are required to park at the **White Rock Visitor Center** (nps.gov/band; ✆ **505/672-3861, ext. 517**), along NM 4 on the way into the park, and ride the **free shuttle,** which delivers you to the Main Loop Trail, Frijoles Canyon Visitor Center, and the trail head for Falls Trail. The shuttle runs about every 30 minutes on weekdays and every 20 minutes on weekends, and also stops at Juniper campground. Before 9am and after 3pm, you can drive into the park if you have a disability tag on your vehicle, if you're going to Juniper Campground, if you're on a bicycle, if you have a pet in your vehicle, or if you are an overnight backpacker. Park admission is $25 per car or truck, $20 motorcycles, $15 individuals and bicycles. No pets are allowed on trails, and the park is closed on Christmas.

Valles Caldera National Preserve ♥♥

Talk about a big boom: This delightful, peaceful area of forests, meadows, peaks, and valleys, with elk by the thousands and historic ranch buildings, was created some 1.25 million years ago by a tremendous volcanic eruption—from what scientists believe is one of only three super volcanoes in the United States. The eruption created a huge crater, which is the heart of this nearly 89,000-acre preserve, purchased by the federal government in 2000 and part of the National Park Service since 2015. It's about 14 miles west of Los Alamos, on NM 4.

The name, Valles Caldera, refers to the numerous valleys (*valles* in Spanish) that occupy the caldera—a large crater formed by the volcanic eruption. The caldera is over a half-mile deep and 12 to 15 miles wide. Scientists say that the volcano's eruptions released some 50 cubic miles of ash and rock, more than 16 times the material that spewed from Mount St. Helens when it erupted in 1980.

After becoming a private ranch in 1860, the area had remained off limits to the public except for some guided elk hunts. Ranch owners also did timber harvesting; there are still miles of old logging roads providing relatively easy public access to much of the ranch's backcountry. Many of these roads are open only to hikers, bikers, and equestrians; motorized vehicles are allowed only on designated routes and require a permit. Today, the Valles Caldera is known primarily for its magnificent herds of elk—estimated at more than 5,000 animals—but it is also home to a wide range of wildlife, including mule deer, mountain lions, black bear, golden-mantled squirrels, chipmunks, and coyotes. Birds here include mourning doves, black-chinned hummingbirds, violet-green swallows, mountain bluebirds, and peregrine falcons. There are 54 miles of hiking and biking trails (also open to cross-country skiers in winter), plus some 30 miles of trout streams.

The Valle Grande Entrance Station (nps.gov/vall; ✆ **505/889-4100, ext. 3**) is along the main road, about 2 miles in from the main entrance from NM 4 near MM 39.2. It's open 8am to 6pm May 15 through October, 9am to 5pm the rest of the year, closed Christmas and Thanksgiving. There's a bookstore on-site with maps and books on the preserve and its environs, but it's credit card only—no cash or checks accepted. Entrance is free.

The High Road to Taos ♥♥

The quick way to Taos from Santa Fe is about 70 miles on a route that partly follows the Rio Grande. It's a pretty enough drive, especially scenic in summer when the river is dotted with colorful rafts and autumn when the cottonwoods gleam golden in the sun. But an alternate route, only about a dozen miles longer, offers a much deeper sense of the region's history, as it winds through historic Spanish Colonial villages known for beautiful weaving, where you'll also see some of the most picturesque churches in the Southwest.

Both routes go to Española via US 285, but where the shorter route continues north on NM 68, the High Road (highroadnewmexico.com), takes off east from Española on NM 76, wandering through the mountains. Your first stop will be in the tiny village of **Chimayo,** settled in 1598. Be sure to stop at **Ortega's Weaving Shop** ♥♥ (ortegasweaving.com; ✆ **877/351-4215** or 505/351-4215), where the seventh, eighth, and ninth generations of weavers still work the looms. They produce a wide range of woven items, from large rugs and blankets to vests and coats, plus small items including placemats, coasters, and purses. Considering the work and skill involved, prices here are quite reasonable. Next head to **Centinela Traditional Weaving Arts** ♥ (chimayoweavers.com; ✆ **505/351-2180**), a delightfully arranged store featuring a working loom on one side and a variety of smaller, more reasonable rugs that make great souvenirs. Chimayo is also your best bet for food between Santa Fe and Taos. **Rancho de Chimayó Restaurante ♥♥♥** (300 Juan Medina Rd./County Rd. 98; ranchodechimayo.com; ✆ **505/351-4444**) serves authentic northern New Mexico food for lunch and dinner daily and breakfast Saturday and Sunday. Some items can be hot (that's spicy hot), so ask your server for suggestions if you have a tender tummy. The restaurant is open daily May to October, closed Mondays the rest of the year. It also has two shops, one with beautiful but very pricey high-end jewelry and pottery, the other with more affordable items, including a wonderful Rancho de Chimayo cookbook.

Nearby, off NM 76 on County Rd. 98, the inspiring **El Santuario de Chimayó ♥♥** (15 Santuario Dr., www.holychimayo.us; ✆ **505/351-9961**), built in the early 1800s, is visited annually by thousands of people seeking relief from medical problems by means of what many consider the "miraculous dirt" found in a corner of the chapel. A room leading to the dirt even features rows of crutches that visitors claim they no longer needed after its healing qualities. An active Roman Catholic church, it is open to the public daily, with free admission, 9am to 5pm year-round. Check the website for the Mass and confession schedule. If you click on the website's "Holy Pilgrimage" section, you will see a map and descriptions of the other historic churches in the area.

Continuing east and north on NM 76, you soon come to the village of **Truchas,** one of the most isolated of the Spanish Colonial towns, which was the scene for much of Robert Redford's 1988 movie *The Milagro Beanfield War,* based on the novel by Taos author John Nichols. There are spectacular mountain views from here, and some good art galleries. A short detour just south of Truchas leads to **Cordova,** a tiny village known for its woodcarvers.

Back on NM 76, the next village to stop in is **Las Trampas,** home to the **Church of San Jose de Gracia,** one of the most beautiful churches built during the Spanish Colonial period. For background information, see the website of El Santuario de Chimayó, above.

The road continues through the mountains, passing through the village of **Chamisal** before arriving in **Peñasco.** On NM 76 near its intersection with NM 75, you can stop to visit **Picuris Pueblo** (picurispueblo.org; ✆ **575/587-2519**),

HIGH ON art

If you really like art and want to meet artists, check out one of the region's **Art Studio Tours** held in the fall season. Artists spend months preparing their best work, and then open their doors to visitors. Wares range from pottery and paintings to furniture and woodcarvings to *ristras* and dried-flower arrangements.

The most notable tour is the **High Road Studio Art Tour** (highroadnewmexico.com) in mid- to late September. If you're not in the area during that time, check newspapers (such as the *Santa Fe New Mexican*'s Friday edition, "Pasatiempo") for notices of other art-studio tours.

set in what is called "The Hidden Valley." A few original mud-and-stone houses still stand, as does a lovely church, the Mission of San Lorenzo, which has been in use for over 200 years. There's a striking above-ground ceremonial kiva called "the Roundhouse," believed to have been built at least 700 years ago, and some excavated kivas and storerooms are on a hill above the pueblo. Picuris has a long history of creating beautiful arts and crafts—its neighbors called it "Pikuria," or "those who paint." The Picuris people make pottery from micaceous clay that is similar to the pottery at Taos Pueblo. Call to check on closures and for information on self-guided tours and any related fees. The pueblo is usually open to visitors Monday through Friday 8am to 5pm.

Continue on toward Taos via NM 518. This particularly scenic route takes you through the Carson National Forest to the **U.S. Hill Scenic Overlook** and then to **Ranchos de Taos,** where you can turn right and follow the main drag into Taos, or turn left and head back to Santa Fe following the Rio Grande via NM 68.

6 TAOS ESSENTIALS

Ringed on the north and east by the Sangre de Cristo range of the Rocky Mountains, Taos spreads west toward the Rio Grande Gorge, a canyon so narrow it's like a knife-cut in the sagebrush-covered mesa. If you're driving up from Santa Fe along the river, you'll find the most dramatic view of the gorge in the late afternoon. As you top that final hill, pull into the parking area on your right: If the light's just right, the panorama is unforgettable.

Located about 70 miles north of Santa Fe, this town of some 6,000 residents combines 1960s hippiedom (thanks to communes set up in the hills back then) with the ancient culture of Taos Pueblo, where some people still live without electricity and running water, as their ancestors did at least 700 years ago. There are even some people here who completely eschew materialism, living "off the grid" in half-underground houses called earthships. But there are plenty of more mainstream attractions as well—Taos boasts some excellent restaurants, a lively arts and music scene, and incredible opportunities for outdoor action, including world-class skiing and fly-fishing.

For a town of its size, Taos has an incredibly colorful history. Throughout the Taos Valley, ruins and artifacts attest to a Native American presence dating back 5,000 years. The Spanish first visited this area in 1540 and colonized it in 1598, although as late as the 1680s and 1690s, three rebellions at Taos Pueblo challenged Spanish rule. During the 18th and 19th centuries, Taos was such an important trade center that New Mexico's annual caravan to Chihuahua, Mexico, couldn't leave until after the annual midsummer **Taos Fair,** which French trappers had been attending since 1739. Even though the Plains tribes often attacked the pueblos at other times, they called a temporary truce each year so they could attend the market festival. By the early 1800s, Taos had become a meeting place for American mountain men, the most famous of whom, Kit Carson, made his home in Taos from 1826 to 1868.

Taos remained loyal to Mexico during the U.S.–Mexican War of 1846 and rebelled against its new U.S. landlord in 1847, killing newly appointed governor Charles Bent in his Taos home. The town was eventually incorporated into the Territory of New Mexico in

1850, but only a few years later, during the Civil War, Taos fell into Confederate hands for 6 weeks; afterward, Carson and two other men raised the Union flag over Taos Plaza, guarding it day and night.

In 1898, two East Coast artists—Ernest Blumenschein and Bert Phillips—discovered the community by accident while looking for a place to get a broken wagon wheel repaired. They were enthralled with the dramatic, varied effects of sunlight on the land, the picturesque adobe homes, the dramatic church in Ranchos de Taos, and the prominent shape of Taos Pueblo, all of which they captured on canvas. By the early 1900s more artists made their way to Taos, and the **Taos Society of Artists** was founded. Since then, the town has gained a reputation as an artistic and cultural center.

The town of Taos is merely the focal point of rugged 2,200-square-mile Taos County. Two features dominate this sparsely populated region: the high desert mesa, split in two by the 650-foot-deep chasm of the **Rio Grande,** and the **Sangre de Cristo** range, which tops out at 13,161-foot Wheeler Peak, New Mexico's highest mountain. From the forested uplands to the sage-carpeted mesa, the county is home to a large variety of wildlife. The human element includes Native Americans who still live in ancient pueblos, and Hispanic farmers who continue to irrigate their farmlands using centuries-old methods.

There's a laid-back attitude here, even more pronounced than the general *mañana* attitude for which New Mexico is known. Many Taoseños live to play—and that means outdoors. Some work at the ski area all winter (skiing whenever they can) and work for rafting outfitters in the summer (to get on the river as much as they can). Others are into rock climbing, mountain biking, and backpacking. Yet Taos doesn't feel like an outdoor sports resort—its strains of Hispanic and Native American heritage give it a richness and depth that most resort towns lack.

These days, Taos's biggest task is trying to balance the things that make it so attractive—clean air, outdoor recreation, that laid-back attitude—with a constant stream of newcomers and the development that always accompanies growth.

ORIENTATION

Visitor Information

The official **Taos Visitor Center** is located at 1139 Paseo del Pueblo Sur (taos.org; ✆ **800/732-8267** or 575/758-3873) at its intersection with Paseo del Canon (NM 585), an easy stop on your drive in from Santa Fe. You can get a free Taos map here, as well as information and maps about the Carson National Forest. The center is open daily 10am to 5pm; it's closed on major holidays.

City Layout

The center of town—and Taos's first traffic light—is **Taos Plaza,** just west of the intersection of US 64 (Kit Carson Road) and NM 68, **Paseo del Pueblo**

Sur. US 64 proceeds north from the intersection as **Paseo del Pueblo Norte,** and continues out to the Rio Grande Gorge Bridge and beyond. **Camino de la Placita** (Placitas Road) circles the west side of downtown, passing within a block of the other side of the plaza. Many of the streets that connect these thoroughfares are narrow and winding lanes lined with traditional adobe buildings, many over 100 years old.

Around the plaza are shops and galleries, plus the historic La Fonda Hotel (p. 132), facing the central green where occasionally live entertainment is offered on summer evenings. There are more shops, galleries, and museums within a few blocks of the plaza. The area is best traversed on foot.

Two other areas of interest are **Ranchos de Taos,** a few miles south of the plaza, and **Arroyo Seco,** about 6 miles north.

GETTING AROUND

By Car

Taos is best explored by private vehicle. Although there are a lot of attractions and restaurants within walking distance of Taos Plaza, there are some really good spots away from the plaza that you shouldn't miss. Aside from a few too many potholes, roads are fairly decent, and most are paved to the areas you'll want to visit. Finding a place to park in downtown Taos is usually not too difficult, although it can be a problem during the summer and winter rush, when an unceasing stream of tourists' cars rolls north and south through town. Street parking is metered, as are several of the lots closest to the plaza; there's free parking at Kit Carson Park (US 64), at Town Hall, and along Quesnel Street. The town recently upgraded all of its paid parking meters from coin-operated to accept payment by card and an app.

Warning for Drivers

En route to many recreation sites, reliable paved roads often give way to rough forest roads, where gas stations and cafes are virtually non-existent. Four-wheel-drive vehicles are recommended on much of the unpaved terrain of the region and are imperative in snow. If you're doing any off-road adventuring, it's wise to go with a full gas tank, extra food and water, and warm clothing—just in case. At the higher-than-10,000-foot elevations of northern New Mexico, sudden summer thunderstorms are frequent, and even freak summer snowstorms can occur.

By Bus & Shuttle

If you're in Taos without a car, there's a mostly free local bus service, provided by the **North Central Regional Transit District** (p. 235), that has a variety of routes around Taos and the Enchanted Circle.

By Bicycle

Bicycle rentals are available from **Rift Cycles** ♥, 1029 Paseo del Pueblo Norte (riftcycles.com; ✆ **575/694-2096**); daily rentals start at $120, and weekly rates are available. It's open Tuesday to Saturday 10am to 5pm.

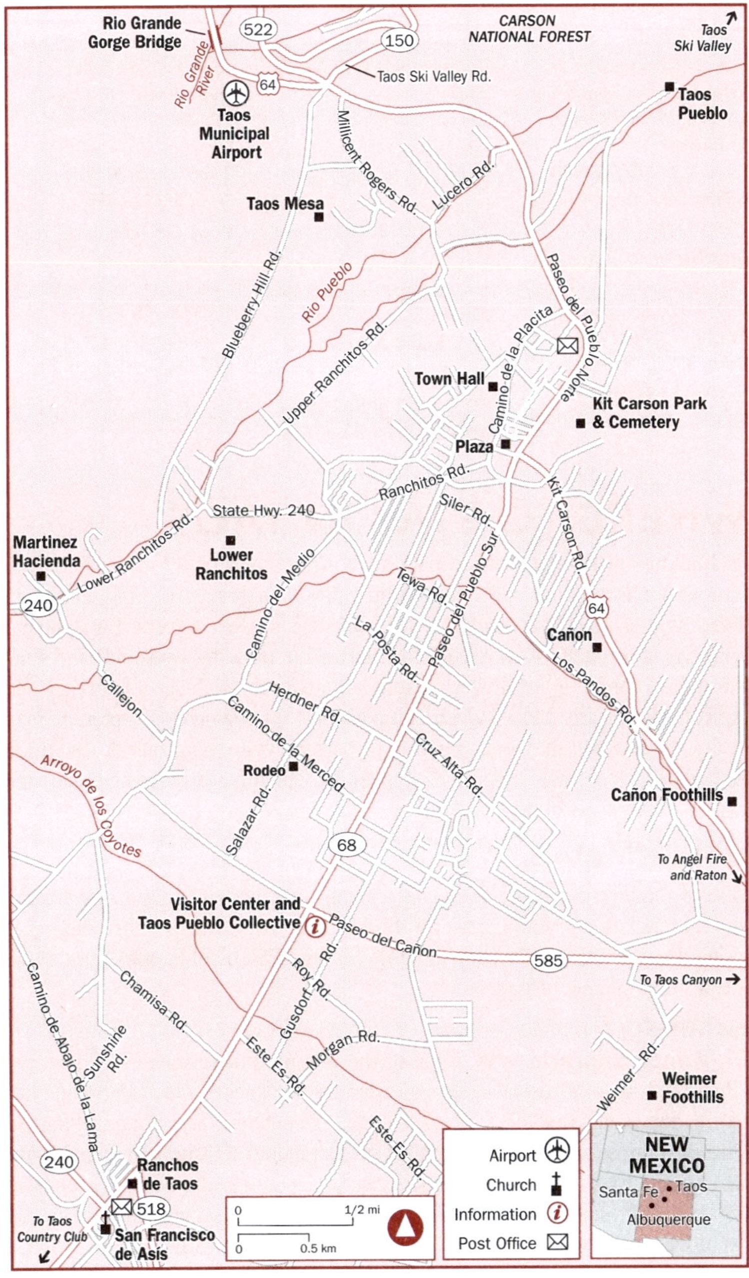

Rio Grande Gorge Bridge
522
150
CARSON NATIONAL FOREST
Taos Ski Valley
Taos Ski Valley Rd.
64
Rio Grande River
Taos Municipal Airport
Taos Pueblo
Millicent Rogers Rd.
Lucero Rd.
Taos Mesa
Blueberry Hill Rd.
Rio Pueblo
Paseo del Pueblo Norte
Camino de la Placita
Upper Ranchitos Rd.
Town Hall
Kit Carson Park & Cemetery
Plaza
Ranchitos Rd.
State Hwy. 240
Siler Rd.
Kit Carson Rd.
Lower Ranchitos Rd.
Martinez Hacienda
Lower Ranchitos
240
Camino del Medio
Tewa Rd.
Paseo del Pueblo Sur
La Posta Rd.
Cañon
Los Pandos Rd.
Callejon
Herdner Rd.
Camino de la Merced
Cruz Alta Rd.
Arroyo de los Coyotes
Rodeo
Salazar Rd.
Cañon Foothills
68
To Angel Fire and Raton
Visitor Center and Taos Pueblo Collective
Paseo del Cañon
585
To Taos Canyon
Camino de Abajo de la Lama
Chamisa Rd.
Roy Rd.
Gusdorf Rd.
Sunshine Rd.
Este Es Rd.
Morgan Rd.
Weimer Rd.
Weimer Foothills
Ranchos de Taos
518
To Taos Country Club
San Francisco de Asís
0 1/2 mi
0 0.5 km
Airport
Church
Information
Post Office
NEW MEXICO
Santa Fe
Taos
Albuquerque

[FastFACTS] TAOS

Car Rentals Car rental agencies in Taos include **Wheeler Peak Rent a Car** (✆ **575/776-4904**) and **Enterprise,** 1350 Paseo del Pueblo Sur (✆ **575/758-5553**), only open weekdays 9am to 3pm.

Doctors For a medical emergency, dial ✆ **911.** Walk-in medical services are available at **Taos Urgent Care,** 330 C Paseo del Pueblo Sur (✆ **575/758-1414**), open 9am to 7pm.

Emergencies Dial **911.**

Hotlines The 24-hour **Crisis Hotline** (✆ **575/758-9888**) is available for emergency counseling.

Libraries The **Taos Public Library** is at 402 Camino de la Placita (taoslibrary.org; ✆ **575/758-3063** or 575/737-2590).

Newspapers ***The Taos News*** (taosnews.com; ✆ **575/758-2241**) is published weekly.

Police In case of emergency, dial ✆ **911.** For non-emergencies, call the **Town of Taos Police Department** (✆ **575/758-4656**), or outside town limits contact the **Taos County Sheriff** (✆ **575/737-6480**).

Post Offices The main **Taos post office** is at 318 Paseo del Pueblo Norte (✆ **575/758-2081**), a few blocks north of the plaza traffic light; it's open Monday to Friday 8:30am to 5pm and Saturday 10:30am to 2pm.

WHERE TO STAY IN TAOS

A small town with a big tourist market, Taos has thousands of rooms in hotels, motels, condominiums, and bed-and-breakfasts. There are two high seasons in Taos: winter (the Thanksgiving-to-Easter ski season, except for January, which is notoriously slow except for Martin Luther King weekend) and June through October. In the slower seasons—January through early February and April through early May—when competition for travelers is steep, rates may be lower, and you may even be able to bargain your room rate down. Book well ahead for ski holiday periods, especially Christmas and spring break, and expect to pay top dollar.

Hotels/Motels

One of the advantages of a relatively small town is that it has fewer streets, and that makes everything easier to find. In the town of Taos, most lodging is along the main drag—Paseo del Pueblo Sur and Paseo del Pueblo Norte, with a few on Kit Carson Road.

EXPENSIVE

El Monte Sagrado ♥♥ One of the premier properties in the state, the "Sacred Mountain" resort has an eco-friendly focus, with a lush landscape full of flowing water (recycled, of course) that's centered on a tranquil "Sacred Circle" of grass and trees. Accommodations range from standard Taos Mountain rooms to small, self-contained casitas to suites, including 12 bi-level two-bedroom suites. The varied interior design draws inspiration from the Southwest and South America to Morocco and Tibet. Suites boast either a patio or balcony (private of course), and virtually every room has stunning views of Taos Mountain and the surrounding landscape. Over-the-top luxury suites are the real draws here, all with wet bar, kiva fireplace, huge bathrooms,

Taos Area Hotels

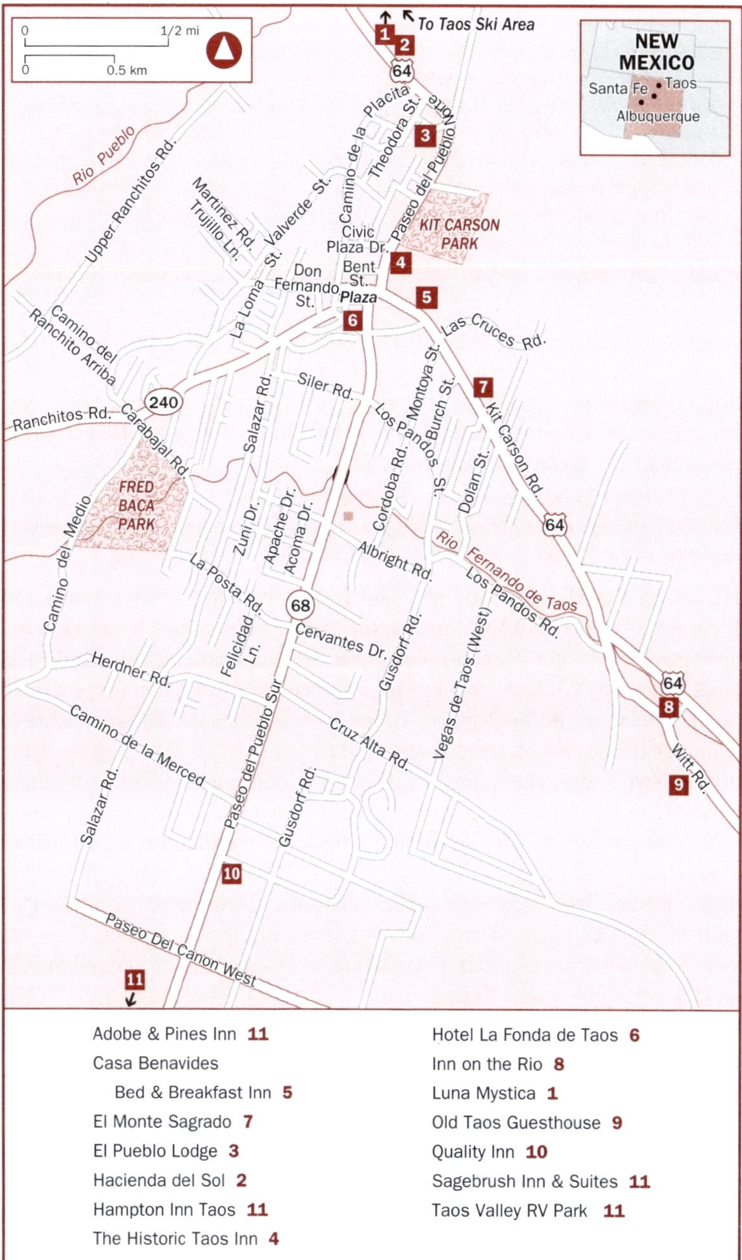

Adobe & Pines Inn **11**
Casa Benavides Bed & Breakfast Inn **5**
El Monte Sagrado **7**
El Pueblo Lodge **3**
Hacienda del Sol **2**
Hampton Inn Taos **11**
The Historic Taos Inn **4**
Hotel La Fonda de Taos **6**
Inn on the Rio **8**
Luna Mystica **1**
Old Taos Guesthouse **9**
Quality Inn **10**
Sagebrush Inn & Suites **11**
Taos Valley RV Park **11**

CHAIN MOTELS IN taos

South of Taos, along Paseo del Pueblo Sur, you'll find a string of chain motels. Of these we recommend the **Quality Inn ♥**, 1043 Paseo del Pueblo Sur (choicehotels.com; ✆ **877/424-6423** or 575/758-2200), which has a pool, accepts pets ($25 per pet per night), and includes a hot breakfast in its rates of $86 to $172 double and suites from $98. Another good nearby choice is **Hampton Inn Taos ♥**, 1515 Paseo del Pueblo Sur (hilton.com; ✆ **877/461-1402** or 575/737-5700), which also has a pool and accepts pets ($50 one-time fee for stays up to 4 days, $75 for 5 days or more); its rates ($116–$275) include a hot breakfast. Both have free Wi-Fi.

and decor that would make Indiana Jones jealous. All rooms have mini-fridges. There's also a spa that features a lush saltwater pool and a large selection of treatments. A plus is that El Monte Sagrado is within fairly easy walking distance of Taos Plaza. For food and drink, stop in the **De La Tierra** restaurant (p. 138) and the Anaconda Bar.

317 Kit Carson Rd. elmontesagrado.com. ✆ **888/213-4419** or 575/758-3502. 84 units. $174–$474 double, suites from $294. Dogs accepted ($75 per day per dog). **Amenities:** Restaurant; bar; concierge; business center; health club; free Wi-Fi.

Hotel La Fonda de Taos ♥ This is the only hotel right on Taos Plaza. It dates back to 1820, when a mercantile/saloon with rooms for travelers first appeared on this spot. Famous guests over the years have included Judy Garland, Tennessee Williams, and D. H. Lawrence (his presence lingers on in the "D. H. Lawrence Forbidden Art Exhibit," where you can see nine of his oil paintings risqué enough to be confiscated by police in 1929, if pretty tame by modern standards). The rooms, while not large, have undeniable historic elegance, with hand-tiled bathrooms and fireplaces in some. If you want more space, opt for a larger suite, or spring for the luxury penthouse on the top floor (1 to 4 bedrooms that go for $499–$1,400). The property is right in the middle of the action, Taos-wise, so expect some noise from the plaza, although a policy of no kids under 8 helps keep interior ruckus to a minimum. The south side of the hotel, facing away from the plaza, is very quiet. Although there is an elevator, some rooms require stairs, so contact the hotel directly if accessibility is an issue.

108 South Plaza. lafondataos.com. ✆ **575/758-2211.** 25 units. $149–$289 double, suites $199–$299. Children under 8 not permitted. **Amenities:** Coffee shop; lounge; free Wi-Fi.

MODERATE

El Pueblo Lodge ♥ The sign and vibe may say "old school," but this motel about a half-mile north of the plaza doesn't scrimp on comfort. Rooms in the 1940s South Building and in the "Casita," the original 1920s motor lodge, ooze with Route 66 atmosphere, although the rooms from the 1920s are a bit smaller than more modern motel rooms. Units in the newer West

Building are larger, with kiva-style fireplaces. There's also a three-bedroom condo with full kitchen facilities. All in all, this is a good value, especially considering that it's within walking distance of the plaza.

412 Paseo del Pueblo Norte. elpueblolodge.com. ✆ **800/433-9612** or 575/758-8700. 50 units. $130–$220 double. Rates include breakfast. Pets welcome ($25 for 1–2 nights, $50 for 3–5 nights). **Amenities:** Pool; hot tub; fitness room; coin laundry; barbecue grills; horseshoe pits; free Wi-Fi.

The Historic Taos Inn ♥♥ The name is no hyperbole: Some of the buildings that make up the Historic Taos Inn were bought by the town's first physician in the 1890s, and the guest list has included Greta Garbo and D. H. Lawrence. The buildings surround a small plaza, which was enclosed in the mid-1930s to become the inn's delightful lobby. In the middle of the lobby, a fountain encircled by vertical vigas rises two-and-a-half-stories to a stained-glass cupola. Across the lobby from the carved reception desk is the **Adobe Bar** (p. 165), still a local gathering place with live music nightly, and to the left of the front door is the entry to **Doc Martin's** (p. 138) restaurant. The hotel encompasses both the older buildings, where the rooms can be pretty small and even low-ceilinged, and a newer section with fancier digs done up in contemporary Southwestern decor including Saltillo tile floors and kiva fireplaces. The whole package radiates warm Old Taos character, overlaid with a modern comfort level.

125 Paseo del Pueblo Norte. taosinn.com. ✆ **855/961-1143** or 575/758-2233. 45 units. $129–$195 double, suites from $189. **Amenities:** Restaurant; lounge; access to nearby health club; free Wi-Fi.

Sagebrush Inn & Suites ♥♥♥ This sprawling property about 3 miles south of town has two main draws: its quiet location amid the sagebrush away from downtown, and a wide range of accommodations from cozy historic rooms with kiva fireplaces (in the original 3-story adobe building) to executive suites with all the modern conveniences for the business traveler. The seasonal pool is located in the large original tree-shaded courtyard, and there's a second, more intimate courtyard with rooms and suites behind the conference center. Many units have their own patios or balconies, and the view of Taos Mountain to the north is stupendous. The spacious lobby bar livens up most nights with live music and dancing.

1508 Paseo del Pueblo Sur. sagebrushinn.com. ✆ **800/428-3626** or 575/758-2254. 156 units. $116–$289 double. Pets accepted in designated rooms, subject to availability ($15 per pet per night and $150 cleaning deposit). Free parking. **Amenities:** Restaurant; bar; outdoor pool (year-round); 3 hot tubs; fitness center; bocce ball courts; free Wi-Fi.

INEXPENSIVE

Luna Mystica ♥♥ Set on 12 acres at the northwestern edge of town, this collection of 22 vintage trailers has considerable charm. Each trailer—many of which are from the '50s and '60s—has a different layout, feel, and capacity. The "Soy Capitan," a 42-foot Imperial Mansion trailer, has two bedrooms and mid-century decor, while the "Apollo" is a spaceship-themed Airstream that sleeps two. All accommodations come with air-conditioning and heating, mini-fridges, cooktops, and outdoor decks, and most have full baths, though opting for the communal shower area might give you more room. The hotel also has 60 camping sites that cost $25 per night and come with access to shower facilities and a guest lounge with free Wi-Fi. Across the dirt road is The Mothership, an outpost of Taos Mesa Brewery that serves beers and pub food like burgers and wings. In the summers, keep an eye out for concerts at its outdoor stage.

25 ABC Mesa Rd. hotellunamystica.com. ✆ **575/613-1411.** 82 units. $99–$200 double. Pets $20 per night. Free parking. **Amenities:** Showers; guest lounge; free Wi-Fi.

Bed & Breakfasts

EXPENSIVE

Adobe & Pines Inn ♥♥♥ You may feel you're taking a step back in time as you drive down the tree-lined entrance onto this 3-acre property, built around an 1832 adobe hacienda ⅓ mile south of San Francisco de Asis church in Ranchos de Taos. You enter its lobby through a carved wood door after stepping onto an 80-foot-long grand portal that stretches across the front. This is a perfect spot to relax in the evening and enjoy the changing light of the sunset reflected on the Sangre de Cristo Mountains. The grounds are lush in summer, with a babbling brook—part of the original *acequia* (irrigation ditch) system flowing through and traversed by a charming old stone bridge. Five rooms are in the original hacienda; all rooms are richly colored with artistic Southwest furnishings, and have at least one fireplace, plus private entrances. The most requested room is Puerta Rosa, with its large sunken bathroom where you can pamper yourself in a deep two-person soaking tub or a dry cedar sauna. Puerta Violeta on the second floor has its own oversize jetted tub and a private balcony where you'll feel as though you can pluck the stars right out of the velvet sky. Although it's close to the highway, once you're inside the thick-walled adobe building, the traffic sounds disappear.

4107 State Road 68, about 4 miles S of Taos Plaza. adobepines.com. ✆ **800/723-8267** or 575/751-0947. 8 units. $170–$370 double. Rates include breakfast. Dogs under 20 lb. accepted with prior arrangement, one-time $25 fee. **Amenities:** Concierge service; kitchen facilities; hot tubs; Zen garden; electric car chargers; free Wi-Fi.

Casa Benavides Bed & Breakfast Inn ♥♥♥ This eclectic place stretches the boundaries of what a B&B can be: 37 rooms spread across a multitude of properties, each done in a different style (and for different prices), but all sharing a traditional New Mexico aesthetic of wood-burning fireplaces and Mexican-tile bathrooms. Some have kitchens. The owners' families have lived in Taos for generations. They opened Casa Benavides in 1989 in what was an art gallery and artists' residence just a few blocks from Taos Plaza. The lounge and dining room are in the main building, with a patio and two outdoor hot tubs. Don't miss the homemade granola at breakfast.

137 Kit Carson Rd. casabenavides.com. ✆ **800/552-1772** or 575/758-1772. 37 units. $140–$288 double. Rates include breakfast. No pets. **Amenities:** Complimentary afternoon tea; free Wi-Fi.

Hacienda del Sol ♥♥ The first thing you notice about Hacienda del Sol is the magnificent mountain backdrop. Even though it's just off the main drag, the property edges up against Taos Pueblo land, which means the scenery is virtually unspoiled. It's easy to see why art patron Mabel Dodge Luhan bought the place in the 1920s as a private retreat and guesthouse. Eventually you'll notice the rest of it: the 200-year-old main house with two courtyards, arched doorways, curved adobe walls, and viga ceilings. All 14 rooms are filled with Southwest-style furniture and original art. Most rooms have kiva fireplaces, and some have private hot tubs and steam showers. Bathrooms have Mexican tile. There's even an "earthship" home available for guests looking for an authentic experience living "off the grid." Guests can sign up for private use of the main outdoor hot tub. Gourmet breakfasts are cooked by owner Gerd Hertel, who also hosts group cooking lessons. The newer Southwest Villa has a full kitchen, heated floors, and French doors leading to a private grassy spot. The property boasts lots of flowers, tall trees, and Southwest sculptures.

109 Mabel Dodge Ln. taoshaciendadelsol.com. ✆ **866/333-4459** or 575/758-0287. 14 units. $129–$299 double; $229–$295 suite; villa from $299. Rates include breakfast. No pets. **Amenities:** Free Wi-Fi.

MODERATE

Inn on the Rio ♥♥ There is no shortage of lodgings in Taos that qualify as quaint, charming, or even adorable. It takes a little something special to rise above the crowd, as the Inn on the Rio does. Away from the hustle and bustle of downtown Taos in the foothills of the Sangre de Cristo Mountains, the inn provides a relaxing setting by old rustling cottonwoods along the bank of the Rio Fernando. Each room is unique, with colorful decor and touches such as hand-carved log beds, Western memorabilia, and American Indian–style wall hangings. Each of the private bathrooms has been whimsically hand-painted by area artists. The gracious hosts, Robert and Julie, cook up gourmet breakfasts, keep the hot tub bubbling, and make every guest feel like an actual guest instead of a paying client.

910 E. Kit Carson Rd. 1½ miles E of Taos Plaza. innontherio.com. ✆ **575/758-7199.** 12 units. $99–$211 double. Rates include breakfast. **Amenities:** Outdoor pool; whirlpool tub; free Wi-Fi.

Old Taos Guesthouse Inn ♥ A historically registered cultural landmark, this hacienda-style B&B fills a 2-century-old adobe home set high on 7½ acres on the quiet outskirts of town. Each cozy room has a private entrance and hand-carved doors and furniture; some have kiva fireplaces, mountain views, and kitchens, and the bathrooms have hand-painted Mexican tiles. There's a veranda over the well-tended courtyard for shade in the summer, and the views from the outdoor hot tub go on forever.

1028 Witt Rd. oldtaos.com. ✆ **575/758-5448.** 11 units. $149–$199 double. Pets accepted, $25 per night. Rates include breakfast. **Amenities:** Free Wi-Fi.

Ski Area Lodges & Condominiums

Taos Ski Valley is in the middle of a major, multiyear upgrade, but everything remains open. For more information on what's going on at Taos Ski Valley, see p. 155, and check out skitaos.com.

EXPENSIVE

The Blake ♥♥♥ Owned and operated by Taos Ski Valley, Inc. and named for ski valley founder Ernie Blake and his family, this is the premier lodging at Taos Ski Valley. Adjacent to lift 1, the Blake's rooms and suites are both luxurious and comfortable, with thick carpeting, solid wood furnishings, plush seating, top-quality beds, and large windows providing views of the ski runs and surrounding mountains. They're simply but tastefully decorated with Alpine touches. Most bathrooms have large walk-in showers; a few have bathtubs. Basic rooms have one king bed or two queens, and the deluxe king rooms also have a queen-size sofa bed. There are also one- and two-bedroom suites, larger than some people's houses. A restaurant, **192 at The Blake,** serves breakfast, lunch, and dinner daily; its somewhat eclectic menu changes, but might include several pizzas; a bison burger on a brioche bun; espresso-crusted antelope leg loin; chile relleno; a 12-ounce rib-eye; and rainbow trout dusted with blue cornmeal. Prices range from the mid-teens to the upper 30s. The Blake also has the **Spa and Wellness Center** (p. 160). Throughout the hotel's public areas you'll see photos of the Blake family, some dating to the ski area's beginnings in the 1950s.

116 Sutton Pl. skitaos.com/stay. ✆ **888/569-1756** or 575/776-5335. 115 units. Ski season $252–$413 double, $454–$756 suite; rest of year $151–$296 double, $226–$494 suite. Pets accepted, $25 per pet per night. **Amenities:** Restaurant; bar; pool; fitness center; spa; valet parking; ski valet; free Wi-Fi.

Edelweiss Lodge & Spa ♥♥ This classy condominium property located in the heart of the resort's main base area offers one-, two-, and three-bedroom condos, each individually furnished by their owners, with a range of bed types. All have fully equipped kitchens, living rooms, dining areas, washers and dryers, and gas fireplaces, with ski-in/ski-out convenience. Many have grand views of the ski slopes and the highest peaks of the Sangre de Cristo mountains. Small hotel rooms are available as lock-outs from a larger condominium at most times of the year. Rooms are medium size with comfortable beds and mid-size baths. There is on-site underground parking and ski valet service. The full spa offers deep-tissue massage, all-natural facials, and body scrubs among its treatments. The Edelweiss's main restaurant, the **Blonde Bear Tavern,** is a great place to wind down after a day on the slopes, with food and drink specials and comfortable seating around a four-sided stone fireplace. The dinner menu (ski season only) ranges from chicken pot pie and a half-pound burger to sage-brined pork chops, sautéed duck breast, and steaks, including an 18-ounce rib-eye. Dinner prices run $13–$48. The restaurant also serves breakfast daily during ski season and breakfast and lunch

Friday through Monday in summer. Eggs are local and organic, and the breakfast burritos are especially popular. Lunch selections ($9–$19) include burgers and sandwiches.

106 Sutton Place. edelweisslodgeandspa.com. ✆ **575/737-6900.** 31 units. 3- to 5-night min. stay in winter; 2-night min. in summer at certain times. Winter $240–$900; off-season $240–$525. **Amenities:** Restaurant; cafe; bar; concierge; exercise room; health club and full spa; hot tub; dry sauna; ski valet; boot lockers; free Wi-Fi.

MODERATE

Alpine Village Suites ♥♥ This pet-friendly, family-owned hotel just a few steps from the ski lifts includes within its "village" two ski shops and the Stray Dog Cantina, a popular, family-friendly bar and restaurant. A variety of suites filled with rustic mountain charm can accommodate two to six people; condo and home rentals are also available, accommodating up to ten. All suites have kitchenettes; some rooms have fireplaces and balconies, and some suites have sleeping lofts for the young and nimble. All are attractively and comfortably furnished with Southwestern touches. In addition, there's a wonderful massage and spa service.

100 Thunderbird Rd. alpine-suites.com. ✆ **575/776-8540.** 31 units. 3- to 5-night min. stay at certain times in winter. Winter $110–$725 double, off-season $199–$355 double. Call for condo and home rates. Pets accepted ($20 per pet per day). **Amenities:** Hot tub; massage and spa services; dry sauna; ski lockers; business center; free Wi-Fi.

RV Parks & Campgrounds

Carson National Forest ♥♥ There are national forest campgrounds east of Taos along US 64, southeast via NM 518, and north along the road to Taos Ski Valley. These developed areas are generally open during the summer, although exact dates vary. They range from woodsy, stream-side sites to open lowlands with lots of sagebrush. There are also dispersed camping areas in the Questa and Tres Piedras ranger districts. Check the forest service website (under "Recreation"), or stop at the office to discuss locations and pick up maps.

Carson National Forest Supervisor's Office, 208 Cruz Alta Rd. fs.usda.gov/carson. ✆ **575/758-6200.** Free–$22 per night. No credit cards. Pets welcome. **Amenities:** Vault toilets; no Wi-Fi.

Taos Valley RV Park ♥♥ For almost-in-town camping, this is the place to be, just 2½ miles south of Taos Plaza but set back far enough on a side road that you won't be hearing traffic noises all night. It's well-maintained (very clean bathhouses), mostly open with some well-established trees, offers all the usual commercial campground amenities, and has grand views of the surrounding mountains. Each site has a picnic table and grill.

120 Este Es Rd., off NM 68 (½-block east of Paseo del Pueblo Sur). taosrv.com. ✆ **575/758-4469.** 91 sites. $35 tent; $43 water and electric; $49–$56 full hookup. Pets welcome. **Amenities:** Playground; convenience store; coin-op laundry; dump station; propane; free Wi-Fi.

WHERE TO EAT IN TAOS

Taos offers great food in great comfort; nowhere is a jacket and tie mandatory. Alongside fine-dining spots, you'll also find basic comfort food—northern New Mexico–style, of course. As in Santa Fe and Albuquerque, the chile can be hot (spicy hot), so if you're not sure your tastebuds and stomach can handle it, ask for a sample before ordering. For many dishes you can also ask for your chile on the side and add a little bit at a time to your meal. Reservations are recommended for dinner when the town's jammed in summer or during the height of ski season.

Among national chains, you'll find a **McDonald's** in the middle of town at 200 S. Santa Fe Road (mcdonalds.com; ✆ **575/758-9762**) and a **Domino's Pizza** at 710 Paseo del Pueblo Sur (dominos.com; ✆ **575/779-3030**), which delivers throughout the area.

Expensive

De La Tierra ♥♥ NEW AMERICAN Located in El Monte Sagrado (p. 130), this restaurant features plush leather seating, attractive Southwest artwork, and a light and airy feel. The menu blends French and Southwestern cuisine, using organic and regional ingredients as much as possible. Breakfast offers such items as shakshuka, breakfast burritos, and crème brûlée French toast. De La Tierra dinner entrees include a tender beef tenderloin with whipped crème fraiche potatoes, roasted corn pico, and blue-corn onion strings, as well as a cumin-spiced lamb rack with cauliflower-labneh puree. The Sunday brunch menu includes huevos rancheros, a breakfast burrito, piñon buttermilk pancakes, and for the adventurous, lobster Benedict. A lovely outdoor space for al fresco dining, The Gardens is tucked inside the walls of the resort, and you can also eat in the Anaconda Bar. There is full liquor service.

In El Monte Sagrado Hotel, 317 Kit Carson Rd. elmontesagrado.com. ✆ **575/758-3502.** Breakfast $16–$27; brunch $15–$36; dinner main courses $39–$58. Mon–Sat 7–11am and 5–9pm; Sun 8am–noon and 5–9pm.

Doc Martin's ♥♥♥ AMERICAN/NEW MEXICAN Doc Martin's serves delicious and innovative meals in the former home and office of the first doctor in Taos, Dr. Thomas Paul Martin—also the place where painters Ernest Blumenschein and Bert Phillips plotted the beginnings of the Taos Society of Artists in 1912. The old adobe building oozes with Taos history, while keeping up-to-date in comfort and style. Local art graces the walls, tables are comfortably spaced, and there's a nice courtyard in back for warm-weather dining. There's also patio dining in front, along the street, if you don't mind a little traffic noise. This is where we come for our green chile cheeseburger and fries at lunch, although we also like the Southwest chicken torta sandwich with griddled Chihuahua cheese and bacon and the blue-corn chicken enchiladas. The dinner menu offers a steak of the day, Doc's chile relleno platter, and the ever-popular grilled rainbow trout. The brunch menu includes chilaquiles, a smothered burrito, and blue-corn blueberry piñon pancakes. The

Taos Area Restaurants

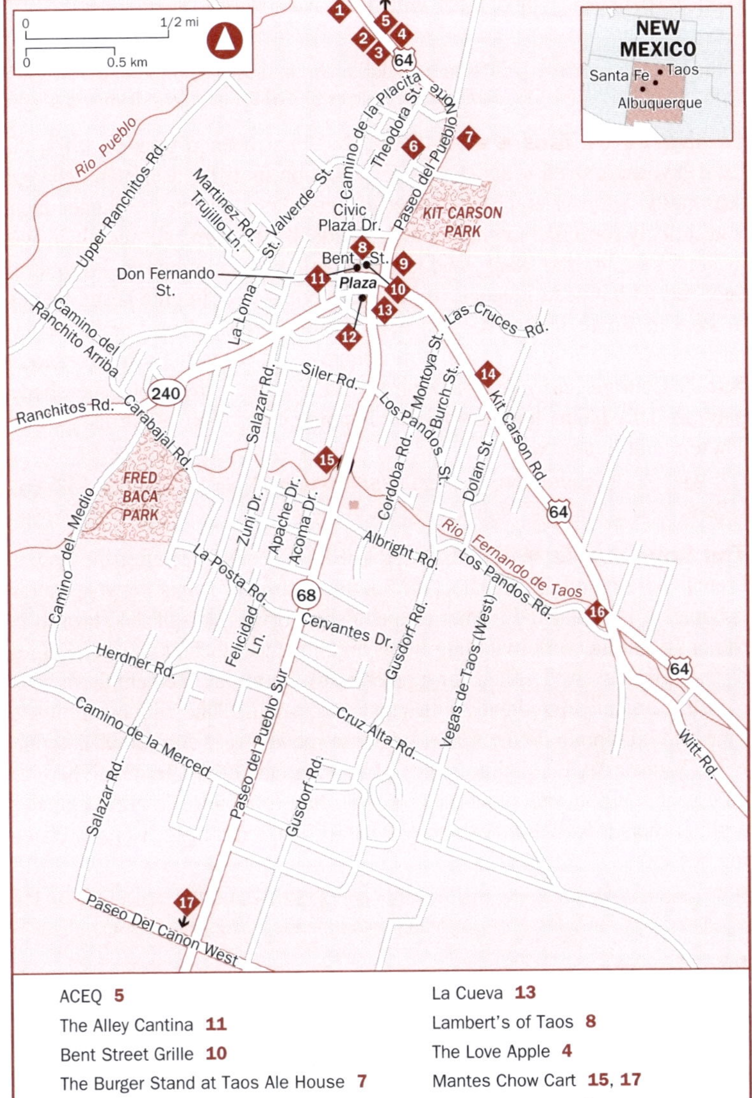

ACEQ **5**
The Alley Cantina **11**
Bent Street Grille **10**
The Burger Stand at Taos Ale House **7**
De La Tierra **14**
Doc Martin's **9**
The Gorge Bar & Grill **12**
Guadalajara Grill **1**, **17**
Gutiz **2**
La Cueva **13**
Lambert's of Taos **8**
The Love Apple **4**
Mantes Chow Cart **15**, **17**
Michael's Kitchen **6**
Orlando's New Mexican Café **1**
Ranchos Plaza Grill **17**
Taos Cow **5**, **16**
Taos Pizza Out Back **3**

Adobe Bar, across the lobby from the restaurant, is often referred to as the "living room of Taos" and offers live music (a changing menu of bluegrass, jazz, gospel, Celtic, and folk) with no cover charge. There is full liquor service.

In the Historic Taos Inn, 125 Paseo del Pueblo Norte. taosinn.com. ✆ **575/758-1977.** Brunch and lunch $14–$19; dinner main courses $22–$40. Daily 7am–1pm and 4–9pm.

Lambert's of Taos ♥♥ AMERICAN First opened back in 1989, this local favorite moved to its Bent Street location in 2013. The menu changes seasonally, with an emphasis on local ingredients, but on the dinner menu you'll likely see a filet mignon, which practically melts in your mouth, as well as lamb loin, braised shank, seafood, and perhaps zucchini pasta—ribbons of zucchini with grape tomatoes, oyster mushrooms, and arugula pesto. Be sure to save room for one of the decadent desserts prepared by Lambert's own pastry chef. For a more casual atmosphere, head upstairs to the **Treehouse Bar & Lounge** (daily 4:30–8:30pm), with a view of the apple tree–shaded patio. A daily happy hour from 4:30 to 6pm features food and drink specials. There is full liquor service.

123 Bent St. lambertsoftaos.com. ✆ **575/758-1009.** Main courses $29–$62. Daily 5–8pm.

The Love Apple ♥♥ AMERICAN/FRENCH Named after the original French phrase for the tomato ("la pomme d'amour"), this cozy restaurant occupies a 150-year-old former chapel a short drive north of the plaza. It's a romantic setting, with twinkling lights and huge roof beams overhead, a festive atmosphere well suited for a celebratory night out. The emphasis is on regional, organic ingredients, with standout specialties like rainbow trout with lime and a chipotle crème sauce, or house-made sweet corn tamales topped with Oaxacan-style red chile mole, a fried egg, and crème fraiche. There are plenty of seafood and vegetarian options, like a homemade potato gnocchi with burrata, as well as an extensive wine list and tempting seasonally changing desserts.

803 Paseo del Pueblo Norte. theloveapple.net. ✆ **575/751-0050.** Main courses $14–$25. No credit cards. Reservations highly recommended. Wed–Sun 5–9pm.

Moderate

ACEQ ♥♥ AMERICAN This new kid on the block is veering away from the standard fare available—namely, New Mexican and New American—with a kind of laid-back but refined menu that would look at home in a big city. Located in the small village of Arroyo Seco on the way to Taos Ski Valley, it's a small and bustling space with an open kitchen, communal tables, and a rock-heavy playlist. The menu varies according to the seasons, but expect small plates like mushroom cakes made from lions' mane and bison bone marrow served with hummus, grilled vegetables, and halloumi cheese. For entrees, there's black cod flown in from Alaska and a signature Wangus steak (a cross between Wagyu and Angus) from nearby Lazy6 Cattle Ranch, as well as some

Hungarian-leaning staples like duck paprikash and vegan goulash. For drinks, choose from six renditions of house-infused jalapeño tequila cocktails, plus interesting natural wines.

480 NM-150, Arroyo Seco. aceqrestaurant.com. ✆ **575/776-0900.** Main courses $20–$24. Daily 5–10pm.

The Alley Cantina ♥♥ AMERICAN This busy, noisy, locals' hangout gets our vote for the best fish and chips in northern New Mexico. Not the place to come for a romantic evening out, especially during the daily happy hour (5–7pm) with half-price drinks. Parts of the building date to the 16th century; in the 1800s it was the office of New Mexico's first territorial governor. There's heavy wood furniture and an old Taos atmosphere. The list of burgers and sandwiches includes a club sandwich on focaccia bread, a pulled pork barbecue sandwich, and a cod sandwich featuring the Alley's famed beer-battered fish. You can also get burritos, tamales, or enchiladas smothered with red or green chile, and various seafood items. But you can't beat the fish and chips—Pacific cod, hand-dipped in beer batter and panko breadcrumbs, deep fried and served with house-made tartar sauce. There is live music almost every night of the year, a pool table, shuffleboard, and arcade games—plus full liquor service.

121 Teresina Ln. (just off NW corner of Taos Plaza). www.alleycantina.com. ✆ **575/758-2121.** Main courses $12–$18. Thurs–Mon 11:30am–midnight; kitchen closes 9pm. Tues drinks only 8–midnight.

The Burger Stand at Taos Ale House ♥ AMERICAN The burger reigns supreme here, along with craft draft beer. Specialties include a green chile cheeseburger with fire-roasted Hatch green chile and one the restaurant calls "Bomber," with grilled onions and something called "ski sauce." There are various other types of burgers (even plain ones), all cooked to order from Black Angus chuck. Not in the mood for a burger? How about barbecued chicken with potato salad, fish and chips, a chili cheese dog, or a brie and arugula pizza? Several salads are available as a full meal or a side, and the French fries come either fried the normal way or in duck fat; the beer-battered onion rings are especially good. The atmosphere is a bit funky and casual, which fits well in this old adobe building across the street from Taos Post Office. The Burger Stand also has shakes and floats in addition to beer and wine.

401 Paseo del Pueblo Norte. theburgerstandnm.com. ✆ **575/758-5522.** Main courses $12–$20. Sun–Wed noon–9pm, Thurs–Fri noon–11pm, Sat 11am–11pm.

The Gorge Bar & Grill ♥ NEW MEXICAN/AMERICAN Located on the upper floor of a shopping complex on the northeast corner of Taos Plaza, the Gorge's outside balcony dining area overlooks the plaza and is a great place to watch what's going on (and to hear periodic live concerts in summer). The spacious main dining room has both tables and booths; it's a bit on the dark side, but the food is tasty, with everything made from scratch using homegrown ingredients from around the state. We love the green chile sirloin

family-friendly RESTAURANTS

Michael's Kitchen (p. 144) With a broad menu, comfy booths, and a very casual, diner-type atmosphere, Michael's Kitchen makes both kids and their parents feel at home.

Orlando's New Mexican Café (p. 144) The relaxed atmosphere and playfully colorful walls will please the kids almost as much as the tacos and quesadillas made especially for them.

Taos Cow (p. 145) Burritos and baked goods will fill kids up before they dive into the all-natural ice cream at this outdoor cafe's two locations.

Taos Pizza Out Back (below) Pizza is a natural hit for both parents and kids; even better are all the odd decorations here, such as the chain with foot-long links hanging over the front counter.

stew, but it's quite spicy—you might want to ask for sour cream on the side to cool it down. The many sandwiches—burgers to club to veggie—come with your choice of beer-battered fries, sweet potato fries, or coleslaw. If you're partial to fish and chips, the beer-battered cod is quite good. There are also dinner specials, from Tuesday taco night to meatloaf Fridays. Keep in mind dinner service ends early, even by New Mexico standards, at 7:30pm.

103 E. Plaza. thegorgebarandgrill.com. ✆ **575/758-8866.** Main courses $15–$33. Tues–Sat noon–7:30pm.

Taos Pizza Out Back ♥ PIZZA It's hard to decide what's better at this popular and unpretentious pizza joint: the crispy thin crusts topped with sesame seeds; the homemade sauces; or the choice of creative assemblages like the Bottom Line, with mushrooms, black or green olives, bell peppers, fresh tomato, onion, pepperoni, and Italian sausage. Either way, the slices are monstrous. There's a weekday lunch special of a lunch-size slice with two regular toppings and a side salad for $10.75. Spaghetti, calzones, wings, and a variety of salads are also served, and there's a good selection of microbrews and wine to wash them down. Sit outside on the patio on nice days. The restaurant does a brisk to-go business, but does not deliver.

712 Paseo del Pueblo Norte. www.taospizzaoutback.com. ✆ **575/758-3112.** Slices (large) $8–$13; whole pizzas $16–$35; pastas, wings, and calzones $12–$17. Daily 11am–9pm.

Inexpensive

Bent Street Grille ♥ DELI/CAFE This popular cafe, a short block north of the plaza, serves simple food in a country-home atmosphere. Outside, a flower box surrounds sidewalk seating that is heated in winter. Inside, wood floors and lots of windows provide a country-diner feel. The breakfast menu (served all day) features breakfast burritos, numerous other egg dishes, pancakes, and fresh-baked breads; for lunch you can choose from deli sandwiches, burgers, or a variety of salads. The dark-brown bread matched with a changing selection of soups is a good choice. If you'd like a picnic to go, the deli offers carryout service plus free delivery in downtown Taos. Beer and wine is served.

120-M Bent St. in the John Dunn Shops. bentstreetgrille.com. ✆ **575/758-5787.** Breakfast $11–$18; lunch $6.50–$17. Daily 8:30am–3:30pm, last seating 3:15pm.

Guadalajara Grill ♥ MEXICAN All too often, Mexican food—even in New Mexico—is a bland heaping of rice, beans, and sauces, generously portioned but often tasteless. Not here, where dishes such as the Aztec quesadilla (with chicken, beef, pork, or shrimp, plus peppers, onion, scallions, mushrooms, salsa, and chipotle sauce) are crisp and spicy enough to make your lips sing. The fish tacos of grilled tilapia are the best in town, and the extensive menu includes practically everything Mexican, from fajitas to *campechana* (a seafood cocktail of octopus, squid, mussels, shrimp, and cuttlefish). The fried ice cream is big enough for a table to share, and burgers and steaks are also available. There are two Guadalajara Grills in town; the other is at 822 Paseo del Pueblo Norte (✆ **575/737-0816**). Beer and wine are served. ***Note:*** This is Mexican food, the type you'll find in Mexico, not the New Mexican food you'll find in most northern New Mexico restaurants.

1384 Paseo del Pueblo Sur. guadalajaragrilltaos.com. ✆ **575/751-0063.** Main courses $11–$24. Daily 10:30am–8:30pm.

Gutiz ♥♥ LATIN AMERICAN/FRENCH Serving a creative blend of Latin American and French cuisines, Gutiz is a popular spot for breakfast and lunch, preparing excellent Parisian crepes, eggs Benedict, and caramelized French toast. Green chile sausage bowls, *pollo borracho* (drunken chicken), and a variety of sandwiches on homemade bread are also available, and you might top your meal off with a chocolate truffle or blueberry crumb cake. No alcohol is served.

812B Paseo del Pueblo Norte. gutiztaos.com. ✆ **575/758-1226.** Main courses $9–$20. Wed–Sun 8am–2pm.

La Cueva Cafe ♥ MEXICAN One block south of Taos Plaza, this no-frills restaurant is run by a couple originally from Mexico, who churn out classic staples like mole enchiladas, chimichangas, and fajitas, with a focus on seafood dishes. Breakfast, served all day, includes New Mexican favorites plus diner items like steak and eggs. All ingredients are prepared fresh daily and the entire menu is gluten-free. Beer, wine, and margaritas are served.

135 Paseo del Pueblo Sur. lacuevacafe.com. ✆ **575/758-7001.** Breakfast $11–$13; lunch and dinner $10–$20. Mon–Fri 10am–8pm, Sat 10am–5pm.

Mantes Chow Cart ♥♥ NEW MEXICAN/AMERICAN For years, Taoseños crowded around the actual Chow Cart parked in a grocery store lot to get their breakfast or lunch burrito of choice. Then Mantes moved into a fast food–style location south of Taos Plaza, and more recently added this slightly more upscale facility. Housed in an octagonal building with long low windows and a central four-sided fireplace, Mantes serves good traditional northern New Mexico food. There's banco seating at tables along the walls, and Southwestern decor complete with niches for pottery and kachina dolls. In addition to the usual burritos, tacos, and stuffed sopapillas, there are croissant sandwiches, fajita plates (marinated beef or chicken grilled with onions and peppers), and burgers; our favorite is the chile rellenos—roasted Hatch green chile stuffed with cheese and cooked in a secret batter. Almost all of the New Mexico dishes can be smothered with your choice of red or green chile, or "Christmas"—a combination of both. Beer and wine are served. The second-generation fast-food version of Mantes is at 402 Paseo del Pueblo Sur (✆ **575/758-3632**). No alcohol is served there.

1541 Paseo del Pueblo Sur, about 3 miles S of Taos Plaza. manteschowcart.com. ✆ **575/758-4855.** Dishes $3–$12. Mon–Fri 7am–7pm, Sat 7am–2pm.

Michael's Kitchen ♥ NEW MEXICAN/BAKERY A local landmark for 4 decades or so, Michael's serves what some call the best green chile in town, but that's just the start. Breakfast, served all day, is the star attraction, with choices like strawberry-banana-pecan pancakes and the "Moofy" (egg, ham, and cheese on a croissant), drawing folks from far out of town. The extensive and varied menu runs from Philly cheesesteaks to breakfast burritos to steaks and pork chops. It also features what Michael's calls "Health Food," a double order of fries with your choice of chile and cheese. There's also a full bakery turning out pies, breads, donuts, and cookies. Don't miss the pumpkin empanadas. No alcohol is served.

304 Paseo del Pueblo Norte. michaelskitchen.com. ✆ **575/758-4178.** Baked goods $3–$6; main courses $7–$22. Wed–Sun 7am–2pm. Often closes for a month in the fall.

Orlando's New Mexican Cafe ♥♥ NEW MEXICAN A family-run cafe in El Prado, about 2 miles north of the plaza, Orlando's doesn't cook anything too flashy, but what they do, they do well—witness the dozens of awards on the walls. Red and green chile are the standouts, but the *carne adovada* and taco salad are also popular with the crowds that pack the place at lunchtime. One way you can tell it's authentic New Mexican cooking is that they serve *posole* (hominy stew) instead of rice on the side. There's a casual backyard strung with Christmas lights and a warm local crowd. Definitely save space for a slice of banana split cake. *¡Delicioso!* Beer and wine are served.

1114 Don Juan Valdez Ln. (on US 64). facebook.com/OrlandosNewMexicanCafe. ✆ **575/751-1450.** Main courses $11–$22. Mon–Sat 10:30am–3pm and 5–9pm.

Ranchos Plaza Grill ♥♥ NEW MEXICAN Remember the good old days? You'd go into your local family-run cafe and be greeted by name and order your favorites from a menu that hadn't changed in years. This is what you'll find at Ranchos Plaza Grill. Located in part of a hacienda built in the 1700s, next to San Francisco de Asis Church in Ranchos de Taos, the Ranchos Plaza Grill reminds us of early 1970s Taos. Decorated with murals and art by local artists, it has a comfortable and welcoming feel. It also has some of the best genuine northern New Mexico food you'll find, and at very reasonable prices. The chile sauces are excellent; both red and green chile are made with fresh ground pork, although a vegetarian green chile salsa is available. The chile is spicy and flavorful, but not too hot. Expect all the usual northern New Mexico dishes—enchiladas, tacos, carne adovada, chile rellenos, tamales, burritos, huevos rancheros—we recommend ordering a combo plate for a sampling of items. Entrees are served with pinto beans, Spanish rice, and a not-to-be-missed homemade sopapilla with honey. There are also gringo items, including a club sandwich, pasta, salads, and burgers. Service is fast and portions are generous. No alcohol is served.

8 Ranchos Plaza Rd., Ranchos de Taos. ✆ **575/758-5788.** Main courses $8–$16. Wed–Sun 8am–2pm.

Taos Cow ♥♥ ICE CREAM/CAFE What could inspire skiers fresh off the mountain to stop at a food trailer in Arroyo Seco or travel to the Anglada building in Cañon, east of Taos, for ice cream? Taos Cow, that's what—a cafe and scoop shop that's been churning out all-natural, hormone-free ice cream since 1993, in flavors like raspberry dark chocolate, piñon caramel, cafe olé (coffee with cinnamon and dark chocolate), and coconut. Although neither location has indoor seating, both have outdoor seating and take-out. In addition to its locally famous ice cream, Taos Cow offers burritos, bagels, sandwiches, bowls, and baked goods. This is a must-stop on the way to or from the slopes or hiking trails. No alcohol is served.

483 NM 150, in Arroyo Seco, about 8 miles N of Taos; and 736 Kit Carson Rd., Cañon, 1½ miles E of Taos Plaza. taoscow.com. ✆ **575/776-5640.** Ice cream $5–$8; other items $3.50–$14. Daily 7:30am–5pm.

EXPLORING TAOS

7

With a history shaped by pre-Columbian civilization, Spanish Colonialism, and the Wild West, boasting outdoor activities that range from hot-air ballooning to hiking to some of the West's best skiing, and graced by an abundance of artists, writers, and musicians, Taos has something to offer almost everybody. Its museums offer an amazing display of regional history and culture, and Taos Pueblo should be on everyone's must-see list.

WHAT TO SEE & DO IN TAOS

Top Attractions

Millicent Rogers Museum of Northern New Mexico ♥♥♥

MUSEUM Thank Millicent Rogers, the late Standard Oil heiress, for popularizing turquoise and silver Native American jewelry among the masses and turning it into such a Southwestern fashion standard. Her collection of jewelry and Navajo weavings forms the core of this museum. The wide-ranging exhibits include Hispanic, Native American, and Anglo pieces from Pueblo jewelry to Apache baskets; Hopi *kachina* dolls; and more recent decorative tinwork. The museum boasts one of the largest public collections of works by San Ildefonso Pueblo potter Maria Martinez, arguably the Southwest's most famous Native American potter. Another focus is carved Catholic images called *santos,* with many examples from master carvers of the 18th and 19th centuries. Rogers' own jewelry collection includes the famous "Tab Necklace," made of three pounds of Zuni-worked turquoise, for which she paid a mere $5,000 in the 1940s. Sign up for a docent-led tour ($5) at least 48 hours in advance.

1504 Millicent Rogers Rd., off US 64 about 4 miles N of Taos Plaza. millicentrogers.org. ✆ **575/758-2462.** Adults $20; $15 for seniors (60+), veterans, active duty military, and students 7–18 with ID; children under 6 free. Daily 10am–5pm (closed Wed Nov–Mar). Closed New Year's Day, Easter, July 4, September 30, Thanksgiving, Christmas; closes 3pm Christmas Eve and New Year's Eve.

Taos Attractions

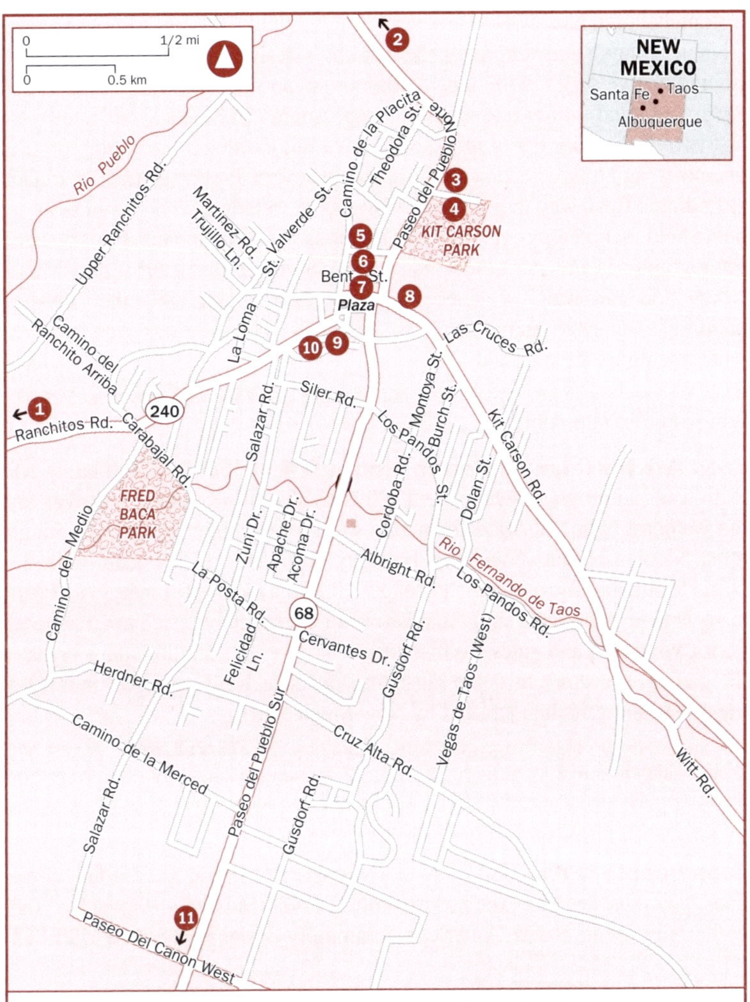

Blumenschein Home & Museum **9**	Millicent Rogers Museum of Northern New Mexico **2**
D. H. Lawrence Ranch **2**	Rio Grande Gorge Bridge **2**
Governor Bent House Museum **6**	San Francisco de Asis Church **11**
Harwood Museum of Art **10**	Taos Art Museum at Fechin House **3**
Historic County Courthouse **7**	Taos Firehouse Collection **5**
Kit Carson Home and Museum **8**	Taos Pueblo **2**
Kit Carson Park and Cemetery **4**	
La Hacienda de Los Martinez **1**	

San Francisco de Asis Church ♥♥ CHURCH If this massive adobe edifice about 4 miles south of Taos looks familiar, it's because this Spanish Colonial church has inspired artists since it was built in 1816. Almost elemental in its strength and simplicity, the building's design is a classic mix of Spanish and Native styles, with huge buttresses supporting the walls and twin bell towers adorned with white crosses. Ansel Adams and Georgia O'Keeffe are just two of the long list of artists who have immortalized the church on film or canvas, and today it's practically a law that every Taos artist tries their hand at finding a fresh way to portray it. Visitors are welcome when services aren't being held, but please remember this is a house of worship and not a museum. Photography is not permitted inside the church or the nearby parish hall, where you can watch a video about the church and view the "mystery painting"—an 1896 image of Christ that shows a mysterious glowing cross when the lights are dimmed.

60 St. Francis Plaza, Ranchos de Taos. sfranchos.org. ✆ **575/758-2754.** Free. Mon–Sat 9am–4pm, Sun 9am–3pm.

Taos Art Museum at Fechin House ♥♥ MUSEUM A rotating collection of paintings, drawings, and prints by the Taos Society of Artists and the Moderns who followed them fills the former home of Russian émigré artist Nicolai Fechin (*Feh*-shin). Between 1927 and 1933, Fechin built this home for his family, carving and shaping it into a wonderful merging of Russian, Native American, and Spanish motifs. The elaborate carved wooden doors, windows, and gates are his work. Visit Fechin's studio, take a break in the garden, and don't miss the museum store, which offers books on most of the artists and gifts handcrafted by New Mexico artists.

227 Paseo del Pueblo Norte. taosartmuseum.org. ✆ **575/758-2690.** Adults $10, seniors and military $9, students $6, ages 12 and under free. Tues–Sun 11am–5pm (noon–4pm Nov–Mar). Closed New Year's Day, Easter, July 4, Thanksgiving, Christmas; early closure Christmas and New Year's eves.

Taos Pueblo ♥♥♥ HISTORIC LANDMARK If you see nothing else in Taos, you must see this. The northernmost of New Mexico's 19 pueblos, Taos is the only living Native American community designated both a UNESCO

The Thing About Adobe...

Each June (usually the first 2 weeks), parishioners from **San Francisco de Asis Church** (see above) undertake the annual task of re-plastering its soft-mud exterior walls. Built in Spanish Colonial times before foundations were common, the church was refurbished with an exterior coat of hard plaster a number of years ago—but it turned out that sealing the outer walls, with no foundation to protect them from ground run-off, allowed moisture to seep up inside the walls, melting the adobe from within. Off came the hard plaster, and back came the annual ritual. The church is closed during this work, but the workers are very friendly and happy to take a break and chat a bit, and watching them is a one-of-a-kind experience.

feast days AT TAOS PUEBLO

Timed to celebrate the patron saints of the Catholic religion, feast days at Taos Pueblo also correspond to the traditional Pueblo religion's holy days. These fascinating religious ceremonies are open to the public, although no photography is allowed.

The most important is the **Feast of San Geronimo** (the patron saint of Taos Pueblo), September 30, which marks the end of the harvest season. This feast day is reminiscent of an ancient trade fair for the Taos Indians, when tribes from as far south as South America and as far north as the Arctic traveled here to trade for wares, hides, clothing, and harvested crops. Today the celebration is marked by foot races, pole climbs performed by traditional Indian clowns, and artists and craftspeople dressed in the garb of early traders.

The pueblo's Christmas celebration begins on **Christmas Eve,** with bonfires and a procession of the Blessed Mother. On **Christmas Day,** a variety of dances take place. These may include the **deer dance,** or the haunting **Matachines dances** (p. 26), an intriguing blend of Native and Spanish traditions.

Other annual events include a turtle dance on **New Year's Day;** buffalo or deer dances on **Three Kings Day** (January 6); and corn dances on **Santa Cruz Day** (May 3), **San Antonio Day** (June 13), **San Juan Day** (June 24), **Santiago Day** (July 25), and **Santa Ana Day** (July 26).

World Heritage Site and a National Historic Landmark. This awe-inspiring five-story adobe structure has been home to Taos Puebloans since before Columbus claimed his "New World" for Queen Isabella. Though the Tiwa were essentially a peaceful agrarian people, they also spearheaded the most successful revolt by Native Americans. Launched by Pope (Poh-*pay*) in 1680, the uprising drove the Spanish from Santa Fe until 1692 and from Taos until 1698.

The largest multi-story pueblo in existence, Taos remains home to about 150 people, who live without electricity or running water. Some 1,900 more Taos Indians live nearby on other pueblo lands. Taos Pueblo comprises two main multistory buildings, one on each side of the Rio Pueblo de Taos, which is traversed by footbridges. The plaza runs along the riverbanks, and Taos Mountain stands sentinel to the northeast. Both structures are coated with a soft straw-and-mud plaster, requiring constant upkeep (if you're there on a winter morning after a snowfall, you'll see the inhabitants shoveling the snow off their flat roofs). This is a life that goes back centuries.

As you explore the pueblo, stop in shops and studios, buy some homemade fry-bread baked in a traditional *horno* oven, look into the **San Geronimo Chapel,** a handsome Roman Catholic church still in use today, and wander past the ruins of the nearby mission church and cemetery. The place is incredibly photogenic, but always ask permission before taking a photo of someone (some may request a small payment), and do not attempt entrance to kivas (underground sacred chambers) or any area marked as restricted. If you would like to try traditional feast-day meals, stop at **Tiwa Kitchen,** near the entrance to the pueblo.

Taos Pueblo may be closed for an extended period in late winter into early spring for tribal rituals, and at other times for tribal reasons, so call ahead. Guided tours are offered year-round at 9am; call to confirm availability. The guides are often unpaid college students or volunteers, so donations are encouraged.

Like many New Mexico pueblos, Taos has opened a casino. **Taos Mountain Casino** (taosmountaincasino.com; ✆ **575/737-0777**) is on the main road to Taos Pueblo and is entirely smoke-free.

120 Veterans Hwy. From Paseo del Pueblo Norte, travel 2 miles N on Veterans Hwy. taospueblo.com. ✆ **575/758-1028.** Adults $25; seniors, students, and military $22; ages 10 and under free. Camera, video, and sketching fees subject to change; be sure to ask about telephoto lenses and tripods, as the pueblo may not allow them; photography not permitted on feast days. Daily 9am–4pm, with a few exceptions.

More Attractions

Blumenschein Home & Museum ♥♥ MUSEUM/HISTORIC HOME Talk about eclectic—this mishmash of pretty old and very old shows how the artists of the early 20th century lived and worked. Parts of this historic adobe building date from the 1790s; in 1919 it became the home and studio of Blumenschein, one of the founders of the Taos Society of Artists. The building, with its garden walls and courtyard, has been maintained much as it was when the artist and his family lived here; period furnishings include European antiques and handmade Taos furniture in Spanish Colonial style. An extensive collection of works by early 20th-century Taos artists, including some by Blumenschein's wife, Mary, and daughter, Helen, are on display.

222 Ledoux St. taoshistoricmuseums.org. ✆ **575/758-0505.** Adults $10, seniors $8, children $4. Mon–Sat 10am–5pm.

D. H. Lawrence Ranch ♥♥ HISTORIC HOME Although the controversial early-20th-century author D. H. Lawrence spent a total of just 11 months in New Mexico, the state made such an impression on him that he wrote, "I think New Mexico was the greatest experience from the outside world that I have ever had. It certainly changed me forever." Today you can visit his retreat, the remote Kiowa Ranch on Lobo Mountain above San Cristobal, where he lived on and off between 1922 and 1925. His mornings were frequently spent writing at a small table under a mammoth pine tree—the Lawrence Tree. When he died in southern France in 1930, his wife Frieda returned to the ranch, where she eventually constructed a shrine to her husband. Frieda willed Kiowa Ranch to the University of New Mexico for educational, cultural, and recreational purposes, providing they made "a perpetual D. H. Lawrence Memorial and Foundation." Now under the auspices of UNM and the D. H. Lawrence Ranch Alliance, the Lawrence Memorial and the Lawrence Tree are open to visitors, plus Frieda's gravesite, two cabins, and a small visitor center. A docent tour can be arranged.

About 15 miles N of Taos via NM 522, in San Cristobal. Turn right at sign and travel about 5 miles on well-maintained dirt road. dhlawrenceranch.unm.edu. ✆ **575/776-2245.** Free. Tues–Thurs 9:30am–3:30pm.

Governor Bent House Museum ♥ HISTORIC HOME This small and disorderly museum's claim to fame is that this is the exact spot where the New Mexico Territory's first American governor was murdered. The museum is housed in the residence of Charles Bent, a former trader who helped establish Bent's Fort in Colorado. He was killed during the 1847 Taos Pueblo and Hispanic revolt, while his wife and children escaped by digging through an adobe wall into the house next door. The mishmash of items on display represent the era but not Governor Bent specifically.

117 Bent St. ✆ **575/224-4754.** Adults $3, ages 8–15 $1, free for kids 7 and under. Daily 10am–5pm. Closed New Year's Day, Easter, Thanksgiving, and Christmas.

Harwood Museum of Art ♥♥ MUSEUM If you only have time to stop at one museum, make it this enormous collection of Taos art, from the early 20th-century Taos Society of Artists through the Taos Moderns of the 1940s and contemporary works of the 1970s, right up to the present, plus art by Latino and Indian artists. This of course means that only a small selection can be on view at any one time, but you can be sure there will be something worthwhile. One gallery, for example, was specifically built for seven paintings by Agnes Martin. Martin was so thrilled with the gallery that she suggested the addition of its central Donald Judd–designed benches and would often visit her works. The museum also schedules changing exhibitions throughout the year.

238 Ledoux St. harwoodmuseum.org. ✆ **575/758-9826.** Adults $10, seniors (64+) and students $8, ages 18 and under free. Tues–Fri 10am–5pm, Sat–Sun noon–5pm. Closed New Year's Day, Easter, July 4, Thanksgiving, Christmas Eve, Christmas, and New Year's Eve.

Historic County Courthouse ♥♥ HISTORIC BUILDING Located in the middle of the north side of Taos Plaza, this is the third courthouse built in Taos County (the fifth is in use south of town), standing on the site of the burned-down second one. After its completion in January 1934, the WPA commissioned four Taos artists—Emil Bisttram, Victor Higgins, Ward Lockwood, and Bert Phillips—to create frescos in the second-floor courtroom.

Art Classes

If you're in Taos, why not pretend to be a famous Taos artist? To pursue an artistic adventure of your own, check out the variety of classes in such media as painting, sculpture, Native American pottery, photography, and Navajo weaving offered by **Taos Art School** ♥ (taosartschool.org; ✆ **575/758-0350**). Open since 1989, the school is a virtual campus in which classes are held wherever they need to be. For instance, the plein air painting class takes place on the school's 18,000-acre ranch, a pottery class might be at a local artist's home, another painting class at an interesting church; equine arts classes are held in a local barn with the horses present (bring carrots). Fees vary from class to class and usually don't include the cost of materials.

After years of neglect, they were restored in 1994, and two more were added. Downstairs you'll find the old, and pretty wretched, Taos jail—just follow the signs. The courthouse is also home to the Taos Community Center Co-op (✆ **505/758-1054**), a good place to see and buy arts and crafts by Taos County artisans. As of writing, the courthouse is temporarily closed for a major refurbishment that seeks to return its original floorplan and exterior.

121 North Plaza. Free. Daily 10am–5pm.

Kit Carson Home and Museum ♥ HISTORIC HOME Everyone has heard about Kit Carson, Taos's most famous frontiersman, but if you want the real scoop on who he was and why he's famous, this is the place. Carson bought this adobe home in 1843 as a wedding gift for his bride Maria Josefa Jaramillo. They lived here until 1868, when they both died, a month apart, in Colorado. Some rooms have been restored and furnished as it's believed they were when the couple was in residence, with buffalo hides, leather clothes, a Civil War saber, and a replica of the famous scout's Hawken rifle. A 20-minute video about Carson is shown, and there are photos of Carson and his family. A visit offers a glimpse of life during Taos's frontier heyday.

113 Kit Carson Rd. kitcarsonmuseum.org. ✆ **505/758-4082.** Adults $10; seniors $8; teens, students, and veterans with ID $7; free for ages 12 and under. Tues–Sat 11am–4pm. Closed Thanksgiving, Christmas, and New Year's days.

Kit Carson Park and Cemetery ♥♥ PARK Major community events are held in this pleasant park north of Taos Plaza, a relaxing grassy place to take a break while exploring Taos. At the southeast corner of the park you can wander around a cemetery, established in 1847, which contains the graves of many historical figures connected to the sites you'll be visiting: Kit Carson, his wife Josefa, the murdered Governor Charles Bent, the Don Antonio Martinez family, Mabel Dodge Luhan, and others. Their lives are described briefly on plaques.

211 Paseo del Pueblo Norte. ✆ **575/751-2001** (Taos Parks & Plaza Dept.). Free. Daily 7am–-8pm, gate closes 5pm in winter.

La Hacienda de Los Martinez ♥ HISTORIC SITE To step back into New Mexico in the early 19th century, begin at this imposing adobe complex. Built along the Rio Pueblo between 1804 and 1827 by a farmer and trader, this was the northern terminus of El Camino Real (the Royal Road), a major trade route that ran all the way to Mexico City. Thanks to occasional raids by Indian tribes, it's part residence, part fortress—notice the lack of windows in the outer walls—with 21 rooms arranged around two courtyards, or *placitas*. Colonial clothes, foods, and other items fill the restored rooms; there's a working blacksmith's shop and other living-history-type crafts on display. Old-time Taoseños tell tales of the ghosts that supposedly haunt the hacienda.

708 Hacienda Way (off NM 240/Lower Ranchitos Rd.). taoshistoricmuseums.org. ✆ **575/758-1000.** Adults $8, seniors $7, ages 5–15 $4, under 5 free. Mon–Sat 10am–5pm, Sun noon–5pm.

Rio Grande Gorge Bridge ♥♥ LANDMARK This magnificent 1,272-foot-long bridge, west of the Taos airport, spans the mighty Rio Grande. At 650 feet above the canyon floor, it's one of America's highest bridges. If you can stand the vertigo—and the vibration when a truck drives over—it's a grand view to the river below. Sometimes you can spot rafters or kayakers on the water, and occasionally you'll see a hot-air balloon dipping into the gorge. If you park in the rest area on the west side of the bridge and follow the West Rim Trail south, you'll get a fine view of the expanse of the bridge. You might even glimpse a few of the bighorn sheep that make the gorge their home. Movie trivia: The wedding scene in the 1994 movie *Natural Born Killers* was filmed here.

US 64, 10 miles W of Taos. Free. Daily 24 hr.

Taos Firehouse Collection ♥♥ MUSEUM Tucked away at the back of the Taos Fire Station, behind the fire trucks, hoses, and pool tables, is an unexpected trove of more than 100 paintings, among the most eclectic collections in Taos. The works have only two things in common: All the artists lived and worked in the Taos area, and each piece was donated to the fire department. Just about every square inch of wall space in the fire department's recreation hall is covered with this somewhat haphazardly hung exhibit. It's a fascinating collection spanning more than a century of Taos art. Look for the delightfully whimsical painting by Eugene Dobos of a man dressed in a tux wearing a firefighter's helmet, and the colorful, somewhat casually mounted "Fire Season" by George Chacon. While at the fire station, say hello to Maria, the department's 1936 American LaFrance fire engine. She comes out for parades and special events if she starts; Maria can be a bit temperamental.

323 Camino de la Placita. No website. ✆ **575/758-3386.** Free, donations welcome. Mon–Fri 9am–4:30pm, Sat–Sun by appointment (unless everyone's out fighting a fire).

Organized Tours

Heritage Inspirations ♥♥ (heritageinspirations.com; ✆ **575/779-5516**) offers a number of tours of the area, most leaving from **El Monte Sagrado Resort** (p. 130). The half-day Cultural Tour includes a visit to iconic **Taos Pueblo** (p. 148), the **Hacienda de los Martinez** (p. 152), the **San Francisco de Asis Church** (p. 148), and the **Rio Grande Gorge Bridge** (above). Another tour heads to the bridge first, then takes an interpretive guided hike in the Río Grande del Norte National Monument. If you love chocolate—and who in her right mind doesn't?—you might sign up for the Taos Artisan Walking Tour + Chocolate, a guided wander around the backroads and alleyways of downtown Taos, describing the history and culture along the way. You'll finish at Chokola Bean to Bar for a sample of the miracle that's chocolate and even some data about the bean. Other tour options include serious hiking, fly-fishing, and even snowshoeing in winter. Prices vary considerably depending on the number of people, duration of tour, and where you're going. Check the website for details and booking.

SPORTS & RECREATION

Thanks to the federal government, the area around Taos is one big public playground, with forests, mountains, lakes, streams, and the mighty Rio Grande. There is hiking, camping, fishing, downhill and cross-country skiing, snowshoeing . . . the list goes on and on. Most of this public land is managed by two federal agencies with their headquarters in Taos. For information on many of the activities and locations discussed below, contact **Carson National Forest,** 208 Cruz Alta Rd. (fs.usda.gov/carson; ✆ **575/758-6200**), or the **Bureau of Land Management,** 226 Cruz Alta Rd. (blm.gov/new-mexico; ✆ **575/758-8851**). At press time, the Taos office of the BLM was planning a move to Paseo del Pueblo Sur, so call before going.

Downhill Skiing

Four alpine ski resorts are within an hour's drive of Taos; all offer complete facilities, including lodging, restaurants, equipment rentals, and just about every type of ski gear and clothing you might want to buy. Although exact opening and closing dates vary depending on snow conditions, the season usually begins anywhere from mid-November to mid-December and continues into late March or early April. Basic ski pass prices are included below, but be sure to check each resort's website for special deals and packages.

Angel Fire Resort ♥♥ About 20 miles east of Taos, and over a mountain, Angel Fire is a good family-friendly ski area. The 80 runs are heavily oriented to beginner and intermediate skiers and snowboarders, although there is plenty for those more advanced. Instead of an old village, like other ski areas listed here, this is a Vail-style resort, with a variety of activities other than skiing (see "The Enchanted Circle," p. 166). Snowmaking capabilities here are excellent, as is the popular ski school. There's a 2,077-foot vertical drop from the summit (10,677 ft.) to the base. Two high-speed quad lifts whisk skiers to the top; there are also three double lifts and two surface lifts. The 86 trails are rated 27% beginner, 49% intermediate, and 23% advanced, with four glade (tree trail) areas covering 30 acres designated as advanced. There are also three terrain parks, including Liberation Park at the summit, with multiple jumps, rails, fun-boxes, and other features for advanced riders. Cross-country skiing, snowshoeing, and snow-biking are also available.

angelfireresort.com. ✆ **800/633-7463** or 575/377-6401. Full-day lift ticket adults $85–$120, ages 13–17 $74–$104, ages 7–12 and ages 70–74 $59–$83; seniors 74+ and children under 7 $22–$24. Daily 9am–4pm in ski season.

Red River Ski & Summer Area ♥♥ Since opening in 1959, this family-owned business provides a unique family experience year-round. The village sits at the base of the lifts, giving easy access to winter skiing and summer adventures. The area doesn't depend on Mother Nature as much as most other ski areas—good snow is almost guaranteed early and late in the season by snowmaking that can cover 85% of the runs. There's a 1,600-foot vertical drop to a base elevation of 8,750 feet. Lifts include one double chair, three triples, a quad, and two surface lifts. There are 64 trails—rated 31% beginner, 31% intermediate, and 38% expert, plus three terrain parks and one glade. In summer, Red River offers a refreshingly cool mountain retreat with an aerial adventure ropes course, zip line, tubing, scenic lift rides, and disc golf, with everything pretty much within walking distance.

redriverskiarea.com. ✆ **575/754-2223.** For lodging see redriver.org, ✆ **575/754-3030.** Full-day lift ticket adults $106, ages 6–12 $76, seniors 70+ and ages 5 and under free. Daily 9am–4pm (open until 5pm Fri–Sat March–Thanksgiving).

Sipapu Ski and Summer Resort ♥ The oldest ski area in the Taos region, founded in 1952, Sipapu is located on NM 518 in the tiny village of Vadito, tucked into the mountains about 20 miles southeast of Taos. It prides itself on being a small, family-friendly ski area—small enough so your kids won't get lost, with 215 skiable acres and 40 trails—and claims to have the longest ski season in the state. It also has the lowest lift prices in the Taos area, with deep discounts for early- and late-season skiers; first-timers are welcomed with free ski lessons. Lifts include a quad, two triples, a platter, and two surface tows. There's a vertical drop of 1,055 feet to the 8,200-foot base. Of Sipapu's 41 trails, 20% are for beginners, 40% are intermediate, and 40% are advanced; there are also three terrain parks.

sipapu.ski. ✆ **505/587-2240.** Full-day lift ticket adults $15–$44; free for seniors 75+ and children under 12. Daily 9am–4pm late Nov–Apr.

Taos Ski Valley ♥♥♥ This is the big one: New Mexico's best and most famous ski area; some would call it the preeminent ski resort in the southern Rocky Mountains. It was founded in 1955 by Swiss-German immigrant Ernie Blake, who had been managing ski areas while searching for somewhere to build his own. Flying over northern New Mexico in his Cessna 170, Blake spotted the perfect place: the abandoned mining site of Twining, north of Wheeler Peak and high above Taos. The rest, as they say, is history. Owned and managed by several generations of Blakes for years, the resort was sold in 2013 to Louis Bacon of New York. Bacon instigated a major construction and improvement project, which included upgrades to practically every aspect of the resort, from new energy-efficient snowmaking equipment to construction of The Blake (p. 136), an elegant 80-room hotel in the heart of the base area.

So, why do you want to ski or snowboard Taos? For starters, there's light, dry powder (usually more than 300 in. annually), one of the best ski schools in the country, and its personal, friendly service. And then there are the superb trails. Taos Ski Valley offers steep, high-alpine, high-adventure skiing, perfect for the expert skier, but beginners and intermediates aren't left out, either. Of the resort's 110 trails, 24% are for beginners, 25% for intermediates, 33% advanced, and 18% are hike-to terrain. Between the 12,481-foot Kachina Peak and the 9,207-foot base, the area has an uphill capacity of more than 15,000 skiers per hour on its gondola, double chairlift, three triples, four quads, one high-speed quad, and four surface tows.

Skiing with Kids

Although known primarily for its wonderful expert terrain, Taos Ski Valley is also a good family destination. It welcomes snowboarders and has an excellent ski school. The Rio Hondo Learning Center offers daycare, lessons for ages 3 to 14, and evening programs. The Ernie Blake Snowsports School has classes for all ages and abilities, from the beginner to the expert looking to work on technique. Check skitaos.com for details.

There are numerous lodges and condominiums at Taos School Valley, with some 1,500 beds; most offer ski-week and other packages. There are several restaurants on the mountain as well, in addition to the many facilities of Village Center at the base.

skitaos.com. ✆ **575/776-2291** for general information; ✆ **844/828-5601** for snow reports; ✆ **888/569-1756** for lodging reservations. Full-day lift ticket adults $80–$175, ages 7–17 $55–$130, seniors 65+ $70–$130; $65 novice lift ticket give you access to the Pioneers Lift, Rueggli Lift, and Pioneers Zippers. Prices lower with multi-day and advance purchase. Daily 9am–4pm Thanksgiving–mid-April.

Cross-Country Skiing

There are dozens of popular Nordic trails in the **Carson National Forest,** which covers much of the area around Taos. One of the more popular trails is **Amole Canyon Trail # 10 ♥♥**, off NM 518 near the Sipapu Ski Resort. This is actually a stacked loop system of trails of various difficulty levels, with trail signs at intersections. Part of the system is groomed and tracked periodically. It's open to cross-country skiers and snowshoers, but closed to snowmobiles—a comfort to lovers of serenity. Details on this and numerous other trails are available from the Carson National Forest office (p. 154). Recreation officers emphasize that these trails are not patrolled; for your safety, they recommend that you not go alone.

Just east of Red River, with 20.5 miles of groomed trails (in addition to 9.3 miles of trails strictly for snowshoeing), the **Enchanted Forest Cross Country Ski Area ♥♥** (enchantedforestxc.com; ✆ **575/754-6112**) spreads over 400 acres of forestlands atop Bobcat Pass. There's even a 3.1-mile section where you can ski with your dog. In addition to cross-country ski and snowshoe rentals, the ski area rents pulk sleds—high-tech devices in which children are pulled by their skiing parents. There's a full ski shop and snack bar, and instruction in cross-country classic as well as freestyle skating is available, plus guided snowshoe tours. A yurt is also available for a ski-in accommodation. Full-day trail passes, good 9am to 4:30pm, are $25 for adults, $24 for ages 13 to 17 and 60 to 69, $10 for seniors 70 and up, and free for children 12 and under.

For access to high-mountain terrain, the **Southwest Nordic Center ♥** (southwestnordiccenter.com; ✆ **575/758-4761**) offers rentals in a yurt that can accommodate 10 people, in an area called Bull of the Woods near Taos Ski Valley. Skiers trek to the hut, backpacking their clothing and food in, either with a guide or on their own (following directions on a provided map). The yurt is rented by the night (2-night minimum), and fees range $80 to $145 per group. Guide service is extra. Call for reservations as far in advance as possible.

Adventure Ski Rentals & Snowboard Shop ♥ (adventureskishops.com), with two locations—1337 Paseo del Pueblo Sur (✆ **575/758-1167**) and 303 Paseo del Pueblo Norte (✆ **575/758-9744**)—should be able to set you up with whatever snow gear you need, from snowshoes to cross-country skis, with various packages available, plus a full range of ski and snowboard repair and tuning services.

Other Sports & Recreation

BALLOONING

As in many other towns throughout New Mexico, hot-air ballooning is a top attraction. Recreational trips over the Taos Valley and Rio Grande Gorge are offered year-round by **Eske's Paradise Balloons** ♥ (taosballooning.com; ✆ **575/751-6098**), and from June through September by **Taos Balloon Rides** ♥ (taosballoonrides.com; ✆ **575/224-6022**).

BIKING

The **West Rim Trail** ♥ is a scenic and easy 10-mile ride along the Rio Grande Gorge. To reach it, head west on US 64 and cross the Rio Grande Gorge Bridge, pulling into the rest area. Or start at the southern end: Head south on NM 68 for 17 miles to Pilar, turn west onto NM 570, and travel along the river for 6¼ miles. Cross the bridge and drive to the top of the ridge.

If you're looking for a technical and challenging ride, try the steep **Devisadero Loop Trail 108** ♥ in the Carson National Forest. This 5.1-mile trail, also used by hikers and horseback riders, is 3 miles east of Taos via Kit Carson Road (US 64), and provides splendid panoramic views of the Taos Valley. You can follow it to Devisadero Peak and stand guard to watch for invading Apaches, as the people of Taos Pueblo once did.

Bicycle rentals for cruising the town or riding the back country are available from **Rift Cycles** ♥, 1029 Paseo del Pueblo Norte (riftcycles.com; ✆ **575/694-2096**); daily rentals on a 29-inch full-suspension carbon bike start at $120, and weekly rates are available. It's open Tuesday to Saturday 10am to 5pm, with trail maps available.

Annual touring events include Red River's **Enchanted Circle Century Bicycle Tour** ♥♥ (redriver.org; ✆ **575/754-2366**) on the weekend following Labor Day.

FISHING

The rivers and streams of Taos County are great for fishing, and although you can go out on your own, we recommend going with a guide, who will know where the fish are biting. The family-owned **Taos Fly Shop** ♥♥ (taosflyshop.com; ✆ **575/751-1312**), 338 Paseo del Pueblo Sur, has gear, maps, and knowledgeable people to help you; "Super Fly" Taylor Streit, who's been guiding in the area since 1980, runs the guiding side of things. Gear and guides are also available from **The Solitary Angler** ♥ (thesolitaryangler.com; ✆ **866/502-1700** or 575/758-5653), 303 Paseo del Pueblo Norte. Licenses are required and can be purchased at local sporting goods and fly shops.

FITNESS FACILITIES

The **Taos Spa and Tennis Club** ♥♥, 111 Dona Ana Dr. (across from Sagebrush Inn; taosspa.com; ✆ **575/758-1980**), is a fully equipped fitness center that rivals any you'd find in a big city. It has a variety of cardio machines, bikes, and weight-training machines, as well as saunas, indoor and outdoor Jacuzzis, a steam room, and indoor and outdoor pools. The club offers a wide range of exercise classes from yoga to Pilates to water fitness. In addition, it has tennis and racquetball courts. Therapeutic massage, facials, and physical therapy are available daily by appointment. Children's programs include a tennis camp and swimming lessons, and childcare services are available. Open hours are Monday to Thursday 5am to 9pm, Friday 5am to 8pm, and Saturday and Sunday 7am to 8pm. The daily rate is $20, but short-term memberships and multi-day passes are available.

High Altitude Health and Fitness ♥, on the north side of town at 1307 Paseo del Pueblo Norte (highaltitudehealthfitness.com; ✆ **575/751-1242**), is also a full-service facility, with free weights and Cybex and cardio equipment. It offers aerobics and yoga classes, indoor and outdoor pools, and four tennis courts, plus children's and seniors' programs. The center is open weekdays 5am to 9pm, Saturdays 7am to 8pm, and Sundays 7am to 7pm. The daily rate is $13.

Located just a short distance south of the plaza, **Deliberately Fit** ♥ (deliberatelyfit.com; ✆ **575/758-2900**), 324 Paseo del Pueblo Sur, offers premium equipment, top-notch training, and 24-hour access to those who buy multi-day passes. It's open Monday to Friday 9am to midnight for day-use visitors. A day pass costs $15; a week pass is $30.

GOLF

Golfers love the 18-hole course at the **Taos Country Club** ♥, 54 Golf Course Dr., Ranchos de Taos (taoscountryclub.com; ✆ **575/758-7300**), with its Jep Wille–designed course and four sets of tees. The rolling greens are edged and surrounded by a sea of sagebrush against a stunning backdrop of the Sangre de Cristo Mountains. Located off NM 68 and CR 110, just 6 miles south of Taos Plaza, it's a first-rate championship golf course designed for all levels of play. It has open fairways and no hidden greens, a driving range, practice putting and chipping greens, and private and group lessons. The country club also has a clubhouse with a restaurant and full bar. It's always advisable to call ahead, or book online, for tee times. Greens fees start at $60 in summer, and $50 spring and fall; cart and club rentals are available. Closed December through February.

The par-72, 18-hole course at the **Angel Fire Resort Golf Course** ♥ (angelfireresort.com; ✆ **800/633-7463** or 575/377-4488) is surrounded by stands of ponderosa pine, spruce, and aspen. At 8,500 feet, it's one of the highest regulation golf courses in the world. It has a driving range, putting green, carts and clubs for rent, and a club pro who gives lessons. Greens fees start at $99 in summer, $73 spring and fall; tee times should be scheduled 7 days ahead.

HIKING

There are hundreds of miles of hiking trails in Taos County's mountain and high-mesa country. The nights turn chilly by September, and mountain weather is always changeable, so layers are recommended. Take plenty of water and sunscreen, wear sturdy hiking shoes and a hat, and pop a snack in your pack. For maps and advice on all **Carson National Forest** trails and recreation areas, look online (fs.usda.gov/carson) or visit the **U.S. Forest Service** office in Taos (p. 137). Gear and advice are available from **Taos Mountain Outfitters ♥**, 113 N. Plaza (taosmountainoutfitters.com; ✆ **575/758-9292**).

One of the easiest hikes to access is the **West Rim Trail ♥**, which follows the rim of the Rio Grande Gorge. Drive west from Taos on US 64, crossing the Rio Grande Gorge Bridge, and turn left into the picnic area. Walking a short distance south along this trail affords a spectacular view of the full span of the bridge. The full trail is 10 miles long, but you can go however far you like, remembering you have to hike the same distance back to your car!

The 18,897-acre **Wheeler Peak Wilderness ♥♥♥** is a wonderland of alpine tundra, encompassing New Mexico's highest peak (13,161 ft.). A favorite (though rigorous) hike to Wheeler Peak's summit (15 miles round-trip with a 3,700-ft. elevation gain) makes for a long but exciting day. The trail head is at Taos Ski Valley (p. 155). A favorite short hike is the **Williams Lake ♥♥** trail with its parking lot and trail head near the Kachina chairlift and Bavarian lodge above Taos Ski Valley. The 2-mile trail starts out on private land, so please be respectful and stay on the trail as you follow the east side of Lake Fork Creek. The trail begins among stands of Engelmann spruce, opening into meadowlands and scattered rock as you climb. Williams Lake is a natural lake and untenanted by fish as it freezes in winter. You may encounter avalanche debris along the unmaintained trail, so watch your step, and in winter be alert to the danger. Elevation gain is just 900 feet. In Hondo Canyon, the popular **Italianos Canyon ♥♥** trail can get quite crowded on summer weekends. You'll walk among mixed conifers along its 3.5 miles; it gains 2,800 feet in elevation and affords access to Lobo Peak, Flag Mountain, and Gold Hill. The trail head is on the north side of NM 150, about 3 miles southwest of Taos Ski Valley and 8 miles from Arroyo Seco. Nearby **Yerba Canyon Trail ♥**, just 2 miles west of Italianos along NM 150, boasts an abundance of aspen and willows along its southern stretch, gradually giving way to spruce and fir as you approach the ridge. It's 4 miles long, with an elevation gain of 3,700 feet. Both trails follow a drainage path, meaning avalanches are a possibility in winter and early spring. Both trails are open to horseback riding and backcountry camping.

HORSEBACK RIDING

The expansive sage mesas and tree-covered mountains around Taos make it a fun and exciting place to ride, and the hiking trails described above are open to horses. **Rio Grande Stables** ♥ (riograndestables.net; ✆ **888/508-7667**) offers a variety of guided rides along the mountain trails of the ski valley. There's something for everyone regardless of ability or experience. A 3-hour adventure (2 hr. of actual riding) starts at $85 per person.

ICE SKATING

In winter there's ice skating at the **Taos Youth and Family Center** ♥♥, 407 Paseo del Cañon East, 2 miles south of the plaza and about ¾ mile off Paseo del Pueblo Sur (taosnm.gov; ✆ **505/758-4160**). Cost is $4 for adults and $3 for children, which includes skate rentals. Hours are Monday through Friday 9am to 7pm, Saturdays 9am to 6pm, and Sundays 10am to 6pm, although weekend hours may be shortened during hockey season.

RIVER RAFTING

Half- or full-day whitewater rafting trips down the Rio Grande and Rio Chama originate in Taos and can be booked through a variety of outfitters in the area. The wild and wonderful **Taos Box** ♥♥♥, a steep-sided canyon south of the Wild Rivers Recreation Area of Río Grande del Norte National Monument (p. 170), offers a series of class IV rapids that rarely let up for some 17 miles. The water drops up to 90 feet per mile, providing one of the most exciting 1-day whitewater tours in the West. May and June are prime rafting months. Experienced rafting companies in Taos are **Los Rios River Runners** ♥♥♥ (losriosriverrunners.com; ✆ **575/776-8854**), and **Far Flung Adventures** ♥♥♥

GETTING PAMPERED: the spa scene

For a luxurious pampering, head to **Ojo Caliente Mineral Springs Resort and Spa** ♥♥♥ (50 Los Banos Dr., Ojo Caliente; ojosparesorts.com; ✆ **888/939-0007** or 505/583-2045), about 45 minutes southwest of Taos in the village of Ojo Caliente. Over 100,000 gallons of geothermal mineral waters steam to the surface from four springs, revitalizing those who soak in one of their 11 sulfur-free mineral pools. Each spring provides a different mineral: lithia, iron, soda, or arsenic, and the pools are filled with different types and combinations with temperatures ranging from 80 to 109 degrees Fahrenheit. In addition, you'll find a mud pool, a full-service day spa, plus—our favorite—outdoor private pools, where clothing is optional and there's a kiva fireplace for chilly evenings. There's also a restaurant and wine bar, hiking and mountain biking trails, plus lodging and camping on premises.

In Taos, **El Monte Sagrado** ♥♥ (317 Kit Carson Rd.; elmontesagrado.com; ✆ **800/828-8267** or 505/758-3502) offers a variety of treatments (see p. 130); and you can get a massage at **Taos Spa and Tennis Club** ♥ (116 Sutton Place, Taos Ski Valley; see "Fitness Facilities," p. 158).

In Taos Ski Valley visit **The Spa and Wellness Center at The Blake** ♥♥ (116 Sutton Place, Taos Ski Valley; skitaos.com; ✆ **575/776-5340**) for facials, massages, body treatments, and more.

(farflung.com; ✆ **800/359-2627** or 575/758-2628). You will be required to wear a life jacket (provided), and you should expect to get wet. Half-day trips cost $70 to $75 for adults and $60 to $65 for kids. The season usually runs from March to October.

Note that only experienced river runners should attempt these waters without a guide. Check with the **Bureau of Land Management** (blm.gov/newmexico; ✆ **575/758-8851**) to make sure that you're fully equipped to go whitewater rafting. Have them check your gear to make sure it's sturdy enough—this is serious rafting and kayaking!

ROCK CLIMBING

Mountain Skills ♥ (climbingschoolusa.com; ✆ **575/776-2222**) has been offering rock-climbing instruction since 1994 for all skill levels, from beginners to more advanced climbers, who would like to find the best area climbs.

SKATEBOARDING

Try your board at **Taos Youth and Family Center** (see "Ice Skating," p. 160), which includes an in-line-skate and skateboarding park, open daily from dawn to dusk; admission is free.

SNOWMOBILING

Traversing the hiking and horseback trails of the ski valley on a snowmobile makes for some of the best rides anywhere. Big Al of **A.A. Taos Ski Valley Wilderness Adventures** ♥♥ (aataosskivalleywildernessadventures.com; ✆ **575/751-6051**) knows these trails inside and out, and he'll take you on the ride of your life. Never been on one? No matter: Big Al prides himself on providing personal service to ensure that you'll enjoy every minute. Rides start at $120 for 2 hours. Call to reserve.

SWIMMING

The Town of Taos **Youth and Family Center** (see "Ice Skating," p. 160) includes the **Taos Aquatic Center** ♥♥ (✆ **575/737-2583**), which has an excellent pool and slide. Swim sessions cost $4 adults and $3 children and seniors. Times are set aside for recreational swimming, lap swimming, water aerobics, and toddler swim times. Check the website for the current schedule.

TENNIS

The **Taos Spa and Tennis Club** (p. 158) has four outdoor courts, and the **High Altitude Health and Fitness** (p. 158) has three tennis courts. In addition, there are four free public courts in Taos—two at **Kit Carson Park,** on Paseo del Pueblo Norte, and two at **Fred Baca Memorial Park,** on Camino del Medio, south of Ranchitos Road.

TAOS SHOPPING

For those who love to shop, Taos offers countless choices. The place to start is **Taos Plaza,** with shops and galleries all around, plus a restaurant or two and even the La Fonda Hotel (p. 132). After perusing what the plaza has to offer, head east on **Kit Carson Road,** then north on Paseo del Pueblo several blocks, taking a side trip down **Bent Street**—so named not because of the sharp bend about two-thirds of the way down, but rather because the first governor of the territory lived here (see p. 151).

Once you've finished with downtown Taos, head south to **Ranchos de Taos** and the shops and galleries on the plaza behind San Francisco de Asis Church (p. 161). Finish up with a visit to the charming village of **Arroyo Seco,** about 5 miles north of Taos along NM 150. While you're there, stop by the lovely 1834 church, La Santísima Trinidad, tucked away a short walk off the highway.

Galleries and shops are generally open daily in summer and closed Sundays or one day midweek in winter. Hours vary but generally run from 10am to 5 or 6pm. Some artists show their work by appointment only.

Art

Bryan's Gallery ♥♥ Since its opening in 1982, this gallery has specialized in art of the Southwest and New Mexico's Eight Northern Pueblos. Here you'll find paintings, jewelry, sculpture, pottery, rugs, baskets, and more. 121 Kit Carson Rd. bryansgallery.com. ✆ **575/758-9407.**

Carol Dee's Art Joint ♥ Offering contemporary art with an elaborate sculpture garden, this is a fun place to browse for works on paper or of clay. Lyman Whitaker's wind sculptures catch the eye of everyone driving by on US 64. 1405 Paseo del Pueblo Norte (in the Overland Sheepskin Complex), El Prado, 3 miles N of Taos Plaza. caroldeesartjoint.com. ✆ **505/751-1344.**

Navajo Gallery ♥♥♥ On display here are numerous R. C. Gorman works: oil pastel drawings, lithographs, giclées, bronzes, and more. 104 S. Plaza. rcgormannavajogallery.com. ✆ **575/758-2211.**

R. B. Ravens ♥♥ This longtime gallery specializes in pre-1930 Navajo weavings, Pueblo pottery, Hopi kachinas, and American Indian paintings. 4146 NM 68 (near the church plaza), Ranchos de Taos. rbravens.com. ✆ **575/758-7322.**

Robert L. Parsons Fine Art ♥♥♥ Located in the 1859 Ferdinand Maxwell home, this gallery displays works of the early Taos and Santa Fe artists, including Nicolai Fechin, Joseph Sharp, and O. E. Berninghaus. Fine Pueblo pottery and antique Navajo blankets dress the space. 131 Bent St. parsonsart.com. ✆ **575/751-0159.**

Steppin' Out

Explore the Taos Plaza galleries and shops, then take a turn down Juan Largo Lane to explore the delightful pedestrian walkway that connects to Bent Street. The **John Dunn House Shops** ♥♥ (johndunnshops.com) line the walkway, offering fine and folk art, fashion for men, women, and children, a bookstore and a kitchen shop, a coffee shop, and a nice deli with outside seating in decent weather. Take a stroll.

Taos Blue ♥ You can't miss this gallery at the corner of Bent Street, with its colorful metal flower sculptures in the front yard and string of huge canister bells hanging from the portal. Inside you'll find room after room filled with fine art, weavings, and Native American handcrafts, plus wearables, jewelry, and fetishes. 101A Bent St. taosblue.com. ✆ **575/758-3561.**

Books

Brodsky Bookshop ♥ Come here for the exceptional inventory of fiction, nonfiction, Southwestern and Native American studies, children's books, used books, cards, tapes, and CDs. 226A Paseo del Pueblo Norte. facebook.com/people/Brodsky-Bookshop/100057361364887. ✆ **575/758-9468.**

Children

Twirl ♥♥ This is an adventure as well as a terrific place to shop. A play structure, hobbit home, and fountain entertain kids while those of all ages hunt for musical instruments, toys, and clothing. 225 Camino de la Placita. twirlhouse.com. ✆ **575/751-1402.**

Crafts

Moxie ♥♥ A "fair trade and handmade" shop with unique gifts, clothing, home decor, and so much more—all colorful and fun. 204 Paseo del Pueblo Norte. taosmoxie.com. ✆ **575/758-1256.**

Fashion

Artemisia ♥♥♥ This shop carries lovely wearable art and accessories in bold colors, all hand-woven or hand-sewn, all for women. 103 Bent St. artemisiataos.com. ✆ **575/737-9800.**

Overland Sheepskin Company ♥ You can't miss the romantically weathered barn just off the highway in a meadow a few miles north of town. Inside, you'll find anything you can imagine in leather: coats, gloves, hats, slippers, and more. 1405 Paseo del Pueblo Norte. overland.com/stores/taos-nm. ✆ **575/758-8820.**

Furniture & Home

At Home in Taos ♥ If you're looking to brighten your abode, head to this brilliant shop in McCarthy Plaza just off a corner of the main plaza. You'll find colorful handmade placemats and bowls as well as cards, pottery, and bags made from recycled materials. 117 S. Plaza. facebook.com/athomeintaos123. ✆ **575/751-1486.**

CFT Décor and Gifts ♥ Here you'll find unique pottery, art, unusual gifts, and home furnishings spread through seven rooms. 303 Paseo del Pueblo Norte. facebook.com/cftaos. ✆ **575/613-3486.**

Nambé ♥♥ This company made a name for itself producing serving platters, picture frames, and candlesticks from a metal alloy. Over the years,

Nambé has expanded into production of crystal and wood designs, all lovely additions to your home. 109 N. Plaza. nambe.com. ✆ **575/758-8221.**

Gifts & Souvenirs

Arroyo Seco Mercantile ♥ This funky building is chock-full of cowboy hats, antiques, and country home items. 488 NM 150, Arroyo Seco. secomerc.com. ✆ **575/776-8806.**

Chimayo Trading del Norte ♥ Specializing in Navajo weavings, Pueblo pottery, and early Taos artists, this is a fun spot to peruse on the Ranchos Plaza. There's also jewelry, sculptures, and baskets. 1 St. Francis Church Plaza, Ranchos de Taos. chimayotrading.com. ✆ **575/758-0504.**

El Rincón Trading Post ♥ This century-old shop has a real trading-post feel, making it an interesting place to browse. In the back of the store is a museum full of American Indian and Western artifacts. 114 Kit Carson Rd. ✆ **575/758-9188.**

Taos Gems and Minerals ♥♥♥ Locally owned and operated for several decades, this intriguing shop offers a huge assortment of stones, polished and not, in all shapes and sizes. There's jewelry, carvings, and lovely polished bowls with fossils, plus unique wooden vessels. Don't rush your visit here. The well-informed staff is pleased to answer your questions and help you find the perfect piece to take home. 637 Paseo del Pueblo Sur. facebook.com/TaosGemsMinerals. ✆ **575/758-3910.**

Taos Rockers ♥ Wander among the myriad minerals and fossils, gems and jewelry in this fascinating shop. Additionally, there are healing stones and crystals, rough and polished geodes, mineral lamps, and candleholders. Something for everyone. 229-A Camino de la Placita. taosrockers.com. ✆ **575/758-2326.**

Touchstone Mineral & Fossil Gallery ♥♥ This fine showroom, one of three in the Touchstone chain, offers an adventure into an ancient world of stunning geodes and fossils, both decorative and functional. Look for jewelry and fetishes here as well. 110 S. Plaza. touchstonegalleries.com. ✆ **575/737-5001.**

Two Graces Gallery ♥♥ For a wide range of old and new, step off the beaten track and visit this gallery. You'll find art, Southwestern pottery, kachinas, curios, and books—mostly used but a few new—on Taos or the Southwest. 105 Barela Lane off Kit Carson Rd. near the Taos Inn. twograces.com. ✆ **575/770-5580.**

Jewelry

Artwares Contemporary Jewelry ♥♥ For "a departure from the traditional," stop in this shop where each piece offers classic and unusual settings of sterling silver, gold, platinum, and other metals, often combined with precious or semiprecious stones. Many present a new twist on traditional Southwestern and Native American designs. 129 N. Plaza. ✆ **800/527-8850** or 575/758-8850.

Claireworks Gallery ♥♥♥ Claire Haye has been designing her unique jewelry for several decades. She began her career as a ceramic sculptor, and her jewelry reflects this background—each piece is a tiny sculpture or made up of a series of same. Pieces come in silver, bronze, or gold, accented with gemstones. Claire also creates marvelous bronze or painted steel sculptures for the home, plus ceramic murals. 482A NM 150, Arroyo Seco. claireworks.com. ✆ **575/776-5175.**

TAOS AFTER DARK

For a small town, Taos has its share of top entertainment. The resort atmosphere and the arts community attract performers, and the city enjoys annual programs in music and literary arts. Many events are scheduled by the **Taos Center for the Arts (TCA),** 133 Paseo del Pueblo Norte (tcataos.org; ✆ **575/758-2052**), at the Taos Community Auditorium. The TCA imports regional and national artists and also hosts local performances in theater, dance, and music.

You can obtain information on current events in the *Taos News* (taosnews.com; ✆ **575/758-2241**). The **Taos County Chamber of Commerce** (taoschamber.com; ✆ **575/751-8800**) is also a good resource, as is the **Taos Visitor Center** (taos.org; ✆ **800/732-8267** or 575/758-3873).

The Performing Arts

Music from Angel Fire ♥♥ If you enjoy classical music, be sure to attend one of the concerts presented by Music from Angel Fire. World-renowned performers appear in a short season that runs from mid-August to Labor Day. Based in the small resort town of Angel Fire (about 21 miles east of Taos, off US 64), programs take place in surrounding communities, including Taos. Angel Fire. musicfromangelfire.org. ✆ **575/377-3233.**

Taos School of Music ♥♥♥ If you're in Taos during the summer, you owe it to yourself to catch a performance by Taos School of Music. The school attracts the best and brightest young musicians every year, and takes them to the next level of violin, viola, cello, and piano performance of chamber music. The 8-week **Chamber Music Festival** (mid-June to mid-August), an important adjunct of the school, offers 16 concerts and seminars for the public, with performances by big names, plus the students themselves. Programs are held at the Taos Community Auditorium and the Hotel St. Bernard in Taos Ski Valley. taosschoolofmusic.com. ✆ **575/776-2388.**

The Club & Music Scene

Adobe Bar ♥♥ Nightly live music, with no cover charge, and some of the best margaritas in Taos draw folks to the small bar at the Taos Inn, across the lobby from Doc Martin's restaurant (p. 138). Music ranges from folk to jazz to bluegrass and beyond. The place is often packed, so get there early to grab some food and a drink and claim a place to sit. The Taos Inn, 125 Paseo del Pueblo Norte. taosinn.com/adobe-bar. ✆ **575/758-1977.**

Alley Cantina ♥♥ One of Taos's old standby nightspots, the Alley Cantina has gone through various owners and names through the years, but it hasn't changed much. Parts of the building date back some 400 years, and of course there's the resident ghost—Teresina Bent, daughter of the 19th-century territorial governor who was murdered less than a block away. There's an old saloon feel to the place, live music of some sort most nights, good drinks, and locals' favorite fish and chips. What more can you ask for? 121 Teresina Ln. alleycantina.com. ✆ **575/758-2121.**

KTAOS Solar Bar ♥♥ Look for the solar panels at the start of the road to Taos Ski Valley to find this family-friendly bar, flanked by two operating radio stations. Watch the DJs at work and, if it's nice out, send the kids to play on the grassy knoll outside, pre-stocked with toys. The tacos are great, and there's often live music indoors or out. 9 State Rd. 150. ktaos.com. ✆ **575/758-5826 ext. 206.**

The Mothership ♥♥ In addition to a tap room in town, Taos Mesa Brewing runs this sprawling venue 8 miles northwest. An outdoor stage hosts concerts spring through fall. The backdrop of the Sangre de Cristo range during sunset is reason enough to stop by. 20 ABC Mesa Rd. taosmesabrewing.com. ✆ **575/758-1900 (ext. 2).**

Sagebrush Grill & Cantina ♥♥ For years one of the most popular bars in Taos, this is where locals go Friday and Saturday nights to practice their two-steppin' in a genuine Old West setting, complete with local bands and a rustic wooden dance floor. 1508 Paseo del Pueblo Sur. sagebrushinn.com. ✆ **575/758-2254.**

EXCURSIONS FROM TAOS

The Enchanted Circle ♥♥

This just might be the perfect driving tour. The 84-mile Enchanted Circle loop winds through some of northern New Mexico's most spectacular mountain scenery—including views of 13,161-foot Wheeler Peak, the state's highest point—with stops at towns rich in history and culture, such as the old Hispanic villages of Arroyo Hondo and Questa and the Wild West mining town of Red River. You'll roll through a pass that the Apaches, Kiowas, and Comanches once used to cross the mountains to trade with the Taos Pueblo people; travel along the base of some of New Mexico's tallest peaks; then skim the shores of a high mountain lake at Eagle Nest before heading back to Taos along the meandering Rio Fernando de Taos. Although you can drive the entire loop in 2 hours, most folks prefer to take 5 or 6 hours, stopping in Red River or Eagle Nest for lunch.

Traveling north from Taos via NM 522, it's a 9-mile drive to **Arroyo Hondo,** the remains of an 1815 land grant along the Rio Hondo. Along the dirt roads that lead off NM 522, you may find a windowless *morada* or two,

Enchanted Circle & Taos Excursions

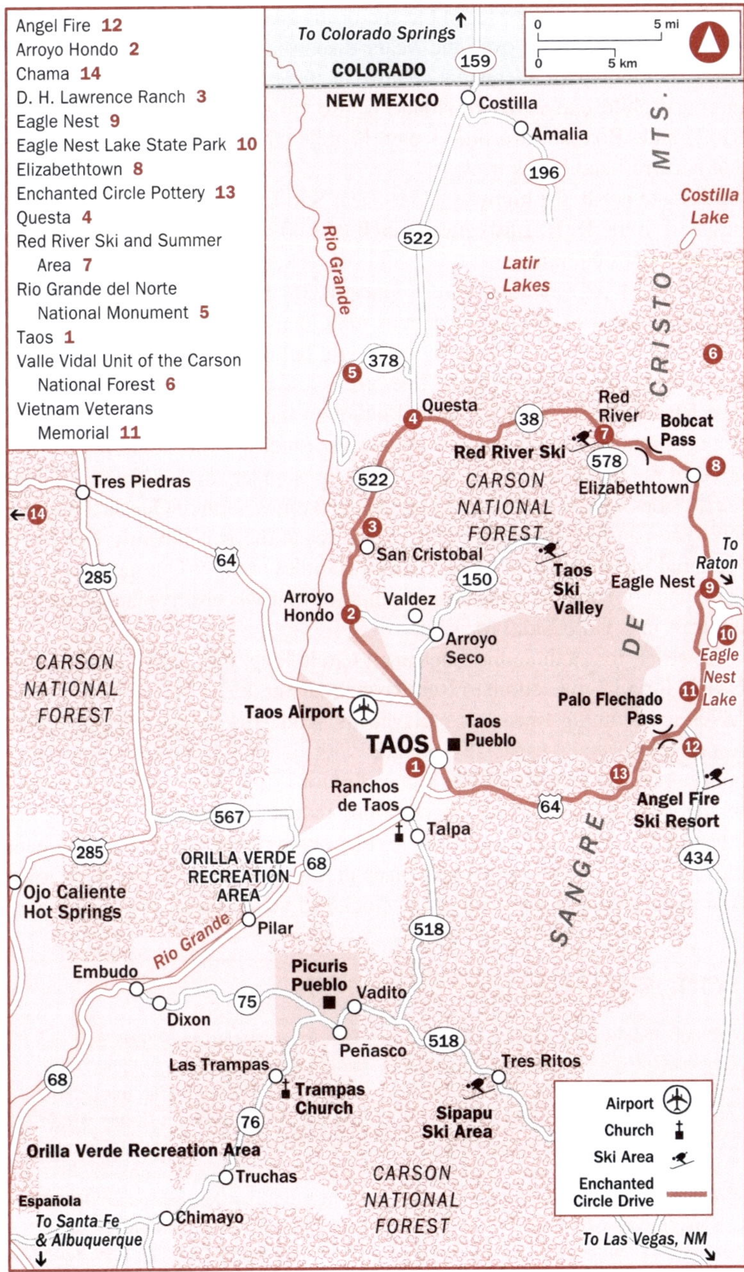

marked by plain crosses in front—places of worship for the still-active Penitentes, a somewhat secretive religious order known for self-flagellation. In the 1960s, Arroyo Hondo was also the site of the New Buffalo hippie commune, whose members have over the years dispersed throughout northern New Mexico, bringing an interesting creative element to the state's food, architecture, and philosophy. Arroyo Hondo is also the turnoff point for trips to the Rio Grande Box, an awesome 1-day, 17-mile whitewater run for which you can book raft and kayak trips.

En route north, the highway passes near **San Cristobal,** where a side road turns off to the **D. H. Lawrence Ranch** (p. 150) and **Lama,** former home of another 1960s commune.

Next, NM 522 passes through **Questa.** Most residents here are former employees of a nearby molybdenum mine that ceased operations in 2014. Mining molybdenum (an ingredient in light bulbs, television tubes, and missile systems) was controversial. The process raked across hillsides along the Red River, using groundwater, and although the mine's owners treated the water it used before returning it to the river, studies showed that it adversely affected the fish life. Now, a major clean-up is underway, but the scars along the hillsides will be visible for years. About 3 miles north of Questa along NM 522, you can turn west onto NM 378 to reach the **Río Grande Del Norte National Monument** (p. 170). Another 20 miles north of Questa on NM522, the village of **Costilla** is the turnoff point for four-wheel-drive jaunts and hiking trips into **Valle Vidal** (p. 171).

However, to continue the Enchanted Circle loop, turn east at Questa onto NM 38 for a 12-mile climb to **Red River** (redriver.org). This rough-and-ready 1890s gold-mining town has parlayed its Wild West image into a pleasant resort village that's especially popular with families from Texas and Oklahoma. At 8,750 feet, Red River is a center for skiing, snowmobiling, fishing, hiking, off-road driving, horseback riding, mountain biking, river rafting, and other outdoor pursuits. Frontier-style celebrations, honky-tonk entertainment, plus numerous annual events take place in this charming and fun small town. And it's a good spot for lunch if the clock and your stomach say it's time.

ghosts OF ELIZABETHTOWN

Although only a few trodden clues remain, the gold-mining Elizabethtown once boasted 7,000 residents and was the first seat of Colfax County. It was called Virginia City when founded in 1865, but the name was changed to honor Elizabeth Moore, daughter of a leading citizen. What has become known as E-town had plenty of gold-town perks: five stores, two hotels, seven saloons, and three dance halls. By the early 1900s, most of the gold had run out, and in 1903 fire blazed through the town, leveling much of it. Today, visitors can still see the stone walls of a hotel, some foundations, and remnants of a cemetery. It's on the west side of NM 38, about 10 miles east of Red River, just before you get to the Eagle Nest turnoff.

From Red River, it's a beautiful 16-mile drive over the 9,850-foot Bobcat Pass, especially pretty in fall when the aspen trees turn bright yellow. About 6 miles down from the pass sits the ghost town of **Elizabethtown,** where gold was mined as early as 1866. All that's left of this once booming mining town are a few grave markers and the crumbling rock walls of a ruined hotel. Another 5 miles brings you to US 64 and **Eagle Nest,** nestled in the Moreno Valley on the shore of Eagle Nest Lake. This small Old West town (pop. just under 300) finally incorporated in 1976.

If you're heading to Cimarron or Denver, turn east on US 64 from Eagle Nest. But to complete the Enchanted Circle back to Taos, head west on US 64, passing by Eagle Nest Lake, where the 4-square-mile **Eagle Nest Lake State Park** ♥♥ (emnrd.nm.gov; ✆ **575/377-1594**) stretches out below the village. Facilities include restrooms, camping (19 sites), a boat ramp and dock, and a visitor center. The lake is considered one of the top trout producers in the U.S. and attracts ice fishermen in winter as well as summer anglers. It's too cold for swimming, but sailboats and windsurfers ply the waters when it isn't covered in ice. The park is also a good spot for bird-watching, and there's a 1.2-mile hiking trail.

About two miles past the lake, perched on the hill above you to the right is the **Vietnam Veterans Memorial** ♥ (vietnamveteransmemorial.org; ✆ **575/377-6900**), a stunning structure with curved white walls soaring high against the backdrop of the Sangre de Cristo Range. Consisting of a chapel and an underground visitor center, it was built by Dr. Victor Westphall in memory of his son, David, a Marine lieutenant killed in Vietnam in 1968. The 6,000-square-foot memorial houses exhibits, videos, memorabilia, and a changing gallery of photographs of Vietnam veterans who lost their lives in the Southeast Asian war.

If you like outdoor activities, you may want to plan a night or two at **Angel Fire,** south of US 64 along NM 434. Opened in the late 1960s, this resort offers a hotel, condominiums, and cabins. Winter is the biggest season, especially with skiing families (see p. 154). In spring, summer, and fall, **Angel Fire Resort** (p. 154) offers golf, tennis, hiking, mountain biking (you can take your bike up on the quad lift), fly-fishing, river rafting, and horseback riding. There are other fun family activities, such as a video arcade, a miniature golf course, theater performances, and, throughout the year, a variety of festivals, including a hot-air-balloon festival, Winterfest, and concerts of both classical and popular music. For more information on the Moreno Valley, including lodging and restaurant listings, contact the **Angel Fire Chamber of Commerce** (angelfirechamber.org; ✆ **800/446-8117** or 575/377-6353).

Returning to US 64, turn left (west) for the final 21-mile leg back to Taos. Soon the road reenters the **Carson National Forest,** and you begin a slow, winding, mountain drive through a forest of firs and pines. The road seems to point straight up to Palo Flechado Pass, at 9,101 feet elevation. Its name is Spanish for "tree pierced with arrows," and in the 18th and 19th centuries, the pass was used by American Indians, Spaniards, and Anglo-Americans traveling from the eastern plains to the trading center of Taos. As the road goes downhill, about 4 miles past the pass you'll see **Enchanted Circle Pottery ♥♥**, where owner-artists JoAnne and Kevin DeKeuster have been creating one-of-a-kind pieces to "make people fall in love with our work" since 2003. Their totally green studio-gallery offers all manner of things from platters and plates, pitchers and bowls, to decorative pieces (enchantedcirclepottery.com; ✆ **575/737-9640**).

Continue your drive past a number of U.S. Forest Service recreation sites, including some good spots for picnicking, camping, hiking, cross-country skiing, and snowshoeing. Finally, you arrive back in Taos via Kit Carson Road, which delivers you to the historic Taos Plaza.

Río Grande del Norte National Monument ♥♥♥

Created by Presidential Proclamation in March 2013, this vast Bureau of Land Management property encompasses about 17% of Taos County, or a quarter-million acres stretching from the New Mexico/Colorado border south to Pilar along the Rio Grande. Here can be found rugged, wide-open plains dotted with sagebrush, a deep chasm carved by the Rio Grande, and ancient volcanic mounds with piñon and juniper covering the slopes. Ute Mountain climbs to 10,093 feet, and the Rio Grande flows 600 to 800 feet below the gorge rim. Rocky Mountain elk, mule deer, pronghorn, and Rocky Mountain bighorn sheep often winter in the monument and can often be seen traversing it. Evidence of ancient human activity crops up everywhere—petroglyphs, prehistoric dwelling sites, and other archaeological finds—as well as evidence of more recent activity in abandoned homesteads from the 1930s. For 21st-century visitors, recreation opportunities abound: hiking, mountain biking, horseback riding, camping, picnicking, hunting, fishing, canoeing, kayaking, river rafting, or soaring aloft in a hot-air balloon.

A good starting place is **Orilla Verde Recreation Area** (blm.gov/visit/orilla-verde-recreation-area; ✆ **575/791-4718**), near the community of Pilar, 14 miles south of Taos via NM 68 and NM 570, along the banks of the Rio Grande. Views here range from rugged mesas to deep river canyons. Anglers catch native brown trout, German brown trout, rainbow trout, and northern pike, and there is an easy-to-moderate 1.25-mile (one-way) hiking trail that leads past prehistoric petroglyphs and wonderful scenic views. You'll find picnic tables, a visitor center with a variety of exhibits, and easy access to a relatively calm section of the Rio Grande, especially inviting to those with small inflatable boats. There are both primitive campsites ($5 per night) and developed campsites ($7 per night for one vehicle), as well as a limited number with RV electric hookups ($15 per night). Drinking water and restrooms are available. The day-use fee is $3 per vehicle.

The scenery's more rugged at **Wild Rivers Recreation Area** (blm.gov/visit/wild-rivers-recreation-area; ✆ **575/758-8851**), which sits on a plateau above the Rio Grande, with trails leading into the gorge. It's north of Taos, past the community of Questa along NM 522 and then NM 378, which takes

rock art IN THE RIVER GORGE

Modern-day outdoor types weren't the first to explore the dramatic gorges of the **Wild Rivers Recreation Area,** so don't be surprised if you find petroglyphs on its boulders and rock faces. One especially good site is accessed by hiking into the gorge from the Big Arsenic Springs Campground. ***Warning:*** The hike, which is only a little over a mile each way, is rated moderate-to-difficult because of the 1,000-foot elevation change—not bad going down, but a little rough coming back up. Look for a big round rock near the river, standing about 7 feet high: It's covered with a wealth of petroglyphs, including numerous animal images, which are believed to have been created between A.D. 1000 and 1600. It can be difficult to find, so ask for directions at the visitor center before you head down the trail.

you west to the recreation area. The level mesa top provides a point where you can look down into the awesome canyons where the Rio Grande and Red River converge. About two dozen miles of hiking trails wind through the area, including several leading down from the mesa campgrounds to the Rio Grande (the only way to get down to the river). The recreation area also has several mountain-biking trails, and fishing for northern pike and brown and rainbow trout. The day-use fee is $3 per vehicle, and there are river-view campsites along the canyon rim ($7 per night for one vehicle, $10 for two), with water and toilets but no showers or RV hookups.

A **Río Grande del Norte National Monument** map is available for download, and there's detailed information on the monument's website (blm.gov/visit/rgdnnm). The monument is open year-round, with day-use hours 6am to 10pm. There's a daily fee of $3 per vehicle for those staying 30 minutes or more.

The Valle Vidal ♥

If you want to spend a few days fishing, hiking, and camping, or just take a long scenic day trip from Taos, this unit of the Carson National Forest may be the place for you. Covering about 100,000 acres, Valle Vidal offers plenty of wide open spaces, sparkling lakes, tall pines, snow-capped peaks, historic sites, and some of the area's best wildlife viewing. Access is via US 64 and the communities of Eagle Nest and Cimarron to the east, and from NM 522 and the towns of Costilla and Amalia to the west. The main route through the unit is Forest Road 1950. For maps and information, contact the **Carson National Forest** (p. 154).

Back in the late 19th century this was a busy place, dotted with pioneer logging and ranching communities. Although it is far from pristine today, after years of ranching and logging, the Valle Vidal offers a rugged beauty, while the remains of old ranch houses and railroad beds convey a sense of the genuine Old West.

The scenery is spectacular, but what sets the Valle Vidal apart is the richness and diversity of its wildlife. At last count there were well over a thousand elk and several hundred mule deer, wild turkeys, hawks, bobcats, cougar, beaver, coyotes, and black bear. Abert's squirrels are often seen on the east side, and bald eagles occasionally soar overhead. The Valle Vidal also contains one of the Southwest's largest pure stands of bristlecone pines, a species considered the world's oldest living tree. Located northwest of **Clayton Corral,** about a half-mile off Forest Road 1950, the stand includes what is believed to be the world's largest bristlecone, a healthy 76-footer with a trunk almost 4 feet across.

There are few marked hiking trails in Valle Vidal, but numerous old logging roads lead to pioneer homesteads, railroad buildings, and cemeteries. Of about 350 miles of dirt roads open when Valle Vidal was donated to the Forest Service in 1982, all but 42 miles are now closed to motor vehicles and available for hiking, mountain biking, and horseback riding. The area's pioneer heritage is especially evident at the imposing **Ring Ranch House,** along Forest Road 1950 in the eastern section of the park. In the 1890s, this two-story log building was headquarters for a 320-acre ranch, home to Irish immigrant Timothy Ring, his wife Catherine, and seven daughters. An interpretive trail leads about a half-mile from **McCrystal Campground** to the ranch house, with photo exhibits that describe the history of the ranch.

Anglers catch Rio Grande cutthroat trout in the unit's 67 miles of streams, with the best luck usually in Costilla Creek and Middle Ponil Creek, plus the two Shuree Ponds, which also contain rainbow trout. All streams are catch-and-release, and other special regulations apply. (One of the Shuree Ponds is open for fishing only by children under 12.) Valle Vidal is also a popular hunting destination during the fall elk season.

There are 93 campsites total across **Cimarron Campground** (off FR 1910 at 9,400 ft. elevation) and **McCrystal Campground** (off FR 1950 at 8,100 ft.). Both have grills, picnic tables, and vault toilets, but no showers or RV hookups. Cimarron has drinking water; McCrystal does not. Camping costs $11 to $40 at Cimarron; $8 to $16 at McCrystal.

Chama ♥♥

Sitting at the base of 11,403-foot Brazos Mountain and surrounded by some of the most beautiful mountain scenery in the West, Chama has a wonderful location. At 7,850 feet above sea level, this former mining town of about 1,000 people is one of New Mexico's highest communities, which helps explain why it gets so much snow every winter; chilly nights are the rule even in July. The town's main claim to fame today is as a base for year-round outdoor recreation—fishing, hunting, hiking, cross-country skiing, snowshoeing, snowmobiling, you name it—plus (and it's a big plus) the absolutely wonderful narrow-gauge **Cumbres & Toltec Scenic Railroad** (see below).

Chama is on US 64/84 at its junction with NM 17, about 89 miles west of Taos. Much of the 2- to 3-hour drive there is a beautifully scenic route through the mountains of the Carson National Forest. Note that in winter, snow often causes road closures, so check road conditions (see p. 241) before heading out.

In 1880, the Denver and Rio Grande Western Railroad began construction on a rail extension from Alamosa, Colorado to Durango, Colorado, by way of Chama. The first rail travel began in February 1881, and for the next 30 years, Chama was a wild little place, complete with honest-to-goodness holdups of the payroll train, lots of saloons, and a great influx of both good guys and bad guys. You can get a walking-tour brochure, describing about two dozen points of interest in the Chama railroad yards, from the 1899 depot in Chama.

A registered National Historic Site owned by the states of Colorado and New Mexico, the **Cumbres & Toltec Scenic Railroad** ♥♥♥ (500 S. Terrace Ave.; cumbrestoltec.com; ✆ **888/286-2737** or 575/756-2151) runs steam trains daily from both Chama and Antonito, Colorado, between late May and October. Trains run 64 miles through some incredible mountain scenery, passing through forests of pine and aspen, past striking rock formations, and over the magnificent Toltec Gorge of the Rio de los Pinos. At 10,015 feet elevation, it tops Cumbres Pass. Halfway through the trip, the two trains meet at Osier, Colorado, where a buffet lunch is served (included with all fares).

There are a couple of ways to enjoy a full day on the Cumbres & Toltec. You can board the train in Chama—our favorite, since you get to chug up the steep incline to the top of Cumbres Pass, and if you're really lucky to be on a long enough train this will require two engines—and either switch trains after lunch and ride back to Chama, or stay on for the full excursion to Antonito, taking a motor coach back to the Chama train station. Alternately you can start with the motor coach ride from Chama and begin your train trip in Antonito, ending in Chama. These options, in reverse, are also available from Antonito, Colorado. There are also half-day excursions, dinner trains, and other special trips.

Seating is assigned, in three levels of train cars: classic coach cars with comfortable bench seating, deluxe tourist cars with extra room and individual seating, and premium parlor cars (open only to those 21 and older), which are top-of-the line, restored historic cars with lounge-style comfort. All three are enclosed. Passengers can walk through the train to the snack car, restrooms, and the gondola caran open-air car that provides the best cinders-in-your-hair views of scenery unchanged for over a century.

Special cars with wheelchair lifts are available with a 7-day advance reservation. Full-day tickets cost $115 to $275 for adults, $60 to $135 for ages 6 to 12, and $40 to $70 for children 2 to 5; reservations are highly recommended. Trains leave Chama daily at 10am; motor coaches depart for Antonito at 8:30am.

Meanwhile, the woods, streams, and lakes of the **Carson National Forest** offer practically unlimited opportunities for hiking, mountain biking, cross-country skiing, snowshoeing, snowmobiling, camping, fishing, and hunting. Information, including contact information for local outfitters and guides, is

THE lake-to-lake CONNECTION

El Vado Lake and Heron Lake are connected by the 5.5-mile **Rio Chama Trail,** a nice hiking trail open to foot travel only. It's a great place to view wildlife such as wild turkeys, peregrine falcons, red-tailed hawks, white-throated swifts, scrub jays, and mountain bluebirds, as well as the occasional elk and mule deer. From the El Vado Lake trail head, it follows the Rio Chama to a mesa on the south side of the river, which offers tree-framed views of both El Vado and Heron lakes. The trail then winds down the side of the canyon, through a piñon-juniper forest, and crosses the Rio Chama on a cable footbridge before heading up a steep set of redwood stairs to the Heron Lake trail head. It's mostly an easy hike, but the last half-mile climb is moderately strenuous.

available at the **Northern New Mexico Welcome Center** in Chama (northwest corner of the junction of US 64/84 and NM 17, ✆ **800/477-0149** or 575/756-2306), and at the **Chama Valley Chamber of Commerce** website (newmexico.org). For details on activities in the national forest, contact the Carson's **Canjilon Ranger Station,** located in the community of Canjilon, about 33 miles south of Chama via US 84 and NM 115 (fs.usda.gov/carson; ✆ **575/684-2489**).

South of Chama are two state parks (emnrd.nm.gov) that offer great recreation opportunities. Day-use fees are $5 per vehicle, camping fees $8 to $18. **El Vado Lake State Park** (27 miles south of Chama via US 64/84 and NM12; ✆ **575/588-7247**) boasts a 3,200-acre lake for anything that floats, from high-powered speedboats to sailboats, canoes, and small inflatables. Swimming is permitted, although there are no designated swimming areas and the water is somewhat chilly. Anglers catch rainbow and German brown trout, kokanee salmon, and channel catfish. There are also hiking trails and plenty of wildlife viewing. The park's campgrounds have 80 campsites (17 with electric hookups plus 2 with full hookups), restrooms, showers, and an RV dump station. ***Note:*** The park is closed December to March. **Heron Lake State Park** (640 NM 95, 20 miles south of Chama via US 64/84 and NM 95; ✆ **575/588-7470**) has an even bigger lake, tucked away in a mountain forest of ponderosa pines, piñons, and junipers. Although motorized boats are allowed, this is a no-wake lake, and its broad expanse gives sailboats plenty of tacking room. A marina has a dock and slips for rent on a nightly basis, but no boat rentals or supplies; businesses within a few miles of the park offer boat rentals, plus groceries and camping and fishing supplies. Swimming is permitted anywhere in the lake. Although there are no established trails, cross-country skiers can ski along some of the lesser-used unplowed roads; snowshoers can traipse along the hiking trails, or just head out across the fields and through the woods. There are 192 developed campsites (54 with electric hookups), restrooms, showers, and an RV dump station.

ALBUQUERQUE ESSENTIALS

As the gateway to northern New Mexico, Albuquerque is often regarded simply as the portal through which most domestic and international visitors pass before traveling on to Santa Fe and Taos. But don't sell this city short. Albuquerque is a comfortable city, easy to explore, with a small-town attitude and relaxed environment. It's also an economical place to visit, with some of the lowest lodging and meal prices in the state. It's a smart idea to spend a day or a week here—or even make Albuquerque your base camp for exploring the region.

From the rocky crest of Sandia Peak at sunset, one can see the lights of this city of more than half a million people spread out across 20 miles of high desert. As the sun drops toward the western horizon, it reflects off the Rio Grande, flowing through Albuquerque more than a mile below. This waterway is the bloodline for the area, the feature that made it possible for a city to spring up in this vast desert. Nowadays, however, the farming communities that once lined its banks are giving way to subdivisions and shopping centers. With continuing sprawl on the west side of the city, more means for transporting traffic have been built on the river.

The railroad, which set up a major stop here in 1880, prompted much of Albuquerque's initial growth, but that was nothing compared to what happened after World War II, when Albuquerque was designated a major national center for military research and production. People from across the nation and around the world came for jobs, and as the city grew, it became a center of commerce for New Mexico and beyond. Look closely and you'll see Anglo ranchers, Native Americans, and Latino villagers stocking up on goods to take back to the New Mexico boot heel or the Texas panhandle.

ORIENTATION

Visitor Information

Official Albuquerque visitor information centers, operated by **Visit Albuquerque** (visitalbuquerque.org; ✆ **800/733-9918** or 505/842-9918), are at the airport and in Old Town at 522 Romero St. NW.

The Old Town visitor center is open weekdays 10am to 5pm and weekends 10am to 3pm.

City Layout

Albuquerque's sprawl takes a while to get used to. A visitor's first impression is of a grid of arteries lined with shopping malls and fast-food eateries, with residences tucked behind on side streets.

The center point of all this is the crossroads—referred to locally as the "Big I"—of I-25 and I-40. In the southwest quadrant formed by that intersection, you'll find both **downtown Albuquerque** and **Old Town,** the site of many tourist attractions. Lomas Boulevard and Central Avenue, aka historic Route 66 (US 66), flank downtown on the north and south. They come together 2 miles west of I-25 near **Old Town Plaza,** the historical and spiritual heart of the city. Lomas and Central continue east across I-25, running parallel about half a mile apart as they pass the **University of New Mexico** and the **Expo New Mexico** fairgrounds. The airport is directly south of the UNM campus, about 3 miles via Yale Boulevard. Kirtland Air Force Base—site of Sandia National Laboratories—is south of the fairgrounds via Louisiana Boulevard.

A bit north of the Big I, **Menaul Boulevard** runs east-west and is the focus of midtown and uptown shopping, as well as the hotel districts. The other major east-west thoroughfare in the northeast quadrant is **Montgomery Boulevard,** about 1½ miles north of Menaul. As Albuquerque expands northward, the **Journal Center** business park, about 3 miles north of Montgomery along the west side of I-25, has grown. East of Eubank Boulevard are the **Sandia Foothills,** where the alluvial plain slants toward the mountains.

When looking for an address, it is helpful to know that Central Avenue divides the city into north and south, and the railroad tracks—which lie just east of First Street downtown—comprise the dividing line between east and west. Street names are usually followed by a directional: NE, NW, SE, or SW.

MAPS Comprehensive Albuquerque street maps are available at visitor centers (see above), and also from the **American Automobile Association** (AAA), 10501 Montgomery Blvd. NE (aaa.com; ✆ **505/291-6611**), and 9231 Coors Blvd. NW, Ste. R (✆ **505/792-1938**), if you're a member.

GETTING AROUND

Albuquerque is easy to get around, thanks to its wide thoroughfares and grid layout, combined with its efficient transportation systems.

By Bus

ABQ Ride (cabq.gov/transit; ✆ **505/243-7433**) travels the arterials with its city bus network. For information on routes, call or check the website. Standard buses are free to use.

Greater Albuquerque

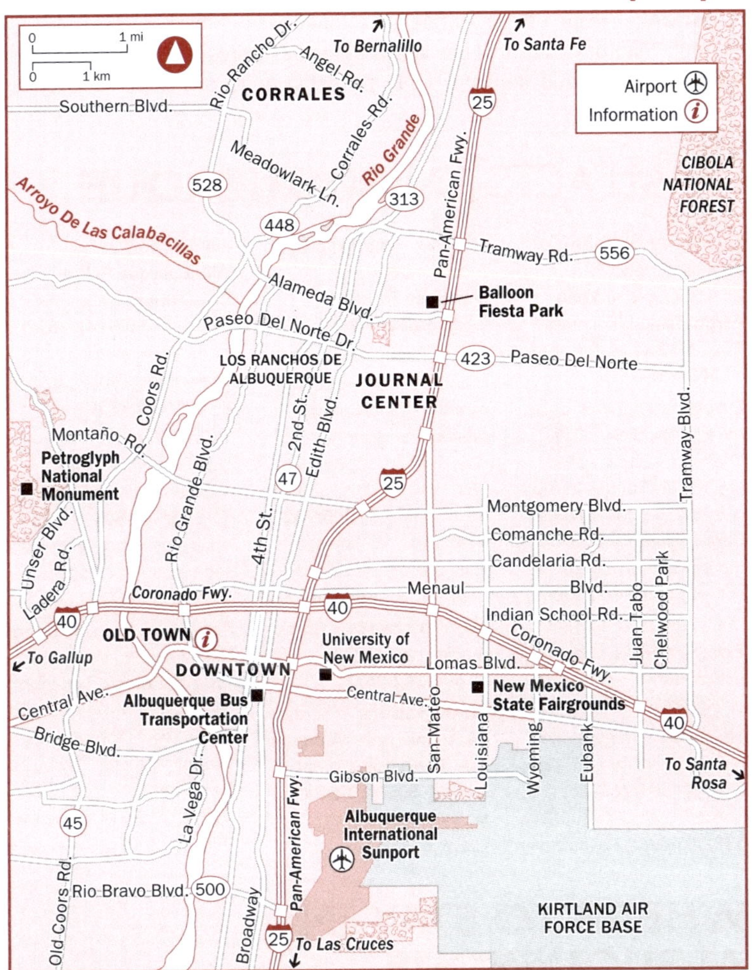

By Car

Albuquerque is a good place to have a car, in large part because attractions, restaurants, and lodgings are spread throughout the city. Also, it's a fairly easy city to drive in once you get the hang of its peculiarities, as mentioned in "City Layout," above. Traffic can be pretty stiff during rush hour—generally 7:30 to 9:30am and 4 to 6pm—but isn't bad the rest of the time. However, be aware that wherever you're heading you'll probably be slowed by road construction, which seems unending. A local joke is that the city of Albuquerque doesn't need a storage yard for its orange barrels; they just move them from place to place.

Parking is generally not difficult in Albuquerque. Meters operate Monday through Saturday 8am to 6pm and are not monitored at other times or on federally recognized holidays. Only the large downtown hotels charge for parking.

[FastFACTS] ALBUQUERQUE

Currency Exchange Foreign currency can be exchanged at **Wells Fargo Bank,** 200 Lomas Blvd. NW; wellsfargo.com; ✆ **505/766-6415.**

Doctors For a medical emergency, dial ✆ **911.** There are several walk-in urgent care centers in Albuquerque, including **Next-Care Urgent Care,** 5504 Menaul Blvd. NE (nextcare.com; ✆ **505/348-2868**), open daily 8am to 8pm.

Emergencies For police, fire, or ambulance, dial ✆ **911.**

Hotlines The following hotlines operate 24/7: rape crisis (✆ **505/266-7711**); poison control (✆ **800/222-1222**); thoughts of suicide (✆ **988**); and emotional, mental health, and substance abuse (✆ **855/662-7474**).

Libraries There are 18 branches of the **Albuquerque Bernalillo County Library,** including the main branch at 501 Copper Ave. NW, between Fifth and Sixth streets (✆ **505/768-5141**). You can find the locations of other library branches at **abqlibrary.org**.

Lost Property Contact the city police at ✆ **505/242-2677.**

Newspapers The daily newspaper is the ***Albuquerque Journal*** (abqjournal.com; ✆ **505/823-4400**).

Police For emergencies, call ✆ **911.** For other matters, contact the **Albuquerque Police Department** (cabq.gov/police; ✆ **505/242-2677**) or the **New Mexico State Police** (sp.nm.gov; ✆ **505/841-9256**).

Post Offices The main U.S. Post Office is at 1135 Broadway Blvd. NE (✆ **505/346-8051**). For other post office locations, see usps.com or dial ✆ **800/275-8777.**

Taxis You won't find cabs to hail on the street here, but **ABQ Metro Taxi** (abqmetrotaxi.com; ✆ **505/450-8580**) serves the city and surrounding area 24 hours a day. **Uber** (uber.com) and **Lyft** (lyft.com) also operate their ride-share services here.

WHERE TO STAY IN ALBUQUERQUE

Finding a place to sleep in Albuquerque usually isn't difficult. There are plenty of hotels and motels, and most are far less pricey than those in Santa Fe or even Taos. The only downside to the Albuquerque lodging scene is that, with a few exceptions, it's really boring. There are numerous chain motels, all pretty much the same as you would find in any other area. Sure, they'll put a few local prints on the walls and use deep red and brown colors to signal Southwestern decor, but that's about it. We suggest that unless you want to stay in one of the high-end properties or a neat bed and breakfast, you stick with a reputable chain.

While Albuquerque lodging is usually a very good value, during special events—specifically, the New Mexico State Fair (Sept) and especially the

Albuquerque Hotels

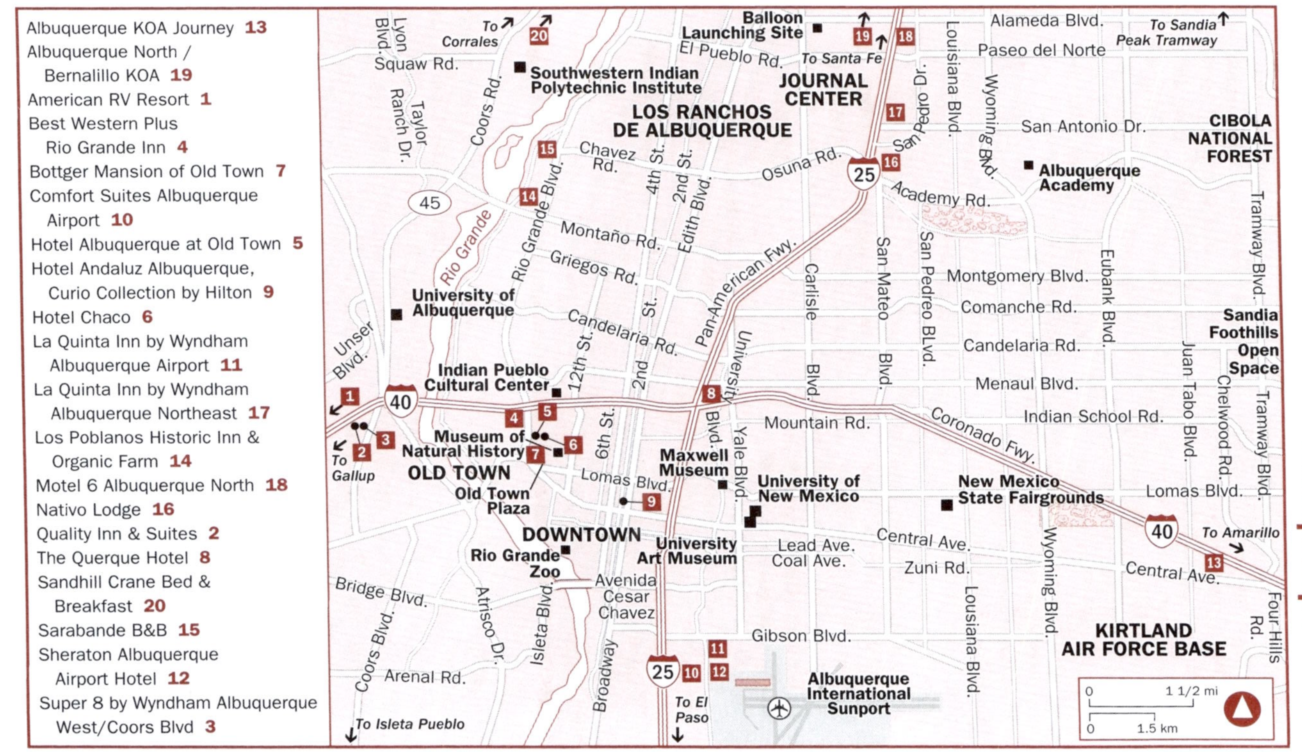

chain hotels IN ALBUQUERQUE

You don't need us to describe the dozens of chain motels—you've probably seen them before—but we can give you some of the locations, contact information, and current rates. All of these properties offer free Wi-Fi. The rate ranges quoted here do not include the special event times mentioned above.

We're fans of the **La Quinta** chain (wyndhamhotels.com/laquinta; ✆ **800/753-3757**), now part of the Wyndham family, in part because La Quintas generally accept pets with no extra charge, and also because we've found these facilities to be clean, generally well-maintained, and a good value. Albuquerque has five La Quintas, with rates usually $50 to $100 double. We suggest the **La Quinta Inn by Wyndham Albuquerque Airport ♥♥**, 2116 Yale Blvd. SE (✆ **505/243-5500**), and the **La Quinta Inn by Wyndham Albuquerque Northeast ♥**, 5241 San Antonio Dr. NE (✆ **505/821-9000**).

Super 8 (wyndhamhotels.com/super-8; ✆ **800/454-3213**), also now part of the Wyndham family, has two motels in the Albuquerque area, including the **Super 8 by Wyndham Albuquerque West/Coors Blvd ♥**, 6030 Iliff Rd. NW (✆ **505/836-5560**), with rates of $50 to $90 double. Wyndham has 26 properties in the Albuquerque area. See wyndham hotels.com for a complete list.

Choice Hotels (choicehotels.com; ✆ **877/424-6423**) has quite an array of motel brands, including Econo Lodge, Comfort Suites, Quality Inn, Sleep Inn, and Rodeway Inn. At last count, Choice had 22 properties in the Albuquerque area, with rates mostly $50 to $115 per night. We recommend the **Comfort Suites Albuquerque Airport ♥♥**, 1401 Woodward Rd. SE (✆ **505/705-6500**), and the **Quality Inn & Suites ♥**, 6100 West Iliff Rd. (✆ **505/234-7569**).

A popular choice for the budget-minded is the **Motel 6** (motel6.com; ✆ **800/899-9841**) chain, which has six motels in Albuquerque. One of its nicest is the **Motel 6 Albuquerque North ♥**, 8510 Pan American Freeway NE (✆ **505/821-1472**), with rates of $50 to $65 double.

Albuquerque International Balloon Fiesta (early Oct)—lodging will not only be hard to find, rates will be higher, sometimes double. The solution? If you want to participate in those events, grin and bear it. But if you don't really care about the State Fair, or the Balloon Fiesta, plan your New Mexico trip for some other time. ***Note:*** Rate ranges discussed below do not include these special events, when rates are essentially whatever the market will bear.

Lodging **taxes** totaling 8% are added to every hotel bill, in addition to sales tax.

Hotels/Motels

EXPENSIVE

Hotel Albuquerque at Old Town ♥♥ Elegant Southwestern furnishings, authentic art, and excellent service make this hotel, just steps from Old Town, a good choice. Although not large, the rooms are quite comfortable, and south-facing ones overlook Old Town. Many rooms have private balconies, offering great views of mountains or mesas; and junior suites have a separate sitting area. If you come during the Balloon Fiesta (p. 210), request a room on the north side so you can watch the display in total comfort. The spacious high-ceilinged lobby is a grand place to meet friends. The Hotel Albuquerque also offers wedding planning services, either in its own 19th-century-style non-denominational chapel or another Albuquerque venue.

800 Rio Grande Blvd. NW. hotelabq.com. ✆ **800/237-2133** (reservations) or 505/843-6300. 188 units. $150–$250 double, junior suites from $200. Free parking. **Amenities:** Restaurant; lounge; concierge; fitness center; whirlpool tub; outdoor pool; business center; room service; free Wi-Fi.

Hotel Andaluz Albuquerque, Curio Collection by Hilton ♥♥
This luxury hotel, built by New Mexico native Conrad Hilton, opened in 1939 as the first Hilton Hotel in the state and is on the National Register of Historic Places. A $30-million renovation was completed in 2009. The lobby is grand and atmospheric, with its soaring ceiling, intimate alcoves, and a central fountain. The elegant guest rooms are decorated in a contemporary fusion of cool colors balanced by warm earth tones, and boast environmentally sustainable custom furniture and allergen-free carpets. The rooftop bar and patio (at press time undergoing renovation), provides sweeping views of the city and mountains to the east plus lively entertainment many evenings.

125 2nd St. NW, at Copper Ave. hotelandaluz.com. ✆ **877/987-9090** or 505/242-9090. 107 units. $150–$190 double, suites from $200. Valet parking $21 per day. Pets accepted, $75 fee per stay. **Amenities:** Restaurant; lounge; concierge; exercise room (nearby); room service; free Wi-Fi.

Hotel Chaco ♥♥♥ At the center of the Sawmill District's transformation from a dwindling industrial area to a commercial hub just north of Old Town, this elegant hotel is one of the few of its caliber to open in Albuquerque in recent years. Its unique design is inspired by ancestral Puebloan great houses. Upon entering the lobby, you'll find a sculpture by famed artist Roxanne Swentzell of Santa Clara Pueblo and a chandelier by Ira Lujan of Taos and Ohkay Owingeh Pueblos, which sets you up nicely for what will be an Indigenous art-filled stay. This carries on to the rooms, with their contemporary decor of earthy colors and natural materials (the sinks are carved out of petrified wood). There's also a downstairs bar, a rooftop restaurant with views of the Sandia Mountains (dinner served daily 5–10pm, weekend brunch 8am–1pm). The hotel also recently opened a spa with treatments that use local ingredients, like body wraps featuring sage, cacao, and honey.

2000 Bellamah Ave. NW. hotelchaco.com. ✆ **505/246-9989.** 118 units. $183–$469 double. Resort fee $35, including parking. Pets accepted, $75 fee per stay. **Amenities:** Restaurant; bar; concierge; fitness center; spa; rooftop pool; room service; free Wi-Fi.

Los Poblanos Historic Inn & Organic Farm ♥♥♥ Designed in 1932 by famed New Mexico architect John Gaw Meem, this boutique inn is listed on the National Register of Historic Places. Located in northwest Albuquerque in the village of Los Ranchos de Albuquerque, with the Rio Grande flowing southward less than a quarter-mile to the west, it's set on 25 acres of formal flower gardens, ancient cottonwoods, fields of lavender, and organic vegetable gardens. "Meem" rooms in the original hacienda offer king or queen beds and have kiva fireplaces, hardwood floors, and New Mexican furnishings. The slightly upscale "Field" suites were inspired by the original 1930s dairy buildings and have private patios, full kitchens, separate dining rooms, and spacious bathrooms. They are adjacent to the lavender fields, allowing guests to immerse themselves in the agricultural experience of the farm. The "Farm" rooms and suites are a bit different, with pitched tin roofs and simpler decor, yet the same 1930s feel, with wood-burning fireplaces and hardwood floors. Many have private patios or open out onto a central courtyard with a fountain. The lavender bath amenities are made on the farm.

4803 Rio Grande Blvd. NW, Los Ranchos de Albuquerque. lospoblanos.com. ✆ **855/486-1380.** 45 units. $330–$480 double, suites from $430. Free parking. **Amenities:** Restaurant; bicycle usage; fitness center; concierge; outdoor pool; free Wi-Fi.

Nativo Lodge ♥ In general, the accommodations at this full-service hotel on the north side of town are modest, though comfortable: Attractively decorated in a Native American theme, each room has a small balcony and a desk, with bathrooms that are small but functional. What lifts the Nativo Lodge into a higher category, however, are its 63 "Artist" rooms, which are something unique indeed: "large-scale, livable installation works of art" commissioned from contemporary Native American artists. Each room is one of a kind, and staying in one will immerse the visitor in the designing artist's vision. The lounge can get noisy in the evenings on weekends, so try to get a room that's not too close if you don't plan to be part of the festivities.

6000 Pan American Fwy. NE, just E of I-25 exit 230. nativolodge.com. ✆ **855/997-8221** or 505/798-4300. 144 units. $100–$220 double. Free parking. **Amenities:** Lobby bar; restaurant; whirlpool tub; indoor/outdoor pool; free Wi-Fi.

MODERATE

Best Western Plus Rio Grande Inn ♥♥ A short walk from Old Town, this attractive Pueblo Revival–style building has a lobby decorated in distinctly Southwestern fashion. Because it's close to the interstate, try for a quieter, south-facing room. The medium-size rooms are accessed from interior corridors and have warm, earth-tone colors on the walls and handcrafted Southwestern furniture. One room option is outfitted with a king-size Murphy bed, giving you more room when it's tucked away during the day. With a restaurant on-site and a lovely, fenced pool, this is a good family choice.

1015 Rio Grande Blvd. NW, on S side of I-40 exit 157. riograndeinn.com. ✆ **800/959-4726** or 505/843-9500. 173 units. $120–$160 double. Free parking. Pets accepted ($30 per night). **Amenities:** Restaurant; free airport transfer; exercise room; hot tub; outdoor pool; free Wi-Fi.

Sheraton Albuquerque Airport Hotel ♥♥ This 15-story building is easy to spot, just 200 yards from the airport, and it is the perfect place to stay when your plane arrives late or you have an early flight the next morning. Or base yourself here while exploring the area. Rooms are simply but colorfully decorated and spotlessly clean, with top-quality beds and wood furnishings. Staff is very accommodating, and there's a very good restaurant and lounge. It's surprisingly quiet considering the hotel's proximity to the airport, but perhaps one of the best things here are the spectacular views from the upper floors.

2910 Yale Blvd. SE. marriott.com. ✆ **888/625-4937** or 505/843-7000. 276 units. $125–$175 double; suites from $170. Parking $11. Pets under 40 lb. accepted ($45 fee per stay). **Amenities:** Restaurant; lounge; concierge; fitness center; outdoor pool; Wi-Fi $5–$10 per day.

INEXPENSIVE

The Querque Hotel ♥ A contemporary Southwestern lobby complete with a fireplace welcomes guests to this hotel (formerly a Fairfield Inn by Marriott). Rooms are vibrant and bright, clean, with plush seating and colorful touches on the bed covers and artwork, including some wonderful photos of the Albuquerque Balloon Fiesta. Each room has a balcony or terrace. Despite its recent change of hands, the hotel shows its age, particularly in the finishes and lack of sound insulation, but it's hard to argue with the low rates. Its location in the NE quadrant of the intersection of I-40 and I-25 makes it central, but you might want to request an east-facing room to avoid the noise and view of the highway.

1760 Menaul Blvd. NE. thequerquehotel.com. ✆ **866/733-8553** or 505/889-4000. 189 units. $61–$114 double. Free breakfast. Free parking. Pets accepted, up to two, $50 fee per stay. **Amenities:** Fitness center; indoor pool; hot tub; sauna; business center; free Wi-Fi.

Bed & Breakfasts

Bottger Mansion of Old Town ♥♥♥ This stunning mansion houses a historic inn in historic Old Town, decorated with historic memorabilia from the coming of the railroad to the Route 66 era. Is that enough history for you? Most of the rooms are named for an interesting but lesser-known historical figure, and include a thumbnail bio for your edification. In summer, the flower-filled courtyard attracts hummingbirds, finches, and other birds, and is shaded by mature trees. Among its choice rooms, there's the first-floor Route 66 Suite, with its own sunroom; the Edward Buxton Cristy room (named for the architect who redesigned this elegant B&B), decorated in blue and white with yellow accents, and encircled by a 1930s-era mural of New Mexico's mountains; and the Bernard Shandon Rodey room (named for the territorial legislator who introduced the bill that founded the University of New Mexico), which is full of historic photos, a vintage map of UNM, and statehood cartoons. Breakfasts are as elegant as the decor, starting with locally roasted coffee, juice, and fresh fruit. The entree might be a savory green chile quiche, blue cornmeal pancakes with pine nuts, or a scrumptious blueberry French toast casserole. And there's generally breakfast sausage, ham, or bacon, plus scones or biscuits.

110 San Felipe NW. bottger.com. ✆ **505/243-3639.** 7 units. $180–$260 double. Rates include breakfast and snacks. Free reserved parking. **Amenities:** Free Wi-Fi.

Sarabande B&B ♥♥ This restored bed-and-breakfast has changed a few hands over the years, and has gotten better in each iteration. Located in Los Ranchos, a former agricultural area along the Rio Grande that's now a quiet upscale neighborhood, the property feels very luxurious for its price point. An adobe compound is connected by a tiled courtyard and houses five room types, from a spacious king room with a kiva fireplace and semi-private patio to a small room with two twin beds and little else. Each is simply decorated, with white walls, either tiled or hardwood floors, and monochromatic furnishings. The open-concept kitchen and dining room, with a similar modern black-and-white aesthetic, serves breakfast every day: from Monday to Wednesday, there's a healthy buffet of granola, yogurt, fruit, fresh juice, and something savory; from Thursday to Sunday, there's full breakfast service with eggs, produce, and meats. In summer a 30-foot lap pool is open.

5637 Rio Grande Blvd. NW. sarabandebnb.com. ✆ **505/348-5593.** 5 units. $180–$320 double. Rates include breakfast. Free parking. Dogs accepted by prior arrangement ($25 fee). **Amenities:** Free Wi-Fi.

RV Parks & Campgrounds

Albuquerque KOA Journey ♥ A good location—not in the middle of the noisy city but close enough so you don't spend all your time driving—this RV park and campground has all the amenities you'd expect in a commercial

CRUISING corrales

If you're heading north, enjoy a leisurely drive on tree-lined streets through meadows and apple orchards by taking the road through Corrales. Home to farmers, artists, and affluent landowners, this is an enchanting place to roam through shops and galleries, and, in the fall, sample fruits and vegetables from roadside stands.

Two excellent restaurants, both serving imaginative new American cuisine, sit on the main street. **Indigo Crow ♥**, 4515 Corrales Rd. (✆ **505/898-7000**), serves lunch (11:30am–2:30pm) and dinner (5–9pm) Tuesday to Saturday, and brunch (10:30am–2:30pm) and dinner (5–9pm) on Sunday. Happy hour runs 3 to 5pm, between lunch and dinner. Lunch entrees range $14 to $18, dinner entrees $29 to $44, and brunch entrees $10 to $16. **Hannah & Nate's ♥♥**, 4512 Corrales Rd. (✆ **505/898-2370**), serves delectable breakfasts, salads, and sandwiches. It is open daily 7am to 2pm, and prices range from $8.50 to $15.

If you'd like to stay in the village, contact the **Sandhill Crane Bed and Breakfast ♥**, 389 Camino Hermosa (sandhillcranebandb.com; ✆ **505/898-2445**). There are three guest rooms in this Southwestern-style adobe hacienda, decorated with works by local artists and Western and Native American items. Rates are $120 double; one large suite, for $160, is available for those traveling with dogs ($25 per dog). A full hot breakfast is served, and there is free Wi-Fi.

Corrales is also home to the **Casa San Ysidro** museum (p. 203) and **Jane Butel's Southwest Cooking School** (p. 206). The **Corrales Bosque Preserve** is a wildlife preserve along the Rio Grande, managed by the village, and in September the **Harvest Festival** (corralesharvestfestival.com) is well worth the trip. For more information about Corrales, contact Corrales Village (corrales-nm.org; ✆ **505/897-0502**).

To get to the village, head north on either I-25 or Rio Grande Boulevard, turn west on Alameda Boulevard, cross the Rio Grande, and turn north on Corrales Road (NM 448). The village is just a few minutes up the road.

campground and even a few extras, such as a miniature golf course and horseshoe pits. It's set in the foothills east of Albuquerque, with easy access off I-40, has good mountain views and some shade trees, and large sites to accommodate big rigs. There are also upscale sites with patios, and some with private dog areas. The camping cabins are especially nice, with TVs and refrigerators. Some share the campground bathhouses and others have private bathrooms. Linens are provided for the cabins with bathrooms but not for the ones that share the campground bathhouses.

12400 Skyline Rd. Off I-40 exit 166. NE. koa.com. ✆ **800/562-7781** or 505/296-2729. 169 sites. $45–$50 tent site, $55–$110 RV site, $70–$160 cabin. Rates for up to 2 people. Pets accepted ($10–$25 per pet in cabins). **Amenities:** Bathhouse; convenience store; horseshoe pits; outdoor pool (May–Nov); indoor hot tub; coin laundry; miniature golf (extra fee); playground; propane; free Wi-Fi.

Albuquerque North/Bernalillo KOA ♥♥ This is one of our favorite KOAs, with more than 1,000 cottonwood and pine trees for shade, lots of flowers in summer, and very friendly and helpful hosts. At the foot of the mountains, 14 miles north of Albuquerque, it has plenty of amenities. Guests enjoy an outdoor cafe and free outdoor movies in summer, and there's a brewpub next door. Six camping cabins are also available.

555 South Hill Rd., Bernalillo off I-25 exit 240. koa.com. ✆ **800/562-3616** or 505/867-5227. 95 sites. $40–$44 tent site; $68–$74 RV site; $80–$94 cabin. Rates for up to 2 people. Additional person $3. Children 6 and under free with parent. Pets accepted. **Amenities:** Restaurant (open weekends 7–10am in summer); playground; outdoor pool (summer only); store; free Wi-Fi.

American RV Resort ♥ About 10 miles west of downtown Albuquerque on the higher west mesa, this RV park is a good choice for those visiting attractions on the west side of the city, such as Old Town or Petroglyph National Monument. It has nice views of the Sandia Mountains and the city lights at night. There are some shade trees and grass, a pleasant pool, a hot tub, two bathhouses, and a dog park. It's gated at night, so you'll need to make a reservation and get the gate code if you'll be arriving late.

13500 Central Ave. SW, off I-40 exit 149. americanrvpark.com. ✆ **800/282-8885** or 505/831-3545. 236 sites. $52–$79 tents and RV sites; cabins $100–$159. Pets accepted. **Amenities:** Two bathhouses; outdoor pool; hot tub; horseshoe pits; playground; coin laundry; propane; store; free Wi-Fi.

WHERE TO EAT IN ALBUQUERQUE

Albuquerque may not be the first American city that comes to mind when you think of fine dining destinations, but you can certainly have a memorable meal or two while visiting here. There are excellent high-end restaurants such as the **Ranchers Club of New Mexico ♥♥♥** (p. 188), quite a few really good moderately priced eateries, and some bargain joints that serve tasty, inexpensive, and sometimes even relatively healthy grub.

SOME FAVORITE brand restaurants IN TOWN

Looking for a familiar restaurant chain? Albuquerque probably has it. **Applebee's Grill & Bar** ♥♥ has six outlets in Albuquerque, including one at 2600 Menaul Blvd. NE (applebees.com; ✆ **505/883-2846**). **Olive Garden** ♥ has three restaurants in town, including one at 6301 San Mateo Blvd. NE (olivegarden.com; ✆ **505/881-8425**). Albuquerque has seven **Chipotle Mexican Grills** ♥♥, including one at 6810 Menaul Blvd. NE (chipotle.com; ✆ **505/884-1716**). There are two **Red Lobster** ♥ restaurants, including one at 5555 Montgomery Blvd. NE (redlobster.com; ✆ **505/884-4445**).

If you're getting in late, leaving early, or just hungry at 3am, there are four 24-hour **Denny's** ♥♥, including one at 2400 San Mateo Blvd. NE (dennys.com; ✆ **505/884-6574**); another choice for night owls are the 24-hour **IHOP** ♥ locations, including at 1400 Mercantile Ave. NE (ihop.com; ✆ **505/508-4935**). An excellent choice for a healthy sandwich or soup is the well-respected chain **Panera Bread** ♥♥♥, with six Albuquerque outlets, including one at 6600 Menaul Blvd. NE (www.panerabread.com; ✆ **505/884-3040**).

Many of the most interesting restaurants here serve traditional northern New Mexican cuisine, which emphasizes spicy chile sauces. We certainly hope you'll try some, because to truly experience northern New Mexico you will want to experience the foods as well as the sights and sounds. However, those not used to spicy food may want to ask the servers how hot the chile is—you'll note that in New Mexico we use the word "hot" to mean spicy, which doesn't have anything to do with actual temperature. Many restaurants will either bring you a sample to taste before ordering, or put the chile on the side, so you can add a bit at a time.

Expensive

Campo at Los Poblanos ♥♥♥ AMERICAN One of Albuquerque's most romantic restaurants is located within the beloved hotel and lavender farm Los Poblanos. Set in a restored dairy building, Campo's main dining room has a casual farmhouse aesthetic; there's also a chef's table that serves a set menu and a private room that features a wine cellar and mountain views. Start your evening with a cocktail at the bar, which showcases the botanicals that Los Poblanos has been growing and distilling for the past two decades (order one featuring its Western Dry gin, with notes of chamomile, rose, hawthorn, and piñon). Upon entering the restaurant, you'll be met with the kitchen's open-fire hearth, used in most dishes on the menu. You won't go wrong with anything on the menu, which changes seasonally, but the pork confit with blue-corn hominy, tortillas, green chile, and fries-like papitas and the carrot cavatelli pasta with lemon-chicken sausage, green-chile cream, and chicken-skin breadcrumbs are especially tasty. There's also breakfast or brunch. Reservations are required.

4803 Rio Grande Blvd. NW. lospoblanos.com. ✆ **505/985-5000.** Dinner main courses $32–$65; breakfast/brunch $12–$24; Mon–Wed 8–10:30am and 5–9pm, Thurs–Sun 8:30am–1pm and 5–9pm.

Albuquerque Restaurants

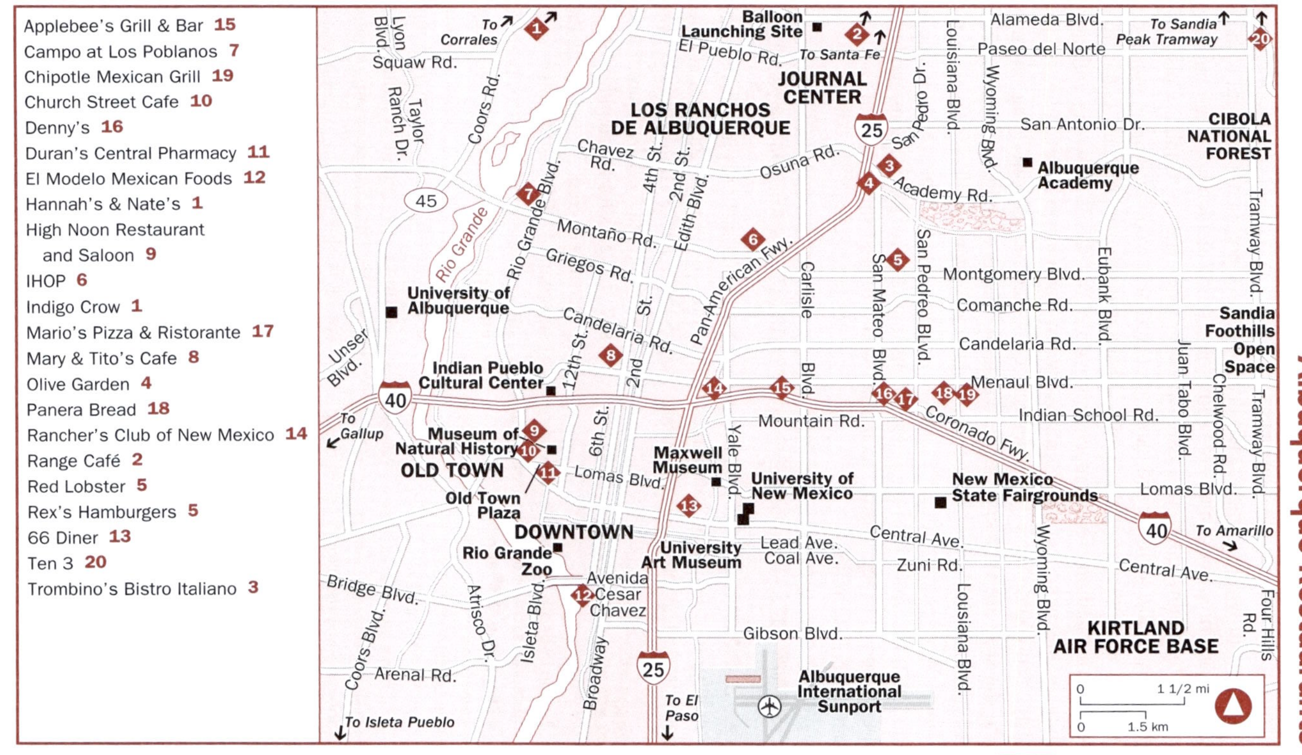

Applebee's Grill & Bar **15**
Campo at Los Poblanos **7**
Chipotle Mexican Grill **19**
Church Street Cafe **10**
Denny's **16**
Duran's Central Pharmacy **11**
El Modelo Mexican Foods **12**
Hannah's & Nate's **1**
High Noon Restaurant and Saloon **9**
IHOP **6**
Indigo Crow **1**
Mario's Pizza & Ristorante **17**
Mary & Tito's Cafe **8**
Olive Garden **4**
Panera Bread **18**
Rancher's Club of New Mexico **14**
Range Café **2**
Red Lobster **5**
Rex's Hamburgers **5**
66 Diner **13**
Ten 3 **20**
Trombino's Bistro Italiano **3**

Ranchers Club of New Mexico ♥♥♥ STEAK/SEAFOOD/GAME Have a special occasion to celebrate? This is the spot. Albuquerque's most luxurious restaurant, the Ranchers Club boasts superb service in an elegant dining room with a refined ranch decor—lots of polished wood and a handsome stone fireplace. There are saddles and ranch memorabilia, and ranching photos by renowned New Mexico photographer Harvey Caplin. Cuisine is primarily steak, seafood, and game, prepared on a wood grill using mesquite, hickory, and other aromatic woods. Meats and other ingredients come from local farms and ranches as much as possible. You won't go wrong with anything on the menu, but the 18-ounce cowboy-cut bone-in rib-eye is especially tasty. You couldn't ask for better service—attentive without being invasive, and the staff are very knowledgeable about the food and the extensive wine list. (There's full liquor service as well.) Live piano music is played in the lounge Wednesday through Saturday evenings. The Ranchers Club is one of the few northern New Mexico restaurants that requires reservations and has a dress code: business casual, men must wear collared shirts, and no shorts or sandals are permitted.

Inside the Crowne Plaza Hotel, 1901 University Blvd. NE. theranchersclubofnm.com. ✆ **505/889-8071.** Main courses $49–$53. Mon–Thurs 5:30–9:30pm, Fri–Sat 5:30–10pm.

Ten 3 ♥♥ AMERICAN The views are the star attraction, plus the fact that you have to ride a tram 15 minutes to get here (p. 198), but the food is quite good, too. The previous restaurant atop Sandia Peak, High Finance, was closed and demolished, and it took several years for this building to be constructed. Ten 3 opened in the summer of 2019 with a new chef and a new mission—to prepare international, American, and New Mexican specialties from scratch, using locally sourced ingredients as much as possible. The view from the handsome main dining room is the best in Albuquerque. From the top of Sandia Peak, at an elevation of 10,300 feet (thus the name), you can see some 11,000 square miles of western New Mexico, with panoramic sunsets and nighttime city-light vistas that are simply phenomenal. The bar, facing east, offers views of Sandia Peak Ski Area and Santa Fe in the distance. The main dining room, with an open floor plan, plush seating, and dark tables, reminds us of a club for the quietly rich, but you can't ignore the wall of windows giving every table a great view. The casual-dining bar menu offers a good variety of American and New Mexican dishes, from a green chile bison smash burger to carne asada tacos to inventive salads. For dinner, we recommend jumbo sea scallops with a sweet corn piñon risotto; the

Gastroblog

For an in-depth look at Albuquerque's restaurants, check out **Gil's Thrilling (and Filling) Blog ♥♥** at nmgastronome.com. Food critic and New Mexico native Gil Garduño has dined at more than 1,000 restaurants in northern New Mexico. In his blog he provides his personal in-depth accounts and ratings, of both the food and the experience of dining at most of them. You can spend hours reading up on his favorites, or just take a quick peek to get a recommendation.

Kurobuta pork tenderloin with white beans, apple puree, and fig mostarda; or New York strip steak with fondant potatoes and a red chile honey broccolini puree. There is full liquor service.

On Sandia Peak, accessible via Sandia Peak Tramway. ten3tram.com. ✆ **505/764-8363.** Main courses lunch/bar $21–$59, dinner $34–$186. Bar daily 11am–10pm, dining room daily 4:30–10pm; last seating 7:30pm.

Moderate

Church Street Cafe ♥♥ NEW MEXICAN/AMERICAN This almost-hidden gem of a restaurant in Albuquerque's Old Town offers well-prepared northern New Mexico standards plus enough American-style diner food to satisfy most visitors. It's located just north of the San Felipe de Neri Church, for which Church Street is named, in an adobe house built by the Ruiz family in the early 1700s; it remained their home until 1991 when the last inhabitant, Rufina Ruiz, died at age 91. There's a lovely mosaic kiva-style fireplace in the main room, which leads to a series of narrow dining rooms decorated with northern New Mexico antiques, rugs, and historic photos. Breakfast items include various egg dishes, pancakes, and breakfast burritos; we recommend the breakfast quesadilla—scrambled eggs, cheddar cheese, green chile, and ham or bacon, on a flour tortilla. Lunch and dinner items include salads, sandwiches such as a tasty Reuben, and burgers, plus fajitas, tamales, tacos, burritos, and enchiladas. Many items are served with chile. There's also an outdoor patio where your dog is welcome. The drinks menu includes beer, wine, and cocktails.

2111 Church St. NW. churchstreetcafe.com. ✆ **505/247-8522.** Sandwiches, salads, and most breakfast items $9–$18, dinner entrees $13–$21. Tues–Thurs 11am–9pm, Fri–Sat 8am–9pm, Sun 8am–4pm.

High Noon Restaurant and Saloon ♥ STEAK/SEAFOOD/NEW MEXICAN Looking for a great steak in a Wild West atmosphere? This is the spot. The Villa family has been serving top-quality steaks in this historic Old Town building since 1974. Believed to have been built between 1750 and 1785, the adobe building is rumored to have been both a gambling parlor and a brothel in its earlier days. Today it's not only a reminder of Albuquerque's wild youth but also a home of excellent steaks, seafood, wild game, and New Mexican classics. Among steaks we suggest the High Noon tenderloin, an 8-ounce hand-cut filet with red wine demi-glace, served with wild mushroom enchiladas, or the 14-ounce rib-eye, with mashed potatoes and a red-chile jus. Not a beef eater? Try the shrimp pappardelle in red-chile cream sauce. The popular green chile cheeseburger and shrimp enchiladas are available for both lunch and dinner. There is a full bar, with an especially wonderful selection of tequila available.

425 San Felipe St. NW. highnoonrestaurant.com. ✆ **505/765-1455.** Main courses $16–$45. Tues–Sun 12–9pm.

Mario's Pizza & Ristorante ♥ ITALIAN Mario's reminds us of the Italian restaurants of our youth in New York and New Jersey, and it's no wonder, since the Burgarello family, immigrants from Sicily, opened their first restaurant in Queens, New York, in 1965. The family moved to Albuquerque in 1972, and the rest, as they say, is history. This is not "fine dining," whatever that is, but well-prepared everyday Italian food, in this case using Mama Anná's made-from-scratch family recipes. The unpretentious dining room is designed to resemble an Italian villa, with plaster walls and half-moon windows, decorated with posters, photos, and old menus. Offerings include practically all the Italian standards, from spaghetti to lasagna to veal parmigiana, along with calzones, Italian subs, and sandwiches (including a French dip!), and of course, pizza. We especially like the lasagna and pizza, but in the years we've been coming here we haven't discovered anything we wouldn't recommend. Beer and wine is available. This is the original, but there are Mario's locations, with the same menu, at 11500 Menaul Blvd. NE (© **505/294-8999**), 5700 4th St. NW (© **505/344-4700**), and 7501 Paseo del Norte Blvd. NE (© **505/797-1800**).

2401 San Pedro Blvd. NE. mariospizzaabq.com. © **505/883-4414.** Main courses $14–$20, pizzas from $14. Sun–Thurs 11am–8pm, Fri–Sat 11am–9pm.

Range Café ♥ NEW MEXICAN/AMERICAN New Mexico comfort food done right is what you'll find at all five Range Cafés in the Albuquerque area. This one, the very first, is in in an old building in downtown Bernalillo, about 20 minutes north of Albuquerque; we like it best, because there's more funky New Mexico ambience here than at the other four, with attractive and colorful artwork—some with a whimsical feel—and a pressed-tin ceiling. The food is pretty much the same at all locations, however—mostly basic American, such as roast turkey and stuffing, grilled chicken breast, burgers, and Tom's meatloaf, with some New Mexican dishes, including their best seller, the award-winning huevos rancheros, and a few surprises. Try the salmon salad—a grilled filet atop mixed greens, berries, candied pecans, and crispy onion. Breakfast, served all day, is tops. We recommend the breakfast burrito with green chile. There's a gift shop and full liquor service. ***Note:*** Street parking is often full, so watch for the little alley across the street that leads to the Range's parking lot. The other Albuquerque-area outposts are at 4401 Wyoming Blvd. NE (© **505/293-2633**), 10019 Coors Blvd. NW (© **505/835-5495**), 1050 Rio Grande Blvd. NW (© **505/508-2640**), and 320 Central Ave. (© **505/243-1440**).

925 Camino del Pueblo (off I-25 at exit 240), Bernalillo. rangecafe.com. © **505/867-1700.** Main courses $13–$20. Mon–Wed 8am–8pm, Thurs–Fri 8am–9pm, Sat 7am–9pm, Sun 7am–8pm. Closed Thanksgiving and Christmas.

Trombino's Bistro Italiano ♥♥ ITALIAN Since 1979 the Trombino family has been serving some of the best genuine Italian food in Albuquerque, prepared from scratch, at very reasonable prices. The dining room and bar have rustic Italian decor—colorful, comfortable, and casually elegant. The menu, much of it from old family recipes, ranges from standards such as veal parmigiana, lasagna, and three-cheese ravioli to specialties such as Shrimp

Fra Diavolo—brandied shrimp tossed with a hot, spicy fire-roasted tomato sauce, served over pasta marinara. You can also create your own main course: Choose among six types of pasta and add different sauces and toppings, ranging from the Trombino family's own marinara sauce to spicy tomato arrabbiata with pancetta and garlic. Especially popular is the house-made Italian sausage, either spicy or mild, grilled and topped with roasted peppers and onions. A pleasant surprise is that this Italian bistro serves especially good steaks. The tiramisu cake is extra special. There is full liquor service.

5415 Academy Rd. NE. bistroitaliano.com. ✆ **505/821-5974.** Main courses $16–$37. Mon–Fri 4–8pm, Sat–Sun 3–8pm. Closed Thanksgiving, Christmas, and Super Bowl Sunday.

Inexpensive

Duran's Central Pharmacy ♥♥♥ NEW MEXICAN Those old enough to remember going to the local drugstore to sit at a counter for a sandwich or an ice cream soda will feel right at home at Duran's. A genuine old-time drugstore, with plenty of stuff to browse through (check out the special-occasion and note cards, and the rather strange religious icons), this busy locals' favorite also offers some of the best genuine northern New Mexico food you'll find in Albuquerque, and at bargain prices. The somewhat noisy restaurant section is in the back of the store, with stainless-steel tables and diner-style orange vinyl chairs. There are also stools along a long, curved counter overlooking the open cooking area, and an outdoor covered patio. You'll find all the usual suspects here—tacos, burritos, enchiladas, and of course, breakfast burritos—but our favorites are the Torpedo (potatoes, chile, and cheese, wrapped in a tortilla) and the turkey and jack cheese wrap, in a tortilla with enough green chile to set your head on fire. Duran's serves seriously hot chile, so ask for recommendations before ordering, or request that the chile be served on the side. No alcohol is served.

1815 Central Ave. NW. duransrx.com. ✆ **505/247-4141.** Menu items $8–$16. Sun–Tues 9am–4pm, Wed–Sat 9am–7pm.

El Modelo Mexican Foods ♥♥ MEXICAN The lunch rush at this no-frills counter-service eatery speaks to its high standing within Albuquerque's Mexican community. For many Burqueños, El Modelo represents one of the few holdouts of a changing city and some of the most authentic Mexican food in the state. The menu is broken up into tacos, burritos, and plates, which includes tender spareribs cooked in red chile, topped with lettuce, cheese, and tostadas. The star of the menu are the tamales, handmade daily, as well as the stuffed sopapillas. There is also a selection of sides available by pint or quart, including the joint's famed red chile. Breakfast is served all day. Most take their orders to go, but next door you'll find a small yard with picnic tables.

1715 2nd St. SW. elmodelomexicanfood.com. ✆ **505/242-1843.** Main courses $5–$9. Daily 7am–7pm.

Mary & Tito's Cafe ♥♥♥ NEW MEXICAN Don't be fooled by the modest exterior—this Albuquerque institution has not only lasted for 60-plus years, but has remained relevant amid the city's changing food scene, even winning a James Beard Award as an "American Classic" in 2010. What's kept it beloved all these years is its very traditional, yet unique, approach to staples: enchiladas smothered in sauces that taste unusually rich, and a different take on a stuffed sopapilla, called a "Mexican turnover," with a crust that more resembles a calzone. The highlight of the menu, though, is the *carne adovada,* a stew of marinated roast pork slow cooked in red chile for hours and served with tomato rice and beans. Dining here feels like being a guest in someone's home, furthered by the warm service and a dining room plastered with the owners' family photographs and mementos. If you still have room for dessert, order the Mexican wedding cake, made with crushed pineapple, walnuts, and cream-cheese frosting.

2711 4th St. NW. No website. ✆ **505/344-6266.** Main courses $7–$11. Mon–Thurs 11am–3pm, Fri–Sat 11am–5pm.

Rex's Hamburgers ♥♥ AMERICAN/NEW MEXICAN Thinking of stopping at one of the national fast-food chains for a burger and fries? Forget it. Instead, head to Rex's, hidden in a little shopping center along busy Montgomery Boulevard, for better burgers, better fries, and great shakes and malts. The dining room is simply decorated diner-style, with some interesting signs, photos, and posters. Chairs and booth seating are upholstered, and the tabletops are tile, a nice touch. In addition to various burgers—we usually get the green chile cheeseburger—there are hot dogs, sandwiches, burritos, and tacos. You can order a la carte or get a platter, which includes your entree plus fries, one onion ring, and applesauce. The fresh lemonade is good, and we especially like the malts. No alcohol is served. There's an outdoor patio where your dog is welcome.

5555 Montgomery Blvd. NE. ✆ **505/837-2827.** Main courses $4–$15. Mon–Sun 10:30am–8pm.

family-friendly RESTAURANTS

Mario's Pizzeria & Ristorante (p. 189) There's a lot of people-watching to be done here, and what kid doesn't like pizza?

Range Café (p. 190) The fun and funky decor, especially at the Bernalillo location, and ice cream specialties make this a good spot for kids.

Rex's Hamburgers (above) Fast food is fun, the burgers are good, and the walls are covered with fascinating posters and photos. It's also a popular spot for kids' birthday parties.

66 Diner (below) A full range of burgers and treats such as root beer floats and hot fudge sundaes will make any youngster happy.

66 Diner ♥♥ AMERICAN This somewhat hokey 1950s-style diner didn't exist during the glory days of Route 66, but it certainly does a good job of capturing the spirit of those times, or at least capturing our rose-colored recollections of it. There are photos of Elvis and Marilyn and plenty of neon and chrome; even the servers dress the part. The food is just as you'd expect—good burgers, sandwiches, meals such as grilled liver and onions or meatloaf with mashed potatoes and gravy, and green chile chicken enchiladas. Daily blue plate specials include chicken pot pie on Thursdays and fried catfish on Fridays, and an old-fashioned soda fountain creates wonderful malts and milkshakes. Breakfasts—all the usual American items—are served Saturdays and Sundays only, 8am to noon. No alcohol is served.

1405 Central Ave. NE. 66diner.com. ✆ **505/247-1421.** Main courses $6–$14. Mon–Thurs 11am–10pm, Fri 11am–11pm, Sat 8am–11pm, Sun 8am–10pm.

EXPLORING ALBUQUERQUE

9

Albuquerque is all too often overshadowed by Santa Fe and Taos, two historic towns with enormous tourist appeal, and it really isn't fair. Yes, Albuquerque has its own Spanish Colonial plaza and historic Old Town area, but it also seems to live more in the 21st century, with a diverse and dynamic selection of cultural draws, an impressive array of urban green spaces, and a large state university adding more museums, performing arts, and spectator sports into the mix. (Frankly, if you're traveling with kids, they may enjoy Albuquerque's family-friendly sights more than artsy Santa Fe and Taos.) And because lodging and dining costs are more reasonable here in the big city, it can be a better base for excursions into northern New Mexico's fascinating desert landscapes.

WHAT TO SEE & DO IN ALBUQUERQUE

Albuquerque's original town site, known today as Old Town, is the central point of interest for visitors. Here, grouped around the plaza, are the venerable Church of San Felipe de Neri and numerous restaurants, galleries, and crafts shops. Several important museums are nearby, and within a few blocks you'll find BioPark, with its excellent aquarium, botanic garden, zoo, and beach. (Yes, a beach in the desert.) But don't get stuck in Old Town. Elsewhere, you'll find the Sandia Peak Tramway, the Balloon Museum, and several natural attractions.

The Top Attractions

Albuquerque Museum ♥♥ Visit the "Only in Albuquerque" history gallery to get a fresh look at the city's history in this fine modern museum on the edge of Old Town. It's interactive and fun, a great introduction to the cultural history of New Mexico. Exhibits tell the city's story from pre-written history up to now, and there are interactive storybooks and theaters, not to mention a chance to electronically send someone a Route 66 postcard and even create your own coat of arms. Don't miss the art portion of this museum, either: The "Common Ground" gallery highlights significant works

Central Albuquerque Attractions

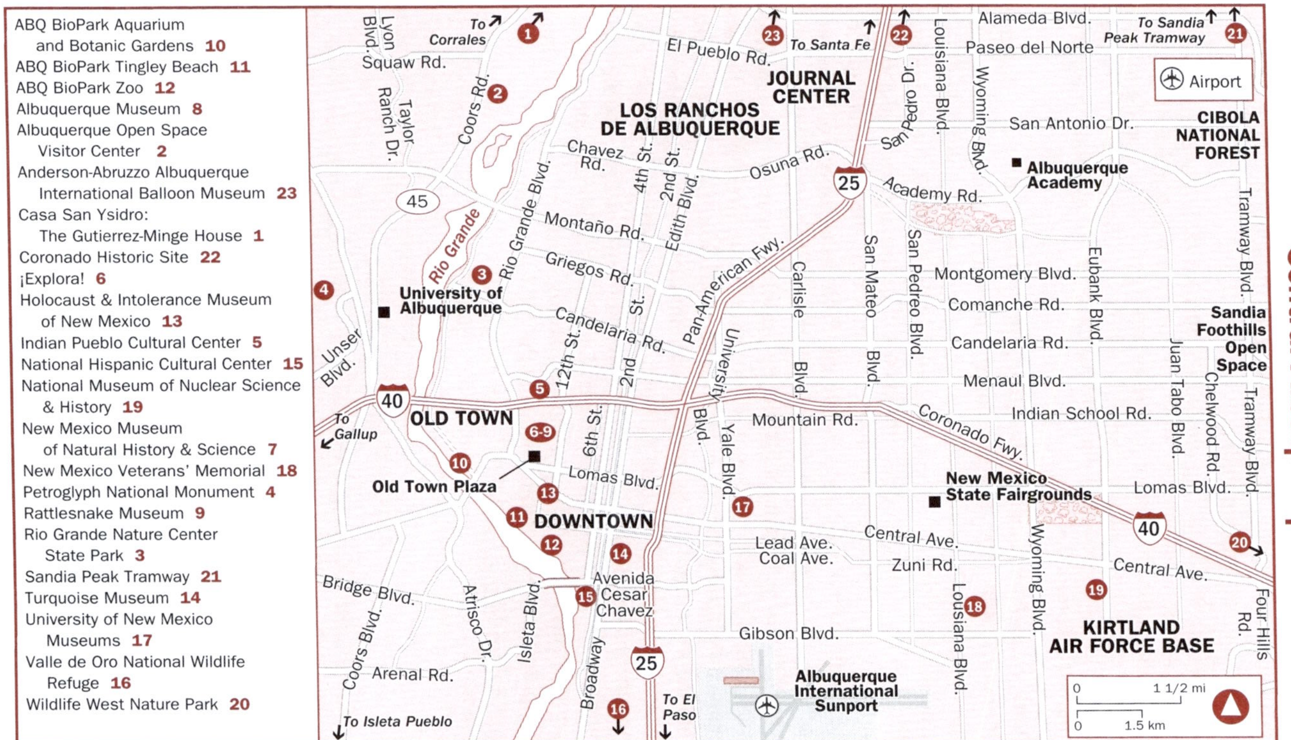

from the museum's permanent collection from the late–19th century to today, most by New Mexico artists. In addition, there are wonderful changing exhibits, often with an unusual focus. Every year a visiting artist installs a temporary show in the museum's lobby.

2000 Mountain Rd. NW. cabq.gov/museum. ✆ **505/243-7255.** Adults $6, seniors (65+) $4, ages 4–12 $3. Free admission 1st Wed of month and 9am–1pm Sun, except during Balloon Fiesta. Extra fees for special exhibits and events. Tues–Sun 9am–5pm. Docent tours by pre-arrangement; Old Town walking tours Tues, Thurs, and Sun 11am; Sculpture Garden walking tours Mar–Nov 11am Wed and Sat. Closed Thanksgiving, Christmas, and New Year's Day.

Anderson-Abruzzo Albuquerque International Balloon Museum ♥♥ Fun and fascinating, entertaining and educational, this sprawling museum is a natural favorite for kids—what's not to love about hands-on activities, multimedia technology, and a balloon flight simulator? The Balloon Museum explores the history of ballooning, from the first flight in France in 1783 (a rooster, sheep, and duck were the passengers, to see if they could survive the trip) to the present. It covers all aspects of ballooning, including the largest lighter-than-air vehicles—dirigibles, which were filled with hydrogen or helium for lift and used gasoline engines to push them forward. One of the scariest uses of balloons was during World War II: Japanese children built them, then their government added bombs and launched them into the jet stream flowing toward North America. Of the 10,000 launched, about 1,000 made it to land in North America. Additional exhibits cover Atlantic and Pacific crossings, the first around-the-world flight, and the beginning of aerial photography. The museum is named for Albuquerque's pioneering aeronauts Maxie Anderson and Ben Abruzzo, who, with Larry Newman, completed the first manned crossing of the Atlantic Ocean in 1978.

9201 Balloon Museum Dr. NE (from I-25 exit 233 for Alameda Blvd., W to Balloon Museum Dr.). balloonmuseum.com. ✆ **505/768-6020.** Adults $6, seniors (65+) $4, ages 6–17 $3, free for children 5 and under. Free admission Sun 9am–1pm and first Fri of month except during Balloon Fiesta. Tues–Sun 9am–5pm. Closed New Year's Day, Thanksgiving, Christmas, and some other city holidays.

Indian Pueblo Cultural Center ♥♥ Owned and operated by the 19 pueblos of New Mexico, this museum has a stated purpose of perpetuating their culture and advancing understanding by presenting the Pueblo people's accomplishments and evolving history. It is an excellent place to begin your exploration of Puebloan cultural history. Start with the permanent exhibit "We Are of This Place: The Pueblo Story," which tells their story in the words and voices of Pueblo people. The South Gallery has rotating exhibits drawn from a collection of more than 2,500 pieces of pottery, jewelry, textiles, baskets, photographs, prints, paintings, and archaeological artifacts. In addition there are over 20 murals by Pueblo artists, vividly depicting the role of the seasons, dance, harvest, agriculture, and animals in Pueblo life. Throughout the year, **Native American dancers perform** in an outdoor arena, on Saturday and Sundays (at noon in winter, 11am and 2pm Apr–Oct, plus 2pm Fridays

May–Aug). During Balloon Fiesta, there is a full daily schedule of dancing and music; check the website about a week ahead if you're planning a trip then. A large shop, **Indian Pueblo Store,** offers fine pottery, rugs, sculptures, fetishes, storytellers, baskets, jewelry, paintings, and more. There's also a very fine restaurant, **Indian Pueblo Kitchen,** serving excellent regional and Pueblo-inspired cuisine. It's open 9am to 5pm Tuesday through Sunday.

2401 12th St. NW. indianpueblo.org. ✆ **866/855-7902** or 505/843-7270. Adults $12; seniors 62+ and ages 5–17 $8; military $10, free for children 5 and under. Daily 9am–5pm. Closed New Year's Day, Memorial Day, July 4, Labor Day, Thanksgiving, and Christmas.

National Hispanic Cultural Center ♥♥ Take a rich cultural journey through hundreds of years of Hispanic world history in this fine museum in the historic Barelas neighborhood on the Camino Real. It explores Hispanic arts and lifestyles with visual arts, drama, music, dance, and other programs. An intriguing 4,000-square-foot concave fresco depicts thousands of years of Hispanic and pre-Hispanic history from the Iberian Peninsula to the Americas. Rotating exhibits feature pieces from the center's permanent collection of over 2,500 pieces of artwork from the United States, Latin America, Spain, and other regions of Spanish emigration. **La Fonda del Bosque** restaurant (lafondadelbosqueabq.com; ✆ **505/238-5316**) serves multicultural Latin and northern New Mexico fare Wednesday through Friday 11:30am to 2pm and Friday 5 to 8pm.

1701 4th St. SW (at Av. Cesar Chavez). nhccnm.org. ✆ **505/246-2261.** Adults $6, military and kids 16 and under free. Free with New Mexico CulturePass (see box below). Tues–Sun 10am–4pm. Closed major holidays; check website for calendar.

A GREAT DEAL FOR museum lovers

If you're a fan of museums and historic sites, and especially if you'll be touring other areas of the state, be sure to pick up a **New Mexico CulturePass.** It's good at some 15 museums and historic sites across the state. The cost is $30 per person and entitles the bearer to one visit at each of the properties in a 12-month period. You can buy the CulturePass at the first museum or historic site you visit, or ahead of time by phone (✆ **505/476-1125**) and have the pass mailed to you within 10 days, or receive a voucher via e-mail, redeemable for the pass upon your first site visit. For the most up-to-date list of included sites statewide, visit newmexicoculture.org.

Sites in the Albuquerque area are the **National Hispanic Cultural Center** (above), the **New Mexico Museum of Natural History and Science** (p. 206), and the **Coronado Historic Site** (see p. 203) and **Jemez Historic Site** (see p. 228).

Sites included in the Santa Fe area are the **New Mexico History Museum** (p. 74), the **New Mexico Museum of Art** (p. 74), the **Museum of International Folk Art** (p. 78), and the **Museum of Indian Arts and Culture** (p. 77) Other sites the pass covers include the **New Mexico Museum of Space History** in Alamogordo, the **New Mexico Farm and Ranch Heritage Museum** in Las Cruces, and several other historic sites around New Mexico.

Old Town ♥♥♥ This plaza was once the heart of town, with mercantile and grocery stores, government offices, and businesses to serve the needs of the public. The importance of Old Town as Albuquerque's commercial center declined after 1880, when the railroad came through 1¼ miles east, and businesses relocated to be closer to the trains. The area fell into disrepair until the 1930s and 1940s, when artisans and shop owners rediscovered it and the tourism industry burgeoned. More than 150 shops, boutiques, galleries, and studios comprise Old Town today. Its central grassy square with benches set under old cottonwood trees is a great place for people-watching.

On the north side of the plaza, you can see where the first building was erected when Albuquerque was established in 1706, the **San Felipe de Neri Church ♥♥** (sanfelipedeneri.org). The original church collapsed in 1782 after a particularly wet season; the present church was erected in 1793. Its 5-foot-thick adobe walls have withstood the years through constant maintenance and occasional renovation. Inside, the plaster walls are off-white above light blue wainscoting, with deep window enclosures strikingly painted in a geometric motif. Oak pews rest on the brick floor (not original) of the sanctuary, whose walls are lined with large paintings of the Stations of the Cross. This simple house of worship has been in almost continuous use for many generations of Albuquerque residents. Its gift shop, set in the Sister Blandina Convent and Chapel to the west of the church, is filled with religious art used in the life and liturgy of the parish, including a charming assortment of angels and lovely crosses at reasonable prices, including many made of brightly painted and glazed terra cotta.

Around the plaza, and a block or two in all directions, you can find food and drink from snacks to fine dining, galleries offering fine art and jewelry, some fun clothing boutiques, and the inevitable souvenir shops. An excellent **Old Town historic walking tour** is offered most days at noon; information on that and other tours, plus reservations (required 2 hr. in advance) are available online or by phone (toursofoldtown.com; ✆ **505/246-8687**). The tour originates at the ticket window at 303 Romero St. NW, Plaza Don Luis #N120, off the northwest corner of the Old Town Plaza across from the church. Public tours are $25 per person; private tours are offered for $60 for a group of up to five people.

North of Central Ave. and east of Rio Grande Blvd. NW. Old Town Visitor Center: 303 Romero St. NW. albuquerqueoldtown.com. ✆ **505/243-3215.** Visitor Center daily 10am–4:30pm, until 6pm in summer.

Sandia Peak Tramway ♥♥ Not for those with vertigo, this fun trip up the face of the Sandias in a metal box hanging from a cable presents wonderful views of the city and to everywhere and nowhere in particular. For a panoramic view, it can't be beaten. The Sandia Peak Tram is a "jigback": as one car approaches the top, the other nears the bottom. The two pass halfway through the trip, in the midst of a 1½-mile "clear span" of unsupported cable between the second tower and the upper terminal. Several hiking trails are available on Sandia Peak, but may not be suitable for children. Call the Sandia Ranger station for information (✆ **505/281-3304**). If you're riding up in late afternoon, plan to dine at **Ten 3** restaurant (p. 188) and watch the sunset—it's an unsurpassed experience. Special tram rates apply with dinner reservations. Be aware that certain weather conditions, such as high winds, can cause the tram to be shut down.

10 Tramway Loop NE (I-25 exit 234 or I-40 exit 167). sandiapeak.com. ✆ **505/856-7325.** Round trip tickets: Adults $34; seniors 62+, military, and ages 13–20 $29; ages 2–12 $24, free for children under 2. Memorial Day to Labor Day and Balloon Fiesta, Wed–Mon 9am–9pm; rest of year Wed–Mon 9am–8pm. Regular maintenance closures in Apr and Nov; call or visit website for details. Parking at base $3.50 daily.

Turquoise Museum ♥♥♥ Located in the prominent "Turquoise Castle" in downtown Albuquerque, this excellent and fun museum is home to what's believed to be the world's largest collection of natural turquoise on display. Turquoise has been the passion of five generations of the Zachary and Lowry

route 66 REVISITED: REDISCOVERING NEW MEXICO'S STRETCH OF THE MOTHER ROAD

You know how the song goes: "Get your kicks on Route 66." The highway that once stretched from Chicago to California was hailed as the road to freedom. During the Great Depression, it was the way west for farmers escaping Dust Bowl poverty, and if you found yourself in a rut in the late 1940s or '50s, all you had to do was hop in the car and head west on Route 66.

Of course, the road existed long before it attracted such widespread fascination. Built in the late 1920s (though not fully paved until 1938), it was a lifeblood of communities in several states. Nowadays, however, US 66 is as elusive as the fantasies about it that once carried hundreds of thousands west in search of a better life. Replaced by other roads, covered up by interstates (mostly I-40), and just plain out of use, US 66 still exists in New Mexico, but you'll have to do a little searching and take some extra time to find it.

In New Mexico there were actually two routes: From 1926 to 1937, Route 66 meandered north from Santa Rosa to Santa Fe before heading south to Albuquerque, where it turned west. But from 1937 onward it made a more-or-less straight shot across the state, bypassing Santa Fe.

Motorists driving west from Texas might be able to find a gravel stretch of the original highway running from Glenrio to San Jon. After San Jon, you can enjoy some paved sections of vintage 66, including the main drags in both Tucumcari and Santa Rosa. In Albuquerque, US 66 follows Central Avenue for 18 miles, from the state fairgrounds, past what's left of some original 1930s motels and the historic Nob Hill district, on west through downtown. Heading west from Albuquerque, you can pick up a 6-mile stretch of old Route 66 in Grants, much of it along Santa Fe Avenue. In Gallup, a 9-mile segment of US 66 is lined with restaurants and hotels reminiscent of the city's days as a Western film capital from the 1920s through the 1960s.

For more information about Route 66 from beginning to end, check out **historic66.com**; for information about Route 66 in New Mexico, see **newmexico.org/route66**.

families. Pieces from their collections are displayed here, with a large number of items from J. C. "Zack" Zachary, Jr., the great-grandfather of the current museum executive director, Jacob Lowry. Amassed from 80 mines around the world, the collection includes the George Washington Stone, named for its resemblance to the United States' first president (the most valuable gem in the museum, according to Lowry). In addition to countless turquoise gemstones in all manner of settings, the 8,500 square-foot museum has exhibits that explain the stone's geology, history, and mythology; there are maps showing mine locations from Egypt to Kingman, Arizona. The museum provides a great service for those interested in purchasing turquoise: exhibits help you learn how to determine the quality of the stones you're considering. There are lapidary demonstrations, special events, and the popular Turquoise 101 class, plus numerous hands-on exhibits. It is also worth stopping by just to see the building. Built as a private residence in 2008, it resembles a castle—there are 132 chandeliers inside. The museum staff can provide appraisals of your turquoise (call for rates and an appointment); there's a well-stocked gift shop and a cafe offering soups, salads, and sandwiches. Allow at least 1 to 2 hours, more if you plan to take a class or watch a demonstration.

400 2nd St. SW. turquoisemuseum.com. ✆ **505/433-3684.** Adults $20 plus tax; seniors 55+, active and retired military, children under 18, and AAA members $15 plus tax. Mon–Sat 10am–2pm (last entrance 2pm). Closed major holidays.

ABQ BioPark

This city park complex is our favorite outdoor and nature experience in Albuquerque, where you could easily spend an entire afternoon or day. It combines a fine aquarium, excellent botanic gardens, and the best zoo in the state, with an electric shuttle bus (tickets included with purchase of "combo" pass) connecting them, as well as fishing ponds and walking and fitness trails.

BioPark Aquarium and Botanic Gardens ♥♥ At the Aquarium you can see how shipwrecks provide homes for underwater life; compare the beauty and differences between an Atlantic and Pacific coral-reef; get up close to and actually feel exotic creatures at one of the touch pools (from Wed–Fri 11am–1pm, Sat–Sun 10am–noon and 2–4pm, volunteer schedules permitting); and get to know sea creatures from around the world. There's a 280,000-gallon shark tank, river otters, eels, and jellyfish, a large exhibit describing the myriad ecosystems of the Gulf Coast, and more.

The Botanic Gardens offer a peaceful stroll among fragrant flowers as you wander through gardens en route to a 10,000-square-foot conservatory, with separate sections for desert plants and Mediterranean flora. The summer-only Butterflies and Bees exhibit features 40 species of native butterflies, fluttering around a variety of native pollinator-friendly plants. If you like arachnids and other arthropods, be sure to visit the BUGarium. Heritage Farm is a recreation of a 1930s Rio Grande Valley farm with corrals, a vineyard, orchard, Navajo churro sheep, chickens, and goats (at press time, it's closed for renovation). The Sasebo Japanese Garden, with a koi pond, bell tower, and tiered waterfall, combines aspects of a traditional Japanese garden with New Mexico influences.

2601 Central Ave. NW. cabq.gov/biopark. ✆ **505/768-2000.** Adults $15 ($22 for BioPark combo ticket), seniors 65+ $7.50 ($12 for combo ticket), ages 3–12 $6 ($8 for combo ticket), free for children under 3. Daily 9am–5pm; June–Aug Sat–Sun and holidays open until 6pm. Closed Mondays btw. Veteran's Day and President's Day. Ticket sales stop 30 min. before closing. Closed New Year's Day, Thanksgiving, and Christmas.

BioPark Tingley Beach ♥ The ponds at Tingley Beach provide a refreshing break from the city. Anglers 12 and older must have a New Mexico fishing license, but other than that there is no charge for fishing. Central Pond is the largest; the Children's Pond is for kids 12 and under to try their hand (parents are welcome to accompany them but are not allowed to fish); flyfisherman can enjoy the Bob Gerding Catch and Release Pond; and there's even a Model Boat Pond. Both the Central and Children's ponds are stocked with rainbow trout in winter and channel catfish in summer, and have wheelchair ramps. There are also walking paths and a fitness course. Dogs are welcome but must be leashed and cleaned up after.

1800 Tingley Dr. SW. (from Rio Grande Blvd., head W on Central Ave., turn S on Tingley Dr.). cabq.gov/biopark. ✆ **505/768-2000.** Free. Daily sunrise to sunset. Closed New Year's Day, Thanksgiving, and Christmas.

BioPark Zoo ♥♥♥ Some 250 species—about 1,000 animals in all—call this 64-acre zoo home. Summer 2019 saw the opening of Penguin Chill, a 15,000-square-foot exhibit with more than 30 penguins of multiple species; the building is kept between 39 and 45 degrees Fahrenheit, as most of the penguins are native to the Antarctic and Southern Hemisphere (warm-weather penguins live in the Australian Shores habitat). Specialized ultraviolet lighting mimics seasonal day and night cycles in the sub-Antarctic, while the penguins swim and play in a 70,000-gallon, 12-feet-deep tank, into which visitors can peer to watch them. Other major exhibits include Asian elephants; a polar bear and Andean bear; Birds of the Americas, with parrots; Mexican wolves; an Africa area with everything from hippos to chimpanzees, giraffes to cheetahs, zebras to rhinos, plus an aviary; the Ape Walk, with gorillas; and a reptile exhibit. The most recent addition is an expanded Asia exhibit, featuring Malayan tigers, orangutans, siamangs, snow leopards, and stellar sea eagles. Open-moat exhibits with animals in naturalized habitats give you a feel for what their lives are like in the wild. Check out the various feeding times when you arrive so you can see the animals chowing down.

903 10th St. SW. cabq.gov/biopark/zoo. ✆ **505/768-2000.** Adults $14.50 ($22 for BioPark combo ticket), seniors 65+ $7.50 ($12 for combo ticket), ages 3–12 $6 ($8 for combo ticket), free for children under 3. Daily 9am–5pm; June–Aug Sat–Sun and holidays open until 6pm. Ticket sales stop 30 min. before closing. Closed New Year's Day, Thanksgiving, and Christmas.

Other Museums

Holocaust & Intolerance Museum of New Mexico ♥♥ Although not a fun place, this museum deserves your time and attention. Its purpose is to fight hate and intolerance through education, and it does this through visuals, narratives, and artifacts, presenting a chronological overview of the Holocaust. The photos can be shocking, and the artifacts, such as devices used by the Nazis in World War II, are sobering. On the more uplifting side, there are exhibits depicting how people put themselves in mortal danger to help victims escape, such as Christians who hid Jewish children from the Nazis. In addition to the Holocaust, the museum deals with other genocides and continued forms of social injustice—there are also displays depicting the persecution of Native Americans; slavery in America; genocides in Armenia, Greece, and Rwanda; the power of propaganda; and contemporary hate in America. The lessons learned from these exhibits are a foundation for building understanding and compassion in a troubled world. Predicated on the notion that bad things happen when good people choose to do nothing, the UPSTANDER banners allow visitors to leave with a feeling of empowerment and commitment to engage.

616 Central Ave. SW. nmholocaustmuseum.org. ✆ **505/247-0606.** Adults $6; seniors, military, and college students $4; younger students $2; ages 5 and under free. Wed–Sun 11am–3:30pm, no entry after 3pm. Closed all major holidays.

National Museum of Nuclear Science & History ♥♥ This Smithsonian affiliate is the only congressionally chartered museum in the nuclear field, and an intriguing place to follow the unfolding story of the atomic age from early research through the Manhattan Project and Cold War to today's peaceful uses of nuclear technology. There's something for everyone, with both permanent and changing exhibits, including a 9-acre outdoor exhibit area boasting a B-29 Superfortress, a nuclear submarine sail, and more. This museum challenges visitors to learn, to think, to imagine, and then to draw their own conclusions.

601 Eubank Blvd. SE (at Southern). nuclearmuseum.com. ✆ **505/245-2137.** Adults $22; ages 6–17 and 60+ $20; veterans, active military, and dependents $12; free for ages 5 and under. Daily 9am–5pm. Closed New Year's Day, Easter, Thanksgiving, and Christmas; closes at 3pm Christmas Eve and New Year's Eve.

University of New Mexico Museums ♥♥ On the 70-acre campus of New Mexico's flagship university, about 2 miles east of downtown Albuquerque, there are four campus museums, all with free admission (donations welcome), built in modified Pueblo-style architecture. In the Center for the Arts complex off Redondo Drive NE, the **University of New Mexico Art Museum ♥♥** (1700 Lomas Blvd. NE; ✆ **505/277-4001**) has especially strong collections of prints and rare and printed books, spanning the history of the graphic arts from 1493 to the present, and a photography collection with some 10,000 photographs by over 1,000 different photographers spanning the entire history of the medium. In painting and sculpture, the museum owns many works of modern and contemporary American art as well as historic

European and Spanish Colonial paintings, *retablos,* and polychrome wood sculpture, plus African sculpture. A number of noted New Mexican artists are represented, including Georgia O'Keeffe, Richard Diebenkorn, and Agnes Martin. It's open Tuesday to Saturday 10am to 4pm. Beside the main UNM library, the **Maxwell Museum of Anthropology** ♥♥ (500 University Blvd. NE on Redondo W. Dr.; maxwellmuseum.unm.edu; ✆ **505/277-4405**) is one of the nation's finest anthropology museums, with a number of intriguing changing exhibitions, as well as two permanent exhibits in the Main Gallery: "People of the Southwest," which delves into the history of the area from 10,000 years ago into the 16th century, and "Ancestors," which looks at human evolution. The Maxwell is open Tuesday to Friday 9am to 4pm, Saturdays 10am to 4pm. About midway between these two museums, in Northrup Hall (200 Yale Blvd. E.) are two smaller museums. The **Geology Museum** ♥ (✆ **505/277-4204**) has some fascinating displays of minerals, rocks, and fossils, many of them incredible works of art with nature as the artist, created over the span of eons. It's open 8am to noon and 1 to 4:30pm, Monday to Friday. The highlight of the **Meteorite Museum** ♥ (✆ **505/277-1644**) is a 1-ton piece of the stony meteorite that fell in Kansas in 1948. The Meteorite Museum is currently open on a limited basis; call ✆ **505/277-2747.**

University of New Mexico, 1 University Hill NE, north of Central Ave. unm.edu. ✆ **505/277-0111.** Free admission to all. Parking garage E of the Center for the Arts at Redondo Dr. and Stanford Dr. plus limited metered parking along Redondo Dr. Museums closed on major holidays.

Historic & Cultural Attractions

Casa San Ysidro: The Gutierrez-Minge House ♥ Inside the adobe walls of Casa San Ysidro are artifacts and furnishings used when New Mexico was a remote frontier. Walk through the *zaguán* gate into a central *plazuela,* enclosed corral, and heritage field. View a small family chapel, Hispano tinwork, ironwork, carpentry, and weavings; Pueblo pottery; Navajo textiles; Apache basketry, and furnishings from the Spanish Colonial, Mexican, and Territorial periods. Listed on the State Register of Cultural Properties and El Camino Real de Tierra Adentro National Interpretive Trail, it is named for the original owners who built it in 1875, and the couple who purchased the property in the 1950s, then restored and expanded it to evoke New Mexico's past. In the late 1990s the Minges donated their home to the City of Albuquerque.

973 Old Church Rd., Corrales. cabq.gov/casasanysidro. ✆ **505/898-3915.** Guided tours only: adults $6, students 13–18 and seniors 65+ $5, children under 12 $4, groups of 5 or more adults $5 each. Jun–Aug Tues–Sat 10:30am, noon & 1:30pm; Feb-May & Sep–Nov Tues–Fri 9:30am & 1:30pm, Sat 10:30am, noon & 1:30pm. Closed Dec–Jan.

Coronado Historic Site ♥♥ When Spanish explorer Francisco Vázquez de Coronado traveled through this region in 1540–41, searching for the Seven Cities of Cíbola, he wintered at one of about a dozen Indian villages on the west bank of the Rio Grande, displacing the ancestral Puebloans (called Tiwa) who had lived there since the early 1300s. Coronado's forces also stole their food. In 1541, a short but bloody conflict erupted between the two groups that left hundreds of Tiwas dead and two villages destroyed. Here at Kuaua (Tiwa Indian for "evergreen"), a multistoried building with over 1,200 small rooms was excavated in the 1930s as a Works Progress Administration project. Although the actual ruins remain buried for their protection, their outline has been created in adobe mud to show what this village would have looked like. In addition, a kiva has been reconstructed so that visitors can descend a ladder into the enclosed space, once the site of sacred rites. Unique multicolored murals, depicting human and animal forms, were found on successive layers of wall plaster in this and other kivas here, and some of those murals have been replicated. Some of the original murals are displayed in the site's museum. ***Note:*** Photography is not permitted inside the kiva; photos cannot be taken of the murals in the museum. The site, located along the Rio Grande just north of Albuquerque, also has splendid views of the Sandia Mountains, nature trails, and a birding checklist listing the 150 species that are seen here. Access to the painted kiva is by 45-minute guided tour, offered hourly 10:30am to 2:30pm (subject to docent availability).

Kuaua Rd., Bernalillo. (I-25 exit 242, then 1½ miles W on NM 550). nmhistoricsites.org. ✆ **505/867-5351.** Adults $5, free for ages 16 and under. Free with New Mexico CulturePass (p. 76). Wed–Mon 8:30am–5pm. Closed New Year's Day, Easter, Thanksgiving, and Christmas.

New Mexico Veterans' Memorial ♥♥ Covering 25 acres, the New Mexico Veterans' Memorial park honors the men and women who have served the United States—and New Mexico even before it became a state. The park provides places for reflection as well as events on special days such as Veterans Day and Memorial Day. As you enter the grounds you pass through the Boulevard of Flags, flying the American flag plus those representing the six U.S. military services and the POW/MIA flag. There are about three dozen monuments to various aspects of the military and those who served, from the first encounters between the Spanish and American Indians through more current conflicts including the Gulf War and the War on Terror. There are

A snow-free SNOWMAN?

When one lives in the desert where not much snow falls, how does one build a snowman? One must use one's ingenuity. And that's just what the Albuquerque Metropolitan Arroyo Flood Control Authority, or AMAFCA, does. After clearing seemingly millions of tumbleweeds from arroyos every fall, where they often block drains and cause flooding, the AMAFCA a number of years ago decided to make something with them: It built a snowman. Now it's an Albuquerque tradition, and when the 15-to-20-foot tall fellow appears on I-40 just east of the University exit, people know the holiday season has officially begun. If you're here during the month of December, be sure to drive by there to see a true Southwest "Snowman."

monuments to the Merchant Marines, the Navajo Code Talkers, women in the military, and the Buffalo Soldiers, as well as monuments depicting the stages in a soldier's life: The Call, The Battle, The Fallen Friend, and finally, The Homecoming. Tours of the facilities are available by appointment.

1100 Louisiana Blvd. SE. nmvetsmemorial.org. ✆ **505/768-4495.** Free. Grounds open daily 8am–5pm, visitor center & museum open daily 9am–3pm. Closed New Year's Day, Christmas.

Petroglyph National Monument ♥♥ These lava flows were once a hunting and gathering area for prehistoric peoples, who left a chronicle of their beliefs etched on the dark basalt boulders. Some 25,000 petroglyphs provide a nice outdoor adventure after a morning in a museum. Stop first at the visitor center to get a map, check out the exhibits, and view the short film. Be sure to carry water when you head out—even in winter the sun can dry you out quickly.

From the visitor center, drive north to the **Boca Negra** area, which has an incredible array of images easily seen along three short trails. The 0.3-mile Mesa Point Trail climbs quickly up the side of a hill and offers many petroglyph sightings, including four-pointed stars, handprints, and a human-like mask that seems to look in two directions at once. From the top of the escarpment you can see the Sandia Mountains to the east and the volcanic cones that formed this escarpment to the west. The two other trails here are easy, with an excellent petroglyph of a macaw easily found along the—you guessed it—Macaw Trail. There are restrooms, a drinking fountain, picnic tables, and shaded seating areas available. Boca Negra is open daily 8:30am to 4:30pm, with last entry at 4pm; parking costs $1 per vehicle weekdays, $2 weekends. Pets are not allowed in the Boca Negra area due to the high usage.

Returning south past the visitor center, you'll reach **Rinconada Canyon** where you can hike part of an undeveloped 2.2-mile trail, following a path created by wildlife and used by Spanish sheepherders. Allow 2 hours to explore and locate as many of the 300 petroglyphs in the area as you can. Look for the older images of roadrunners and lizards, handprints, and human and god-like figures, plus more recent images of livestock brands, crosses, and sheep left by Spanish settlers. The parking lot is open 8am to 5pm daily, with foot access sunrise to sunset; vault toilets available but no drinking water.

Piedras Marcadas Canyon is about 6 miles north of the visitor center. It has no water or restrooms but you can see 300 to 500 petroglyphs along the 1.5-mile undeveloped trail. The area is open sunrise to sunset daily, and parking is behind the Valvoline Motor Oil Change station.

Leashed pets are allowed in Rinconada and Piedras Marcadas canyons, but the rocky ground can be hard on their feet. Be sure to clean up after your pet.

6001 Unser Blvd. NW (3 miles N of I-40 at Unser and Western Trail). nps.gov/petr. ✆ **505/899-0205, ext. 335.** Free. Visitor Center open daily 9am–4pm. Closed New Year's Day, Thanksgiving, and Christmas; visitor center closes at 3pm the day before these three holidays.

TAKING HOME A southwest KITCHEN

If the unique and spicy New Mexican cuisine has taken over your taste buds, you might consider taking a cooking class with Jane Butel, a leading Southwest cooking authority and the first to write nationally and internationally about Southwest cooking. She is the author of 32 cookbooks and the former host of the national TV show *Jane Butel's Southwestern Kitchen*. Her **Jane Butel's Southwest Cooking School ♥**, 138 Armijo Court, Corrales (janebutel cooking.com; ✆ **505/243-2622**) offers day classes, weekend, week-long, team-building, and private classes. In all, you'll be treated to Jane's review of the history of the cuisine and its major ingredients, plus hints and techniques for success. Students cook in small groups, most often 2 or 3 people, with guidance provided by Jane and her staff. The week-long sessions allow ample time to explore native breads and main dishes, appetizers, and desserts. Call or visit Jane's website for current schedules and fees.

Especially for Kids

¡Explora! ♥♥ Part science center, part children's museum, ¡Explora! welcomes visitors of all ages; adults often have just as much fun as the kids. ¡Explora! is also part grandparents' garage and part science lab, filled with more than 250 truly hands-on exhibits and experiment spaces that offer opportunities to explore and create. You can investigate the properties of air, water, optical illusions and 3-D puzzles, bubbles, light, electricity, and much more. There's a room for toddlers, and younger kids love the arts and crafts workshop where they use recycled materials to make take-home creations. Older kids and adults appreciate the high-wire bicycle and the Studio Inventivo makerspace. You can spend anywhere from an hour to all day here. Be sure to check to see if there's a special Adult Night happening during your visit.

1701 Mountain Rd. NW. explora.us. ✆ **505/600-6072.** Adults $11; students, military, and seniors 65+ $8, ages 1–11 $7, under a year free. Daily 10am–5pm. Closed New Year's Day, July 4, the week after Labor Day, Thanksgiving, and Christmas; early closing Christmas Eve and New Year's Eve.

New Mexico Museum of Natural History & Science ♥♥ Take a walk through time here, beginning with the early dinosaurs of the Triassic era and the giants of the Jurassic age. See a partial skeleton of a 40-foot theropod Saurophaganax dinosaur discovered in central New Mexico. Play naturalist at a hands-on center where microscopes allow you to inspect live animals and insects, as well as rocks and minerals. Look through the eyes of the museum's own fieldworkers in the Bisti Badlands of New Mexico, where FossilWorks gives visitors a chance to observe the painstaking process of excavating the ancient bones on display. Don't miss the planetarium, or the DynaTheater, with its 2-D/3-D digital 4K dual projection system, five-story-high screen, and surround sound—seeing (and hearing) is believing. The NatureWorks

Discovery Store completes your visit with a wide offering of educational, unique, and fun items.

1801 Mountain Rd. NW. nmnaturalhistory.org. ✆ **505/841-2800.** Adults $8, seniors 60+ and ages 13–17 $7, children 3–12 $5, free for children 2 and under. DynaTheater $7 adults, $6 seniors, $4 children; Planetarium prices in the $7 range for adults, $4 range for children. Discount ticket combinations available. Free admission with New Mexico CulturePass (p. 76). Wed–Mon 9am–5pm. Closed New Year's Day, Thanksgiving, and Christmas.

Rattlesnake Museum ♥ Danger! Look but don't touch! Well, you can't touch the rattlesnakes because they're behind glass, which is just as much for their protection as yours. This fairly small "animal conservation museum" is packed with more than 30 species of rattlesnakes—it claims to be the world's largest collection of different species of live rattlesnakes—each housed in its appropriate habitat with descriptive signs. Other creepy-crawly creatures here include horned lizards and Gila monsters. There's a short film on rattlesnakes, and exhibits of rattlesnake memorabilia, from Native American pottery with rattlesnake designs to a poster for the 1944 film *Cobra Woman.*

202 San Felipe St. NW Suite A. rattlesnakes.com. ✆ **505/242-6569.** Adults $8.95; seniors 60+, military, teachers, and students $7.95; ages 3–12 $6.95; children under 3 free. Tues–Sat 11:30am–5:30pm; Jun–Aug also Sun 1–5pm. Closed Easter, Thanksgiving, and Christmas.

Parks, Gardens & Zoos

Rio Grande Nature Center State Park ♥♥♥ Just a few miles from Old Town, this delightful oasis on the east bank of the Rio Grande is an excellent place for bird-watchers, hikers, and anyone wanting a break from the bustle

IN SEARCH OF adrenaline rushes

For a seriously fun and exciting time, take the kids to **Cliff's Amusement Park ♥**, 4800 Osuna Rd. NE (cliffsamusementpark.com; ✆ **505/881-9373**). Though it's not on the scale of Disneyland, this park has rides that'll thrill every adrenaline junkie. The Cliff Hanger zips 120 feet in the air, then drops like a rock; the SideWinder spins and swings 80 feet up, around, and over; and the Fireball is an 80-foot high looping ride that flips upside-down and back around 13 times a minute. For those with less desire for such thrills, there's the carousel, Demolition Disco (bumper cars), and a pretty train you can ride around the park. There are height limitations on many rides. It's open daily Memorial Day to early August, weekends only in May and September. Day passes start at $28 per person.

The **Hinkle Family Fun Center ♥** offers a different kind of fun: a 220-yard Go Kart track; bumper boats and cars; a couple of miniature golf courses; a bungee jump trampoline; two state-of-the-art game rooms with redemption, merchandise, and video games; and an immersive virtual reality experience. It's located at 12931 Indian School Rd. NE (hinklefuncenter.com; ✆ **505/299-3100**) in the foothills just west of Tramway Blvd. It's open year-round except Thanksgiving and Christmas. Passes start at $33 per person; most individual activities charge $8.59 per person. Check the website for all options, upgrades, and specials.

ALBUQUERQUE open space

In the 1960s, the city of Albuquerque initiated an open space program that is considered one of the most ambitious in the country. It began buying land for as little as $2.50 an acre, and today it has nearly 30,000 acres, both inside and outside city limits. These protected lands include one of the world's largest riverside cottonwood forests and a major winter home for sandhill cranes. Throughout the open space lands are opportunities for hiking, biking, birding, and photography.

One recommended area, the **Elena Gallegos Picnic Area** on the east side of the city, has magnificent views of the Sandia Mountains, covered picnic tables, and a variety of multi-use trails including the Cottonwood Springs Trail, a wheelchair-accessible trail featuring interpretative artwork and a wildlife blind that overlooks a wetland. Another is the **Rio Grande Valley State Park,** a corridor along both banks of the Rio Grande from just above Alameda Boulevard in the north to below Rio Bravo Boulevard in the south where I-25 crosses the river. It includes some 4,300 acres of riverside forest, known locally as the *bosque* (Spanish for forest). This park has picnic areas and multi-use trails, including the Paseo del Bosque Trail, which runs along the eastern bank of the river almost the entire length of the park; it's a favorite of bikers.

Your first stop should be the **Open Space Visitor Center** (6500 Coors Blvd. NW, at the end of Bosque Meadows Rd.; cabq.gov/openspace; ✆ **505/768-4951**), where you can get detailed information on trails, birding checklists, and other aspects of the system. The visitor center is open Tuesday to Sunday 9am to 5pm. Some trails leave from the visitor center, and it also has exhibits.

of the city. The park lies in what is called a *bosque,* a Spanish word for forest that in New Mexico is often used to describe wetlands along rivers, particularly along the Rio Grande. The nature center covers some 270 acres of woods and meadows, with native grasses, wildflowers, willows, Russian olives, and cottonwoods. It also has a 3-acre pond, which attracts more than 260 species of birds. The Rio Grande Flyway, an important migratory route for many birds, is an excellent place to see sandhill cranes, Canadian geese, and quail. The interpretive River Loop and Bosque Loop trails meander through the bosque; the paved Paseo del Bosque Trail, which runs along a flood-control ditch between the visitor center and river, is open to bicycles. The visitor center has exhibits as well as a library, a small nature store, and a children's resource room.

2901 Candelaria Rd. NW. emnrd.nm.gov; ✆ **505/344-7240.** Admission $3 per vehicle (no credit cards). Daily 8am–5pm; visitor center 10am–4pm; nature shop Mon–Thurs 11am–2pm, Fri–Sun 10am–4pm. Closed New Year's Day, Thanksgiving, and Christmas.

Valle de Oro National Wildlife Refuge ♥♥ This work in progress encompasses 570 acres of a former dairy farm along the east bank of the Rio Grande, offering stunning views of the Sandia Mountains, Vulcan volcano tubes, and the lush Rio Grande Bosque. The land is currently in transition from irrigated fescue and alfalfa farm fields to a diversity of Rio Grande floodplain habitats, including shallow seasonal wetlands, bosque, grasslands, and upland habitats. Farming is being phased out as restoration progresses. Stop first at the visitor center for information on the history of the refuge, a list of recent wildlife sightings, and updates on habitat restoration and other projects. Then follow an unpaved road to the outdoor classroom and a 2.5-mile trail into the bosque. Get there early for birding or late to see the magnificent Southwest sunset reflected off the Sandia Mountains. There's also prime fishing along the riverside ditch. The refuge offers ample opportunities for bird-watching, especially cranes (in winter), geese, ground-nesting birds, and various wading birds. Additional wildlife viewing should develop as native habitats are restored, and more nature trails and interpretative programs are planned. You'll want to take a camera, drinking water, sunscreen, and bug spray.

7851 Second St. SW, 5 miles S of downtown Albuquerque (I-25 exit 220, Rio Bravo Blvd., W on Rio Bravo, then S on 2nd St., refuge entrance on right). fws.gov/refuge/valle_de_oro. ✆ **505/248-6667.** Free. Daily 1 hr. before sunrise to 1 hr. after sunset; visitor center Tues–Sat 9am–4pm.

Wildlife West Nature Park ♥♥ They can't go home, but you're invited to visit them here at this rescued wildlife zoo about 20 minutes east of Albuquerque. All the wildlife at this 122-acre nature park, a project of the non-profit New Mexico Wildlife Association, has been injured, orphaned, or for some other reason cannot be released back into the wild. There are 22 species of New Mexico wildlife, including cougars, wolves, raccoons, deer, bear, elk, pronghorn, javelina, and hawks, along with native plants. There's a raptor viewing area and a half-mile birding walk. A variety of festivals, classes, and other events are held; call or check the website for schedules.

87 N. Frontage Rd., Edgewood (I-40 exit 187, head W on N. Frontage Rd.). wildlifewest.org. ✆ **505-281-7655.** Adults $9, seniors 60+ $7, students $5, children under 5 free. Daily mid-Mar to Oct 10am–6pm, Nov to mid-Mar noon–4pm. Closed New Year's Day, Thanksgiving, and Christmas.

Organized Tours

Albuquerque Tourism & Sightseeing Factory ♥ The AT&SF offers one of the best ways to get acquainted with the city: its *Best of ABQ City Tour* offers a fully narrated, multimedia exploration of the city in an open-air trolley. Beginning with Old Town, this 100-minute jaunt takes you to filming locations for major movies and TV shows (including the TV series *Breaking Bad* and *Better Call Saul*), historic Route 66, Tingley Beach, the zoo, museums, and more. AT&SF also sponsors the *Albucreepy Downtown Ghost Walk*—a 100-minute tour of the city's dark side complete with stops for pints of beer at local pubs; plus—believe it or not—a 2½-hour tour on a 14-passenger bike, with stops at pubs, breweries, bars, and restaurants, all of which offer discounts to ticket holders. Another plus for tour participants is the AT&SF All-Stars discounts offered by many Albuquerque businesses. Hang on to your tour sticker and redeem your discount at any businesses displaying the All-Star decal. Details available on AT&SF's website.

Most tours depart from Hotel Albuquerque, 800 Rio Grande Blvd. NW (free parking for trolley riders at hotel). tourabq.com. ✆ **505/200-2642.** Costs and times vary depending on tour—call or check website for times, prices, and current specials.

SPORTS & RECREATION

With sunny skies and pleasant temperatures almost year-round, the Albuquerque area is a perfect locale for outdoor activities, from hiking and biking to fishing and bird-watching. Just remember that summer temperatures can sometimes be scorching and winter winds can produce biting wind chills. Also, especially in summer, be sure to carry drinking water on any outdoor excursion, and drink it. It's dry out there!

Ballooning

Visitors have a choice of several hot-air balloon operators; rates start at about $189 per person per hour. Contact **Rainbow Ryders** ♥ (rainbowryders.com; ✆ **800/725-2477** or 505/823-1111) or **World Balloon Corporation** ♥ (worldballoon.com; ✆ **505/293-6800**). If you'd rather just watch, go to the annual **Albuquerque International Balloon Fiesta** ♥♥♥, which is held the first through second weekends of October (see box below for details).

Biking

With some 400 miles of bike paths and trails, Albuquerque is a major bicycling hub in the summer, for both road racers and mountain bikers. To receive a City of Albuquerque Bicycle Map before leaving home, call ✆ **505/768-2680.**

The city's premier multi-use paved trail, the 16-mile **Paseo del Bosque Trail** ♥♥ follows the Rio Grande from Alameda Boulevard south to Rio

ALOFT OVER albuquerque

From a distance it looks like a kids' birthday party gone wild, but up close it's a delightfully exciting, seemingly endless explosion of colorful hot-air balloons literally filling the skies, accompanied by the deafening sound of the balloons' propane heaters. The **Albuquerque International Balloon Fiesta,** begun in 1972 when 13 balloons launched from a parking lot, now boasts over 500 balloons launching from the event's own 78-acre—that's 54 football fields—launch field in Balloon Fiesta Park in early October, with 9 days of events. Most exciting are the mass ascensions at 7am most mornings (weather permitting), but there are also races and flying competitions, dawn patrol shows, chainsaw carving contests, and morning and evening glows, when the balloons come alive in the darkness with light from the propane heaters shining through the balloon fabric.

You can see the balloons from anywhere in the city (that's free), but the best close-up views are from **Balloon Fiesta Park,** which charges $15 per person 13 and older, per session; 12 and under free. A session is either a morning or afternoon/evening. There are also parking fees, and five-pack tickets ($45) and various other packages. Crowds for some of the events exceed 100,000 people, so you'll want to get to the park between 4 and 4:30am for the morning events. The park is located north of Alameda Boulevard, 1 mile west of I-25, north of the city.

If you want to take to the skies yourself during the fiesta, contact **Rainbow Ryders,** the fiesta's official balloon ride concessionaire (see "Ballooning," above). For additional information see balloonfiesta.com or call ✆ **888/422-7277** or 505/821-1000.

Bravo Boulevard uninterrupted by roadways. Part of Albuquerque's Open Space (p. 208), it has several access points along the route, so pick up a map at the Open Space visitor center. To the east, the **Foothills Trail ♥** runs along the base of the mountains, a fun 7-mile-long trail with stupendous views. Access it by driving east from downtown on Montgomery Boulevard, past the intersection with Tramway Boulevard. Go left on Glenwood Hills Drive and head north about a half-mile before turning right onto a short road that leads to the Embudito trail head.

A great place to mountain bike is **Sandia Peak ♥♥** in the Cibola National Forest (Sandia Ranger Station ✆ **505/281-3304**). You can ride up on the Sandia Peak Tram (p. 198); you can't take a bike with you on the tram, but once you're at the top you can rent a bike at the ski area, and chairlift no. 1 is available for further uphill transportation with a bike. The lift usually runs weekends from July through Labor Day and daily during the Balloon Fiesta. Helmets are mandatory; trail maps are available; and clearly marked trails range from easy to very difficult.

Routes Bicycle Tours & Rentals ♥♥ (routesrentals.com; ✆ **505/933-5667**) rents a wide variety of bikes including several models for kids, plus tandems, children's Trail-a-Bikes, and single and double trailers. They also rent tandems and electric bikes, and offer several tours, plus extended length rentals. Bike rates for adults are $35 to $55 for half-day (4 hr.), $50 to $85 for a full day (24 hr.), and $185 to $265 for 7 days; kids' bikes (20" or 16" with training wheels) rates are $25, $40, and $165 respectively. Extended rentals can be arranged. Helmets and U locks, plus a city map with all the bike trails/routes and attractions marked, are included with all rentals. City Cruisers—with their signature yellow tire—are three-speed bikes with a steel frame, good on easy-to-moderate terrain; the hybrid has a lightweight aluminum frame and 21 speeds—excellent for varied terrain like that found on the Paseo del Bosque Trail; several models of mountain bikes offer hardtail or full suspension; and the road bikes are high performance Cannondale bicycles. The Routes store is open 9am to 5pm daily, except Wednesdays, and is located at 2113 Charlevoix St. NW just north of Old Town. It is closed New Year's Day, Thanksgiving, and Christmas.

Bird-Watching

The Rio Grande is the fourth-longest river on the continent and the basis for the **Rio Grande Flyway,** one of North America's most important flyways for migratory waterfowl and other birds. The river flows through the heart of Albuquerque, and the city area has an abundance of local, state, and federally protected land that serves as ideal habitat for nesting and migratory birds. **Albuquerque Open Space** (p. 208) offers several excellent bird-watching spots around the city, and its visitor center has a bird checklist that indicates what time of year each species has been sighted. Also be sure to check out the **Rio Grande Nature Center State Park** (p. 207). And if you're here from November through March, head south to **Bosque del Apache National Wildlife Refuge** (p. 224), where vast numbers of many bird species winter.

Golf

There are quite a few public courses in the Albuquerque area. The **Championship Golf Course at the University of New Mexico ♥♥♥**, 3601 University Blvd. SE (unmgolf.com; ✆ **505/277-4546**), is one of the best in the Southwest. Check the city's Parks and Recreation Department (see box below) for a complete list of public courses.

Hiking

There are ample hiking opportunities in and around Albuquerque. Open Space (p. 208) is a great place to start for both suggestions and maps to trail heads in the city. A favorite hike is the **Embudito Trail ♥**, which heads up into the eastern foothills, with spectacular views down across Albuquerque. The 5.5-mile one-way hike is moderate to difficult; allow 1 to 8 hours, depending on how far you want to go. Access it by driving east from downtown on Montgomery Boulevard past the intersection with Tramway Boulevard. Go left on Glenwood Hills Drive and head north about a half-mile before turning right onto a short road that leads to the trail head. The premier Sandia Mountain hike is **La Luz Trail ♥♥**, simply bursting with color around every switchback with brilliant wallflowers ranging from vivid orange to deep crimson, violet Rocky Mountain penstemon, and scarlet gilia to name but a few of the wildflowers throwing up their heads after a wet winter. This is a very strenuous 8-mile trek from the Sandia foothills to the top of the Crest, but you can take the Sandia Peak Tramway (p. 198) either up or down. Allow a full day for this hike. The trail head is off Tramway Boulevard and Forest Service Road 333. As always in this high-desert climate, it's best to start out early in the day so you're off the trail before the thunderheads threaten with lightning; be ready for sudden weather changes, and carry plenty of water. The 1½-million-acre **Cíbola National Forest** (fs.usda.gov/Cibola; Sandia Ranger Station; ✆ **505/281-3304**) also has many excellent, well-marked hiking trails.

Skiing

The **Sandia Peak Ski Area ♥** is a good place for family skiing, with plenty of beginner and intermediate runs and 117 inches of average annual snowfall. (If you're looking for more challenge or variety, head north to Taos, p. 154.) The ski area has twin base-to-summit chairlifts to its upper slopes at 10,350

Where's the Nearest Tennis Court or Hiking Trail?

The **Albuquerque Parks & Recreation Department** (cabq.gov/parksandrecreation; ✆ **505/768-5353**) has maps and lists of places for many outdoor activities: bicycle and hiking trails, golf courses, tennis courts, swimming pools, skate parks, a rock-climbing wall, and skiing and snowboarding.

GETTING PAMPERED: THE spa SCENE

If you're looking to get pampered, you have a few options. **Mark Pardo Salon & Spa** ♥ (markpardo.com; ✆ **505/298-2983** all locations) offers treatments at two locations: Wyoming Blvd. NE, Ste. 804 and 10420 Coors Bypass NW.

The Back Porch Day Spa (8525 Indian School Rd. NE; thebackporchdayspa.com; ✆ **505/822-9700**) offers a luxurious variety of massages, facials, body wraps and scrubs, plus retreat packages for one or two people. It's recommended you book at least a week in advance

Albuquerque's top two resort spa experiences are at the **Hyatt Regency Tamaya Resort & Spa** ♥♥ at Santa Ana Pueblo (hyatt.com; ✆ **505/867-1234**), and the **Sandia Resort & Casino** ♥, 30 Rainbow Rd. NE (sandiacasino.com; ✆ **505/796-7500**). Each offers a broad array of treatments, as well as a sauna and a steam room, in refined atmospheres. The Tamaya is 15 minutes north of Albuquerque in Bernalillo, while the Sandia is on the north end of town, off Tramway Road.

feet. The 30 trails are rated as 35% beginner, 55% intermediate, and 10% advanced; there's a day lodge and ski-rental shop at the base. Two chairs whisk skiers to the top; and two Pomas service the beginner slopes. All-day lift tickets start at $19 online, check the website's calendar for ticket prices, which change based on dynamic pricing. Rental packages are available. The season runs late December to mid-March. In 2023, the resort became a part of Power Pass, which includes 12 areas across the country, including Pajarito Mountain and Sipapu in New Mexico. Contact the ski area, 10 Tramway Loop NE (sandiapeak.com; ✆ **505/242-9052**), for more information, or call the hotline for a snow report (✆ **505/857-8977**).

Cross-country skiers can enjoy the trails of the Sandia Wilderness from the ski area, or they can go an hour north to the remote Jemez Wilderness and its hot springs.

Tennis

Albuquerque has 146 public tennis courts. Check with the city's Parks and Recreation Department (p. 212) for a complete list to determine which is closest to your hotel.

SPECTATOR SPORTS

Auto Racing

The **Sandia Speedway** ♥♥ (racesandia.com; ✆ **505/220-4901**) attracts fans of fast cars, with races scheduled most Saturdays from April through mid-October. Tracks include ½- and ¼-mile paved ovals, a high banked ⅜-mile dirt oval, and a 1.7-mile road course. From I-40 west exit 149/Atrisco Vista Blvd., take the south frontage road west for about 3 miles, then Shelby Road south for about another mile to the speedway.

Baseball

The **Albuquerque Isotopes** ♥♥ (albuquerquebaseball.com; ✆ **505/924-2255**), part of the Pacific Coast League, play in Isotopes Park on the UNM South Campus, on the northeast corner of Avenida Cesar Chavez and University Boulevard. Take I-25 south to exit 223 and go east to University.

Basketball

The University of New Mexico team, **the Lobos** ♥♥ (golobos.com; ✆ **505/925-5626**), plays an average of 16 home games from late November to early March. Capacity crowds cheer the team at the 17,000-seat University Arena (fondly called "the Pit") on the southwest corner of Avenida Cesar Chavez and University Boulevard. Take I-25 south to exit 223 and go east to University.

Football

The **UNM Lobos** ♥ football team plays a September-to-November season—usually with five or six home games—at the 30,000-seat UNM Stadium, on the southeast corner of Avenida Cesar Chavez and University Boulevard, opposite both the Albuquerque Sports Stadium and the University Arena at University and Stadium boulevards. Take I-25 south to exit 223 and go east to University. For tickets and information, call ✆ **505/925-5626** (golobos.com).

Horse Racing

The **Downs at Albuquerque Racetrack and Casino** ♥ (abqdowns.com; ✆ **505/767-7171** for post times), at 145 Louisiana Blvd., is on the northeast corner of Central Avenue and Louisiana. Racing and betting—on thoroughbreds and quarter horses—take place late June through late September. The Downs has a glass-enclosed grandstand and exclusive club seating. General admission is free; parking is free if you enter off Central. Simulcast racing occurs daily year-round, and the casino offers more than 700 gaming machines plus an electronic pit area of table games.

ALBUQUERQUE SHOPPING

Many New Mexicans think of Albuquerque as one big shopping center, and come here to stock up on basics, building materials, and appliances. (What? You didn't come to New Mexico to buy a refrigerator?) Albuquerque can't really compete with Santa Fe and Taos as far as art galleries and fancy shops, but the city does have its share of interesting places to leave some coin, and there's a good chance you'll find something you just have to take home with you—and it'll probably be cheaper here than in Santa Fe or Taos. By far, most galleries and top-quality shops are in Old Town; others are spread around the city, and don't forget the museum shops.

Once a month, usually the first Friday, the **Albuquerque Art Business Association** (artscrawlabq.org; ✆ **505/244-0362**) sponsors an **ArtsCrawl** ♥♥, self-guided tours to dozens of galleries and studios. It's a great way to meet the artists, with exhibit openings, receptions, demonstrations, and special events.

The state's best shopping mall is **Coronado Center** ♥♥, 6600 Menaul Blvd. NE (coronadocenter.com; ✆ **505/881-2700**), with more than 125 stores including Macy's, JCPenney, Bath & Body Works, Dick's Sporting Goods, and Barnes & Noble. Smaller but slightly more upscale is **ABQ Uptown** ♥, at Louisiana Boulevard NE and Indian School Road NE (abquptown.com; ✆ **505/792-1929**), where you'll find an Apple Store, Pottery Barn, Warby Parker, Eddie Bauer, Williams-Sonoma, and The North Face.

Arts & Crafts

Albuquerque Photographers' Gallery ♥♥ This fine art photography gallery specializes in unique images of the American West—photos that capture the mind-bending scenery that abounds in New Mexico and the West, plus wonderful imagery epitomizing the photographer's imagination. 328 San Felipe St. NW, Ste. B, Old Town. abqphotographersgallery.com. ✆ **505/244-9195.**

Amapola Gallery ♥ Dozens of New Mexico artists and craftspeople sell their work at this artists-owned gallery established in 1980. You'll find wearable art, photography, jewelry, paintings, fabric art, plus artworks of clay, ceramic, cut paper, fused glass, macramé, wood, and gourds. 205 Romero St. NW, Old Town. amapolagallery.com. ✆ **505/242-4311.**

Bien Mur Indian Market ♥♥♥ Billing itself as the largest retail arts and crafts store in the Southwest, this market, owned and operated by Sandia Pueblo, has been in operation since 1975. It offers top-quality, genuine Native American arts and crafts, including Navajo, Hopi, Zuni, and Santo Domingo jewelry; Zuni fetishes; Navajo rugs; Pueblo pottery; storytellers; sand paintings; and even war bonnets. I-25 at Tramway Rd. NE, next to Bien Mur Travel Center. sandiapueblo.nsn.us. ✆ **505/771-7994;** 800/365-5400 for info on special events with artists.

Mariposa Gallery ♥♥ This fun gallery has been selling contemporary crafts and jewelry since 1974, including ceramics, paintings, mixed media, and wood. Look for Lisa Smith's playful ceramic figurines and Helen Cozza's earthy prints. 3500 Central Ave. SE. mariposa-gallery.com. ✆ **505/268-6828.**

Tanner Chaney Gallery ♥♥ Come here for authentic and unique historic and contemporary Native American jewelry, including old pawn jewelry. It also offers Pueblo and Mexican pottery, wood carvings, and other handmade crafts. 323 Romero St. NW. tannerchaney.com. ✆ **800/444-2242** or 505/247-2242.

Books

Barnes & Noble Booksellers ♥ There are two Barnes & Noble bookstores in Albuquerque, both with everything readable you might want. Each also has a large children's book section, weekly children's story time, and a coffee shop. Coronado Center, 6600 Menaul Blvd. NE. barnesandnoble.com. ✆ **505/883-8200.** Also at Cottonwood Corners, 3701-A Ellison Dr. NW, ✆ **505/792-4234.**

Bookworks ♥♥ This local independent bookstore has been serving readers for more than 30 years from its location in the North Valley. A fine source of books on the Southwest, it's also a good spot to meet authors, with numerous author events, as well as storytelling events for children. Bookworks sells both new and used books, and offers e-book and audiobook downloading. 4022 Rio Grande Blvd. NW. bkwrks.com. ✆ **505/344-8139.**

Page 1 Books ♥♥ Locally owned and operated since 1981, Page 1 is likely to have whatever book you're looking for, including out-of-print and rare books. It also has a popular children's story reading program. Mountain Run Shopping Center, 5850 Eubank Blvd. NE. page1book.com. ✆ **505/294-2026.**

Food

Burque Bakehouse ♥♥♥ For the city's most inventive pastries, head to this take-away window, where you'll find New Mexico–influenced creations like green-chile croissants and carne adovada Danishes. The brainchild of a former pastry chef at Los Poblanos, the bakery has been nominated for multiple James Beard awards. 640 Broadway Blvd. SE. burquebakehouse.com. ✆ **505/234-6294.**

The Candy Lady ♥ Practically every type of candy you've ever heard of, and a few you haven't heard of, are prepared fresh by The Candy Lady. Choose among truffles, caramels, peanut butter crunch, hard rock candy, fudge, and special New Mexico flavors such as chocolate red chile and pecan nut clusters, made with New Mexico pecans clustered in milk, white, or dark chocolate. You can also order a custom cake. 424 San Felipe St. NW, Old Town. thecandylady.com. ✆ **505/243-6239.**

Celina's Biscochitos ♥♥ The official state cookie of New Mexico since 1989, biscochitos are a lard-based cookie flavored with anise seed, brandy, and cinnamon. They're served at weddings, Christmas, and special occasions.

A TASTE OF THE grape

In addition to its many enchanting natural sights, New Mexico also has a 400-year-old winemaking tradition (Spanish monks planted the first vines), and wineries abound across the state. Call or check websites to find out their wine-tasting hours. The top Albuquerque area wineries are **Casa Rondeña Winery ♥♥**, 733 Chavez Rd., Los Ranchos de Albuquerque (casarondena.com; ✆ **800/706-1699** or 505/344-5911), and **Gruet Winery ♥♥♥**, 8400 Pan American Fwy. NE (gruetwinery.com; ✆ **888/857-9463** or 505/821-0055). For additional information on New Mexico's wineries, check the New Mexico Winegrowers Association website: **nmwine.com**.

Celina's bakes the traditional cookie and several specialty flavors including red chile, green chile pecan, and lemon, plus a number of jam-filled options. 404 Osuna Rd. NW. celinasbiscochitos.com. ✆ **505/269-4997.**

Gifts/Souvenirs

The Christmas Shop ♥♥ Want to have a New Mexico Christmas when you get home? This shop offers excellent holiday items by Southwestern artists and crafts workers, including Native American tree ornaments and handmade nativity sets. You can also get chile pepper tree lights, Mexican ornaments, and Southwestern-themed tin cookie cutters, from chile peppers to Kokopelli to geckos. 400 Romero St. NW. christmasinoldtown.com. ✆ **505/843-6744.**

Old Town Emporium ♥ From T-shirts to jewelry, Christmas ornaments to Route 66 souvenirs, you'll find it all at this gift and souvenir shop. And it's not all tacky souvenirs, either—the shop sells handmade pottery from Acoma, San Juan, and Isleta Pueblos, and other quality crafts. 204 San Felipe St. NW. old-town-emporium.square.site. ✆ **505/842-8102.**

Wearables

Old Town Hat Shop ♥♥ From berets to baseball caps to every possible type of fedora and cowboy hat, this is where to shop in Albuquerque if you want to protect your head from the New Mexico sun, or just to make a fashion statement. All the major brands are offered, with some especially fun vintage-style hats for both men and women. The shop also sells belts, scarves, shawls, and purses. 205-C San Felipe St. NW. oldtownhats.com. ✆ **505/242-4019.**

Wild Moon Boutique ♥♥ Are you a wild woman? Then this is your clothing shop. From traditional to chic, mild to wild, this is the place to find your inner wild woman and dress her up in colorful clothing from around the world, or perhaps created by a skilled local artisan using natural fibers. There are dresses, pants and skirt sets, separates, boots, accessories, and Indian jewelry. 400 Gold Ave. SW, Ste. 888 in the Simms Building. wildmoonboutique.com. ✆ **505/247-2475.**

ALBUQUERQUE AFTER DARK

In this city of half a million people, most folks apparently go to bed early and rarely go out at night, judging from the relatively small number of performing-arts groups and venues or other nightlife. However, what *is* available is top-notch. Complete information on all major cultural events can be obtained from the **Albuquerque Convention and Visitors Bureau** (visitalbuquerque.org; ✆ **800/284-2282**).

Tickets for nearly all major entertainment and sporting events can be obtained from **Ticketmaster** (ticketmaster.com; ✆ **800/745-3000**). Discount tickets are sometimes available for midweek and matinee performances; check with individual theater or concert hall box offices.

Major Venues

KiMo Theatre ♥♥ Opened in September 1927, the KiMo is a picture palace in Pueblo Deco style—a flamboyant, short-lived architectural fashion that used Pueblo Indian motifs in an Art Deco design; the elaborate corbels and mosaic tile work here are astonishing. The KiMo offers a variety of entertainment, including film, theater, and musical performances. 423 Central Ave. NW at 5th St. cabq.gov/culturalservices/kimo. ✆ **505/768-3522.** Ticket prices vary by production.

South Broadway Cultural Center ♥♥ This multi-arts hub features a 300-seat theater, an art gallery, a large community meeting/event room, and a library. The John Lewis Theater offers a wide variety of live entertainment throughout the year, from author readings to dance and musical performances. 1025 Broadway Blvd. SE. cabq.gov/culturalservices/south-broadway-cultural-center. ✆ **505/848-1320.** Ticket prices vary.

University of New Mexico Fine Arts Department ♥♥ The university's excellent fine arts department offers programs in theater, dance, and music, and wonderful recitals, performances, and large-scale productions are held during the school year. Most performances are in the Center for the Arts, which houses **Popejoy Hall** (✆ **505/277-3824**), the largest arts venue in the state, with a capacity of 1,985; 284-seat **Keller Hall,** the recital home for the department of music; and 400-seat **Rodey Theatre** for dance and theater productions. The Center for the Arts is on Redondo Drive, just north of Central Avenue between the Yale and Stanford entrances. 1 University Hill NE. unm.edu. ✆ **505/277-0111.**

Dance & Theater Companies

Albuquerque Little Theatre ♥♥♥ The Albuquerque Little Theatre has been offering a variety of productions, from comedies to dramas to musicals, since 1930. The first few years' productions took place in the KiMo Theatre (see above); in 1936 they moved to their current home, designed by famed Southwestern architect John Gaw Meem, the first building in Albuquerque constructed under President Roosevelt's Works Progress Administration. Today seven plays are presented each year, with recent productions including *Jesus Christ Superstar, A Streetcar Named Desire, Beautiful: The Carole King Musical,* William Goldman's *Misery* (based on a Stephen King book), and Disney's *Beauty and the Beast.* Just south of Old Town, the theater has plenty of free parking. 224 San Pasquale Ave. SW (I-40 exit 157A). albuquerquelittletheatre.org. ✆ **505/242-4750**. General admission adults $32–$35.

Musical Theatre Southwest ♥ This theater presents four to five Broadway musicals and several smaller productions throughout the year. Most productions are staged for three consecutive weekends, including some Sunday matinees. The black box theater seats 100. 6320-B Domingo Rd. NE, just N of Central near the state fairgrounds. mtsabq.org. ✆ **505/265-9119.** Tickets $25–$35.

SUMMER shakespeare UNDER THE STARS

Founded in 2010 by the Vortex Theatre (below), the **New Mexico Shakespeare Festival** ♥♥ (nmshakes.org. ✆ **505/247-8600**) is now a collaboration with the City of Albuquerque, producing vibrant outdoor presentations of two of the Bard's plays each June. The first season kicked off with *A Midsummer Night's Dream* and *Romeo and Juliet;* subsequent years have seen productions of *The Taming of the Shrew, Julius Caesar,* and *Much Ado about Nothing,* to name a few. All performances are free and take place at New Mexico Veteran's Memorial Park, 1100 Louisiana Blvd. SE (see p. 204); performances run Thursday through Sunday evenings at 7:30pm. There's lots of free parking and a nice green space perfect for a picnic supper—bring your own or find something at one of the food trucks. All ages are welcome. ***Tip:*** The benches are hard, so bring a cushion or pillow.

New Mexico Ballet Company ♥ Founded in 1972, the state's oldest ballet company holds most of its performances at Popejoy Hall. Typically there's a fall production, such as *Dracula,* a holiday one such as *The Nutcracker* or *A Christmas Carol,* and a contemporary spring production. In addition to ballet, the company also offers dance classes in jazz, tap, ballroom, and hip hop. 6207 Pan American Fwy. NE. newmexicoballet.org. ✆ **505/292-4245.** Tickets $15–$70, depending on performance and venue.

Vortex Theatre ♥ This black-box theater has been a pioneering venue for classic, contemporary, and cutting-edge productions since 1976. It has offered Tennessee Williams' *The Glass Menagerie,* Rudolfo Anaya's *Bless Me, Ultima,* several Shakespeare plays, and *The Underpants* by Steve Martin, among many others. Performances are on Thursday, Friday, and Saturday evenings, with matinees on second and third Saturdays and all Sundays. 2900 Carlisle Blvd. NE, just S of Candelaria Rd. vortexabq.org. ✆ **505/247-8600.** Adults $24, students $19.

The Bar Scene

Santa Fe and Taos may have more cultural programming, but Albuquerque has a much more dynamic nightlife scene, with new venues opening (and old ones closing) all the time. Whether you're looking for salsa clubs, a bar crawl, or one of the best breweries in the state, there's plenty for different ages and interests. In addition, a lot of hotels and restaurants here have good bars, some with live entertainment. Entertainment schedules vary, and cover charges usually range from nothing to $10, with an occasional performance charging more. Check websites or call to see what's happening.

Apothecary Lounge ♥ The rooftop hotspot atop Hotel Parq Central offers great city views, a broad patio, pricey but well-done Jazz Age–inspired cocktails, and a small-plates menu of New Mexican–influenced dishes like elote guacamole and green-chile sliders. Hotel Parq Central, 806 Central Ave. SE. hotelparqcentral.com. ✆ **505/242-0040.**

Billy's Long Bar ♥ Serious beer drinkers should definitely check this one out: The motto is "The World on Tap since 1970" with over 60 draft beers to choose from. The back of the long bar is lined with shelves of bottles, topped by large-screen TVs; the rest of the brick walls are covered with more TVs and numerous beer signs (including some nice neon). Good-looking Tiffany-style lamps overhang several pool tables. 4800 San Mateo Blvd. NE. ✆ **505/889-0573.**

Bow & Arrow Brewing Co. ♥♥ The first Native American woman–owned brewery in the country, Bow & Arrow surpasses every other contender in the city's booming brewery scene. Hoppy recipes use ingredients sourced from Indigenous farmers in the Four Corners area. The warehouse-like space features a lively patio that hosts revolving food trucks. 608 McKnight Ave. NW. bowandarrowbrewing.com. ✆ **505/247-9800.**

The Dirty Bourbon Dance Hall & Saloon ♥♥ For some serious two-steppin', head to this lively spot, which boasts two 53-foot bars and a 1,300-square-foot dance floor. It has frequent live music, line-dancing lessons, pool and shuffleboard tables, and events such as the "ugly sweater party." Open Thursdays through Saturdays. 9800 Montgomery Blvd. NE. thedirty-bourbon.com. ✆ **505/296-2726.**

Happy Accidents ♥ Named the best new cocktail bar in 2022 by the Spirited Awards, this colorful Nob Hill hangout is known for distilling the spirits used in more than 60 craft cocktails on offer. 3225 Central Ave. NE. happyaccidentsbar.com. No phone.

HITTING THE casinos

If you'd like to include a little gambling in your visit to Albuquerque, or maybe see some big-name entertainers, the best spot is the expansive **Sandia Resort & Casino ♥♥**, on the north edge of the city, at 30 Rainbow Road NE—take I-25 exit 140 a quarter-mile east on Tramway Boulevard (sandiacasino.com; ✆ **800/526-9366** or 505/796-7500). The huge complex sits on Sandia Pueblo land and has outstanding views of the Sandia Mountains. Built in Pueblo architectural style, the casino has more than 1,750 slot machines and numerous table games, including blackjack, roulette, craps, mini-baccarat, and one of the largest non-smoking poker rooms you'll find anywhere. There's an amazing 4,000-seat outdoor amphitheater, a huge indoor event space, a large ballroom, several restaurants and lounges, and a par-72 18-hole golf course. Sandia brings in top musical acts such as ZZ Top, Alabama, James Taylor, and Ringo Starr.

Just south of town, the **Isleta Resort & Casino ♥**, 11000 Broadway SE, at I-25 exit 215 (isleta.com; ✆ **877/747-5382** or 505/724-3800), has over 1,700 slots and more than two dozen table games—including craps, blackjack, roulette, baccarat, and poker—in a luxurious casino with a full-service restaurant and bar. Also available are a spa, golf course, and an RV park, plus the "Fun Connection" with bowling, an arcade, and billiards (in the Lucky Strike Lounge). The casino also presents live entertainment like Brian Setzer's Rockabilly, Jay Leno, and Charley Pride.

O'Niell's Pub ♥ With its roots in the Irish public house, O'Niell's is a true community pub, popular with locals and visitors alike. There's a covered patio you can enjoy year-round, plus live music most Sundays. Another branch is at 3301 Juan Tabo Blvd. NE (✆ **505/293-1122**). 4310 Central Ave. SE. oniells.com. ✆ **505/255-6782.**

QBar Lounge ♥♥ You'll find a sophisticated and relaxing atmosphere here, with dancing, a piano lounge, excellent drinks, an extensive wine list, and a media and billiards room. The popular happy hour is 7 to 8pm Thursday through Saturday, complete with DJ music. There are salsa dancing lessons on Thursday evenings. In Hotel Albuquerque at Old Town, 800 Rio Grande Blvd. NW. hotelabq.com. ✆ **505/225-5928.**

Sister ♥♥ Located in the heart of downtown's Central Avenue, which fills up with university students and other revelers on the weekends, Sister is known for its fun roster of live music, pinball games, and affordable drinks. 407 Central Ave. NW. sisterthebar.com. ✆ **505/242-4900.**

EXCURSIONS FROM ALBUQUERQUE

With bargain lodging rates and interstate highways heading in all four directions of the compass, Albuquerque is an excellent base for exploring New Mexico. The following trips can be done in 1 or 2 days, and will take you through old mining towns, to one of the premier bird-watching areas of the West, to ancient sites once occupied by ancestral Puebloan people and Spanish conquistadors, and to a bustling Native Pueblo that may be the longest continuously occupied community in North America.

The Turquoise Trail

Known as "the Turquoise Trail" (turquoisetrail.org), NM 14 begins about 16 miles east of downtown Albuquerque, at I-40's Cedar Crest exit (exit 175), and winds some 46 miles to Santa Fe skirting the east side of the Sandia Mountains. The route takes you through the revived ghost towns of Golden, Madrid, and Cerrillos, where gold, silver, coal, and turquoise were once mined in great quantities. Modern-day settlers, mostly artists and craftspeople, have brought a renewed frontier spirit to the old mining towns.

About 5 miles into the Turquoise Trail is Sandia Park, where you may want to turn left onto Sandia Crest Road and drive about 5 minutes to the **Tinkertown Museum ♥**, 121 Sandia Crest Rd. (tinkertown.com; ✆ **505/281-5233**). Created by the late folk artist Ross Ward and now run by his family, it's primarily a miniatures museum, with an animated mining town and a three-ring circus, odd collections of Western Americana, and plenty of silliness. The building's walls are built from 50,000 glass bottles. It's open daily from late March through October, Friday to Monday 10am to 4pm. Admission is $6 for adults, $3 for ages 4 to 18, and free for kids under 4.

Approximately 10 miles north of the Sandia Park junction on NM 14, you come to the ghost town of **Golden,** first settled in 1839. Its sagging houses, with their missing boards and the wind whistling through the broken eaves, make it a purist's ghost town. There's a general store widely known for its large selection of well-priced jewelry, and across the street, a bottle seller's "glass garden." Be sure to slow down and look for the village church, a great photo op, on the east side of the road. Nearby are the ruins of a pueblo called **Paako,** abandoned around 1670.

Madrid (pronounced "*Mah*-drid") is about 12 miles north of Golden. This town and neighboring Cerrillos were in a fabled turquoise-mining area dating back to prehistory. Gold and silver mines followed, and when they faltered, there was coal, supplying fuel for the locomotives of the Santa Fe Railroad until the 1950s, when the railroad converted to diesel. Madrid used to produce 100,000 tons of coal a year and was a true "company town," but the mine closed in 1956. Today, it's a funky village of artists and craftspeople seemingly stuck in the 1960s hippie era, with numerous galleries and crafts stores. The best way to see Madrid is to park somewhere along the road and walk up one side and down the other. It's only about a mile long, so it doesn't take too long unless you spend a lot of time in the shops. However, beware: Madrid residents don't believe in leashing or confining their dogs, so wandering dogs are everywhere.

When you get hungry, stop at the **Mine Shaft Tavern** ❤ (themineshafttavern.com; ✆ **505/473-0743**), the last of the company-owned buildings in town. It has one of the longest stand-up bars in New Mexico, which you've probably seen in one of the many movies or TV series it's been featured in. Known for its award-winning MadChile Burger, the tavern also offers several other half-pound burgers plus sandwiches; New Mexico favorites like enchiladas, burritos, and tacos; and pub fare such as fish and chips. There's live music on weekends. The Cantina Patio is pet-friendly right down to having bowls of water set out for your four-footed companion. Prices are mostly in the $11 to $27 range; hours vary, so call ahead or just stop by to see if it's open.

Next door to the tavern, the **Old Coal Mine Museum** ❤ (✆ **505/473-0743 ext. 1007**) is constantly being renovated and updated, adding more fun stories (including ghost tales, of course) and replicas. Films of Madrid are shown in the Engine House Theater. The museum's open Friday through Monday in summer, 10am to 4:30pm; admission costs $5 for adults, $3 for seniors and children under 12.

Cerrillos, about 3 miles north of Madrid, is an enchanting village of dirt roads that sprawls along Galisteo Creek. It appears to have changed very little since it was founded during a lead strike in 1879. The whole place still looks very much like an Old West movie set. The top attraction here is **Casa Grande Trading Post** ❤❤, 17 Waldo St. (casagrandetradingpost.com; ✆ **505/438-3008**), a sprawling shop crammed with jewelry (especially turquoise), New Mexico minerals including locally mined raw turquoise, old bottles and glass insulators, and other Western memorabilia. This rambling 28-room adobe is

Excursions from Albuquerque

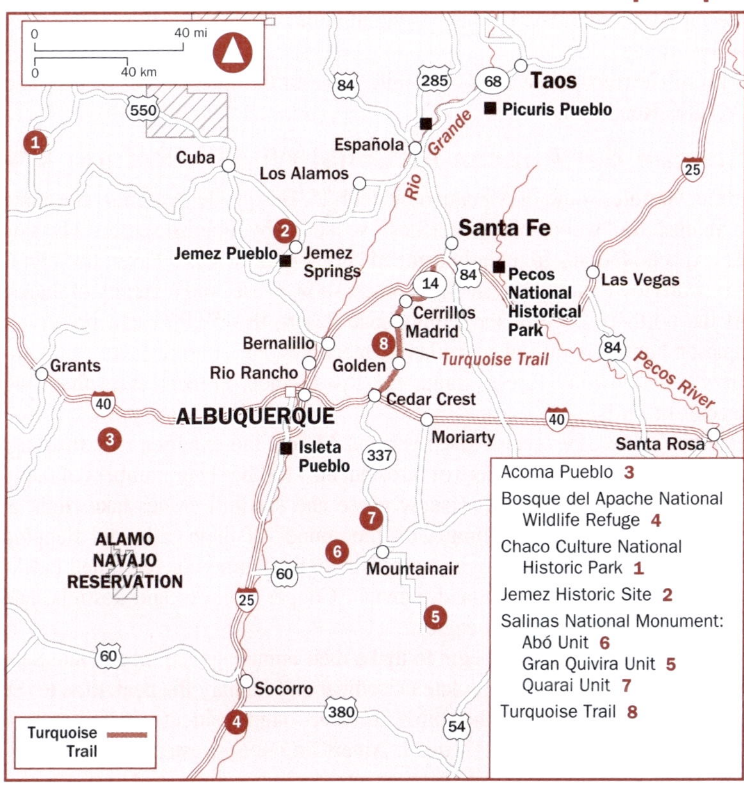

also the home of the **Cerrillos Turquoise Mining Museum** ♥, full of tools and other artifacts from the region's mining era, and a **petting zoo** ♥ with llamas, goats, fancy chickens, and pigeons. The complex is open daily 9am to 5pm. Admission to the museum costs $2, as does a sack of food for the petting zoo. There's also an excellent restaurant, **Black Bird Saloon** ♥♥, 28 Main St. (blackbirdsaloon.com; ✆ **505/438-1821**), which feels like an old-time hangout; it has a stellar menu of comfort breakfasts and sandwiches. Try the elk burger, which features Stilton blue cheese and blueberry mustard. It's open for brunch Friday to Sunday and for lunch and early dinner (it closes at 7pm) Thursday to Saturday.

Just north of the village of Cerrillos, **Cerrillos Hills State Park** ♥ (37 Main St., southwest of the railroad crossing; emnrd.nm.gov; ✆ **505/474-0196**) has 5 miles of trails leading past historic mines to scenic overlooks of the Sandia, Ortiz, Jemez, and Sangre de Cristo mountain ranges. Trails are open to hikers, mountain bikers, and horseback riders. The park is open daily during daylight hours; a visitor center is open Saturday and Sunday 10am to 4pm. Admission costs $5 per vehicle, payable in cash at the visitor center or at a self-pay station when the center's closed. A rack near the door to the visitor center is usually stocked with trail maps, a list of guided hikes and other special events in the park, plus a handout with a map of Cerrillos and history of the village.

From Cerrillos it's a scenic 15-mile drive to the intersection of I-25 and Cerrillos Road in Santa Fe.

Bosque del Apache National Wildlife Refuge ♥♥

About 90 miles south of Albuquerque via I-25, Bosque del Apache—the name is Spanish for "woods of the Apaches," so named by Spanish settlers who saw that Apache Indians frequently camped here—is known as a haven for migratory waterfowl, including sandhill cranes, snow geese, and a variety of ducks. At the northern edge of the Chihuahuan desert, this 57,000-acre preserve's riparian habitat, a mix of marshlands, meadows, agricultural fields, and old-growth cottonwood forests lining the Rio Grande, attracts more than 340 species of birds.

If you're here between November and March, the experience is thrilling, not only because of the variety of birds but also for the sheer numbers of them. Huge clouds of thousands of snow geese and sandhill cranes take flight at dawn and dusk, the air filling with the sounds of their calls and flapping wings. There are also plenty of raptors, including numerous red-tailed hawks and northern harriers (or marsh hawks), Cooper's hawks and kestrels, and even some bald and golden eagles.

Sandhill cranes usually begin to make their annual appearance in late September or early October, with late December and January the peak time to see these spectacular birds. Other birds are year-round residents, including red-winged blackbirds, Gambel's quail, American coots, western meadowlarks, American kestrels, ring-necked pheasants, and wild turkeys. There are also several dozen species of mammals. You might see coyotes (probably in search of a snow goose dinner), and possibly mule deer and elk.

A good first stop is the **visitor center,** where you can examine the exhibits, pick up a free refuge newspaper, rent binoculars, and check on recent bird and wildlife sightings. A 12-mile **self-guided auto tour** loop allows you to explore the refuge (get a map at the visitor center). You will often get closer to the birds and animals by staying in your vehicle, which acts as a blind, but there are some observation decks along the route, and a boardwalk into a marshy area helps you see waterfowl and some mammals up close. There are also about a half-dozen **walking trails,** described in the refuge newspaper, ranging from less than a mile to almost 10 miles. Early and late in the day are usually the best times to see birds and other wildlife.

The refuge grounds are open daily a half-hour before sunrise to a half-hour after sunset. From September through May the visitor center is open daily 8am to 4pm; from June through August it's open 8am to 4pm. It's closed on Tuesdays and Wednesdays. Admission costs $5 per vehicle. For information, see **fws.gov/refuge/bosque_del_apache** or call ✆ **575/835-1828.** The refuge is located 18 miles south of Socorro; from Albuquerque, go south on I-25 to exit

139, at the small village of San Antonio, and then follow signs south on US 380 and NM 1 to the refuge. Because you'll probably want to be in the refuge at sunrise, you may want to find overnight lodging in Socorro, which has a variety of chain motels and a few bed and breakfasts. See **socorronm.gov**.

Acoma Pueblo ♥

This "Sky City," a walled adobe village perched high atop a sheer rock mesa 365 feet above the valley floor, is believed to have been inhabited at least since the 11th century—the longest continuously occupied community in North America (native legend claims people have lived here since before the time of Christ). The name "acoma" in local dialect means "the place that always was." To reach Acoma from Albuquerque, drive west on I-40 approximately 52 miles to the Acoma–Sky City exit (exit 102), then travel about 15 miles southwest, following signs.

Visitors aren't allowed to wander around Acoma Pueblo on their own—you can only see the pueblo on 90-minute guided tours ($25 for adults; $22 for college students, military, and seniors 60 and up; $17 for ages 6–17, and free for 5 and under). Tours run daily year-round beginning at 9:30am. Signing up for one should be your first order of the day when you arrive at the cultural center. You can bring a still camera ($13 fee included in tour price) but no video cameras or sound recording equipment, and you're forbidden to take photos of the cemetery or inside the mission church; no cameras are allowed on feast days or during Christmas events. Should you wish to take a photo of tribal members or their artwork, you must get their permission first. Visitors to the pueblo should not wear what tribal officials consider "revealing clothing."

Home, Home on the Mesa

Officially, the Keresan-speaking Acoma (*Ack*-oo-mah) Pueblo boasts some 6,000 inhabitants, but in fact only a small number still reside year-round on the 70-acre mesa top. The rest come only for ceremonies and other events. The Pueblo is still of vital importance to the tribe, however—not least because the Pueblo people make a fair bit of their living from visitors coming to see their ancient "sky city."

Start your tour at the **Sky City Cultural Center and Haak'u Museum** (acomaskycity.org; ✆ **800/747-0181**), which gives a good look into the Acoma culture, and peruse the gallery, which showcases pottery, textiles, baskets, and other art from the tribe. You can have a meal at the **Y'aak'a Café** and visit the **Gaits'i' Gift Shop.** (In Keres, the language of Acoma, "y'aak'a" means corn—a staple for most Pueblo people—and *gaits'i'* means beautiful.) Then board the **tour bus,** which climbs through a rock garden of 50-foot sandstone monoliths to the mesa's summit. There's no running water or electricity in this medieval-looking village; a small reservoir collects rainwater for most purposes, but drinking water has to be transported from below. Woodhole ladders and mica windows are prevalent among the 300 or so adobe structures. The most striking feature of the mesa-top village, however, is the **San Esteban del Rey Mission,** an impressively large adobe church with two bell towers, which was built by Franciscan friars in the early 1600s—making it the oldest surviving European church in New Mexico. Inside you'll find many examples of Spanish Colonial art. Both the pueblo and the mission church have been named National Historic Landmarks.

As you tour the village, you'll have many opportunities to buy Pueblo crafts, especially their distinctive thin-walled white pottery with polychrome designs. Pottery is expensive here, but you're not going to find it any cheaper anywhere else, and you'll know it's authentic if you buy it directly from the craftsperson. Along the way, be sure to sample some Indian fry bread topped with honey.

The annual **San Esteban del Rey feast day** is September 2, when the pueblo's patron saint is honored with an 8am Mass, a procession, a harvest dance, and an arts-and-crafts fair, which includes homemade games of chance and food stalls. A tribal **Officers' Feast** is held annually in February, and Christmas festivities run December 24 to 28. Guided tours do not operate on the mesa during feast days, but entrance is free for visitors. Note that the pueblo is closed to visitors on Easter weekend (some years), June 24 and 29, July 9 to 14, the first or second weekend in October, and the first Saturday in December. It's best to call ahead to make sure the tour is available when you're visiting, as there are occasional unscheduled closures.

Acoma Pueblo also operates **Sky City Casino Hotel** (I-40 exit 102; skycity.com; ✆ **505/552-6123**), open daily 24 hours, with more than 558 slot machines, table games, live bingo, and live music most weekends in the lounge. They also have a hotel, restaurant, and RV park.

Salinas Pueblo Missions National Monument ♥♥

This national monument, about 80 miles south-southeast of Albuquerque, consists of three separate sites that preserve the ruins of three large Native American pueblos, along with some of the country's best remaining 17th-century Franciscan mission churches. Each site offers a slightly different perspective on the area's history, but all three explain the conflict of cultures between the Pueblo people and the Spanish colonists who arrived in the 1700s. Collectively, these pueblos are now known as **the Salinas**—the Spanish word for salt—which was abundant in the area and an important trade good.

Abó, Gran Quivira (also called Las Humanas), and Quarai were constructed by people of the ancestral Puebloan and Mogollon cultures beginning in the 1300s. The pueblos traded with the Plains tribes to the east and the Rio Grande pueblos to the west and north, and they were thriving communities when Spanish conquistadors first saw them in the late 1500s. One of Spain's goals in exploring the New World was economic—the search for gold and other riches—but converting local people to Christianity was almost equally important. The Franciscan missionaries were partly successful in their conversion efforts, but along with religion they also brought European diseases, to which the natives had little immunity.

The Pueblo people practiced a religion in which Kachina dances and other rituals were intended to take the people's prayers to the gods in hopes of ensuring sufficient rain, good harvests and hunting, and overall harmony. The missionaries considered the Indians' religion to be idolatry, and tried to prevent them from practicing their Kachina dances and other rituals. At first the Pueblo religious leaders thought they could incorporate this new Christian god into their rituals, but after some Franciscans destroyed kivas and Kachina masks, it became obvious that there could be no middle ground. Adding to the animosity of the Pueblo people was that some Spanish colonists were allowed to demand tribute from the Indians, often in the form of grain or cloth.

In the 1660s and 1670s, drought and the resulting famine (along with European diseases) decimated the Pueblo people. The remaining residents abandoned their villages in the 1670s, mostly joining other pueblos. Then in 1680 the pueblos to the north revolted against the Spanish (see "The Great Pueblo Revolt," p. 112), driving them back into Mexico, where they stayed until the reconquest of New Mexico in 1692.

Start your visit at the national monument's **main visitor center** in the community of Mountainair, on US 60, 1 block west of the intersection of US 60 and NM 55 (corner of Ripley Street and Broadway; nps.gov/sapu; ✆ **505/847-2585;** open daily 9am–5pm in summer, closing 4pm Nov–Apr). The visitor center has exhibits on all three pueblos and the missions, a short introductory movie, a bookstore, and restrooms. Armed with the park map, head out to the individual sites, where you can explore the ruins following short, easy paths.

At **Abó** (✆ **505/847-2400;** 9 miles west of the visitor center on US 60 and ½ mile north on NM 513), a short, paved trail leads from the contact station to the towering walls of the Mission of San Gregorio de Abó. You can enter the mission and convento following a side trail, and view an excavated kiva inside the walls. Then continue around the main trail as it loops through some of the unexcavated ruins, with a number of visible walls from the Abó Pueblo and Spanish resettlement structures. There are restrooms and a gift store at the contact station, plus a picnic area a short distance south.

At **Gran Quivira** (✆ **505/847-2770;** 26 miles south of the visitor center on NM 55), a short gravel trail winds among the ruins of two churches—the Mission of San Buenaventura and the Church of San Isidro—plus the excavated and stabilized ruins of the Pueblo de Las Humanas, the largest of the Salinas pueblos. Along the trail you will see several excavated kivas including one quite large one. The contact station houses restrooms and the parking lot is large, allowing for easy RV turnaround.

Although the smallest unit in the monument, **Quarai** (✆ **505/847-2290;** 8 miles north of the visitor center on NM 55 and 1 mile west) has the most impressive mission—the Nuestra Senora de la Purísima Concepción de Quarai—and the unexcavated ruins of a very large pueblo. The half-mile gravel loop trail leads from the contact station past the cemetery into the mission church, meanders around the main convento where you can see a unique square kiva plus a more usual round kiva, then skirts the South Convento before circling back past some partially excavated pueblo ruins. There are restrooms, a museum and bookstore at the contact station. The parking lot is small, so park mid-to-large RVs on the hill above.

The three pueblos have different opening days and times, so check the website for information. The visitor center and sites are closed New Year's Day, Thanksgiving, and Christmas. Inclement weather—particularly heavy winter weather—occasionally causes the park to close, so it's best to call ahead.

Jemez Historic Site ♥♥

Some of the best preserved prehistoric and historic ruins in New Mexico are at **Jemez Historic Site** (18160 NM 4; nmhistoricsites.org; ✆ **505/829-3530**), where you'll see the ruins of a 500-year old Indian village once occupied by the ancestors of today's Jemez Pueblo people, and the massive San José de los Jemez Church, built in the early 1620s. It's about 60 miles north of Albuquerque; take I-25 north to Bernalillo, take exit 242, follow NM 550 north about 20 miles to San Ysidro, turn right on NM 4, and drive about 18 miles to Jemez Springs.

Start at the **museum,** which tells the tale of Giusewa, "place of boiling waters," the area's original Indian name, a reference to the many hot springs (see p. 229) found here. Then take the quarter-mile-long **interpretive trail** through the impressive ruins of the pueblo and the mission church, with its massive stone walls built about the same time the Pilgrims landed at Plymouth Rock. Small plaques along the trail tell the story, juxtaposing the missionaries' first impressions against the reality of Jemez life. The missionaries saw the Jemez people as barbaric and set out to civilize them—a process which included forcing them to haul river stones to the site to erect 6-foot-thick walls for their mission. The church was abandoned less than 20 years after it was

Historic Culture with a Hint of Honey

The nearby **Jemez Pueblo** does not welcome visitors except on selected days. However, visitors can get a taste of the Jemez culture at the **Walatowa Visitor Center,** on NM 4, 8 miles north of the junction with US 550 (jemezpueblo.org; ✆ **575/494-1965**). A museum presents the history and culture of the Jemez people and the gift shop offers works by Jemez artists, including sculpture, pottery, baskets made of yucca fronds, belts, and drums including painted hand drums. You can sign up for a self-guided hike ($6 per person) along the Red Rock Canyon Trail to learn more of the history and culture of the Jemez, and incidentally enjoy the beauty of the surrounding red rocks. While in the area, you may encounter Jemez people sitting under *ramadas* (thatch-roofed lean-tos) and selling home-baked bread, cookies, and pies. If you're lucky, they may also be making fry bread, which you can smother with honey for one of New Mexico's more delectable treats. The visitor center is open daily 9am to 4pm in summer and 10am to 4pm the rest of the year. In mid-October is their Open Air Market, with tribal dances and music, oven bread baking demonstrations, and Jemez cuisine to temp you. Call for the exact dates.

built, and the Jemez people abandoned their pueblo about 40 years later, during the Pueblo Revolt (see p. 112). In the early 20th century, excavations unearthed this massive complex, which you enter through a broad doorway to a room that once held elaborate fresco paintings, with a giant bell tower.

Admission to the site costs $7 for adults, and is free for ages 16 and under and for those with a New Mexico CulturePass (p. 76). The site is open Wednesday through Sunday 10am to 4pm; it's closed New Year's Day, Thanksgiving, and Christmas, and has special Easter hours.

Jemez Hot Springs

Also called the "Home of the Giggling Springs," the **Jemez Hot Springs** (jemezhotsprings.com; ✆ **505/829-9175**) rests in the bottom of San Diego Canyon in the heart of Jemez Springs. Nestled between Virgin Mesa on the west and Cat Mesa on the east, it offers four outdoor mineral pools of 100°F to 104°F in this serene setting.

The springs emanate from deep beneath the Valles Caldera National Preserve (see p. 122) just 17 miles to the north. Trapped beneath the mountains eons ago, the mineral-infused waters have been used by the Jemez people for both healing and spiritual rites. The high mineral levels are very therapeutic and soothing to the skin, but you will need drinking water to stay hydrated—bring a reusable water bottle and they'll keep it filled during your visit. There are benches in the pools, hammocks and chaise lounges for relaxing by the pools in the pavilion or cabanas, and a gift shop with snacks, drinks and smoothies, towels, robes, and even a limited number of bathing suits for rent.

Located in the heart of the village on the west side of the road, the springs open 10am to 5:30pm on Monday, Wednesdays, and Thursdays, and 9am to 7pm on Fridays to Sundays year-round. Entry costs $25 per person for 1 hour, $50 for 2 hours; kids 14 and older are welcome when accompanied by a parent. Pets, alcohol, and glass containers are not allowed.

Chaco Culture National Historical Park ♥♥♥

The combination of a stunning setting and well-preserved ruins makes the long drive to **Chaco Culture National Historic Park,** about 150 miles northwest of Albuquerque in the middle of nowhere, worth the trip. A trip to Chaco is a journey to another time and place, to the prehistoric world of a people who dominated the Four Corners area (where the states of New Mexico, Colorado, Arizona, and Utah meet today) more than 1,000 years ago. This remote park offers not just another ruin, but a feeling for the immensity of what we now call the Chacoan culture, a link with a distant past that provides an awe-inspiring look into the very center of a remarkable civilization.

No matter which route you take into this national historic park, often referred to simply as Chaco Canyon, you drive in on a dusty road. But that's only if you're lucky—with a bit of rain the road turns to mud. When you finally arrive, the stark desert country seems perhaps ill-suited as a center of culture. But centuries ago, the ancestral Puebloans built a complex culture

chaco canyon: **A WINDOW ON THE PAST**

Despite the harsh and unforgiving desert climate, the ancestral Puebloan people successfully farmed these lowlands. Some 1,200 years ago, they launched an ambitious building project here. Instead of simply starting with a few small rooms and adding more as the need arose, as was usual at the time, the Chacoans constructed massive stone buildings of multiple stories. More significant, though, is that these buildings show evidence of skillful planning. Obviously, a central government was in charge. Within a century, six large pre-planned public buildings, or "great houses," were underway. New communities, each consisting of a large central building surrounded by smaller villages, sprang up; established villages followed the trend by adding large public and ceremonial buildings.

Eventually there were more than 150 such communities, most of them closely tied to Chaco by an extensive system of roads. You can't see them from the ground, but get up in a plane and spread out below is evidence of hundreds of miles of roads connecting the outlying settlements with the large buildings at Chaco. These communities appear to have been established along the roads at precise intervals, one day's travel apart. Not simply trails worn into the stone by foot travel, these were carefully engineered roadways 30 feet wide, with a low wall of rock to contain the fill. Where the road went over flat rock, walls were erected along the edges.

By C.E. 1000, Chaco had become the area's center of commerce, ceremony, and culture, with as many as 5,000 people living in some 400 settlements. Artifacts found at Chaco—including shell necklaces, turquoise, copper bells, and the remains of Mexican parrots—indicate that their trade routes stretched from the California coast to Texas, and south into Mexico.

The decline and abandonment of Chaco in the 12th century coincided with a drought in the area, although archaeologists are not certain that this was the only or even the major reason why the site was eventually abandoned. Some argue that an influx of outsiders may have brought new rituals to the region, causing a schism among tribal members. A somewhat controversial theory maintains that cannibalism existed at Chaco, practiced either by the ancestral Puebloans themselves or by invaders, such as the Toltecs of Mexico. Even though archaeologists do not agree on why Chaco Canyon was abandoned, they generally concur that the Chacoans' descendants live among today's Pueblo people.

here, the ruins of which offer a tantalizing glimpse of a mysterious and long-ago past.

Begin at the **visitor center** (nps.gov/chcu; ✆ **505/786-7014**), which has background exhibits on the Chacoan culture and construction of this prehistoric city, plus artifacts discovered during excavations. A video program tells about the ancestral Puebloans. Trail maps for the sites are available to purchase, ranger programs are held daily, and rangers lead guided hikes and walks. The visitor center is open daily 9am to 5pm May through October, closing at 4pm November through April; closed New Year's Day, Thanksgiving, and Christmas. Trails and archaeological sites are open 7am to 9pm May to October, until 5pm November to February, and until 7pm March to April.

Guided tours of the great house sites and night sky programs—Chaco boasts perfectly dark night skies—are offered regularly from May through October and occasionally in April depending on staffing availability. Call ✆ **505/786-7010 ext. 0** (zero) for information on what's available during your visit.

The partially excavated **Una Vida,** a short walk from the visitor center, was one of the first Chacoan buildings to be constructed. Considered a "great house," it had 150 rooms and five kivas, including a Great Kiva. A walking trail leads from Una Vida to several petroglyph sites; it's about 1 mile round-trip, returning to the visitor center, with some rocky or steep sections.

The first great house along the road (about 2 miles from the visitor center) is the unexcavated **Hungo Pavi**, still a dust- and vegetation-covered mound over its more than 150 rooms, great kiva, and enclosed plaza.

Another 2½ miles farther is the impressive **Pueblo Bonito** (Spanish for "beautiful town")—a must-see for every Chaco visitor. Believed to have been the largest structure in the Chacoan system, as well as the largest prehistoric dwelling ever excavated in the Southwest, Pueblo Bonito is the most thoroughly investigated, researched, and celebrated cultural site in Chaco Canyon. It covers more than 3 acres, and contains some 800 rooms surrounding two plazas, in which there were over two dozen kivas.

Accessible from the same parking area is **Chetro Ketl,** the second-largest Chacoan great house, with about 500 rooms, 16 kivas, and an impressive enclosed plaza. It rose up three stories in places. Or you can follow the **Petroglyph Trail** between Pueblo Bonito and Chetro Ketl, which follows the cliff face between the sites and offers many opportunities to view petroglyphs.

A short distance off the loop road is **Pueblo del Arroyo,** a four-story, D-shaped structure with about 280 rooms and 20 kivas. Finally, 6 miles from the visitor center, you come to the largest Great Kiva in the park, **Casa Rinconada.** It was astronomically aligned to the four compass points and the summer solstice, which suggests it may have been a center for the community at large, used for major religious observances.

The park also has four longer **backcountry trails,** ranging from 3 to 7 miles, which lead to additional archaeological sites. Backcountry permits must be obtained (free) at the visitor center. Wear good hiking boots and take drinking water (the visitor center is the only place in the park where you can buy drinking water). There is a surprising amount of **wildlife** at Chaco, considering its harsh landscape. You are quite likely to see white-tailed antelope squirrels, and also watch for collared lizards, desert cottontails, black-tailed jackrabbits, prairie dogs, gray foxes, deer, coyotes, and even bobcats. Birds seen here include western meadowlarks, mountain chickadees, western bluebirds, white-crowned sparrows, canyon towhees, scaled quail, rock and canyon wrens, and golden eagles. You'll want to avoid the rattlesnakes.

Gallo Campground, inside the park about 1 mile from the visitor center, has 24 individual sites and two group sites with picnic tables and fire grates (bring your own wood or charcoal). The water in the campground is not potable, though you can get drinking water at the visitor center. There are two restrooms with flush toilets but no showers; although there are no RV hookups, there is a dump station. The campground cannot accommodate trailers and motor homes over 35 feet long. Camping costs $20 per night; reservations can be made at least 3 days in advance at recreation.gov; ✆ **877/444-6777.** Maintenance is in progress at the campground after a rockfall occurred near its cliff dwelling, but should be completed soon.

To get to Chaco from Albuquerque, take I-25 north to Bernalillo, then US 550 northwest 112 miles. Turn off US 550 onto CR 7900 and follow signs for about 21 miles to the park entrance. This route includes 8 miles of paved road (County Road 7900) and 13 miles of rough dirt road (County Road 7950). Call the park office (✆ **505/786-7014**) to inquire about road conditions. By the way, many people have reported that GPS devices are not reliable in the Chaco area. Park admission, for up to 7 days, is $25 per car, truck, or RV; $20 per motorcycle; and $15 per person on foot or bicycle.

The closest motels and restaurants are 1½ hours away in several directions, so unless you camp in the park, you'll be doing some traveling. Along the route from Albuquerque, the quiet little town of **Cuba** on US 550 will be your last chance to get a bed and a meal before arriving at Chaco, 69 miles away. Cuba has several mom-and-pop motels, two bed and breakfasts, several commercial campgrounds, a half-dozen or so restaurants, and some small grocery stores. See villageofcuba.com or call the Cuba Visitor Center at ✆ **575/289-3808.**

PLANNING YOUR TRIP TO NORTHERN NEW MEXICO

10

A trip to northern New Mexico may affect your attitude. You may return home and find that your responses to the world are different than they used to be. (That is, if you return at all—you wouldn't be the first person to vacation in northern New Mexico, fall in love with it, and move here!) In fact, in many ways northern New Mexico is not simply a destination, but a state of mind, and it can be very addictive. The pace is slow and the objectives are less obvious than in most places. As many transplants to the area report, once they've lived here for 5 years or so, they're not fit to go back to the real world.

Travelers often think that because this is the desert, it should have saguaro cactus and always be warm. Think again. Much of northern New Mexico lies upward of 5,000 feet in elevation, which means that four full seasons act upon the land. So, when you're planning your trip, be sure to take a look at the "When to Go" section in chapter 2 so you will be prepared.

That said, preparation is simple. Even though many people mistake New Mexico for our neighboring country to the south, traveling here is much like going anywhere in the U.S. You can drink the water and eat all the food you care to eat, being mindful of your tolerance for the heat of our chile. The sun at these elevations can also be scorching, so come with a hat, plenty of sunscreen, and sunglasses with good UV protection. In fact, the elements here may present the greatest challenge, so be sure to review "Staying Healthy" (p. 238).

Another point to be aware of is the distance between cities. It's easiest to drive your own vehicle, so you can go where you want when you want, and there are few enjoyments as great as driving in the sparkling light through unpretentious farming villages, past ancient ruins, and over mountain passes. However, public transportation can be useful in some places, such as downtown Santa Fe, where parking can be a frustration during summer's festival weekends.

As with any trip, a little preparation is essential. This chapter provides a variety of planning tools, including info on when to go and how to get there.

ARRIVING

By Plane

Most visitors to northern New Mexico fly into the **Albuquerque International Sunport** (**ABQ;** abqsunport.com; ✆ **505/244-7700**), which is served by most national airlines. It's in the southern part of the city, between I-25 to the west and Kirtland Air Force Base on the east. An Albuquerque visitor information center desk on the lower level is open weekdays 10am to 5pm, weekends 10am to 3pm.

Many Albuquerque hotels have courtesy vans to meet their guests. Limousine service is available from **American Limo** (americanlimosabq.com; ✆ **505/877-7576**) and **Carey Southwest Limousine** (carey.com; ✆ **505/766-5466**). Taxis wait outside the airport terminal, or you can take a city bus operated by **ABQ Ride,** the Albuquerque public transit system (cabq.gov/transit; ✆ **505/243-7433**).

All national car rental chains operate out of the Albuquerque Sunport (see p. 235), and most travelers bound for Taos or Santa Fe rent a car for the next leg of the trip. The Sunport is about an hour's drive from Santa Fe and 1½ hours from Taos. **Groome Transportation** (groometransportation.com; ✆ **505/474-5696**) runs shuttles daily from the Sunport to Santa Fe and back again at a cost of $34 to $46 per person one-way. **New Mexico Rail Runner Express** trains (riometro.org; ✆ **866/795-7245**) also run from the Sunport to Santa Fe, at a cost of $9 per person. Purchase a ticket in advance to access a free shuttle bus from the airport to the train.

It is also possible, though less convenient, to fly directly into Santa Fe or Taos. The **Santa Fe Regional Airport** (**SAF;** flysantafe.com; ✆ **505/955-2900**), just outside the southwestern city limits off Airport Road, has non-stop service from Dallas/Fort Worth and Phoenix with **American Airlines** (aa.com; ✆ **800/433-7300**), plus non-stop service from Denver with **United Airlines** (united.com; ✆ **800/864-8331**). Many Santa Fe hotels offer free shuttles from the airport, or you can get a ride into town with Uber (uber.com) or Lyft (lyft.com). The **Taos Regional Airport** (taosairport.org; ✆ **575/758-4995**) is about 8 miles northwest of town on US 64. During ski season, Taos Ski Valley provides non-stop air service several days a week between Taos and Austin, Dallas, Carlsbad/San Diego, and Hawthorne/Los Angeles, with a free shuttle to Taos Ski Valley. See skitaos.com/taos-air or call ✆ **833/359-8267.**

By Train

Amtrak's *Southwest Chief* (amtrak.com; ✆ **800/872-7245**), which provides east-west service between Los Angeles and Chicago, arrives and departs daily in Albuquerque at the Alvarado Transportation Center, 100 1st St. SW. The train also stops in Lamy, about 20 miles from Santa Fe. **New Mexico Rail Runner Express** (see above) runs trains daily from the Albuquerque train station to various points in Santa Fe, with connecting buses to Taos; the **North Central Regional Transit District** (**NCRTD;** ncrtd.org; ✆ **866/206-0754**) also offers free shuttle bus service from Santa Fe to Taos (service is direct on weekends and requires a transfer in Española on weekdays).

By Bus

Greyhound buses (greyhound.com; ✆ **800/231-2222**) arrive and depart in Albuquerque from the Alvarado Transportation Center, 100 1st St. SW.

By Car

Albuquerque is intersected by two major interstates, the east-west I-40 and the north-south I-25. An hour's drive north on I-25 gets you to **Santa Fe.** (From the east, travelers exit I-40 at Clines Corners and continue 52 miles to Santa Fe on US 285.) For those coming from the northwest, the most direct route to Santa Fe is via Durango, Colorado, on US 160, entering Santa Fe on US 84.

Most visitors arrive in **Taos** via either NM 68 or US 64. From Santa Fe, follow US 285 to Española, and then continue on the divided highway when it becomes NM 68. Southbound travelers on I-25 should exit about 6 miles south of Raton and follow US 64 West about 95 miles to Taos. Coming from the Four Corners area, take US 64 East from Farmington, about 214 miles. Snow often closes this route in winter between Tres Piedras and Chama, but you can get around the closure by detouring up to Colorado. (Check road and driving conditions by calling the state's **Road Advisory Hotline** at ✆ **800/432-4269,** or check out nmroads.com.)

GETTING AROUND

By Car

The most convenient and scenic way to get around northern New Mexico is by private vehicle. If you're visiting from abroad and plan to rent a car in the United States, keep in mind that although foreign driver's licenses are usually recognized in the U.S., you may want to consider obtaining an international driver's license. Check with the agency that issues your local driver's license for the proper procedure and the required documents for driving outside your home country.

CAR RENTALS Auto and RV rentals are widely available for those who arrive without their own transportation. At the Albuquerque airport, rental counters are located at the Sunport Car Rental Center at 3400 University Blvd. SE; a free handicap accessible shuttle (✆ **505/315-7770**) runs every 5 minutes from the airport terminal commercial lane, outside the first level of the airport terminal, to the rental center. The following national car rental firms have

TURNING TO THE internet or apps FOR A HOTEL DISCOUNT

Before going online, it's important that you know what "flavor" of discount you're seeking. Currently, there are several types of online reductions:

1. **Extreme discounts on sites where you bid for lodgings without knowing which hotel you'll get.** You'll find these on such sites as **Priceline.com** and **Hotwire.com**, and they can be money-savers, particularly if you're booking within a week of travel (that's when the hotels resort to deep discounts to get beds filled). As these companies use only major chains, you can rest assured that you won't be put up in a dump. For Priceline, you can install the browser extension **Hotel Canary** for free on your computer, and it will tell you the name of the hotel Priceline is trying to hide from you. There's not as easy a hack for Hotwire, but if you search for it on Frommers.com you'll find a four-step method we figured out for correctly guessing which hotel you're being shown.
2. **Consider joining Room Steals, Travel + Leisure's Go, or one of the travel clubs associated with many professional organizations.** These clubs have access to the "fire sales" of the hotel industry: room rates that are slashed to a level hotels would never want to surface on a Google search. These clubs work best for frequent travelers because there are initial membership fees. Another alternative is **@Hotels** on Instagram, which unlocks the same types of discounts, but with no membership fee (it does have a slightly more cumbersome research and booking method, involving messaging @Hotels for access). But all these entities unlock wholesale prices that consistently shave 25% off the nightly rate at hotels, more for really pricey ones.
3. **Use the right hotel search engine.** They're not all equal, as we at Frommers.com learned in 2023 after putting the top 20 sites to the test in 20 cities around the globe. We discovered that **HotelsCombined.com** and **Google/Hotels** both listed the lowest rates for hotels in the city center 20 out of 20 times—the best record, by far, of all the sites we tested.
4. **Last-minute discounts.** Booking last minute can be a great savings strategy, as prices sometimes drop in the week and days before travel as hoteliers scramble to fill their rooms. But you won't necessarily find the best savings through companies that claim to specialize in last-minute bookings. Instead, use the sites recommended above.

It's a lot of surfing, I know, but in the hothouse world of hotel pricing, this sort of diligence can pay off.

pickups at the Albuquerque airport: **ACE** (acerentacar.com; ✆ 877/822-3872); **Alamo** (alamo.com; ✆ 800/462-5266); **Avis** (avis.com; ✆ 800/331-1212); **Budget** (budget.com; ✆ 800/527-0700); **Dollar** (dollar.com; ✆ 800/800-4000); **Enterprise** (enterprise.com; ✆ 800/736-8222); **Hertz** (hertz.com; ✆ 800/654-3131); **National** (nationalcar.com; ✆ 800/227-7368); **Payless** (paylesscar.com; ✆ 800/729-5377); **Sixt** (sixt.com; ✆ 888/749/8227); and **Thrifty** (thrifty.com; ✆ 800/847-4389). International visitors should note that insurance and taxes are almost never included in quoted rental-car rates in the U.S. Be sure to ask your rental agency about additional fees for these. They can add a significant cost to your car rental.

Drivers who need wheelchair-accessible transportation should call **Wheelchair Getaways,** which rents accessible vans through United Access Albuquerque, 3825 Osuna Rd. NE, Albuquerque (wheelchairgetaways.com; ✆ **888/433-3904**).

DRIVING LAWS Unless otherwise posted, the speed limit on interstate highways in New Mexico is 75mph; on most other two-lane open roads it's 50 to 65mph. The minimum age for drivers is 16. Seat belts or approved child restraint seats are required for all drivers and passengers. Motorcyclists under 18 must wear helmets.

SPECIAL-INTEREST TOURS

See the "Exploring" chapters for each city for additional special interest and guided tours.

Academic & Cultural Trips

Those who like a scholarly bent to their vacations can hook up with Santa-Fe-based **Southwest Seminars** (southwestseminars.org; ✆ **505/466-2775**) and its Travels with a Scholar program. It offers tours around the Southwest led by museum directors, historians, geologists, archaeologists, anthropologists, and authors. These tours often visit sites that aren't open to the general public, such as archaeological sites, petroglyph panels, volcanic calderas, contemporary Indian pueblos, and Native artists' homes and studios. ***Note:*** Most Mondays at 6pm, lectures by regional scholars on a variety of topics are held at Hotel Santa Fe (1501 Paseo de Peralta) or the Santa Fe Women's Club (1616 Old Pecos Trail).

Bike Tours

Bicycle Adventures (bicycleadventures.com; ✆ **800/443-6060**) offers tours through northern New Mexico. Riders get to experience some of the region's loveliest routes, such as the High Road to Taos and the Enchanted Circle. Participants visit major sights, such as Santa Fe's Canyon Road and Taos Pueblo, and can even opt for a river trip. In business since 1984, this company knows how to put together a good tour.

Outdoor Adventures

If you're looking for an active adventure with some relaxation thrown in, one excellent operator is **Santa Fe Mountain Adventures** (santafemountainadventures.com; ✆ **505/988-4000;** see p. 95), which combines outdoor adventures, such as hiking and river running, with cultural activities, such as visits to pueblos or museums, with more relaxing ones, such as spa treatments and meditation practices. The business is eco-conscious.

Photography Trips

Some of the world's most outstanding photographers convene in Santa Fe at various times during the year for the **Santa Fe Workshops,** at a delightful campus in the hills on the east side of town (santafeworkshops.com; ✆ **505/983-1400**). Course lengths range from 2 to 6 days.

STAYING HEALTHY

One thing that sets New Mexico apart from most other states is its elevation. Santa Fe and Taos are about 7,000 feet above sea level; Albuquerque is more than 5,000 feet above sea level. The reduced oxygen and low humidity can yield some unique problems, and the desert environment can also present some challenges. Those with heart or respiratory problems should consult their doctors before planning a trip to higher elevations. If you're in generally good health, you don't need to take any special precautions, but it's advisable to ease into high elevations by changing altitude gradually. Stay in Albuquerque for a few days before venturing to Santa Fe and Taos. Also, get plenty of rest, avoid large meals, consume less alcohol, and drink plenty of water.

One of the most common ailments in northern New Mexico, especially in the mountains above Santa Fe and Taos, is **acute mountain sickness,** the mildest and most common form of high altitude sickness. Rather similar to a hangover, it causes headache, nausea, and fatigue, and can usually be treated by taking aspirin, resting, and drinking lots of water. However, if the condition persists or worsens, it could be serious. You should see a doctor—there are urgent care centers in Santa Fe, Taos, and Albuquerque—and you will most likely be told to go to a lower altitude.

Other dangers of higher elevations include hypothermia and sun exposure, and these should be taken seriously. To avoid dehydration, drink water as often as possible.

Limit your exposure to the sun, especially between 11am and 2pm. Liberally apply sunscreen with a high protection factor, and wear a wide-brimmed hat and sunglasses with good UV protection.

[FastFACTS] NORTHERN NEW MEXICO

Airline Websites The airlines currently serving Albuquerque are **Advanced Air** (advancedairlines.com), **Alaska Airlines** (alaskaair.com), **American Airlines** (aa.com), **Delta Air Lines** (delta.com), **JetBlue Airways** (jetblue.com), **Southwest Airlines** (southwest.com), **Spirit Airlines** (spirit.com), **Sun Country Airlines** (suncountry.com), and **United Airlines** (united.com).

Area Codes The telephone area code for the Albuquerque and Santa Fe areas is **505.** Taos's area code is **575.**

ATM Networks As in most U.S. destinations,

you'll find automated teller machines practically everywhere in the cities of northern New Mexico. However, they may be more difficult to locate in small mountain towns. Usually someone in a store or other business can direct you. ATMs are linked to a network that most likely includes your bank at home. **Cirrus** (mastercard.com; ✆ **800/424-7787**) and **PLUS** (visa.com; ✆ **800/843-7587**) are the two most popular networks in the United States.

Business Hours **Offices** and general merchandise **stores** are usually open Monday to Friday 9am to 5pm, with larger stores also open Friday evening, Saturday, and Sunday. In tourist areas such as Santa Fe and Taos, many art galleries and gift shops open at 10am. Major grocery stores are often open 7am to 10pm. Most **banks** are open Monday to Friday 9am to 5pm, and sometimes until 6pm Friday. Some may also be open Saturday morning. Most branches have ATMs available 24 hours.

Cellphones Cellphones from practically all major networks will work fine in Santa Fe, Taos, and Albuquerque, and along most sections of I-25 and I-40, but service is spotty in rural areas. As of this writing there is no statewide ban on using handheld phones while driving, but there are local laws prohibiting it in Albuquerque, Santa Fe, Las Cruces, Gallup, Taos, and Española. There is a statewide ban on typing/texting on handheld mobile devices and the use of websites while driving.

Disabled Travelers Throughout New Mexico, measures have been taken to provide access for travelers with disabilities. Hotels will often have several rooms that comply with the Americans with Disabilities Act (ADA), and many bed-and-breakfasts have made one or more of their rooms completely wheelchair accessible. Most restaurants have at least two marked accessible parking spaces. Some historic properties, however, including museums and historic sites, may not be able to accommodate those with disabilities, so if this is an issue for you, we suggest you call the site before visiting to check on its accessibility.

Doctors See "Fast Facts" in each city's "Essentials" section for information on the nearest urgent care facility and other medical contacts.

Drinking Laws In New Mexico, the legal age for purchase and consumption of alcoholic beverages is 21; proof of age is required and often requested at bars, nightclubs, restaurants, and retail outlets, so it's always a good idea to carry a picture ID when you go out.

Bars may remain open until 10pm Monday to Friday and until 11pm on Saturday and Sunday. Wine, beer, and spirits are sold at licensed supermarkets and liquor stores, but there are no package sales on Sundays before noon. It is illegal to transport liquor through most Native American reservations.

It is illegal to carry open containers of alcohol in your car or in any public area that isn't zoned for alcohol consumption.

Electricity Like Canada, the United States uses 110 to 120 volts AC (60 cycles), compared to 220 to 240 volts AC (50 cycles) in most of Europe, Australia, and New Zealand. Downward converters that change 220 to 240 volts to 110 to 120 volts are difficult to find in the United States, so bring one with you.

Embassies & Consulates All embassies are in the nation's capital, Washington, DC Some consulates are in major U.S. cities, and most nations have a mission to the United Nations in New York City.

The embassy of **Australia** is at 1601 Massachusetts Ave. NW, Washington, DC 20036 (austemb.org; ✆ **202/797-3000**). Consulates are in Chicago, Houston, Los Angeles, New York, and San Francisco.

The embassy of **Canada** is at 501 Pennsylvania Ave. NW, Washington, DC 20001 (canadianembassy.org; ✆ **202/682-1740**). Other Canadian consulates are in Atlanta, Boston, Chicago, Dallas, Denver, Detroit, Los Angeles, Minneapolis, New York, and Seattle.

The embassy of **Ireland** is at 2234 Massachusetts Ave. NW, Washington, DC 20008 (dfa.ie/irish-embassy/usa; ✆ **202/462-3939**). Irish consulates are in Atlanta, Austin, Boston, Chicago, New York, and San Francisco.

The embassy of **New Zealand** is at 37 Observatory Circle NW, Washington, DC 20008 (mfat.govt.nz; ✆ **202/328-4800**). New Zealand consulates are in Los Angeles, Honolulu, and New York.

The embassy of the **United Kingdom** is at 3100 Massachusetts Ave. NW, Washington, DC 20008 (gov.uk/world/usa; ✆ **202/588-7800**). Other British consulates are in Atlanta, Boston, Chicago, Denver, Houston, Los Angeles, Miami, and San Francisco.

Emergencies In case of emergency, dial ✆ **911.**

Family Travel You may find family travel in northern New Mexico a bit different from what you're accustomed to. The state doesn't have huge Disney-like attractions, but it does have colossal mountains, vast mesas, an immensely deep gorge, and Indian dwellings that are hundreds of years old. Then there are the cultural offerings: history and art, museums and craft shows, musical performances ranging from classical to rock, opera to bluegrass.

Many of the hotels and resorts listed in this book have inviting pools to laze around in or on-site activities planned especially for kids. Wherever you wander, northern New Mexico will definitely give your children a new perspective on the United States by exposing them to ancient ruins, Southwestern cuisine, and Hispanic and Native American cultures that they may not experience elsewhere.

The Santa Fe quarterly ***Tumbleweeds*** (sftumbleweeds.com; ✆ **505/500-4676**) offers useful articles on family-oriented subjects in the Santa Fe area, as well as a quarterly day-by-day calendar of family events and a seasonal directory of kids' classes, camps, and programs. It's available free in locations all over Santa Fe.

Insurance Because of the high cost of travel, travel insurance is always a good idea. If you find that option costly, consider that in this region it is unlikely that your trip will be canceled because of major weather problems or other factors, so you may consider travel insurance unnecessary. For information on traveler's insurance, trip cancellation insurance, and medical insurance while traveling, please visit frommers.com/tips.

Internet Access Wi-Fi and traditional Internet access are widely available in the cities in the region, although sometimes difficult to find in rural areas. Most hotels and commercial campgrounds offer free Wi-Fi, as do all the municipal libraries, and all cities in the region have cafes with wireless access.

Legal Aid If you are pulled over for a minor traffic infraction (such as speeding), never attempt to pay the fine directly to a police officer; this could be construed as attempted bribery, a much more serious crime. Pay fines by mail, or directly into the hands of the clerk of the court. If accused of a more serious offense, say and do nothing before consulting a lawyer. Here the burden is on the state to prove a person's guilt beyond a reasonable doubt, and everyone has the right to remain silent, whether they are suspected of a crime or actually arrested. Once arrested, a person can make one telephone call to a party of their choice. The international visitor should call their embassy or consulate (see above).

LGBTQ+ Travel Northern New Mexico is mostly LGBTQ+ friendly, especially Santa Fe and Taos. The state's best resource for gay, lesbian, bisexual, and transgender visitors is **Pride Guide New Mexico** (gogaynewmexico.com). The guide and website offer information about LGBTQ-friendly areas and community information, and will be an aid in planning your visit.

Liquor Laws The legal drinking age is 21 throughout New Mexico. Bars may remain open until 2am on weekends. Wine, beer, and spirits are sold at licensed supermarkets and liquor stores.

Mail See "Fast Facts" in each city's "Essentials" section for post office locations, or go to **usps.com** or call ✆ **800/275-8777.** If you aren't sure what your address will be in the United States, mail can be sent to you, in your name, c/o General Delivery at the main post office of the city where you expect to be. The addressee must pick up mail in person and must produce ID (driver's license, passport, etc.).

Road Conditions For statewide road and driving conditions, call the state **Road Advisory Hotline** at **511** or 800/432-4269, or see nmroads.com.

Safety Although the frequently visited tourist areas are generally safe, northern New Mexico is by no means crime-free. In fact, Santa Fe, Albuquerque, and Taos all have higher crime rates than the rest of the state and considerably higher than the national average. When walking city streets, guard your purse carefully; there are many bag-grab thefts, particularly during the summer tourist months. Also, be as aware of your surroundings as you would in any other cities.

Senior Travel Publications offering travel resources and discounts for seniors include the Albuquerque-based monthly tabloid ***Prime Time*** (primetimenm.com; ✆ **505/242-2428**), offering a variety of articles aimed at those 50 and older.

Smoking Smoking in indoor public places, including restaurants and nightclubs, is illegal in New Mexico. Some hotels offer a limited number of rooms that allow smoking, though the number of these is dwindling.

Taxes The United States has no value-added tax (VAT) or other indirect tax at the national level. Every state, county, and city may levy its own local tax on all purchases, including hotel and restaurant checks and airline tickets. These taxes will not appear on price tags. In Albuquerque the tax on goods and services is just under 8%, in Santa Fe, just over 8%, and in Taos it is more than 9%. But outside city limits it changes, and it can change twice a year. Lodging tax totals about 15% in all three cities.

Time New Mexico is on **Mountain Standard Time,** 1 hour ahead of the West Coast and 2 hours behind the East Coast. When it's 10am in Santa Fe, it's noon in New York, 11am in Chicago, and 9am in San Francisco.

Daylight Saving Time is in effect from 1am on the second Sunday in March to 1am on the first Sunday in November, except in most of Arizona, Hawaii, the U.S. Virgin Islands, and Puerto Rico. (The Navajo Nation, which is partly in Arizona and partly in New Mexico, does recognize Daylight Saving Time.) Daylight Saving Time moves the clock 1 hour ahead of standard time.

Tipping In hotels, tip **bellhops** at least $2 per bag. Tip the **hotel housekeeping staff** $1 to $2 per day (more if you've left a big mess for them to clean up), and tip daily because different people will be cleaning your room. Tip the **doorman** or **concierge** only if they have provided you with some specific service (like calling a cab for you or obtaining difficult-to-get theater tickets). Tip the **valet-parking attendant** $2 every time you get your car. In restaurants, bars, and nightclubs, tip **servers** 18% to 20% of the check and **bartenders** at least $1 per drink. **Checkroom attendants** usually get $1 per garment. As for other service personnel, tip **cab drivers** 15% of the fare, tip **skycaps** at airports at least $2 per bag, and tip **hairdressers** and **barbers** 15% to 20%.

Visitor Information Numerous agencies can assist you with planning your trip. The best place to start is the state website at **newmexico.org** or call the office at ✆ **505/795-0343.** Santa Fe, Taos, and Albuquerque each have their own information services for visitors (see the

"Orientation" sections in chapters 4, 6, and 8, respectively).

Weather Northern New Mexico's weather is fickle. You don't like the clouds? Wait a few minutes and they'll be gone. Or maybe it will start hailing (even in summer) and the temperature will plummet. So make sure to take jackets, sweaters, rain gear, and hats when going out on hikes, and keep them handy in your vehicle while driving. For weather reports, see weather.gov, weather.com, or wunderground.com.

Index

See also Accommodations and Restaurant indexes, below.

General Index

G

H

I

J

K

L

M

N

O

P

Q

R

S

T

U

V

W

X-Y-Z

Accommodations

Restaurants

Map List

Photo Credits

p. i: TOURISM Santa Fe; p. ii: Tazbah McCullah; p. iii: Sean Pavone / Shutterstock; p. iv: Margaret Wiktor / Shutterstock; p. v, top: Sean Pavone / Shutterstock; p. v, bottom left: William Cushman / Shutterstock; p. v, bottom right: jdpphoto / Shutterstock; p. vi, top: Courtesy of Tourism Santa Fe / Brenda Kelley; p. vi, middle: Danita Delmont; p. vi, bottom: TOURISM Santa Fe; p. vii, top left: TOURISM Santa Fe; p. vii, top right: jdwfoto / Shutterstock.com; p. vii, bottom: Brent Coulter; p. viii, top: TOURISM Santa Fe; p. viii, bottom left: Kristi Blokhin / Shutterstock; p. viii, bottom right: PICTOR PICTURES / Shutterstock; p. ix, top: Dan Kaplan / Shutterstock; p. ix, middle: NMTD New Mexico True; p. ix, bottom: douglas knight; p. x, top left: Rosemarie Mosteller / Shutterstock; p. x, top right: NMTD New Mexico True; p. x, bottom: J. Michael Jones / Shutterstock.com; p. xi, top: Roschetzky Photography; p. xi, middle: emattil / Shutterstock; p. xi, bottom: lunamarina; p. xii, top: Courtesy of Ojo Caliente Hot Springs; p. xii, middle: Courtesy of Cumbres & Toltec Scenic Mountain Railway; p. xii, bottom: Courtesy of Farflung Adventures / Michael DeYoung; p. xiii, top: Sean Pavone / Shutterstock; p. xiii, bottom left: New Mexico Tourism Department; p. xiii, bottom right: Traveller70 / Shutterstock.com; p. xiv, top: Dirt Road Travels / Visit Albuquerque; p. xiv, middle: Nagel Photography; p. xiv, bottom: Picturesque Japan / Shutterstock; p. xv, top: Greg Meland / Shutterstock; p. xv, bottom left: Courtesy of Visit Albuquerque / MarbleStreetStudio.com; p. xv, bottom right: Courtesy of Visit Albuquerque / MarbleStreetStudio.com; p. xvi, top: Markus Mainka / Shutterstock; p. xvi, middle: William Cushman / Shutterstock; p. xvi, bottom: Abbie Warnock-Matthews / Shutterstock.

Frommer's Santa Fe, Taos & Albuquerque

Published by
FROMMER MEDIA LLC

ISBN 978-1-62887-641-3 (paper), 978-1-62887-642-0 (ebk)

Editorial Director: Pauline Frommer
Editor: Holly Hughes
Production Editor: Erin Geile
Cartographer: Andy Dolan
Photo Editor: Liza Schoenfein
Cover Design: Dave Riedy
Compositor: Lissa Auciello-Brogan
Indexer: Cheryl Lenser

Front cover photo: Chile peppers and falsa blankets in Old Town, Albuquerque. © Kip Malone / www.kipmalone.com © www.kipmalone.com.

Back cover photo: Ancient dwellings in Taos Pueblo in New Mexico. Taos Pueblo is believed to be one of the oldest continuously inhabited settlements in the US. © Nick Fox/ Shutterstock.com Image #1253346616

For information on our other products or services, see www.frommers.com.

FrommerMedia LLC also publishes its books in a variety of electronic formats. Some content that appears in print may not be available in electronic formats.

Manufactured in Malaysia

5 4 3 2 1

ABOUT THE AUTHOR

Erin Vivid Riley is a writer and editor whose work has appeared in the *Washington Post*, *Bloomberg Businessweek*, and the *New York Times*. Before going freelance, she was a travel editor at *Outside* and *Departures* magazines. She lives between Santa Fe, New Mexico, and Istanbul, Turkey.

ABOUT THE FROMMER TRAVEL GUIDES

For most of the past 65 years, Frommer's has been the leading series of travel guides in North America, accounting for as many as 24% of all guidebooks sold. I think I know why.

Though we hope our books are entertaining, we nevertheless deal with travel in a serious fashion. Our guidebooks have never looked on such journeys as a mere recreation, but as a far more important human function, a time of learning and introspection, an essential part of a civilized life. We stress the culture, lifestyle, history, and beliefs of the destinations we cover, and urge our readers to seek out people and new ideas as the chief rewards of travel.

We have never shied from controversy. We have, from the beginning, encouraged our authors to be intensely judgmental, critical—both pro and con—in their comments, and wholly independent. Our only clients are our readers, and we have triggered the ire of countless prominent sorts, from a tourist newspaper we called "practically worthless" (it unsuccessfully sued us) to the many rip-offs we've condemned.

And because we believe that travel should be available to everyone regardless of their incomes, we have always been cost-conscious at every level of expenditure. Though we have broadened our recommendations beyond the budget category, we insist that every lodging we include be sensibly priced. We use every form of media to assist our readers and are particularly proud of our feisty daily website, the award-winning Frommers.com.

I have high hopes for the future of Frommer's. May these guidebooks, in all the years ahead, continue to reflect the joy of travel and the freedom that travel represents. May they always pursue a cost-conscious path, so that people of all incomes can enjoy the rewards of travel. And may they create, for both the traveler and the persons among whom we travel, a community of friends, where all human beings live in harmony and peace.

Arthur Frommer
(1929–2024)

NOTES